W9-BBC-786

AUSTRIA-HUNGARY
AND GREAT BRITAIN
1908-1914

DB49
G7
P72
1971

Alfred Francis Pribram

AUSTRIA-HUNGARY AND GREAT BRITAIN 1908-1914

With an Introductory Chapter on
the diplomatic relations between
Austria and England
up to 1908

Translated by

Ian F. D. Morrow

GREENWOOD PRESS, PUBLISHERS
WESTPORT, CONNECTICUT

AUG 8 1972

170223

Originally published in 1951
by Oxford University Press, London, New York, Toronto

Reprinted with the permission
of Oxford University Press

First Greenwood Reprinting 1971

Library of Congress Catalogue Card Number 70-138174

ISBN 0-8371-5631-9

Printed in the United States of America

ALFRED FRANCIS PRIBRAM, 1859-1941

PROFESSOR OF MODERN HISTORY, UNIVERSITY OF VIENNA

WHENEVER I am asked to name a famous portrait that closely resembles Alfred Francis Pribram I reply: "Sargent's Wertheimer in the Tate Gallery." For when I think of Pribram (who was my mentor and friend for twenty years) I always think of that portrait, which reveals so many of his outstanding traits—wit and humour, force of intellect and poise, shrewdness and fairness in judgement of men and events, an epicurean outlook upon life, human sympathy and respect for the dignity of man. It was these qualities as well as his inborn courtesy, kindliness, and self-sacrificing generosity that caused Pribram to be regarded with affectionate admiration by men of his own mental calibre no less than by the great throng of students whose progress along the path of historical knowledge was hastened and made easier by his wise guidance. To say this is to say much of any man. Yet there was in Pribram something more—something out and beyond these mundane qualities—that placed him upon the summit of a pinnacle not always reached even by great intellects and that illumed his whole being. This quality is not capable of exact definition, if only because it was a spiritual quality which he doubtless inherited with his Jewish blood and that, charged as it was with the memories of the terrible sufferings of his ancient race, suffused his whole personality. Intellectually and emotionally Pribram stood upon a Pisgah whence he surveyed the vast panorama of human history. No one who attended his crowded lectures failed to marvel not only at his mastery of his subject but also at the skill with which he brought contemporaneous events into their true perspective against the confused background of modern European history. But brilliant lecturer though he was, Pribram was at his happiest in the less formal atmosphere of his seminar surrounded by his favourite students before whom he could give untrammelled play alike to his learning and his wit.

In his happy home life in the Billrothstrasse, where his many friends from artistic as well as academic circles in Vienna met weekly, Pribram the man as distinct from Pribram the historian displayed to the full the charm and warmth of his many-sided personality. He was widely travelled and exceptionally widely read in four or five languages, a fine linguist keenly appreciative of the *nuances* in a foreign tongue, and a brilliant talker and *raconteur* who always had something wise and witty to say about any and all of the multifarious subjects under discussion. Above all, Pribram possessed that rare gift of stimulating diffident or taciturn people to talk and of drawing out what each had to contribute to the discussion. For like all great conversationalists he never sought to dominate the conversation and knew when to remain silent.

For an historian of modern Europe Pribram was born at a singularly fortunate moment. His long life spanned the rise and fall of the Second German Empire, the downfall and disappearance of the Austro-Hungarian and Russian Empires, the economic and political rearrangement of Europe in the Treaty of Versailles and its fateful consequences, and finally the emergence and triumph of Nazism in Germany and Austria. He lived to witness the outbreak of the Second World War which he had long foreseen, and he died in the unshakeable belief that the England of which he was by birth a son would once more triumph over her enemies. From his coign of vantage in Vienna in the very heart of Europe, Pribram watched these stupendous events taking shape, and he was personally acquainted with many of those who helped to shape them. Hence he spoke and wrote with an unrivalled authority upon *Austrian Foreign Policy, 1908-1918* (London, 1923), *England and the International Policy of the European Great Powers, 1871-1914* (London, 1931), *The Secret Treaties of Austria-Hungary, 1879-1914* (Harvard, 1920), and on *Österreich-Ungarns Aussenpolitik, 1908-1914* (the great collection of Austro-Hungarian diplomatic documents published in Vienna in 1930, of which Pribram was a co-editor). It is evident from these titles that England was never far from his thoughts, and in *Die Oesterreichischen Staatsverträge England* and his massive biography of Lisola Pribram made a valuable contribution to English no less than Austrian history.

Shortly before his death Professor Pribram made me his literary executor and entrusted me with the manuscript of the present work. Owing to wartime conditions it was for years impossible even to contemplate its publication. Further financial support from the Rockefeller Foundation to which I wish here to express my gratitude and the liberality of the Oxford University Press in undertaking its publication have made its public appearance finally possible.

IAN F. D. MORROW

November 1950

CONTENTS

The national egoism of States has always been the accepted foundation of international policy. As long as national egoism is not replaced by a more ideal World-order than the present one, the foreign policy of States must be judged by the consideration whether the national egoism of rival States has been met by the right or the wrong methods.

The Memoirs of Count Bernstorff

PREFACE

WHEN I left Vienna, where my lifework had been done in order to live in my birthplace, London, I proposed to myself the task of completing the history of the diplomatic relations between Great Britain and Austria-Hungary which I had already written from the outset of these relations down to the end of the Napoleonic Wars. The first portion of this history entitled *Die Oesterreichischen Staatsverträge England* was published in two volumes during the years 1907-1913, and was based upon the documents housed in the Vienna State Archives and the Public Record Office in London. I now hoped to continue the story of Anglo-Austrian diplomatic relations throughout the nineteenth century and to bring it down to the outbreak of the First World War in 1914. But I was speedily forced to recognize that conditions rendered the carrying-out of any such project an impossibility. My advanced age alone made it very doubtful whether I would be able to read through the enormous number of documents in the Public Record Office and by order of the new Government in Austria I was deprived of access to the documents in the Vienna State Archives. Hence I was compelled to abandon my original plan. What I therefore offer my readers in the present work is a detailed account of the diplomatic relations between Great Britain and Austria-Hungary during the years 1908-1914 prefaced by a brief survey of the diplomatic relations between these two States from their remote beginnings down to the year 1908—a survey that I do not think anyone has previously made.

For the years 1908-1914 the documentary materials are to be found in two vast publications—*Oesterreich-Ungarns Aussenpolitik 1908-1914*, of which I was one of the editors, and *British Documents on the Origins of the War, 1898-1914*, edited by G. P. Gooch and H. W. V. Temperley. I must at once draw the reader's attention to the fact that I have made no attempt in the following pages to narrate the diplomatic relations of either Great Britain or Austria-Hungary in their entirety in regard to the three great international questions of the time but only the diplomatic relations between Great Britain and Austria-Hungary in the narrower sense. Hence mention will only be made of the influence exercised by other Powers on the course of events in so far as it appears indispensable to an understanding of my particular subject. I have also abstained from entering into any fresh discussion of the innumerable controversies that have arisen during the past twenty years over the conduct and policies of the leading Austro-Hungarian and British statesmen. The use of the envenomed criticism so often employed in discussions of the War Guilt (*Kriegsschuldfrage*) problem renders the achievement of any impartial narration of events quite impossible. Anyone who doubts the sincerity of every word spoken or written by a leading statesman, and who reads a double meaning into every utterance, will be as incapable of attaining to a fair judgement of the speeches and actions of statesmen, and other influential personalities, as will he who never thinks of doubting them. In my reading and in the selection of documents no less than in my narration of events I have tried to approach my subject without preconceived notions and without mistrust in regard to any individual statesman. But I have not wholly refrained from criticism. The literature that has grown up round the subject of the origins of the First World War has become so enormous that it is no longer possible to master the whole of it. To give a bibliography of only the books and articles that I myself have read would occupy more space than can be afforded here. Hence I have only mentioned the most important books and articles in the Bibliography, with the exception of those relating to Chapter II, among which I have included many titles simply because by consulting these for himself the reader will be able to compare two or more frequently conflicting points of view. But I would refer the reader in search of further information to the volumes on England and Austria that have appeared in the Bibliographies published by the Weltbücherei in Stuttgart, to A. Wegerer's *Bibliographie zur Vorgeschichte des Weltkrieges* (1934), and to the 4th Edition of G. P. Gooch's *Revelations of European Diplomacy*, which was published in 1940 under the title *Recent Revelations of European Diplomacy*.

For the Balkan Wars, Helmreich, in *The Diplomacy of the Balkan Wars, 1912-13*, pp. 473-495, gave an exceptionally comprehensive bibliography.

No German books that have been published since the outbreak of the Second World War, and especially Wegerer's

Der Ausbruch des Weltkrieges (two volumes), have been available to me.

I cannot conclude this Preface without expressing my gratitude to the Rockefeller Foundation for the financial support which it so generously afforded me, as also the London School of Economics, and in particular Professor Sir Charles Webster, for assistance given me in carrying out my task.

A. F. PRIBRAM

1940

Chapter One

AUSTRIA AND ENGLAND THROUGH SEVEN CENTURIES, 1200-1908

B EFORE beginning a brief survey of the diplomatic relations—and this survey is concerned with these alone—
between England and Austria down the centuries, a few
general observations seem desirable in order to make clear the
standpoint from which the survey has been taken.

In old and new history books alike there constantly appears
the phrase "traditional friendship" as describing the relations
that have subsisted between England and Austria through the
centuries. In the opinion of the present writer this description
is false. Friendship between man and man—yes; sympathy
between peoples—yes; but friendship between States—never!
Ever since States came into existence their actions and policies
have been guided solely by self-interest. If their interests
happen to run parallel to one another, then they enter into
friendly relations one with another and work together in
harmony. The moment differences arise between them their
relations undergo a change. Not indeed that a state of open
enmity invariably follows. Differences are often smoothed out.
This, however, rarely happens without one or other State,
and indeed often both, feeling that it has had the worst of the
bargain and accusing the other of egoism and ruthlessness. If
no bargain or compromise is achieved then friendship is
replaced by open enmity and there follows an appeal to arms.
It is from this standpoint that one must survey the relations
between England and Austria if one is to attain to an
impartial judgement. It is indeed not a question of Right
against Wrong, but of Right against Right, Might against
Might.

For centuries the relations between England and Austria
were very indefinite. Their interests seldom came into contact.
The quarrel between Richard Coeur de Lion and the Baben-
berg Duke, Leopold V, was a personal one that was eventually
settled by agreements concluded between the Austrian ruler
and the Emperor Henry VI and between Henry VI and
Richard Coeur de Lion, but not directly between Leopold V

and Richard Coeur de Lion. An attempt to bring about permanent relations between the two States was made by King Edward I in 1277 when he betrothed his six-year-old daughter Johanna to the fourteen-year-old son of Rudolph of Habsburg. But it failed of success since the marriage never took place. Nor were the agreements concluded in 1339 between the Austrian rulers Albrecht II and Otto with Edward III productive of results. These agreements were the outcome of the war that broke out between France and England over the succession to the French throne on the death of the last male in the direct line of the House of Capet. Edward III as a Plantagenet laid claim to the French throne and sought allies in the Empire for his war with France. Among the German princes with whom he negotiated were the Austrian dukes. As early as 1335 negotiations were in progress for a marriage between Duke Otto's eldest son Frederick and Edward III's daughter Johanna, while in 1339 an alliance was concluded at Antwerp between Edward III and the Dukes Otto and Albrecht II that pledged both parties to mutual support and authorised the Habsburg dukes to attack and occupy Burgundy during "the present war between Edward III and Philip of Valois who calls himself King of France". The alliance was of short duration. Once it became clear that it was not going to produce the hoped for results Otto and Albrecht turned to France, and, after a long sojourn in Germany, Johanna went home. Nearly a century later when war again broke out between France and England, Duke Frederick of Austria signed a treaty in 1430 with King Charles VII of France by which he undertook to wage war on England's ally, Duke Philip of Burgundy. Shortly afterwards an armistice was arranged between Charles VII and Philip of Burgundy that was extended to cover Frederick's military operations.

Henry VI again tried unsuccessfully to regain Austria's friendship, and, after his failure, there is nothing to report of Anglo-Austrian relations even during the long reign of Frederick III. It was not indeed until the accession of Maximilian I that durable and valuable relations were established between England and Austria. Yet it was not as Duke of Austria, but as the heir of Mary of Burgundy, that Maximilian found himself of necessity called upon to establish durable relations with England. For this reason they do not come within the scope of this survey. In view of the serious disputes that were to arise between England and Austria when at the beginning of the eighteenth century the Austrian Habsburgs became rulers of the Spanish Netherlands, it is nevertheless necessary to point out here that, even in Maximilian's days, mercantile problems stood in the way of agreement between the Netherlands and England. Flemish merchants were ready to come to a political understanding with England if the English merchants were prepared to supply wool to the Flemish weavers and then to buy the manufactured articles in Flanders. The English, however, began not only to manufacture for themselves, and in quantities nearly sufficient to cover their own requirements, but they started exporting and selling the manufactured articles to the Netherlands. The Flemish merchants and weavers consequently demanded that their rulers should pursue an anti-English policy. But Maximilian for long had worked to maintain friendly relations with England, and for this purpose had concluded commercial treaties with Henry VII that were injurious to the Flemish traders with whom he consequently found himself involved in serious conflicts.

Maximilian's relations with Henry VII, and with his successor Henry VIII, underwent frequent changes because they were determined by Maximilian's relations with the French rulers. If he needed England's support against France, then he naturally pursued an Anglophil policy. This policy led to the conclusion of a number of agreements for joint action against the common enemy. Nevertheless mutual mistrust as well as profound political and commercial differences placed obstacles in the way of the carrying out of every agreement. Hence it came about that Maximilian and the English kings at one time were allies and shortly afterwards were at war with one another as a consequence of a change of policy. Under these circumstances of quick and ceaseless change from friend to foe, ally to enemy, it was obviously impossible for the signatories to these agreements to fulfil the stipulations. Time and again Maximilian and Henry VIII found themselves involved in acrimonious controversies. Maximilian complained that the English did not keep their word while Henry criticized Maximilian's selfish conduct. And both with good reason. Their differences grew steadily greater until in 1516 it seemed as if a break was inevitable. The material support of England was nevertheless so indispensable to him that Maximilian, despite his complaints about Henry VIII's conduct, concluded another agreement with him. The Emperor entertained such doubts of its duration that he simultaneously made peace with their common enemy, the King of France.

Maximilian's death made an end to the regular diplomatic relations that had existed between Vienna and London during his reign. His successor as Emperor, Charles, in 1522 gave the Austrian lands to his brother Ferdinand who in 1526 with the union of the Habsburg hereditary lands with the Bohemian and Hungarian Crowns founded a new Austrian State that, although for centuries in intimate connection with the Holy Roman Empire, henceforth pursued its own independent existence. For a long time there was no sufficient reason for this new State to enter into serious political negotiations with England, and in any case it was Charles V, as Holy Roman Emperor, who carried on diplomatic relations with Henry VIII and his successors chiefly for the purpose of obtaining English assistance in the struggle with France that he had carried on for decades. Austrian policy was very largely determined by the policy of Charles V and his successors on the Imperial throne who were one and all simultaneously members of the German branch of the House of Habsburg and rulers of Austria. Until the beginning of the Thirty Years War Austria and England were seldom in direct diplomatic contact, and when they were the problem that usually formed the subject of their discussions was the attitude to be adopted by both States towards Near Eastern affairs. England frequently intervened in the struggles carried on by Austrian rulers in the sixteenth century both with the Sublime Porte and the Princes of Transylvania. Again and again Austrian rulers implored the English Court to help them in their struggle against the enemy of Christendom. All their endeavours failed of success. The English Government was guided solely by self-interest in its attitude towards all these questions and its interest did not often coincide with that of Austria's rulers. A plan evolved by Ferdinand I to marry his younger son Charles to Queen Elizabeth gave rise to negotiations that lasted for twelve years and at one time promised to result in an agreement that would have been of the greatest importance for the political relations between the two countries. Eventually the negotiations ended in failure. Elizabeth had certainly never seriously thought of marrying a Catholic prince and only continued the negotiations with the Imperial Court for political reasons. Moreover Elizabeth's inimical policy towards the Spanish Habsburgs was not without influence upon her relations with the German Habsburgs, and undoubtedly stood in the way of friendly relations between Austria and England.

The accession of the House of Stuart to the English throne saw a speeding-up of the diplomatic relations between Austria and England. True, James I, like his great predecessor, pursued an anti-Habsburg policy that found expression in his alliance with the anti-Imperialist Protestant Union in 1612, and was strengthened by the marriage of his daughter Elizabeth to the Elector Palatine Frederick. In the war which broke out in 1619 James I none the less refused to support his son-in-law not only because as a strict legitimist he felt he could not side with the Elector Palatine against his legitimate sovereign, but also because he was hoping at this time to marry his son to a Spanish Infanta in order to have the support of Spain in his continuous struggle with Parliament. The defeat sustained by the Elector at the Battle of the White Mountain was not unjustly blamed upon James's conduct. Although the vast majority of the English nation was well-disposed towards the Elector, James sought to pave the way for a compromise between his son-in-law and the Emperor, but his efforts were unsuccessful because of the Elector's stubborn opposition. It was only towards the end of his reign, and after the failure of his plan for a Spanish marriage for his son, that James bowed to the demand put forward by Parliament for an anti-Spanish policy, although to the day of his death he successfully avoided an open breach with Spain and the Habsburgs.

Charles I at the beginning of his reign seemed inclined to resume the struggle with the Habsburgs and for this purpose concluded alliances with the States-General and Denmark. But he was unable fully to support his allies because of his conflicts with Parliament and the deterioration that had taken place in Anglo-French relations. After Denmark's defeat in 1629 Charles made peace with Spain and sought an understanding with the Emperor, which he nevertheless failed to achieve because of the Emperor's refusal of Charles's demand for the restoration of the Elector to his dominions. All further attempts on the part of Charles to make a compromise with the Emperor broke down over this divergence of interests. Even after the death of the Elector Frederick the settlement of the Palatinate question remained Charles's chief concern, whereas the Emperor's was to secure English help in his fight with those inveterate enemies of the House of Habsburg— France and Holland. It was in vain that the English Ministers in Vienna, like the diplomatic representatives of Ferdinand II and Ferdinand III in London, sought by mutual concessions to arrange a compromise. The demands put forward by Spain and Maximilian of Bavaria, who in their own interest wanted to prevent any agreement between the Austrian and English monarchs, and the opposition to its conclusion manifested by Parliament, caused the failure of the constantly renewed endeavours made by the men who in the 1640's tried to surmount the obstacles, and especially those made by Baron von Lisola who was the outstanding Austrian diplomatist of that day. Lisola could not prevent Charles I's decision that the settlement of the Palatinate question was to be sought not in direct negotiation with the Emperor but within the framework of a general peace settlement. Nevertheless diplomatic relations with England were not broken off and instead the Government in Vienna instructed Lisola to continue to strive for an alliance between Charles I and the Habsburgs. In event of this plan proving incapable of execution Lisola was instructed at least to prevent an Anglo-French alliance. In this Lisola was successful. At the beginning of 1644 he was able to report to Vienna that the danger was over of the conclusion of an Anglo-French alliance. On the other hand Lisola failed to bring Charles I into the Habsburg camp. "As far as we are concerned," Lisola wrote, "we have nothing to fear nor anything to hope for from England." The Imperial Government felt satisfied with this result and all the more so because in the succeeding years as Charles fought his losing battle with Parliament the Emperor came to set less and less store by an alliance with him. Lisola left London at the close of 1644 and with his departure direct diplomatic relations between Austria and England ceased for a long time.

The news of the beheading of King Charles I filled the Imperial Court in Vienna with horror and indignation. Many thought that the Emperor as the supreme guardian of Right and the Moral Law should inflict punishment upon the King's assassins. While he took no punitive measures against England Ferdinand III did not hesitate to recognize Charles's son, Charles II, as King of England and was willing to fulfil his request for monetary as well as moral support. Ferdinand III and his successor, Leopold I, were uncompromising opponents of the Republican Government in England as well as of the Lord Protector Oliver Cromwell who would never have been recognized by the Viennese Court even if his policy had not been so strongly anti-Habsburg. Through all the fierce conflicts that shook the peace of western and north-eastern Europe during the second half of the 1650s England was to be found in the ranks of the enemies of the House of Habsburg, and on more than one occasion—for example, at the election of Leopold I as Holy Roman Emperor—the Austrian rulers suffered from the Lord Protector's enmity. The Viennese Court was therefore overjoyed by the news of Cromwell's death and soon afterwards by the restoration of Charles II in whom the Habsburgs hoped to find a strong support in their fight against the supremacy of France in Europe. They were doomed to disappointment. Gratitude was foreign to Charles II's nature. He, like his father, was solely guided in his policy and actions by self-interest. Charles I thought that his interest was best served by a policy of neutrality in the great struggle between the Habsburgs and the Bourbons, and therefore abstained from wholly committing himself to either party. Charles II, on the other hand, fought at one time beside Louis XIV and immediately afterwards against him, and was always ready to exchange allies if his former opponent was prepared to pay more for his desertion of his former ally than that ally was prepared to pay to retain the alliance. Since Louis XIV was wealthier than his Habsburg rivals he generally topped the bidding at the English Court, while the mutual distrust between the Emperor and Charles II prevented the conclusion of an alliance between them against Louis XIV, notwithstanding the fact that the general European political situation often forced them to approach one another with this end in view. The rivalry between the Courts of Vienna and London grew sharper with the accession of James II who yearly became more and more dependent upon Louis XIV because the Sun King skilfully made use of the perilous situation in which James II found himself *vis-à-vis* the English nation to bind James II more closely to him. The anti-French party in

Europe by the end of 1687 gave up all hope of seeing England fighting at their side against France as long as James II remained on the throne.

Hence Vienna rejoiced in the late autumn of 1688 when James II was forced to fly from England and was succeeded on the throne by his nephew and son-in-law William of Orange and his wife Mary. All the obstacles that had hitherto stood in the way of a lasting and sincere friendship between England and Austria disappeared as it were overnight. A vast majority of the English nation had long recognized that far less danger threatened them from the Habsburgs than from the absolutist Catholic Kings of France, and now they were ruled over by a monarch who had devoted his life to the struggle against the French bid for supremacy in Europe. The change of monarchs that had taken place in England was all the more welcome to the Emperor Leopold I because he had now been for months past at war with Louis XIV, and consequently he eagerly grasped the helping hand held out to him by William of Orange despite the fact that as a zealous Catholic he was strongly attracted by Louis XIV's simultaneous proposal that they should unite to restore James II to the throne of England in order to advance the Catholic cause in Europe. As ruler of the United Netherlands William III had already had dealings with Leopold I and now as King of England he declared his readiness to take part with these two Powers in the war against France. He therefore pressed for the conclusion of the alliance between the States General and Austria that was signed on 12 May 1689, and shortly afterwards on 9 September England became a partner in this alliance and guaranteed the fulfilment of its obligations including the—for Leopold extremely important—stipulation that in the event of the failure of the Spanish line of the House of Habsburg the signatories would champion the interests of the German line. Although their interests were not seldom in conflict, and notwithstanding the fact that each set great store by the safeguarding of its own interest, Austria and England fought side by side for many years against Louis XIV in defence of the European Balance of Power.

In a pamphlet published in 1692 the idea was ventilated that in the general interest of Christendom, and also the particular interests of England, Austria should be supported by England in her struggle against France.

"It is to the general interest of the whole of Christendom to bring
the House of Austria again into equality with France. This equilibrium
is necessary as well for the safety of the peoples as for that of the princes.
But it is to the special interest of England to establish again this
equality, so that she may again hold the scales in her hand and turn
them to whichever side she desires, for this is the one possible rôle for
us, not only that we may continue to be mistress of the sea, but also
that we may be capable of deciding the event of war and the terms of
peace."[1]

Louis XIV was at last successful in persuading William III,
as well as Leopold I, to engage in separate negotiations with
him with the result that he sowed mistrust between the two
monarchs and their Governments. The Duke of Savoy—ally
of Austria and England—went over to Louis XIV's camp
while Leopold I, in consequence of his war with Turkey,
found himself compelled to conclude a treaty with Louis XIV
which bound both to withdraw their troops from Italy. Hence
William III was forced to declare that any continuance of the
war against France had become impossible and to give his
assent to the opening of peace negotiations. His example was
followed by the Dutch and the Spaniards, and in consequence
Leopold was compelled to agree in 1697 to the signing of the
Peace of Ryswick. The tension thus aroused in Anglo-Austrian
relations was heightened by William III's attitude in the
question of the Spanish Succession. William III and the
States General had bound themselves in a secret article
appended to the Treaty of 1689, "in event of the death of
Charles II without legitimate descendants to place all their
forces at the disposal of the Emperor and his heirs in asserting
their legitimate right to the succession." When, however,
Leopold in connection with the negotiations that led up to
the conclusion of the Peace of Ryswick soon afterwards reminded William III of this undertaking, William III adopted
an attitude of reserve and said that while he was ready to renew
the alliance of 1689 he must, like the States General, make
any declaration in favour of the Austrian Habsburgs' rights
in the Spanish Succession Question dependent upon a previous
public declaration by Charles II of Spain in favour of Leopold's
second son Charles. Charles II, however, was too afraid of
Louis XIV, and too much under the influence of the powerful
French party at his Court, to make any such declaration
regarding the succession. Under these circumstances a

renewal of the alliance for which William III and the States General were pressing had no longer any value in Leopold's eyes. The Imperial Ambassador in London said: "I cannot see what good will come of renewing an alliance just after it has been broken." And one of the most powerful Ministers in Vienna, Count Kinsky, said: "The maritime Powers indeed declare that their object is the safeguarding of Austria's rights after the death of Charles, but they put off doing anything about it to an indefinite future."

The Emperor shared his advisers' opinions. He, too, held firmly to the claim to the entire Spanish inheritance. William III and the States General, however, regardless of Austria's attitude, signed a treaty on 11 October 1698 with Louis XIV by which, as next heirs of the Spanish inheritance, Ferdinand, Elector of Bavaria, was given the Netherlands and the Spanish colonies, the Dauphin Naples and Sicily, and Archduke Charles only the Duchy of Milan. The unexpected death of the Elector of Bavaria occasioned fresh negotiations between all the interested parties. William III was again unsuccessful in his attempts to persuade Leopold to accept his—and the States General's—proposals for the partition of the Spanish inheritance. Leopold stated in the formal declaration with which he answered the proposals of the maritime Powers that he deemed the acceptance of these proposals incompatible with his honour, and that he was firmly resolved in event of the maritime Powers insisting upon carrying out their unjust decisions "to bear what he could not prevent and calmly to await whatever fate the Governor of earthly destinies chose to impose upon the King of Spain and his Kingdom in the firm conviction nevertheless that a just God would bring to nought the schemes of those who contrary to Divine and human law sought to divide up and to distribute foreign kingdoms among others."

Leopold's protest was unavailing. In March 1700, England, Holland, and France agreed on another partition by which Archduke Charles was to get Spain, the Netherlands, and the Spanish colonies while the Dauphin was to receive Spain's Italian possessions. In vain did William III try to persuade the Emperor to accept this partition and in vain did he point to the fateful consequences that must follow from a refusal. In refusing William III's proposal Leopold reckoned on the dislike of the Spaniards for any partition of the Spanish inheritance—a dislike which Charles II had taken into his calculations at the time of the first partition. Moreover Leopold was strengthened in this attitude by a declaration that shortly afterwards reached him from Charles II according to which Charles announced his determination to leave his Crown and all his possessions in their entirety to Archduke Charles.

At the eleventh hour the French party at the Spanish Court was nevertheless successful in getting the dying Charles II to draw up a will by which he left the whole Spanish inheritance to Louis XIV's grandson, Philip of Anjou. Notwithstanding the existence of the partition agreements which he had contracted with the maritime Powers, Louis XIV decided to claim the Spanish heritage for his grandson. The great question that for decades had occupied monarchs and statesmen thus found a temporary settlement. The event that England and the States General had sought to prevent had come about. Spain and France, who had for so long fought one another for the supremacy in Europe, were now ruled over by a common dynasty, and the Balance of Power in Europe, to preserve which so much blood had been spilt, seemed threatened anew. The wish to ward off this danger was as ardent in Vienna as it was in London and The Hague. Different ends were, however, pursued in these capitals. For the Emperor it was, above all else, a question of territorial aggrandizement for his House. England and Holland, on the other hand, feared that their existence as great trading Powers would be threatened, and at least severely restricted, by the union of France and Spain, and therefore in the negotiations for an alliance with the Emperor pursued first and foremost the aim of preventing the transfer of the Spanish overseas possessions into the hands of Philip of Bourbon who was dependent upon France. The compromise that was finally embodied in the treaty of 7 September 1701 was more favourable to the maritime Powers than to the Emperor. True, England and Holland undertook to devote all their resources to the conquest of Naples and Sicily for the Emperor, yet Leopold bitterly regretted the omission of any assurance that they would not lay down their arms before this had been done. Leopold for his part had to agree that the Spanish territory in the West Indies captured by the maritime Powers in the course of the war should remain in their permanent possession. A time limit was set at the insistence of England and Holland within which another attempt was to be made to induce Louis XIV to fulfil the objects set out in the treaty without recourse to war. Much against his will, and after long hesitation, Leopold finally agreed to this condition. These projected negotiations with Louis XIV were in fact never even begun.

After the death of James II, Louis XIV recognized his son as King of England. William III felt that his personal position as King was in jeopardy while the majority of the English people, who had hitherto been against war with France, changed their sentiments when menaced by a Stuart restoration and through Parliament placed the necessary funds at William's disposal for waging war with France. Henceforward England and Austria for years victoriously fought together as allies in the war against France. Any differences that arose between them were easily disposed of. This harmonious relationship came to an end in 1710 when a Tory Cabinet came to power in England and at once changed England's foreign policy. It was not, however, until the death of Joseph I that relations between England and Austria were finally broken off. The reason for this momentous step lay in the fear that the European Balance of Power would now be threatened from Austria's side by reason of the union of the lands which Joseph bequeathed to his heir, Charles, with the entire Spanish inheritance, which it had been intended should pass to Charles. Without the least regard for its ally's interests, and without its ally's knowledge, the English Government negotiated with France, and then, in October 1711, communicated to the Austrian Minister in London, Count Gallas, the conditions under which it was prepared to join with France in a peace conference. Gallas expressed his opinion of the conduct of the English Government in such terms that he was refused admission to the Court and English Ministers declined to speak with him. He thereupon left London. His Government approved his conduct and declined to take part in a peace conference on the English terms. Shortly afterwards Prince Eugene of Savoy appeared in London where he tried to induce the English Government to make some concession but without success. Marlborough's fall revealed to him the hopeless nature of his mission. The Tory Government continued on its course, and, while the Emperor took up arms to attain his ends, concluded in April 1713 at Utrecht peace with France.

The Treaty of Utrecht was a brilliant success for English policy. Gibraltar and Port Mahon remained in English hands to promote the development of English commercial power in southern Europe. The destruction of Dunkirk set the seal upon England's mastery over the North Sea. Vast additions were made to English colonial possessions in America at the expense of England's most dangerous rival—France. The Emperor Charles VI was profoundly hurt by the conduct of his former comrade in arms and gave full vent to his annoyance. Although large portions of Italy and the Spanish Netherlands were given to him by the Treaty of Rastatt, his dream of seeing the Spanish and Austrian sceptres held by one hand was doomed to disappointment. The acquisition of the Spanish Netherlands also gave rise in time to serious conflicts with the maritime Powers that first found expression in the Barrier Treaty of 1715, and that towards the middle of the eighteenth century contributed, above everything else, to a rupture of Anglo-Austrian relations that was to prove fateful for Austria.

The Emperor Charles VI's anger was directed chiefly against Queen Anne and the Tory Government. After Anne's death, and the substitution of a Whig for the Tory Government, an opportunity offered itself of improving the relations between London and Vienna, more especially because the new Government favoured open enmity towards—if necessary war with—France. George I and his advisers sought to restore the former friendly relations with the Imperial Court and proposed to Vienna a defensive alliance which should also be joined by the States General. At first Charles and his counsellors maintained an attitude of reserve, stressing that England had not played the game with Austria in recent years, and declaring that Austria was therefore justified in treating English proposals with suspicion. It was not long, however, before the desire to have England as an ally in a war with France and Spain (which was ruled over by a Bourbon) overcame the doubts entertained by the Imperial Government of English sincerity. After prolonged negotiations the difficulties that arose out of the desire of both parties to safeguard their individual interests were finally overcome. At the end of May 1716, a defensive alliance was signed that bound both parties to defend each others' rights and possessions. The Imperial Government must nevertheless have been bitterly disappointed that England refused to enter into any obligation to assist Austria in a war with Turkey, while the Emperor very unwillingly agreed to take active measures to support the Hanoverian dynasty in its struggle with the Pretender James Stuart. The chief reason for the far-reaching concessions made by Charles VI to England lay in his wish to secure England's support in a new war with Spain. The treaties of peace that had been signed in 1713 and 1714 had not led to a reconciliation between Charles VI and Philip V, and Charles VI was determined at the first favourable opportunity to make good his claims to certain parts of the Spanish dominions. He knew that he could only attain this objective after a victorious war against France and Spain, and also that victory in such a war could only be won if the maritime Powers fought at Austria's side. The defensive alliance of 1716 nevertheless only guaranteed the existing English and Austrian possessions, and consequently did not assure the Emperor England's support in a war with France and Spain in which Austria was the aggressor. It was in order to secure the assurance of English support in this eventuality that the Imperial Government after 1716 carried on negotiations in Vienna and London that encountered a well-nigh insuperable obstacle in England's unwillingness to fight for such far-reaching Austrian interests. England was indeed ready to fulfil certain of Charles VI's demands, and notably to give her support to his acquisition of Sicily, which Victor Amadeus of Savoy was to hand over to the Emperor in exchange for Sardinia. But England refused to accede to the most vitally important of all the Emperor's demands—to enter a war for Austria's sake in which France would be counted among their enemies. Instead, England, in the autumn of 1716, reached an agreement with the French Regent (who showed himself very desirous of it) that in January 1717, with the inclusion of the States General, acquired binding force, and she then continued her endeavours to achieve a settlement between Philip V and Charles VI by peaceful means. In this England undertook an exceptionally difficult task. Charles VI did not want irrevocably to renounce his claim to Spain. The Bourbon Philip under Alberoni's guidance refused to give Charles his Italian possessions. A Spanish Fleet appeared in the Mediterranean and captured Sardinia where the Spaniards once more established their rule. Under the impact of these events England and Austria actively resumed their negotiations in the autumn of 1717, and, after many difficulties had been overcome, were finally successful in bringing about a reconciliation between Charles VI and the Regent of France and in persuading the former to agree to England's two principal demands—Charles VI's renunciation of Spain and the succession to the Grand Duchy of Tuscany for one of the Queen of Spain's sons.

The treaty was signed on 2 August 1718 by the representatives of England, France, and Austria. The Spanish Government categorically refused to accept the decisions taken by the Powers and at Alberoni's instigation the war went on despite a heavy defeat sustained by the Spanish Fleet. France and England therefore found themselves obliged to declare war on Spain, although they had no intention of waging it seriously. On the contrary they continued their endeavours to persuade Spain to become a signatory to the treaty of August 1718, and in this they were finally successful towards the end of 1719 after Alberoni—the begetter and promoter of all the ambitious and warlike plans that circulated at the Spanish Court and the most resolute opponent of peace and of Spain's submission to the behests of the Powers who were seeking to mediate—had been overthrown. Peace was thus formally restored between Spain and the Empire. But it was another five years before a real reconciliation was effected between the Spanish and Austrian monarchs on an entirely different basis. This reconciliation came about largely through the animosity that grew up between England and Austria as a result of their opposing interests in the Netherlands which—it will be remembered—had been given to Charles VI. In order to compensate the inhabitants of the Netherlands for the heavy losses sustained by their trade as a consequence of his agreements with the maritime Powers Charles VI gladly approved a plan drawn up by Ostend merchants for the creation of competitive trading conditions with England and Holland. The plan proved successful and consequently aroused the jealousy of the Dutch and English merchants. Disputes grew more and more violent with the passing of the years until the maritime Powers finally demanded that the Emperor should suppress the Ostend Company. This the Emperor not only refused to do, but instead gave the Company all the help he could, with the result that the attitude of the maritiine Powers steadily grew more and more inimical. In the debates in the House of Commons, as well as in direct negotiations between English and Austrian statesmen, the two countries aired their mutual dissatisfaction. The discussions that were held in Cambrai from the close of 1724 onwards clearly proved that the anti-Austrian party at the English Court had gained the upper hand. It was at this juncture that the Emperor's former enemy, Philip of Spain, who was annoyed by the refusal of the maritime Powers to fulfil his wishes in regard to Gibraltar and Port Mahon, and who hoped by allying himself with the Emperor to secure for his son, Don Carlos, Italian territories and also to assure for his House the dominions of the German Habsburgs by marrying his sons to Austrian Archduchesses, proposed to the Austrian Government the conclusion of treaties by which he would bind himself not only formally to recognize the Ostend Company but also to open Spanish ports to the Company and all the Emperor's subjects, grant them extensive privileges in Spain and the Spanish colonies, and guarantee to them the same freedom of trade that had for long been enjoyed by the Dutch and the English traders. The Emperor for his part renounced his claims to Spain and held out the hope of a marriage between his daughters and the Spanish princes. When news of the signature of this treaty reached Paris and London it created a profound sensation. The English accused the Emperor of ingratitude and said they would not tolerate the injury that would be inflicted upon their commerce. Moreover they substituted deeds for words. In concert with France they took steps to ward off the danger that threatened from Spain and Austria, and they were successful in getting the King of Prussia to join with them.

The Emperor Charles VI became alarmed by these proceedings. He concluded yet another and closer alliance with Spain by which Spain undertook to promote the interests of the Ostend Company and in case of war to give Austria large financial subsidies. The year 1726 was spent by all parties in seeking allies. The Imperial Government induced the Tsar of Russia and many of the Wittlesbach princes to join with Austria while the King of Prussia, disappointed with the conduct of his new allies, deserted to the Emperor. On the other hand France and England were successful in gaining the support of Holland, Denmark, and Sweden, as well as of some of the German princes. Tension increased steadily, as did also the profits of the Ostend Company, with the result that English merchants seeing in this a direct threat to their trade with Spain and the East demanded that the English Government should take strong measures. A general European war seemed unavoidable and every country armed itself. In January 1727 King George I opened Parliament with a Speech from the Throne in which he said that the treaties between Spain and the Emperor "gave, at the first appearance, just grounds of jealousy and apprehension to the neighbouring Powers of Europe; the subsequent proceedings and transactions in those two Courts, and the secret and offensive alliances concluded between them about the same time, have laid the foundations of a most exorbitant and formidable power; and are so directly levelled against the most valuable and darling interests and privileges of this nation, that we must determine either tamely to submit to the peremptory and unjust demands of the King of Spain in giving up Gibraltar, and patiently to acquiesce in the Emperor's usurped and extended exercise of trade and commerce; or must resolve to be in a condition to do ourselves justice, and to defend our undoubted rights against these reciprocal engagements entered into, in defiance and violation of all national faith, and the most solemn treaties."

Parliament unanimously approved the Speech and large sums of money were voted for the strengthening of the Army and Navy in readiness for the coming war. Stormy exchanges at Court between the Imperial Ambassador and the English Ministers led to the former's departure from London. Yet the war that had seemed inevitable never broke out. The mediation of the French Minister, Fleury, resulted in a resumption of the negotiations, and since influential men in Vienna, and among them Prince Eugene of Savoy, were able to demonstrate to the Emperor that under the existing circumstances there was little hope of his winning the war, Charles VI most unwillingly and hesitatingly resolved to give his representatives full powers to sign the preliminary peace. Among other onerous conditions Charles was forced to agree to the suppression of the Ostend Company for a period of seven years. Although the definite peace treaty was subsequently to be drawn up by a congress, France and the maritime Powers had already regained the commercial privileges that they had enjoyed in Spain and the Indies before the Treaty of Vienna of 1715.

These peace preliminaries were a signal triumph for England and for Austria a severe defeat. Anglo-Austrian relations continued in a state of tension. The Diplomatic relations had been broken off ever since the recall of the ambassadors of both Powers from Vienna and London and were not resumed after the accession of George II. Negotiations that went on through the intermediary of France did not promise any speedy improvement. A detached examination of the situation nevertheless led to one conclusion only—the restoration of the former friendly relations between the two States was highly desirable. George II, as King of Hanover, wanted to be on good terms with the Emperor. Charles VI desired an agreement with the maritime Powers because, lacking a male heir, he wished to secure the succession to the Imperial throne of his daughter, Maria Theresa, in accordance with the Pragmatic Sanction. Many of the most influential men in the Emperor's *entourage*, and, above all, Prince Eugene, believed that in view of the claims to the succession put forward by various princes the Emperor's plan could not be carried out without the assistance of the maritime Powers. Yet Charles VI only assented most unwillingly to the resumption of negotiations with England whose egotistic policy, as it appeared to his eyes, filled him with rancour, and therewith to the abandonment of the policy which he himself had inaugurated in his treaties with Spain, that had for its aim intimate relations with the Catholic Bourbon Courts and with them united resistance to the maritime Powers. Nevertheless the clearer the selfishness of the Spanish Court became the greater became the opposition manifested by the more important German princes to the marriage of Charles VI's daughter and heiress with a Spanish Bourbon prince, while the better-founded did doubts of the sincerity and selflessness of French statesmen, as revealed at the Congress of Soissons, appear, the more necessary did Charles VI feel it to be to follow the advice of those who advocated agreement with the maritime Powers. The real question was whether it was possible to overcome the tremendous obstacles that stood in the way of a new alliance. Charles demanded an unconditional guarantee of the succession of his daughter while the maritime Powers demanded the complete suppression of the Ostend Company and its trade. In addition George II asked that the Emperor should guarantee his Hanoverian dominions.

For a long time it seemed as if agreement were impossible since neither party would yield an iota of its demands. The news that reached Vienna at the close of 1729 of the signature of the Treaty of Seville also brought the Austrian Court the unwelcome information that Spain had joined with France and England, broken off her relations with the Imperial Government, and denounced all the agreements by which she had undertaken to further the Emperor's commercial interests. The Imperial Government was enraged not only by Spain's conduct but also by that of France and more especially by England's. In Vienna public feeling ran high and demanded war. In government circles thoughts were seriously entertained of taking up arms in defence of Austria's interests. Attempts to secure allies for the projected war nevertheless proved fruitless and consequently Austrian statesmen, at whose head was Prince Eugene of Savoy, strongly pressed for an agreement with England, which now seemed possible of achievement because England's ties with the Bourbons in France and Spain were already loosening. The Bourbons wanted to wage what they believed would prove to be a victorious war against Austria, whereas the last thing English statesmen wanted was war. Towards the middle of 1730 negotiations were resumed between England and Austria. Charles VI again pressed for a guarantee of the Austrian succession while England demanded the final liquidation of the Ostend Company, that the promises made to Spain in the Treaty of Seville regarding the Spanish possessions in Tuscany and Parma should be fulfilled, and also that George II as King of Hanover should be supported by the Emperor in his demands regarding his Hanoverian dominions. After prolonged and often heated discussions the negotiations finally came to a successful close. On 16 March 1731 a treaty was signed that satisfied the most important requirements of both parties. In February 1732 the States General became a party to the treaty. Nevertheless Charles VI was fated to be disappointed in his hope that an agreement that had been brought about by such heavy sacrifices on Austria's part would result in England's pursuing an Austrophil policy. He did not receive the support he had hoped for when he became involved in a war with the Bourbon Powers, and the English Minister in Vienna went so far as to declare in the name of his Government that the Emperor need expect no help "even if the enemy were to invade the Archduchy (of

Austria) itself." In Vienna it was generally believed that it was England's fault that the Emperor in October 1735 was forced to sign extremely unfavourable preliminaries of peace. Similarly Austria violently accused England of pursuing a selfish commercial policy and of refusing to help Austria's Belgian subjects who had suffered very severely as a consequence of the loss of the Ostend trade. These complaints nevertheless made no impression. England continued to pursue a pro-Bourbon policy. It was not until it became obvious that France and Spain were contending not merely with Austria but also were beginning to defend themselves against England's increasingly menacing naval power, as well as against the damaging expansion of England's trade in the Spanish colonies in South America, that England changed her policy.

Since all attempts to achieve a peaceful settlement failed, England was forced, in 1739, to declare war on Spain, and as it seemed probable that war with France would soon follow, the English Government thought it might be well to have the Emperor as an ally. But Charles VI absolutely refused to fight at England's side in a war with Spain. Events had indeed come the full circle. At the outset it was Charles VI who sought England's friendship, now George II stretched out his hand to Charles VI in vain. But the Emperor's days were numbered. His death and the opposition manifested to Maria Theresa's accession to the throne made it imperatively and urgently desirable that Austria should secure England's support. George II not only declared himself ready to fight for Maria Theresa's rights, he did in fact fight at her side for many years, furnished her with troops, and by means of large subsidies helped her to meet the immense cost of the war. Through all these years of fighting side by side the divergent interests of the allies nevertheless frequently gave rise to serious quarrels between them. In England's eyes France was the enemy who must at all costs be defeated while Maria Theresa saw in Frederick II of Prussia her chief foe. It was, however, in England's interest that Frederick the Great should be induced to make peace and she was successful in achieving this end. Maria Theresa could not afford to dispense with the English alliance and was therefore forced to make peace with Frederick at the cost of heavy sacrifices. Nor was the pressure any less great that was brought to bear by England in order to secure the participation of Savoy in the war against France.

It was in vain that the Austrian diplomatists sought to induce Carl Emmanuel of Savoy to lessen his extensive demands or at least to give Austria proportionate compensation. Since Austria could not continue the struggle without the promised financial aid from England, she was forced to give way and under English pressure to sign agreements in September 1743 at Worms that involved her in very considerable sacrifices.

A partial compensation for these losses was indeed given to Austria in the following month—October 1743—in a convention by which George II undertook to pay Austria an annual subsidy of not less than £300,000 for the duration of the war and also renewed his promise that Maria Theresa should eventually receive adequate compensation for her losses. George II also renewed the guarantees which he had given to Maria Theresa for the eventuality that Frederick the Great broke the peace he had made with her. When, however, the Austrian Minister in London delivered the ratification of this treaty, he was informed that the majority in the Cabinet were opposed to its ratification and had threatened the King with their resignation if he were to approve it. A protest by the Austrian Minister proved fruitless. Maria Theresa had to content herself with an agreement signed in February 1744, by which England undertook to pay Austria for the current year only the same subsidy—£300,000—that she had paid her in the preceding year. Meanwhile England and Austria were no more successful in settling their commercial than they had been in settling their political differences. In common with all other Powers, Austria sought to promote her own trade and industry, and for this purpose adopted measures that were largely aimed at stopping the import of English goods into the Austrian dominions. England took counter-measures. The prohibition of the import of English woollen goods into Austria was answered by England's raising the additional duty on Silesian linen cloth—Austria's most important industrial export to England—and by placing higher duties on other raw materials and manufactured articles that she exported to Austria either direct or from her colonies. The dispute was further aggravated by the heavy losses sustained by the trade of Charles VI's Belgian subjects as a consequence of the suppression of the Ostend Company and the commercial competition of the maritime Powers. Throughout the seventeen thirties the import of many goods into

Austria was wholly forbidden, while on others high duties were levied. English traders bitterly complained of the losses they sustained as a consequence of the Austrian Government's tariff policy and demanded that their own Government should take strong counter-measures. In answer to English inquiries Austria said that in the interest of her own industry she could not lift the import prohibitions nor lower the high import duties.

A fundamental change in this policy only came after the wars with France and Turkey had ended disastrously for Austria. New English demands for a change of policy were now no longer rejected as a matter of course, and in the middle of 1739 negotiations were begun that, after many years and much hard bargaining arising out of the negotiators' endeavour to secure for their respective countries the largest possible gains with the least possible concessions, finally reached a stage at which the English draft of an agreement could be submitted to the Austrian Government for examination and approval. In her reply to the English draft Maria Theresa declared that it was impossible for her "ever to lose the grateful memory of the noble exertions made on her behalf by English citizens" and therefore that she was ready to tie still more closely together the bonds of friendship that had hitherto joined the two nations. But she added that her subjects must not be asked to make sacrifices that they could not bear. Her reply then went on to list the concessions that had been made to England and to state the counter-demands upon the fulfilment of which Austria must make a stand. There can be no doubt that a commercial treaty drawn up on these lines would have been extremely advantageous for England. Such at least was the opinion of many influential Austrian officials and merchants who did everything that lay in their power to prevent the conclusion of the treaty, in which they proved successful. The Austrian Government dragged out the negotiations and when, at the insistence of England, they were resumed in 1745 they ended in failure. The Austrian Government refused to sign the treaty. A reason that contributed to this decision was undoubtedly the loss of Silesia to Prussia by the treaty which England in 1745 compelled Maria Theresa to sign with Frederick the Great: for the loss of Silesia deprived a commercial treaty with England of one of its greatest benefits for Austria—the lightening of the restrictions on the import into England of Silesian linen cloth. Another consideration that weighed with Austrian statesmen in rejecting the commercial treaty was their dissatisfaction with England's attitude in political questions and their fear lest they might close the door on a compromise with France by granting England commercial privileges. The British delegation charged with the negotiation of the commercial treaty left Vienna in the autumn of 1746 without having attained the object for which they had so zealously striven.

The war between Austria and France went on throughout the years 1746-1748 and Austria continued to receive English subsidies. Nevertheless it became increasingly obvious that English statesmen were wholly averse to a prolongation of the war merely to serve Maria Theresa's longing to regain Silesia and the territories that had been ceded to Sardinia. Her complaints were in vain, her endeavours to put off the evil day hopeless. England and the States General made peace with France in 1748, and, after putting up the strongest possible resistance, Maria Theresa was forced to accept the terms agreed upon by her allies. England's conduct in this instance appeared to Maria Theresa as an unjust injury inflicted upon her own person and she held herself aloof from the attempts at a *rapprochement* made by the English Government in the succeeding years. Nevertheless she never thought of separating herself from her former ally since she still hoped to find England fighting at her side in a war with Prussia. For this reason, too, Maria Theresa hesitated to adopt the advice of her most important and ablest counsellor, Kaunitz, who soon after the signature of the Peace of Aix-la-Chapelle proposed a complete reversal of Austrian foreign policy and the abandonment of the "old system" of an alliance with the maritime Powers against France. And it was not until she recognized that she could not expect England's help in the pursuit of her projects, and also not until she had experienced the great disappointment caused her by the English delegation's rudely negatory attitude in the negotiations for a commercial treaty that were carried on during the years 1753-1755 with the object of improving the economic situation of her Belgian subjects—it was not until all this had happened that Maria Theresa finally listened to the advice of Kaunitz and his supporters. As early as June 1755, Kaunitz said that the statements of the English negotiators were couched in such a fashion "that it would be incompatible with the honour and dignity of your Imperial Majesty patiently to investigate their irritating reproaches and threats and still more to tolerate them since moderation could have the damaging effect that the deceits of the inimical and imperious English would increase in number and become intolerable." Moreover, the more obvious it became as a consequence of the war that had broken out between England and France that Maria Theresa could not count on English support in a war with Prussia, the easier it was for Kaunitz to convince his sovereign that the continuance of the policy that had hitherto been pursued no longer accorded with the interests of the country, and instead that Austria's interests called for close relations with France.

The *rapprochement* between the French and Austrian Governments demanded by Kaunitz followed the conclusion of the Convention of Westminster between George II and Frederick II. Anglo-Austrian relations steadily deteriorated and the tone of their mutual communications grew sharper. The English Government reproached the Austrian Government for making demands such as England's support of Austria in a war with Frederick the Great that England could not possibly fulfil. The Austrian Government retorted by declaring that the Convention of Westminster was an open violation of existing treaties and by saying that England's demand that "we should become reconciled with our greatest enemy Prussia simply on England's account is an astonishing and unbelievable suggestion." The first Treaty of Versailles between France and Austria was signed on 1 May 1756 and was followed by a second treaty a year later after war had again broken out between Austria and Prussia. Now French and Austrians fought against Prussians and English whereas during the forties it had been the Austrians and the English who had fought the Prussians and the French. Nevertheless war was never formally declared between England and Austria during the whole course of the Seven Years War nor was there any formal peace between them after the cessation of hostilities. The Seven Years War ended successfully for England with a considerable acquisition of territory and with her might and influence greatly strengthened throughout the world. On the other hand Maria Theresa had to give up her hopes of regaining Silesia. Hence it is understandable that Maria Theresa should have given a cold reception to English proposals for a resumption of friendly relations between England and Austria, when, soon after the peace of 1763, England was hopeful of securing Austria to replace Prussia as an ally in another war with France. For Anglo-Prussian relations had been somewhat strained during the last years of the war. The Austrian Government in reply to these suggestions said that while Austria was indeed ready to live in peace with England she was also determined to maintain friendly relations with France, and therefore that she was firmly resolved neither to maintain in force nor to renew the Barrier Treaty or any of the subsequent agreements arising out of it. And Maria Theresa, acting on Kaunitz's advice, remained faithful to this policy until her death.

But Anglo-Austrian relations continued to be formally correct. Austria remained neutral throughout the War of American Independence, rejected French suggestions that she should join England's enemies, and assured the English Government that she had no intention whatsoever of going to war with England. Under Kaunitz's guidance the Emperor Joseph II continued this policy, and, when in October 1781 he found himself compelled to join the armed neutrality that came into existence between European Powers as a consequence of England's conduct of maritime warfare, he was careful in announcing his decision to George III to assure him that he would continue as before to observe the strictest neutrality. Beyond this, however, the Emperor would not go. The Austrian Government still doubted England's sincerity and consequently showed itself very reserved towards England's frequent attempts to induce Austria to break with France. In September 1784, Kaunitz, replying to suggestions emanating from England and Prussia for this purpose, said:

"So long as France remains true to us . . . it is useless to hope that we who have never been the first to desert an ally nor to denounce a sincere and mutually advantageous agreement will alter our present system of governance; especially since this system has become virtually indissoluble with our self-preservation ever since Great Britain's earlier incomprehensible policy raised up the King of Prussia to be our lasting and serious rival."

Moreover, when in 1785 the English Minister renewed the proposal for an alliance between England, Russia, and Austria to the accompaniment of the statement that it must be directed against France, and simultaneously threatened Austria with the possibility of an Anglo-Prussian alliance, Kaunitz answered the proposal by making the following statement to the English Government:

"It was always and still is very far from the intention of His Imperial Majesty to display towards the Court of Great Britain anything less than the respect and consideration that is its due as one of the first Powers in Europe. But this respect and consideration is something quite different from a formal alliance. And a formal alliance is useless for so long as one party to it looks solely to the final objective, but never comes forward with the means to this end, and for so long as that one party to the alliance only bears in mind its one-sided and selfish interests, and seeks to build up the common bond on this basis alone. It is well known that a foundation-stone of English policy is the destruction of the Bourbon power while it is no less true that its continuance is a foundation-stone of our policy, and must continue to serve as such—this is an anachronism that the English Government has for too long overlooked and even to-day still overlooks. Ever since that misfortunate and fateful time when, chiefly by England's complicity, Prussia attained to its present strength, and when by its own action the English Court through the collision between this Power [Prussia] and ourselves rendered an alliance for itself with either ourselves or Prussia useless and impracticable, our gaze has been—and must continue to be—turned upon Prussia."

Austria's negative attitude decided the English Government in 1787 to conclude an alliance with Prussia and to intervene in support of Prussian interests in the Eastern Question that had been *the* question of the hour in European politics ever since Joseph II declared war upon Turkey. Kaunitz held firmly to the French alliance with the result that all attempts to bring about a compromise between England and Austria failed of success. At the beginning of 1789 as at the outbreak of the Seven Years War, France, Russia, and Austria were opposed by England and Prussia. A decisive change came over the scene, however, much more rapidly than could have been expected. The increasingly difficult situation in which Joseph II found himself in regard to his war with Turkey, the growing opposition to his plans for reform in Hungary and Belgium, the unceasing rivalry with Prussia, and, above everything else, the outbreak of the French Revolution which seriously lowered the value of his alliance with the French Court—all these considerations decided Joseph II and his aged Chancellor, Kaunitz, to seek to come to terms with England. But English statesmen maintained an attitude of reserve and demanded as a preliminary condition for any agreement with Austria that the Emperor should first settle his disputes with Turkey and with his Hungarian and Belgian subjects, and that he should denounce the Austro-French alliance. For a long time Kaunitz refused to yield to English pressure. Tension grew between the two countries. Finally Austria gave way. England assumed the rôle of mediator in both the Belgian and Eastern Questions and ultimately found solutions to both by restoring the *status quo* in the Near East and by effecting a reconciliation between the Empire and Belgium to the accompaniment of a guarantee of the former Belgian Constitution. A compromise was also brought about between Prussia and Austria that led to close relations between them when both Powers found themselves menaced by the victorious advance of the French Revolution. It was only natural under such circumstances that the wish should become steadily stronger in Vienna for English support in a war with France. But England for a long time showed little disposition to take part in a struggle with France and it was not until after the autumn of 1792, when France seized Belgium and threatened Holland, that British statesmen first suggested in December to the Austrian Minister in London the necessity for a Grand Alliance against France and also for an Anglo-Austrian alliance. The Imperial Government gladly entertained this proposal. The negotiations resulted at the end of August 1793 in the conclusion of a treaty by which both States bound themselves to act jointly in a war against France.

The Austrian Government nevertheless did not succeed in securing the fulfilment of its demands. England refused point blank to support either the Austrian proposal for the exchange of Belgium for Bavaria or for Austrian participation in a new partition of Poland between Russian and Prussia. Nevertheless Austria and England remained comrades in arms for twenty years—apart from brief intermissions—in the struggle against their common enemy, the French Republic, and subsequently Napoleon I. Even when they separated for a time necessity always brought them together again, and new alliances were concluded, even though the negotiations leading up to them were often the scene of heated disputes. The negotiators accused each other of self-seeking and indulged in mutual recriminations. The Austrians complained of insufficient subsidies, delays in the receipt of monies already granted, and the harsh conditions imposed on them when raising loans in England. The English retorted by accusing the Austrians of inefficient conduct of the war and of pursuing aims that had no direct connection with the struggle against France. The Austrian Minister, Thugut, who never trusted the English Government, said at the time of the negotiations in 1797 for a fresh loan that the English terms were tantamount to "unprecedented usury and so conceived that we cannot accept such conditions without completely destroying our credit and without announcing to Europe our speedy and inevitable bankruptcy. Even a young spendthrift in the clutches of his creditors would not put his signature to the English terms." England, too, was blamed for the fact that Austria was forced in October 1797 to conclude the Peace of Campo-Formio with Napoleon—an accusation that England strongly denied while at the same time she condemned Austria's conduct as egotistic. "Fine words and honourable behaviour," said Granville, "are wasted on Austrian politicians. Our conduct and actions in their regard should be guided solely by consideration of the extent to which they will be most useful and profitable for us." Mutual mistrust did not vanish even when in 1799 war again broke out between Austria and France with whom England was also at war. The Emperor Francis II did not fight as England's ally. Instead England and Austria fought independently of each other and pursued different aims. The English Government now as formerly saw its chief aim in the prevention of the permanent occupation of Belgium by the French while Francis II wanted to fight in Italy where he hoped to recoup himself for his territorial losses elsewhere.

Under these circumstances it is hardly surprising that months should have gone by before the negotiations begun in 1799 came to a successful end on 20 June 1800 after the Austrian and English delegations had mutually accused each other of the selfish pursuit of their own ends. Napoleon's victory at Marengo two days later nevertheless deprived Francis II of any hope of acquiring the Italian territory promised to him by England while another defeat at Hohenlinden in December forced him to make peace with Napoleon. After England renewed the struggle with France in 1803 the English Government tried to induce Francis II to enter the war and offered him greater financial support. Francis, however, for long hesitated to abandon the neutrality which he had pledged himself to France to keep and it required Napoleon's successes in Italy, combined with the growing conviction that it would prove impossible to avoid another war with France, to induce him after many hesitations to ally himself with England and Prussia and in 1805 once more to declare war upon France. Once again defeat followed upon defeat. Meanwhile England won the decisive naval victory. Francis found himself again forced to sign a degrading peace. In the succeeding years he refused to listen to English warnings or to renew the war with France in return for heavy subsidies and promises of other support. His answer was invariably the same: Austria is not sufficiently well-armed and must therefore remain neutral. In April 1807, the English Minister in Vienna said that Austria could not be persuaded to take the offensive against France and that financial subsidies alone would not suffice to make the Austrian Government declare war. Austria indeed was willing to mediate between France and England. Her efforts nevertheless proved fruitless. Although the entry of Austria into the Continental Blockade hit England hard, the English Government did not abandon hope of getting the Austrian Government to agree to a resumption of the negotiations that had for their object Austria's participation in the war against Napoleon. Moreover, they were strengthened in their hopes by the openly-expressed desire of the majority of Austrian statesmen to see the day when a re-armed Austria would once more take up the sword against Napoleon. The Austrians explained that their present attitude was due to the necessities of the time.

Napoleon's actions throughout 1808, and particularly his humiliating treatment of the Spanish Bourbons, aroused in ever-wider circles in Vienna the fear lest sooner or later the same fate would overtake the Habsburgs. Count Stadion made himself the mouthpiece of these fears. After long and wearisome negotiations in which the question of subventions again aroused bitter conflicts England and Austria agreed to fight together against Napoleon. The campaign that began well for Austria ended in her defeat and there followed the customary recriminations between the allies. The Austrian Government ascribed Austria's defeat in part to negligence in the payment of English subsidies and also to delays in the execution of England's diversionary operations. England retorted by roundly accusing the Austrian General Staff of poor strategical conceptions and indifferent staff work. On 14 October 1809 Austria was forced to sign the Peace of Schönbrunn by which she undertook to leave the ranks of Napoleon's enemies and of which Article XVI required that the Emperor Francis I should join in the Continental Blockade and break off all communications with England. It was in vain that the Emperor let it be known in London that he profoundly regretted that circumstances compelled him to sign this peace and that it was only after strenuous resistance that he had accepted Article XVI in its existing form. London was greatly incensed by Vienna's action. Diplomatic relations were broken off. Nevertheless hopes were still entertained both in London and Vienna that friendly relations would be resumed as soon as circumstances permitted. But there was little sign of this being possible for a long time to come. The general political situation in Europe, and the marriage between Napoleon and the Archduchess Marie Louise, necessitated Francis I's paying more and more regard to Napoleon's wishes which were chiefly directed towards Austria's active participation in all the coercive measures devised for England's destruction and more especially in the Continental Blockade. Meanwhile England made frequent attempts to convince Austria that in her own interests and those of the whole world she must take her share in the struggle against the common foe. But Metternich, who had been directing Austrian policy since the autumn of 1809, still held that the time had not yet come for placing Austria at the side of Napoleon's enemies. Metternich and Francis I were both convinced that Austria must refrain from taking any step that might cause doubts to arise in Napoleon's mind of the Imperial Court's friendship and all the more so since Russian policy in the Near East had aroused resentment in Austria. Francis I was well aware that his chances of extending his dominions eastwards would be better if he were Napoleon's ally rather than his enemy.

These and other considerations made it appear advisable to Metternich in March 1812 to counsel the Emperor to sign the alliance which Napoleon had brusquely proposed to him and that had for its object the participation of Austria in the Russian campaign. Even after the catastrophic failure of Napoleon's Russian adventure Metternich still refused the invitations that came from Prussia, Russia, and England for Austria to fight with them against France. He did indeed offer to be mediator in an attempt to patch up a peace. But when his efforts met with insuperable obstacles, Russia and Prussia resolved to prosecute the war resolutely, and England made more and more extensive promises for the eventuality that Austria entered the war. Metternich now decided to advance a step. Without advising his sovereign openly to join the Allies, Metternich suggested to him to substitute armed neutrality for mediation because this would result either in a general peace or in Austria's joining in the war, but this new policy also failed to please England who demanded that Austria should openly break with France and in return promised "the restoration of Austria's former frontiers and ancient splendour!" The English Government also made no secret of its disapproval of the Emperor's and Metternich's hesitant policy. Metternich and his Imperial master were nevertheless not to be hurried in changing their policy and only seriously resumed negotiations with England after the failure of their endeavours to induce Napoleon to make peace on terms acceptable to the Allies, and after they had decided that Austria should actively enter the war on the side of the Allies. Once again the negotiators on each side vigorously and stubbornly fought to defend their special interests so that much time passed before they finally came to an agreement. After Castlereagh's suspicions that Metternich might follow an independent policy regardless of England's interests had been allayed, the leading statesmen in both countries for years pursued a common policy in the most important questions of the day. From the beginning of 1814 onwards Metternich found in Castlereagh—"the most European and least insular of all English Foreign Ministers"—a firm supporter of his plans. Both statesmen believed in the old idea of the European Balance of Power, both did not want to see Russia become too powerful, both desired a strong Central Europe, and both pursued identical policies in regard to the Eastern Question. Austrian and English policy in regard to the ordering of Italian and German affairs ran on parallel lines. They were at one in their dislike of the introduction or development of representative government in these countries. And, finally, in regard to the attitude of both Powers towards Napoleon during the war, and towards France after his downfall, Metternich and

Castlereagh held the same opinions, and, when differences did arise, they were always overcome by mutual accommodation. The Treaty of Chaumont signed on 1 March 1814 was largely Castlereagh's work but it fully conformed to Metternich's views. By this Treaty the four Allies—Austria, Prussia, Russia, and England—undertook not to make peace with France separately and to maintain their armies on a war footing until the conclusion of peace. And again at the Congress of Vienna, Metternich and Castlereagh wholeheartedly supported one another in most of the questions that came up for decision. Austria and England, in common with France, opposed in the Treaty of 3 January 1815 Russia's and Prussia's far-reaching territorial demands, and, with Castlereagh's support, Metternich achieved the aim that he had set himself of restricting Russia's demands for Polish, and Prussia's demands for Silesian, territory. In return Metternich assisted England to set up a barrier against France by uniting Belgium and Holland. After Waterloo, England and Austria maintained a common front against France, and, although George IV could not for constitutional reasons enter the Holy Alliance, he thoroughly approved of the plans drawn up by the Austrian, Prussian, and Russian monarchs. Castlereagh, like Metternich, only agreed very unwillingly to this fantastic plan for eternal peace and pressed for the renewal and enlargement of the Treaty of Chaumont, which was in fact renewed for a third time—it had been renewed for a second time on the day of the signature of the Second Treaty of Paris—in November 1815, with the inclusion of an undertaking by the four signatory Powers to maintain the peace settlement in its entirety and in case of necessity to defend, with their united forces, the new order in Europe against any disturber of the peace. A provision for assuring the continuance of the existing order was, at Castlereagh's suggestion, introduced into Article VI of the Treaty by which the rulers of the four signatory Powers, or their Ministers, should meet in conference from time to time in order to concert measures for the preservation of peace. In years to come, however, it was Metternich who became the inspirer and organizer of the system of international conferences and he enlarged the competence of this European Areopagus to an extent and in a manner that did not conform with Castlereagh's ideas or the traditions of English foreign policy. Castlereagh thought that the Alliance of 20 November 1815 should assure the maintenance in force of the two peace treaties of Paris and the Final Act of the Congress of Vienna, and that any congresses that met in the future should be solely concerned to prevent any disturbance of the *status quo* by France. Moreover, he held that the four Allied Powers should only interfere in the domestic affairs of France or other States in the event that these seemed likely to give rise to a disturbance of the general peace. Metternich, on the other hand, from the very outset thought that the Great Powers should dictate to the lesser Powers and also intervene in their domestic affairs if there was a threat of revolution.

Obviously these differences of opinion could under given circumstances cause serious conflicts. The community of interest between England and Austria in the maintenance of a common policy in the great majority of political questions, during the years that immediately succeeded to the establishment of the new order in Europe, nevertheless, was sufficiently powerful to induce the leading Austrian and English statesmen to sink their differences. Thus England and Austria by common action were successful at the Congress of Aix-la-Chapelle in 1818 in restricting its discussions to the formal renewal of the Quadruple Alliance and in securing that France should only be invited to take part in the discussions under certain specified circumstances. The differences of opinion, moreover, between the four Allies on the subject of the limitations to be set to their right of intervention in the internal affairs of other States were kept well in the background. This was all the more necessary in England's case because Canning had already expressed the opinion that out of the holding of congresses by the Great Powers there should not be established a system of laws governing all the European Powers. The English people—Canning declared—would be alarmed for their freedom "if their own Government made a practice of joining in conferences with powerful despotic monarchs." The gulf between the outlooks of Metternich and Castlereagh nevertheless inevitably widened despite their mutual endeavours to avoid any break. Castlereagh could not possibly sympathize with the reactionary Carlsbad Decrees because he wanted a policy of moderation in regard to the South German States, and therefore he refused in 1820 to give the English Government's assent to the Carlsbad and Vienna Decrees. He also rejected Metternich's proposal for common action against revolutionary movements in France, and, when revolution broke out in Spain and Portugal, he made it perfectly clear that he would not listen to any proposals for either joint diplomatic action by the five Great Powers or military intervention or even for a general treaty embodying guarantees of the existing order. In fact Castlereagh was a convinced advocate of non-intervention. Metternich yielded to Castlereagh's demands. He left Spain and Portugal to their fate notwithstanding his fears lest events in the Iberian Peninsula might produce repercussions in Italy. But when what he had feared came to pass and a revolution broke out in Naples that appeared to threaten the peace of Europe, Metternich took strong measures that aroused England's opposition. True England as the rival of France in the Mediterranean perforce sided with Austria, recognized her supremacy in Italy and her right to protect her interests in Naples by force of arms, but refrained from affording her open support.

When the three Eastern European Powers—Austria, Russia, Prussia—declared in the Protocol of Troppau on 19 November 1820 that States in which changes of government were brought about by insurrection should be excluded from the comity of European Powers until such time as the legitimate government and law and order had been restored, and further that the Allies possessed the right by friendly intervention, but also if necessary by force, to show such States the error of their ways and lead them back into the comity of nations, Castlereagh raised his voice in protest against such generalizing decrees. He also protested against the notion of an European right of intervention, of which he strongly disapproved, and also against any supervision of the use made by independent States of their sovereignty in their internal affairs and the exclusion of third-rate Powers from the European family of nations. France supported him. Although an open breach between England and Austria was avoided, Europe was now divided into interventionist and non-interventionist groups of Powers. At Laibach Austria gained the day. Nevertheless England stood aside from Austria's intervention and answered the Troppau Decrees with an equally outspoken statement of her contrary opinions. The English Government did not object to Austria's supremacy in Naples; it did object to Austria's making it appear as if she was acting as Europe's mouthpiece. In other matters Metternich and Castlereagh worked together in harmony. After the outbreak of the Greek War of Independence Austria and England at first pursued the same policy in the Near East because neither wished to see Greece freed, and the Turkish power in Europe destroyed, by Russia whose bid for hegemony in the Mediterranean they feared and sought to oppose. A meeting between Metternich, Castlereagh, and George IV in Hanover in October 1822, resulted in complete agreement and was followed by successful negotiations with Tsar Alexander I. Hence it was a very severe blow for Metternich and for his policy when Canning assumed control of English foreign policy after Castlereagh's suicide. For Canning was an outspoken opponent of intervention and was determined that England should play no part in it.

Matters came to a head at the Congress of Verona in 1822 when acting on Canning's instructions Wellington protested against intervention in Spain. After the Congress, France in agreement with Russia, Prussia, and Austria, sent an army across the Pyrennees. Metternich and the principle of intervention had therewith won a victory. Nevertheless England's abstention split the pentarchy. The Quadruple Alliance directed against France was now replaced by a Triple Alliance between the Central Powers and Russia. The Congress of Verona was the last of the "Metternichean Congresses" and it soon became clear how great a loss Metternich had sustained by Castlereagh's death. For although Castlereagh had pursued his own individually English path since the Congress of Troppau, he had nevertheless continued to work for the maintenance of the Entente, and also through the Alliance for the peace of Europe. But Canning was both personally and politically Metternich's opponent. At Verona he resolutely championed non-intervention and withdrew England from any share in the policy of the Quadruple Alliance. Although at first he only afforded them moral support, Canning was on the side of the Spanish Liberals in their struggle against a powerful and reactionary Restoration while he also strongly supported the South American republics in their fight for independence. England and Austria had formerly pursued identical aims in the Near East. Now their paths diverged and each went her own way. Canning adopted an increasingly accommodating policy towards the Greek rebels, and, despite Metternich's endeavours to convince him that it was in

England's interest not to permit any diminution of Turkey's power, adhered firmly to his plan of preventing Russia from driving Turkey out of Europe while at the same time securing for an independent Greece her proper place in Europe. He treated the Greeks as equals of the Turks and on 4 April 1826 signed with Russia the Protocol of St. Petersburg in which England and Russia agreed by English mediation, supported by Russia, to obtain for Greece an autonomous status under Turkish sovereignty that was to be guaranteed by Austria, France, Russia and Prussia. This Treaty, which Metternich described as "a miserable piece of work" for which he refused to accept any responsibility, smashed the Alliance and excluded Austria from any share in the settlement of one of the most important international questions. Thus it was in reality a complete victory for Canning, and for Metternich a severe defeat, inasmuch as the principle upheld by the Great Powers of the sanctity of treaties and the settlement of all European affairs by the legitimate authority, *i.e.* themselves, was replaced by that of the individual interest of the individual State and the right of intervention in the service of illegitimate, or revolutionary, uprisings. The Treaty of London signed on 6 July 1827 between the Western Powers and Russia, despite the fact that Austria and Prussia were invited to append their signatures, marked the end of the pentarchy, and the victory of the Allied over the Turco-Egyptian Fleet at Navarino secured Greece her independence.

Metternich's policy had suffered shipwreck. No better fate awaited him when he called upon the Powers to take coercive measures against Pedro of Portugal, who had granted the Portuguese a constitution—an act that in Metternich's eyes menaced the social order in Europe with death and destruction. Canning refused to take part in the conference which Metternich wanted to summon, said he was opposed to intervention, and in December 1826 asked Parliament to take measures for the protection of Great Britain's oldest ally against attack from abroad. Hence it is hardly surprising that Canning's death on 8 August 1829 should have caused Metternich to breathe a sigh of relief. A slight improvement in Anglo-Austrian relations did indeed follow upon Canning's disappearance from the political scene. The Peace of Adrianople in 1829 met with a bad reception not only in Austria but also in London. The notion that was mooted of protecting the territorial integrity of the Ottoman Empire by means of a guarantee on the part of all the European Great Powers in order to forestall Russia's achievement of hegemony in the Near East was welcomed by Metternich with enthusiasm. But the negotiations that were set in motion for this purpose led to no really satisfactory result. An identity of interests caused Austria and England to recognize Louis Philippe as the successor of Charles X, and at the same time to oppose his wish to strengthen French influence in Belgium by the election of a French prince as King of Belgium. On the other hand the opposition between their interests and political outlooks found clear expression in the negotiations over the settlement of the Netherlands-Belgium question arising out of the successful Belgian revolution. The English Government, and especially Lord Palmerston, who since the close of 1830 had been Secretary of State for Foreign Affairs, supported non-intervention and the separation of the Netherlands from Belgium as well as the grant of constitutional government to Belgium. True England in 1815 had pressed for the union of the two countries for the purpose of erecting as strong a barrier as possible against France. But now English statesmen believed that an independent Belgium afforded England sufficient protection and they were no longer interested in the continued existence of an economically progressive Netherlands. Metternich looked upon the Belgian revolution as a crime against the spirit of the Holy Alliance and the European order established by the Congress of Vienna. He therefore wanted the Great Powers to intervene to secure as far as possible the rights of the legitimate sovereign. He was fated to experience the disappointment of all his hopes. The Conference of London, regardless of the rightful King, decided in favour of the separation of Belgium and the Netherlands, and also that Belgium should be granted a constitution that violated all the principles of which the maintenance appeared to Metternich to be essential were Europe, as in his opinion it should, permanently to resist all revolutionary movements.

For the same reason Metternich deeply deplored the passing of the Reform Bill in 1832 since he found the admission of the liberal middle-classes into political life incompatible with his conception of what should be the relationship between a government and its subjects. But Metternich was pleased when the English Government held firmly to the principle of non-intervention in the struggle between Tsar Nicholas I and his insurrectionary Polish subjects despite the fact that public opinion in England sympathized with the Polish rebels. He also shared the fears entertained by the Western Powers in 1833 after the signature of the Treaty of Unkiar-Skelessi between Russia and Turkey that it might have as a consequence the establishment by Russia of an exclusive protectorate over Turkey, and he played with the idea of forestalling it by a joint protectorate exercised by Russia, Austria, England, and France. The fear of the outbreak of revolution in Germany and Italy coupled with the knowledge that in Nicholas I he had found a champion of the counter-revolutionary movement, and of the principle of intervention, decided Metternich to enter into closer relations with Russia that found outward expression in the meeting in September 1833 of the Austrian, Russian, and Prussian sovereigns at Münchengrätz where it was agreed that every sovereign should possess the right of going to the assistance of any other sovereign and that "it shall not henceforth be permissible to any Power not so appealed to, to intervene for the purpose of hindering such assistance." Austria, Russia, and Prussia now stood united in defence of this principle against the world Powers—France and England. It was from this standpoint that Metternich viewed the constitutional conflicts and disputes over the succession to the throne in Spain and Portugal, and as a consequence he found himself involved in a serious struggle with England. Palmerston—Canning's pupil—was inspired by the same hatred for Metternich, and both in Spain and Portugal supported the Liberal cause against the absolutist Powers. He gained the day in both countries. Metternich had to stand by while Miguel, whose rights he had championed, renounced all his legal claims to the Portuguese throne, the constitution which he had set aside was re-established, and Maria de la Gloria was acknowledged as Queen. A similar defeat awaited him in Spain where he championed the claims of Don Carlos against those of Ferdinand's daughter, Isabella, in accordance with the legitimist doctrine. The Quadruple Alliance of 22 April 1834, which was Palmerston's work, united England, France, Spain, and Portugal—the last two Powers, that is to say, in so far as they supported Isabella, and furthered her cause, and with it brought the constitutional principle, as opposed to the legitimist principle of the Holy

Alliance, to victory. The gulf dividing the Western and Eastern Powers existed for some years, although from time to time differences arose between France and England that caused France to come closer to Austria, until the Eastern Question in the guise of the war between the Sultan and the Viceroy of Egypt, Mehemet Ali, induced the English and Austrian Governments to take joint action in the Sultan's behalf against Mehemet Ali, who was supported by France. Joint action was nevertheless not achieved without difficulty. Metternich knew that Palmerston was intriguing in Constantinople and that he threatened Austria with popular risings in Galicia, Hungary, and Lombardy-Venetia if she did not join with England in a common policy in the Eastern Question. Hence he refused to agree to a conference in London at which he feared that Palmerston would only pursue selfish aims. Moreover Metternich found it repugnant to turn against Nicholas I in whom he saw the strongest member of the Eastern Alliance. He also never doubted that Palmerston's sole object in trying to rope in Austria was to serve English ends. The defeat of the Turks and the defection of the Turkish Fleet to Mehemet Ali nevertheless forced Metternich to give way and to agree to a conference.

Palmerston acted as chairman of the Conference, and under his guidance it finally drafted the Convention of London, which was signed on 15 July 1840 by England, Prussia, Austria, and Russia. A year later, after France had yielded when confronted with joint action by the four Powers, an agreement was concluded with Turkey in which the five Powers—France was now a signatory—recognized the inviolability of the Sultan's sovereign rights and guaranteed the neutralization of the Black Sea and the Straits of the Bosphorus and the Dardanelles. The settlement of this question was a victory for England over Russia, and Austria could also view the result with satisfaction chiefly because on this occasion the division of the Great Powers into a Liberal Dual Alliance and a Conservative Triple Alliance had been avoided and instead all five Great Powers had united in a common action. Another welcome event for Metternich occurred in September 1841, when Melbourne's Liberal Government, in which Palmerston had served as Foreign Secretary, was replaced by a Tory Government headed by Peel with the Earl of Aberdeen in charge of the Foreign Office. Aberdeen was a sincere admirer of Metternich and his policy, and he at once announced his intention of adhering to the settlement of 1815 and of supporting the Continental Powers in event of a violation by France of the Final Act of the Congress of Vienna. This harmonious relationship between the Austrian Chancellor and the English Foreign Secretary only lasted until the middle of 1846, when Lord John Russell replaced Peel as Prime Minister and Palmerston again became Secretary of State for Foreign Affairs. The gulf between Metternich's views on international affairs and those held by Liberal English statesmen again proved too wide to permit of sincere co-operation. In 1846, for example, when the unwelcome news reached London of the betrothal of two Spanish Infantas to two French princes, and Palmerston suggested to Metternich an agreement between the Eastern Powers and England, Metternich rejected the proposal. And again in the same year when Austria took the opportunity afforded by a rising in Galicia to incorporate Cracow with her dominions, Palmerston protested against Metternich's action and gave a warning to the Eastern Powers that the Final Act of the Vienna Congress must be observed in its entirety, and that it was impossible that a government could be allowed to choose from among the Articles of the Final Act those which it thought fit to observe and those which it intended to violate. Nevertheless England in face of the *fait accompli* contented herself with a formal protest. The enmity between Palmerston and Metternich, however, became more and more obvious. Thus Palmerston in the constitutional struggle that divided Switzerland into two hostile camps in 1847 supported the Liberals who wanted to establish a free and constitutionally-governed federal State as opposed to the maintenance of the old form of government by the *Sonderbund* which had the support of the Powers led by Metternich. But it was again Palmerston, and not Metternich, who emerged victorious from the struggle.

The unbridgeable gulf dividing Metternich from Palmerston in the realm of political ideas was, however, most clearly revealed in the attitudes they respectively adopted to the Italian *Risorgimento*. As early as 1846 Palmerston was already supporting the Italian Liberals, especially with Pope Pius IX, and by so doing aroused the fiercest indignation in Metternich who had described the Liberal movement in Italy as "entirely destructive of the treaty-system established in 1815 under the guarantee of Europe." He added that the Liberals sought to drive Austria out of Italy and to unite Italy in a single body politic—"an absurd object since Italy was merely a geographical expression." Replying to Metternich's appeal for help Palmerston declared that there was no intention of uniting the Italian States and that "the real danger to both Italian and European peace lay in the repression of the legitimate aspirations of the people of the Peninsula towards constitutional government." Palmerston indeed never ceased to sympathize with Italian nationalism notwithstanding the dislike of it displayed by Queen Victoria and Conservative statesmen. Nor did he wish to destroy Austria. "The Austrian Empire is a thing worth saving," he said, "its maintenance is an object of genuine interest to all Europe and to no country more than England." Nevertheless he believed that Austria in her own best interest should relinquish her Italian possessions and that this "would not diminish the real strength nor impair the real security of Austria as a European Power." Austria, however, showed not the slightest inclination to follow Palmerston's advice and Radetzky's victories in Italy in 1848 and 1849 enabled Austria to retain her sovereignty over Lombardy and Venetia for some years.

Palmerston adopted a different attitude to the Hungarian Revolution. He certainly sympathized with the Magyars' desire to maintain their constitutional rights, but he did not want Hungary to become independent of Austria, because he feared she might then be sacrificed to Russian expansionist policy. Consequently he approved of Russian intervention when it became clear that it "meant the restoration of Hungary to Austria intact and this he could not but approve." But he strongly condemned the reactionary measures enforced by the Austrian Government after the suppression of the Hungarian insurrection and offered an asylum in England to the victims of Austrian justice. It was due to Palmerston's efforts that the demand made by Austria, with Russia's support, for the extradition of the Hungarian refugees in Turkey met with no success. Nevertheless Palmerston did not want to see Austria's position as a Great Power in Europe upset in any way and he often publicly expressed this wish. In a speech on 21 July 1849 he said *inter alia*:

"Austria has been our ally. We have been allied with Austria in most important European transactions, and the remembrance of an alliance ought undoubtedly to create in the breast of every Englishman who has a recollection of the history of this country feelings of respect towards a Power with whom we have been in such alliance. It is perfectly true that in the course of those repeated alliances, Austria, not from any fault of hers, but from the pressure of irresistible necessity, was repeatedly compelled to depart from the alliance, and to break the engagements by which she had bound herself to us. We did not reproach her with yielding to the necessity of the moment, and no generous mind would think that these circumstances ought in any degree to diminish or weaken the tie which former transactions must create between the Governments of the two countries. But there are higher and larger considerations which ought to make the maintenance of the Austrian Empire an object of solicitude to every English statesman. Austria is a most important element in the balance of European power. Austria stands in the centre of Europe, a barrier against encroachment on the one side and against invasion on the other. The political independence and liberties of Europe are bound up, in my opinion, with the maintenance and integrity of Austria as a great European Power, and therefore anything which tends by direct, or even remote, contingency to weaken and to cripple Austria, but still more to reduce her from the position of a first-rate Power to that of a secondary State, must be a great calamity to Europe which every Englishman ought to deprecate and to try to prevent."

These views on Austria's rôle in Europe did not stop Palmerston from opposing the reactionary measures of the Austrian Government, nor from supporting every libertarian movement, with the natural result that an increasing tension developed in the relations between the two countries.

When Palmerston resigned towards the end of 1851 his successor endeavoured to pursue an Austrophil policy. On 15 March 1852 Lord Malmesbury wrote to the Austrian Foreign Minister, Count Buol:

"In proportion to the value which H.M. Government place upon the maintenance of a cordial friendship with Austria, the oldest ally of England, cemented not only by the tie of mutual interest, but by the recollection of past efforts in a common cause, was the regret with which H.M. present Government on succeeding to office found that the result of the events of the last years had been to substitute for these friendly relations a tone of mutual suspicion, if not of actual alienation, and to give their diplomatic correspondence a character quite at variance with the dispositions which ought to subsist between them."

An old friend of Austria, Lord Aberdeen, went still further in desiring a friendship with Austria based on practical considerations. Towards the end of March 1853 he wrote to his friend Lord Clarendon:

"I think the greatest misfortune of the present day is our alienation from Austria. It is an entirely new feature in our foreign policy, and deranges all our calculations. Austria is a State with which I should have thought it impossible to quarrel, and however desirable to be on the best terms with France and Russia, is the only Power on whose friendship I should have thought we could confidently rely. Our first object ought to be to convince the Austrian Government of our sincerity and to lead them to believe that we have no object in view but their own real welfare."

An opportunity of affording the Austrian Government a proof of the sincerity of this sentiment seemed to offer itself when the Western Powers resolved to fight at Turkey's side in her war with Russia, and considered making an attempt to get Austria to fight with them. In Vienna at this time there were two opposing parties—one faithful to the Metternichean tradition wanted to fight with Russia against Turkey, while the other desired to join the Western Powers. The Emperor Francis Joseph, who was then twenty-four years of age, thought that he ought not to identify himself with the policy of either party and he therefore pursued a contradictory and inconsequential policy of his own making. On the outbreak of war between the maritime Powers and Russia, Austria proclaimed her neutrality, and then finding her hopes of Russia disappointed, changed round without at the same time definitely deciding to go to war with Russia. In this way Francis Joseph deeply offended Russia while he did not satisfy the Western Powers. Palmerston complained of Austrian unreliability and said she was apparently content with some patchwork in the Balkans instead of working for a really good peace settlement. The English Government was disappointed when the Austrian Government only promised in a treaty signed on 2 December 1854 to enter the war under certain conditions and refused to enter into any agreement for the achievement of the Allies' aims unless Russia had not made peace by 1 January 1855 on the Allies' terms. Palmerston exclaimed: "We will sign a treaty of alliance, but Austria will never go to war with Russia, and the sole result of this treaty will be a state of tension between Austria and the Western Powers." Nor was he proved wrong. The Austrian Government never made war on Russia. Francis Joseph did not want to break completely with Russia nor to come completely under the domination of the maritime Powers. The only result of his policy was that he offended the Western Powers without reconciling himself with Russia.

Palmerston became Prime Minister in February 1855, and in consequence the tension in Anglo-Austrian relations increased while the fact that Sardinia, and not Austria, entered the war at the side of the Allies resulted, as was shown in the immediate future, in a lowering of Austrian prestige in Italy. Isolation was the penalty meted out to Austria for her inconsequential policy. Russia remained inimical and Austrian relations with France and England grew cooler and more tense. At the Congress of Paris in 1856 Austria failed to find support for her interests and was forced to abandon her hopes of acquiring the Danubian Principalities. Among the provisions of the Peace of Paris was one by which the Powers were required in the event of disputes arising between them to seek a compromise through the mediation of a friendly Power before taking up arms. When the relations between the Piedmontese and Austrian Governments became increasingly inimical throughout the years 1857 and 1858, and when Cavour's brilliant diplomacy succeeded in gaining Napoleon III's promise of armed support in a future war with Austria and Victor Emmanuel's and Napoleon III's speeches revealed that a war in which France and Sardinia would be opposed by Austria was threatening, England therefore attempted to mediate. The Tory Government then in power was coolly disposed towards Italian nationalism and did not want to see Austria weakened by France. The Secretary of State for Foreign Affairs, Lord Malmesbury, strongly advised the French Government not to go to war because France would find conservative Europe arrayed in arms against her. The English Minister in Vienna urged the Austrian Government to seek a compromise. Since, however, their efforts failed both in Paris and in Vienna the Government introduced into the Queen's Speech in opening Parliament some words about her anxiety over the maintenance of the inviolability of the treaties of 1815, and at the same time started negotiations in Vienna in accordance with the stipulations of the Treaty of Paris for the holding of a Congress. The English Government also advised the Austrian Government to disarm. The Austrian Foreign Minister, Count Rechberg, in replying to this invitation, said: "If England would give Austria a formal guarantee of security against attack from France, Austria would agree to stop armaments. She would go to a Congress and there settle her differences with Sardinia." But England refused to assume this far-reaching responsibility and therefore Austria sent an ultimatum to Sardinia to disarm. "By this precipitate step," Malmesbury said, "the Cabinet of Vienna forfeits all claim upon the support or sympathy of England whatever may be the consequences that may ensure from it." Further attempts to restrain Austria proved fruitless. Austria embarked on a war that ended after her defeats at Solferino and Magenta in a Franco-Italian victory.

A few days before the Battle of Solferino Palmerston again became Prime Minister and together with the Secretary of State for Foreign Affairs, Lord John Russell, and the Chancellor of the Exchequer, Mr. Gladstone, who were all friends of Italy, supported the movement for unification among the Central Italian States. Consequently they were not satisfied with the preliminaries of peace arranged at Villafranca and Palmerston declared that if Austria were to be a member of a union of Italian States Italy would be at her mercy. He refused to take part in a peace conference except on the condition that no pressure was brought to bear upon the Central Italian population which had risen against its Governments. The idea of a conference was subsequently abandoned and the English Government continued to support the movement for Italian liberation. Meanwhile Viennese public opinion was angered by Garibaldi's March and by Victor Emmanuel II's tolerance of it, protests against this breach of international law were made in Paris and London, and the King of Naples was encouraged to hold out. But the English Government supported by public opinion which was filled with admiration for Garibaldi's exploits championed the movement for liberation and declared that the people possessed the right to summon the King of Sardinia to help them in their struggle against the misgovernment of the Pope and the King of Naples. The victory won by the libertarian movement in Italy was hailed with joy in England, and encouraged Palmerston to carry on his anti-Austrian policy in Italy because he did not believe that after the loss of Lombardy Austria would be able permanently to retain Venetia. As early as 1860 he proposed to the Austrian Government that Austria should give Venetia to Piedmont in return for financial compensation. On 21

September 1860 he wrote to Russell: "Austria as long as she holds Venice will have every Italian her bitter foe . . . They will be forced into a quarrel with Austria about Venice, and the sympathies of Europe will go with them and military success will crown their affairs."

Although Austria indignantly refused Palmerston's suggestion, he did not alter his opinion and told the Austrian Ambassador in London towards the middle of July 1862 on the subject of Venetia: "There are only two ways—to sell it or govern it in a conciliatory way. You Austrians did neither." A similar conversation took place the following year between the Ambassador and Lord John Russell in the course of which the former said that Austria would sooner risk a war than voluntarily give up Venetia. Russell replied that he expected this but that it was questionable if it could be deemed wise.

There was less difference in the standpoints adopted by English and Austrian statesmen towards the Polish rising in 1863 notwithstanding the fact that public opinion in England was more strongly pro-Polish than it was in Austria. The two countries were united in their endeavours to avoid being involved in war with Russia. Rechberg supported Russell's proposal for an amnesty for the Polish rebels and for the summoning of a congress in accordance with the provisions of the Final Act of the Congress of Vienna to settle the Polish Question. And when Austria objected to the holding of a congress on the ground that she had refused Russia's counter-proposal that the Polish Question should be settled solely by the three interested Powers—Austria, Russia, Prussia—because she had feared that she would be out-voted in all questions by Russia and Prussia, England considered the Austrian objection well-founded. Furthermore, Austria's rejection of Napoleon III's suggestion that England, France, and Austria should join in a *démarche* at St. Petersburg was well received and fully understood in London. War with Russia was obviated by a declaration that Palmerston insisted that the English Government should make to the effect that in the Polish Question it would confine itself "within the limits of reciprocal diplomatic communications." This declaration also sealed the fate of the Poles. The English and Austrian Governments nevertheless came to a parting of the ways when the accession of Christian IX to the throne of Denmark caused the Schleswig-Holstein Question to become actual. The

English Government supported Denmark and on 23 December 1863 sent a Note to the *Bundestag* in Frankfurt-am-Main which contained a warning that if the Bund were to take an over-hasty step that conflicted with the stipulations of the Protocol of London of 1852 serious complications might arise. This warning, however, made no more impression upon the two leading German Powers—Austria and Prussia—than had Palmerston's statement on 24 July in the House of Commons that whoever attacked the rights and independence of Denmark would not be confronted by Denmark alone. England then endeavoured to have all military preparations postponed but Rechberg and Bismarck rejected her suggestions to the accompaniment of a statement that in occupying Schleswig-Holstein they had no intention of violating the principle of the integrity of Denmark laid down in the London Protocol. On the outbreak of war with Denmark English public opinion strongly supported Denmark, the English Press fiercely attacked Austria and Prussia for their action in regard to Denmark, Edward, Prince of Wales, and his Danish wife championed the Danish cause at Court, and Palmerston stated in the House of Commons that decisive action must be taken against the German Powers. Nevertheless England did not afford Denmark the military support which the Danes had hoped for.

On 25 April 1864 a conference was opened in London which it was hoped by the English Government would solve the problem. Opinion was divided within the Government itself. Palmerston in opposition to the majority of his colleagues wanted to stand by Denmark while Russell would not consent to taking the final step unless France, of whose help he was by no means certain, also came in. The Central Powers stated in the Conference that they regarded themselves as freed from all obligations existing before the commencement of hostilities, including those contained in the Protocol of London of 1852, and they refused to alter their decision even after England and the other Powers had stated that they regarded the Protocol as still having the force of law. Since Denmark for its part rejected a proposal by the Central Powers for an autonomous Schleswig-Holstein joined to Denmark in a personal union, and since renewed attempts at mediation by the English Government proved unsuccessful, the Conference ended on 20 June without having achieved any result.

Palmerston now tried to change his bellicose words into deeds and made an unsuccessful bid for Napoleon's help without success. The Cabinet held many stormy meetings at which the war and peace parties fought with one another, and in the end the peace party gained the upper hand. Palmerston and Russell were compelled when laying the protocols of the Conference before both Houses of Parliament to seek to minimize their defeat by a declaration that, in event of a threatened bombardment of Copenhagen and of the continued existence of Denmark as an independent State in Europe being jeopardized, the English Government would consider changing its policy. England had indeed left Denmark at the mercy of her foes. Defeated in further battles she found herself forced to conclude a peace with her enemies on their terms in the drafting of which England took no part.

The events of the succeeding years, and especially the Convention of Gastein of August 1865, denoted a further lessening of English prestige in Europe that was bitterly resented in London where feeling ran high chiefly against Prussia but also against Austria. Without sympathizing in any way with either of these Powers, and bearing always in mind its own special interests, the English Government, in which Russell had succeeded to the Premiership on Palmerston's death and in which the Earl of Clarendon served as Foreign Secretary, worked steadily to maintain peace once it became obvious that the Austro-Prussian rivalry was likely to lead to a war in which Italy would fight at Prussia's side. After prior agreement with France and Russia, Clarendon proposed the holding of a congress at which an attempt could be made to settle the Danish and Italian Questions, and discussions could take place over the reforms "to be introduced into the German Federal Constitution as far as they may affect the balance of power in Europe." Prussia and Italy accepted the invitation but Austria only "with a proviso which was regarded by the inviting Powers as a refusal. She demanded that the congress should exclude from its deliberations arrangements which would give to any of the States invited an accession of territory or an increase of power. This condition excluded an arrangement such as the proposal—privately favoured by Clarendon— by which Austria would cede Venetia to Italy and would renounce any claims to Schleswig-Holstein in favour of Prussia while receiving Silesia in exchange from Prussia."

But Austria was determined to go to war for Venetia's sake notwithstanding Clarendon's warning that in such an event she would bear the responsibility for the *Bund's* fate. On the outbreak of war England proclaimed her neutrality. Nor did a change of Government a few days after the decisive battle of Königgrätz by which Russell's Liberal Cabinet was replaced by the Conservatives under the Earl of Derby bring about any change in policy. Derby said that "though not wishing to adopt non-intervention in an absolute manner, we would yet abstain from armed intervention," while his son, Lord Stanley, who was Foreign Secretary, declared: "I am not a supporter of the system of advising foreign governments. I think this right has not only been used but abused of late and that we have lost not gained by it." As a matter of fact England did not play any part in the negotiations that preceded the peace settlement between Austria and her opponents, Italy and Prussia. Italy's acquisition of Venetia conformed to the wishes of English statesmen and public opinion, the incorporation of Schleswig-Holstein in Prussia was accepted as something that could not be avoided, while the English Government was completely indifferent to the fate of Hanover.

The settlement of the Danish and Italian Questions removed the controversies that had prejudicially affected Anglo-Austrian relations. Events during the succeeding years did not occasion important negotiations between the two States and consequently they contented themselves with the maintenance of correct and formal diplomatic relations. The Tory Government under Derby continued to pursue its policy of non-intervention in international affairs and the Liberal Government by which it was replaced in 1868 made no change in foreign policy. The Prime Minister, Mr. Gladstone, and the Foreign Secretary, Earl Granville, held that "England should avoid perspective understandings to meet contingencies which might not occur " and therefore refused to enter into guarantees or alliances. The Austro-Hungarian Foreign Minister, Count Julius Andrassy, towards the close of 1871 asked the English Government—without, however, suggesting any formal agreement—how it viewed the present state of Anglo-Austrian relations. Granville was relieved that Andrassy had not formally raised the question of an understanding between England and Austria-Hungary because to any understanding "whether of a public or private character, it would be difficult for H.M. Government to assent." Nor was Granville more forthcoming during further negotiations. To Andrassy's suggestion that the two Governments "should always communicate their views in foreign affairs to each other in the first instance" Granville replied with a statement that he could not go so far (what he certainly meant was not without the authorization of his colleagues) and he added: "I felt sure that I was only expressing their sentiments when I assured him of our determination to communicate freely and openly at once with the Government of Austria-Hungary on an appearance of any European difficulty." The Austro-Hungarian Ambassador, Count Beust, reminded the Secretary of State for Foreign Affairs, Lord Derby, who had taken office at the beginning of 1874 when Disraeli's Conservative Government came to power, of this utterance in communicating to him the conclusion in the previous year of the Three Emperors' Alliance between Austria-Hungary, Russia, and Germany. Beust emphasized that this alliance was intended to serve the cause of peace— a cause that England had so much at heart—but that his Government also attached great importance to the maintenance of friendly relations and the existing *entente* between Austria-Hungary and England more especially in regard to Near Eastern affairs. Derby welcomed Beust's declaration and told him that he could rest assured that H.M. Government "would at all times be ready to communicate freely with that of which he was the representative and that it would give me sincere pleasure that we were able to act together . . . England had no object except the maintenance of European peace, and such, as it seems to me, was also the natural policy of the Austro-Hungarian Empire."

Of the greatest importance, however, was Disraeli's wish that England should work in common with Austria-Hungary for a settlement of the Balkan Question that would satisfy their individual interests in the event of a conflict in which Russia would be opposed by Austria-Hungary and England. Although Austria-Hungary and England thus pursued the same end mutual distrust prevented harmonious collaboration. Disraeli distrusted Andrassy, "who changes his mind every week or day and has half a dozen intrigues at work which will defeat each other." Disraeli and Derby were afraid that Andrassy would try to avoid war with Russia and to come to a compromise with her regardless of England's interests. Andrassy was not sure that in a war with Russia England would not let Austria-Hungary bear the brunt of the battle. After the Russian declaration of war on Turkey in May 1877, England pressed the Austro-Hungarian Government to agree to common action. And on 26 July the two Governments reached "a verbal agreement . . . affirming solidarity of interests and pledging the two Governments to identical but separate diplomatic action and should their interests be endangered to subsequent united military measures." Nonetheless Andrassy was still determined to avoid war with Russia and did not abandon hope of coming to a peaceful settlement with her. It was not indeed until after the Peace of San Stefano in March 1878 between Russia and Turkey revealed that Russia had played false with Austria-Hungary and imposed upon Turkey terms that were in flagrant contradiction with the agreements contracted between the Russian and Austro-Hungarian Governments during and before the war, and were indeed calculated to undermine Austria-Hungary's position in the Balkans, that Andrassy took energetic action. England and Austria-Hungary had already agreed in February 1878 to inform the belligerent Powers that any alteration of the provisions of the treaties of 1856 and 1871 without previous consultation and agreement with the guarantor Powers would be regarded as null and void. They were successful in obtaining the assent of the other guarantor Powers for the summoning of a congress. Mistrust nevertheless still raised barriers between the two Governments. Salisbury, who had replaced Derby at the Foreign Office, feared lest Andrassy would side with Russia if he were successful in inducing Russia to agree to a division of the Balkans into a Russian and an Austro-Hungarian sphere of influence. On the other hand Andrassy was greatly alarmed when he learnt of the negotiations between England and Russia that in fact resulted at the end of May in the signature of a secret agreement over the settlement of those questions that specially concerned English interests.

Salisbury emphatically declared that Austria-Hungary by her conduct was herself responsible for forcing this course upon the English Government. "If she would have agreed to fuller co-operation at an earlier period," he said, "no special agreement with Russia would have been necessary. But we have been obliged to provide for the case, which is even now possible and three weeks ago seemed very probable, of Austria throwing us over altogether." Hence it was not until the agreement with Russia had virtually been concluded that he instructed the English Ambassador in Vienna to make a final offer to Andrassy which met with acceptance. On 6 June an agreement was signed in which Austria-Hungary gave her assent to England's plans for Bulgaria and in return England promised "to support any proposition with respect to Bosnia." Andrassy was indignant that Salisbury refused to include Herzegovina and the Sandjak of Novibazar among the districts with regard to which England undertook at the forthcoming congress to support Austria-Hungary's proposals. He said he regarded the agreement "as between gentlemen" and hoped that a further understanding would be reached at the congress. The English and Austro-Hungarian delegations at the Congress in Berlin did in fact tread the same path. Disraeli wrote to Queen Victoria: "Throughout the discussions Austria entirely supported England . . . I have gained Andrassy and he supported me in everything." In return Salisbury energetically supported Austro-Hungarian claims to Bosnia-Herzegovina, and it was not his fault that Andrassy gave way to Turkey and contented himself with an Austro-Hungarian occupation of Bosnia-Herzegovina, accompanied by a formal recognition of the Sultan's sovereignty over the two provinces, while at the same time agreeing to Turkey's retention of the Sandjak of Novibazar with the proviso that Austria-Hungary "would keep her garrison there in order to secure military and commercial communication through it."

England and Austria-Hungary were satisfied with the results they had obtained at the Congress of Berlin and were therefore willing to maintain the friendly relations that had grown up between them. Salisbury described the Austro-Hungarian-German alliance of October 1879 as a welcome event tending to promote the interests of the peace of Europe and therefore of Great Britain. Austro-Hungarian statesmen were indeed anxious to see Great Britain permanently allied to the Central Powers. In his negotiations with Bismarck, Andrassy had proposed that Great Britain should be asked to join the Dual Alliance and his successor as Foreign Minister, Haymerle, renewed the proposal despite the fact that in Andrassy's time Bismarck had already rejected it, because he feared lest the entry of Great Britain into the Dual Alliance would involve her partners in Anglo-Russian disputes in the Near East—an eventuality that he wished to avoid at all costs. Haymerle wanted an alliance with Great Britain because he was convinced that Italy whose participation in an Austro-Russian war on Russia's side was a constant cause for alarm to him "would never think of attacking an Austria-Hungary allied to England." In February 1880, he asked in Berlin "whether and to what extent we should further enlighten Beaconsfield and Salisbury in order to obtain promises or declarations pledging England, in case of a conflict with Russia or an indirect collision with her which might threaten our position in the Orient, to use her influence, her direct pressure, or, should occasion arise, a naval demonstration to prevent Italy from attacking us and to safeguard the Adriatic for us." English statesmen were not unwilling to afford Austria-Hungary security against Italy and at that time showed "a disposition to enter into the Dual Alliance with the stipulation that any resumption of relations with Russia, as advocated by Bismarck, should be solely directed to the end of preventing conflicts with Russia." But Bismarck refused to be a party to any such stipulation because he was already seeking to draw Russia into the orbit of the Central Powers and thus to restore the old system of the Alliance of the Three Emperors.[2]

The fall of the Conservative Government and its replacement by a Liberal Ministry with Gladstone at its head was deplored in Vienna where Gladstone's dislike of Austria-Hungary was well known. In March 1880 he made his famous "Hands off!" speech addressed to the Austro-Hungarian Government in the course of which he declared that in the whole world it was impossible to place a finger on a spot and say, "Here Austria did good." Gladstone was indeed forced to withdraw his calumnies. Nevertheless he continued to press for energetic action against Turkey, who was supported by Austria-Hungary, and in the conflict between Turkey and Greece, with whom was Montenegro, he supported Turkey's enemies while the Austro-Hungarian, like the German, Government refused to take any action that might lead to war with Turkey. The Triple Alliance signed on 18 June 1881 between Austria-Hungary, Russia, and Germany was rightly regarded in London as an alliance between the Eastern Powers for the purpose of excluding Great Britain from exerting any influence in the Near East. The tension between Vienna and London continued while Gladstone remained Prime Minister. But in 1885 Salisbury formed his first Government and at once expressed a wish for good relations with Austria-Hungary. Moreover, when in 1886 Russia forced Prince Alexander of Battenberg to abdicate as Prince of Bulgaria, and the differences that subsequently arose between Austria-Hungary and Russia threatened to result in war, Salisbury was willing to act in common with Austria-Hungary. His standpoint was that the *status quo* in the Balkans must be maintained, Bulgaria's independence safeguarded, and resistance offered to Russian expansionism. Since the differences that had arisen between Austria-Hungary and Russia made a renewal of the Triple Alliance—it expired in 1887—unthinkable Austria-Hungary agreed to England's plans and on 24 March 1887 placed her signature on the agreement which Germany had promoted on 3 March between Italy and England in the form of an exchange of notes.[3] The English Note was very carefully drafted with a view to possible questions in Parliament. The Note said *inter alia* that, without attempting in advance to define the form which collaboration between the two Powers might assume in any individual case, it would be the endeavour of H.M. Government to assure for as long as might be possible the *status quo* in the Black Sea, the Aegean, and Mediterranean, and in the unhappy event of a change taking place to prevent the establishment of a domination hostile to the interests of the two countries. It is noteworthy that there is no definite promise of active, *i.e.* armed, support. As he had already said to Italy, Salisbury now said to the Austro-Hungarian Ambassador in London: "No British Ministry could bind itself in advance to co-operate in war." But before the close of 1887 Salisbury had decided to take a further step. After much hesitation and lengthy negotiations with Austria-Hungary and Italy he signed an agreement by which he bound England to joint action with these two Powers for the maintenance of the *status quo*, "especially as regards Bulgaria and the Straits in the Near East and (in which the three Powers) announce their right to occupy suitable strategic localities for the purpose of achieving this aim." England by this agreement drew closer to the Triple Alliance, war with Russia was avoided, and Anglo-Austrian relations continued to be friendly.

The Triple Alliance was renewed in May 1891, and one of

the Articles of the Additional Protocol expressed the wish of the signatory Powers to secure, in the same fashion as England had undertaken to assure the integrity of the Ottoman Empire, her military and diplomatic co-operation with the Triple Alliance for the eventuality that France should attempt to extend her sway in one form or another over North Africa. Although Salisbury in principle was not opposed to it, the attempt failed; but in everything else he was convinced that Great Britain must co-operate with the Triple Alliance. This was certainly not the opinion of Gladstone, who returned to power in 1892, and who remained the enemy of Austria-Hungary that he had always been. The Foreign Secretary, Lord Rosebery, showed himself more accommodating than his aged Prime Minister when Austria-Hungary and Italy in 1893 brought up the question of the renewal of the agreement of 1887. Rosebery said "that it was generally recognized both in the Liberal and the Conservative Party that England's interests in the Balkan Peninsula were identical with those of Austria-Hungary, and that outside there was no question on which the interests of the two States were divergent." As a consequence of the conflict that had arisen between France and Great Britain, and of the danger threatening Great Britain from the Franco-Russian alliance, Rosebery was disposed to collaborate with the Triple Alliance. But he emphasized that having regard to Gladstone's attitude he "could not feel himself therefore compelled, in spite of all the identity of views existing between Count Kalnoky [Austro-Hungarian Foreign Minister] and him, to conform this identity of views by the exchange of notes." And he maintained this standpoint when at the close of 1893 the Austro-Hungarian Ambassador, Count Deym, sought to persuade him to obtain from the Cabinet authority to make a formal and binding declaration on behalf of the British Government with regard to the defence of Constantinople against a Russian attack. "Ce que vous me demandez," said Rosebery, "il m'est impossible de la faire et ce n'est pas dans notre intérèt que je le fasse." The Cabinet would certainly be bound to feel that it must refuse "to form binding resolutions to-day for an eventuality that is still far distant." " England," Rosebery subsequently said, "could defend the Straits alone against Russia . . ." What he did ask was that he might count on the Triple Alliance to prevent France from taking part in the struggle. But Germany refused to undertake any such obligation. Kimberley—Rosebery's successor at the Foreign Office—refused in an equally determined manner to place Austria-Hungary's proposals before the Cabinet, and, as Rosebery before him had done, advised the Austro-Hungarian Government to be content with a verbal assurance that England was resolved to safeguard their common interests at Constantinople. And in 1894 this actually happened.

A change subsequently came over the international scene that was brought about by the conflict which arose between Germany and England over colonial questions. Rosebery was now Prime Minister and he declared that it was impossible for England "to maintain her Entente with the Triple Alliance in European questions" when Germany, in conjunction with France, pursued an anti-English policy in Africa. The Austro-Hungarian Government was anxious to maintain good relations with Great Britain and therefore mediated between her and Germany in the conflicts which arose out of Germany's protest against the Anglo-Belgian treaty concerning the Congo. The increasing tension between the British and German Governments nevertheless adversely affected Anglo-Austrian relations. At the beginning of 1896 Count Deym suggested to the newly-appointed Conservative Prime Minister, Lord Salisbury, the renewal of the agreement of December 1887, with a view to closer collaboration between England and Austria-Hungary in Near Eastern affairs. He met with a refusal. Other attempts made by Austria-Hungary during 1897 were also unsuccessful. Salisbury, like his predecessor, said that he could not undertake obligations such as Austria-Hungary wished for before the events which might cause him to do so actually took place. Henceforward Anglo-Austrian relations were determined by the fact that Austria-Hungary was a member of the Triple Alliance and the ally of Germany. Although their opinions, and consequently their actions, differed in many Balkan questions, there were no fundamental differences between Austria-Hungary and Great Britain in questions arising out of their own special interests. The decisive factor in their relations was the nature of the relationship between Great Britain and Germany.

In 1901, during the negotiations between Germany and Great Britain for the conclusion of an alliance, Germany proposed that Great Britain should conclude the alliance with all the members of the Triple Alliance. Salisbury refused and motivated his refusal by saying that the obligation which would rest upon Great Britain of defending Germany and Austria-Hungary against Russia was far heavier than the obligation that would rest upon the Triple Alliance of defending the British Isles against France. Besides he did not want Great Britain to be involved in the conflict which it was expected in England would arise after the death of the old Emperor Francis Joseph.

The greater the tension in Anglo-German relations consequent upon the failure of the attempts made in the years 1898-1901 to effect a compromise the dimmer became the prospect that Great Britain would fight for Austria-Hungary's special interests in the Balkans. After the conclusion of the Anglo-Russian Agreements of 1907 and 1908 no doubt was left in the minds of the Austro-Hungarian Government that in a war with Russia (which seemed likely at this time) Austria-Hungary could not count even upon the adoption by Great Britain of a friendly attitude.

Chapter Two

MONARCHS AND STATESMEN OF AUSTRIA-HUNGARY AND GREAT BRITAIN, 1908-1914

A PROBLEM that will certainly never be solved is that of the extent to which an individual does and can influence the course of history. Those who think that history is made up of an ordered progression of events will attach less importance to the influence of the individual than those who believe that it is first and foremost the individual who determines the course of events. Nevertheless nobody can deny that the influence exerted even by the greatest and most powerful of men is subject to limitations of time and circumstances. But it is no less certain that there have been men who have decisively influenced the course of history. This is true both of men of action and of thinkers. It was therefore a misfortune that during the years preceding the outbreak of the First World War no really great statesman made his appearance on the international political stage to act as the guide and leader of his fellowmen and by his personal magnetism and strength to compel them to follow his leadership. In the two countries—Austria-Hungary and Great Britain—whose diplomatic relations throughout the years 1908-1914 are the subject of this study, there was no man who possessed the outstanding ability and strength of will to enable him to shape the policy of his country, as in an earlier age had been done in their own countries by Pitt, Palmerston, Gladstone, Napoleon, Metternich, and Bismarck. Nevertheless it seems desirable briefly to sketch the characters and personalities of the men who in these years exerted a decisive influence upon the course of events.

THE EMPEROR FRANCIS JOSEPH

In Austria-Hungary it was the old Emperor Francis Joseph who made the decisions and thus exercised the greatest influence upon the course of events. He was already seventy-eight years old in October 1908, and only a few weeks later he celebrated the sixtieth anniversary of his accession to the throne. He had drunk the cup of sorrow to the dregs. He had lived through revolutions and upheavals that shook the very foundations of the throne. He had waged wars against France, Italy, and Prussia, and had emerged the loser from each of them. He had been forced at the sword's point to cede fertile provinces of his empire to Italy and to reconcile himself to the exclusion of Austria from a united Germany ruled over by the King of Prussia as German Emperor. Nor was he any more successful in his domestic policy. He had been compelled to make ever-increasing concessions to Hungary in order to maintain the unity of his empire in foreign policy and military organization. All his endeavours to induce the many nations inhabiting his vast empire to lay aside their national rivalries in the interest of the commonweal had failed of success. In his private life the Emperor was equally unlucky. His brother Maximilian, Emperor of Mexico, fell before a firing-squad. His only son and heir, Rudolph, committed suicide. His wife, Elizabeth, was assassinated at Geneva. The Heir-Apparent after the Crown Prince Rudolph's death was the Emperor's nephew, Archduke Francis Ferdinand, who died in July 1914 at Serajevo as the victim of an assassin's bullets. A deep un-bridgeable gulf of mutual dislike and misunderstanding separated the Emperor and the Archduke Francis Ferdinand, and with many other members of the House of Habsburg the Emperor lived on terms of barely concealed disapproval and dislike. The fact that the Emperor did not break down under the many misfortunes that overtook his family and empire does not mean that these tragic events left no trace upon his mind and character and did not influence his attitude towards life. In the evening of his days Francis Joseph stood quite alone. Death had taken away the few friends he had ever made in his long life and it was only in the company of his favourite daughter, Maria Valerie, and her children, and in that of his faithful friend Frau Schratt, that the old man found some consolation and relaxation. It is not difficult to under-stand that under these conditions his elasticity gradually gave place to immobility and an overwhelming desire for repose. The impulsive and passionate young Emperor of 1848 who had believed that he could rule as he liked had been changed by the events of the passing years into a man who had learnt how to adapt himself to changing times. Until his death,

Francis Joseph nevertheless remained convinced that his subjects were not sufficiently experienced in politics for parliamentary government and that they still needed to be governed from above. He did indeed strictly observe the parliamentary constitution which he had granted in 1867 at the insistence of the Hungarians, and which he had sworn to uphold, while in his Austrian dominions he continually enlarged the right of representation to include larger numbers of people until in 1907 Austria received universal suffrage in which Francis Joseph himself was a firm believer.

As the years succeeded to each other the Emperor's attitude towards his advisers also underwent a profound change. Throughout the first half of his reign, and not until after the death in 1852 of Prince Schwarzenberg to whom he gave a free hand, Francis Joseph did indeed listen to what his Ministers had to say but invariably took the decision himself in each and every case. There were occasions when he bluntly told the Council of Ministers before he opened the formal discussion that he had summoned them to consider such and such matters and to take decisions that he himself would presently announce to them. But there is no record of any such high-handed action throughout the second half of his reign. He accorded his Ministers greater freedom of action in their own individual spheres and listened attentively to what they had to say to him. Moreover, he now tolerated criticism of his own views and was even prepared to adopt suggestions that ran contrary to those views provided only that he felt that they were well grounded in reason and fact. Francis Joseph nevertheless now as formerly maintained that he—and he alone—had the right to take the final decision in all matters. Nothing indeed could change his attitude in regard to his duties and privileges as a ruler, since that attitude sprang from the unshakable belief that God had placed him as ruler over his people and had laid upon him the duty of governing them for their own good. So strong was his belief in his God-given mission that his duty to his people took precedence in his mind over every other interest and consideration. Hence his tireless devotion to his work. He passed the greater part of each day at his desk and occupied himself with the least important administrative issues as well as with the great questions of State policy. His memory was faultless and in consequence as year succeeded to year he acquired an astounding knowledge of people and things that evoked the admiration and astonishment of anyone who had occasion to discuss personal or other matters with him. The orderliness instilled into him by his early education finally became no more than a pedantic regard for the dotting of the "i"'s and the crossing of the "t"'s. Conrad von Hötzendorff once said of Francis Joseph: "The Emperor's brain is like a very well-run grocery store in which each spice or condiment is kept in its own box, and each box can only be opened by a shop-assistant who has been given that particular task to perform. This box contains pepper and that over there ginger. But God help the assistant who tries to put his hand into any box except his own. He will get a sharp rap over the knuckles for interfering with what does not concern him."

Francis Joseph expected the same self-abnegation from his subordinates that he himself displayed in his daily work. But it never occurred to him to feel grateful to them for their services. If a Minister or official was dismissed—Francis Joseph dismissed them as soon as they ceased to serve his purpose or when they showed themselves incapable of over-coming difficulties—the Emperor never again inquired about him or asked for his advice. But he bore them no resentment. He approved or rejected the suggestions that were put before him according to what he deemed to be their usefulness at the time. Francis Joseph was never a party man in the political sense of the word. For the many conflicting political parties in the Empire Francis Joseph entertained no feelings what-soever either of sympathy or dislike. Although he looked upon himself as a German sovereign, he spared no pains in attempting to fulfil the demands that reached him from the many races inhabiting his dominions in so far as he deemed them to be legitimate and justifiable. It has often been said that Francis Joseph played off one nationality against another and that "Divide et Impera" was his guiding political principle. Nothing could be farther from the truth. The motto that he had chosen for his government, "Viribus Unitis", fully ac-corded with his convictions and he was faithful to it throughout his reign.

In private life Francis Joseph was extremely reserved in manner, even towards the members of the Imperial family, and notwithstanding his habitual courtesy he kept people of every rank at a distance. He was so conscious of being an emperor that he never felt any need to impress people. He disliked and avoided pomp and ceremony. But what did impress the people who came into personal contact with him was his dignity and chivalrous temperament, his tact, and, above all else, his high sense of honour. Everyone carried away the lasting impression of a man of his word who would keep his promise at all costs. He was wholly lacking in personal wants or desires and hunting was his sole recreation. He was quick-minded and could very skilfully sum up the results of a conference. He had no imagination and his mind was extremely prosaic. But he was witty and not lacking in humour. A celebrated professor of law Joseph Unger once told the Emperor of a Swiss professor who came to Vienna to attend a congress that was opened by the Emperor and was so captivated by Francis Joseph's personal charm that he subsequently declared that it had almost converted him to a belief in monarchical government. Francis Joseph thereupon observed: "When I was in Switzerland recently I found everything so well-ordered that I almost became a republican!" On one occasion the Emperor was asked to read a private letter written in French by an Austro-Hungarian ambassador of whom the Emperor had heard that he spent much of his time in the society of *demi-mondaines*. On reading the letter the Emperor found that it contained numerous grammatical and other mistakes. He wrote on the margin: "Count K. should get a French tutor and learn French rather than pass his time with lovely *demi-mondaines*."

For art and science Francis Joseph had not the slightest interest. Even as a young man he found Shakespeare and Goethe dull and in later life he read only the newspapers. He occasionally opened an art exhibition and commanded his Chamberlain to purchase a few pictures on condition that they did not emanate from any modern school of painting. He had neither taste nor understanding for serious music. In religion he was a good Catholic and personally very pious. It therefore went much against the grain with him to have to give up the Concordat concluded in 1855 with the Vatican. At the same time Francis Joseph was not a bigot and he resolutely opposed any interference by the Church in State affairs. Francis Joseph was not a stupid man. His misfortune was that he did not possess the outstanding ability that he would have required in order to enable him successfully to solve the very complicated and difficult problems that constantly confronted him during his long reign. He disliked, and was himself incapable of indulging in, theorizing and he showed no understanding for universal problems. Besides Francis Joseph had not got that passionate temperament that is the hall-mark of all great rulers and statesmen. He had no imagination and therefore no ideas, and was utterly incapable of planning for a distant future. He was also wanting in initiative and intensely disliked having to make an irrevocable decision. As an old man Francis Joseph's chief concern was to avoid conflicts and quarrels at all costs rather than to have his own way, and this overmastering longing for peace powerfully influenced his domestic and foreign policy throughout the last years of his reign. In domestic affairs he let events take their own course, avoided change as much as possible, and refused to follow the advice of those among his Ministers who wished to make an end to the steadily growing conflicts between the different nationalities inhabiting the Empire by means—if there were no other way of doing so—of a *coup d'état*. In these last years of his life the guiding principle of his foreign policy (which Francis Joseph even in his old age regarded as his own special responsibility) was the maintenance of peace in so far as this was consonant with his own and the Empire's honour. When the Chief of the Austro-Hungarian General Staff, Conrad von Hötzendorff, wanted to wage a preventive war against Italy and came into conflict with the Foreign Minister, Count Aehrenthal, who would not consent to any such project, Francis Joseph said to Conrad: "Your unending attacks (upon Aehrenthal), and especially your dispute with him over Italy, are directed against me. It is I who formulate policy, it is *my* policy. My policy is pacific. Everyone must accept it and make the best of it. It is in this sense that my Minister of Foreign Affairs carries on my policy." Francis Joseph only consented to the dispatch of the Austro-Hungarian ultimatum to Servia in July 1914 after long hesitation and only after he had convinced himself that his own and Austria-Hungary's honour could no longer tolerate Servia's actions.

ARCHDUKE FRANCIS FERDINAND

It has already been said that after Prince Schwarzenberg's death in 1852 Francis Joseph never again allowed foreign policy to escape his control. In the last years of his reign he certainly accorded his Foreign Ministers greater liberty in the conduct of affairs yet at the same time they got their instructions from him and were compelled to follow them. Moreover, he never permitted anyone else to influence him in matters of foreign policy. He even refused his only son and heir, Crown Prince Rudolph (who had political ambitions and would gladly have played a part in the formulation of his father's foreign policy with which he was not always in agreement), any share whatsoever in the task of government and especially in foreign affairs. He adopted the same attitude towards his nephew, Archduke Francis Ferdinand, who, as Heir-Apparent, considered he had a right to be consulted both in matters of internal and foreign policy and who in the last years of his life became embittered by the Emperor's persistent and brusque refusal to concede him any part or influence in governmental affairs. Francis Ferdinand's bitterness was increased by the fact that he was wholly out of sympathy with his uncle's weakly passive policy that had for its aim the avoidance of every possible conflict, and also by his recognition of the danger threatening the Empire over which he would one day have to rule. The brutal frankness with which the Archduke voiced his dislike for the prevailing system of suppressing or glossing over unpleasant facts out of regard for the aged Emperor brought him into conflict not only with the Emperor himself, but also with the Ministers and Generals by whom Francis Joseph was surrounded and with many of the aristocracy. His bitterest foes were those members of the Hungarian nobility who shrank from nothing in their opposition to the endeavours of the non-Magyar races to obtain their proper share in the government of the polyglot empire.

Despite the frequent conflicts with the Emperor into which they brought him Francis Ferdinand held fast to his plans and was often successful in achieving their adoption. At the same time he was careful to avoid an open breach with his uncle. Indeed Francis Ferdinand closely resembled Francis Joseph in many aspects of his character. He, like Francis Joseph, was an Austrian and a soldier, into the very marrow of his bones, and like him was filled with pride by the thought of the greatness of the Habsburg House to which he belonged. In common with his uncle he asked little of life, hated hypocrisy, and cared nothing for popularity. He had the same unfailing memory and quick apprehension. He shared Francis Joseph's love of nature and hunting. Nevertheless there were marked differences between the two men. Francis Ferdinand was neither industrious nor tactful. Unlike Francis Joseph he was a fierce hater who never forgot a real or imaginary injury or slight. He lacked self-control and his outbursts of fury shocked and terrified all who were compelled to witness them. His inborn suspiciousness attained pathological heights after he suffered a serious illness, during which it seemed, for a time, that he might never succeed to the throne. For the sycophants around him deserted him and began to pay court to his brother, Otto, as the future emperor. Indeed, Francis Ferdinand became a despiser and contemner of men. He once said to Conrad von Hötzendorff: "You think everyone is an angel and some day you'll be disillusioned. When I meet a man for the first time I regard him as a thorough cad and never change my opinion of him until I have cause to know better."

It is only just to Francis Ferdinand's memory to recall that he had been terribly embittered and angered by the attitude of the Court, and a great many of the nobility, towards his wife whom he had married against the Emperor's wish and not until he had overcome almost insuperable obstacles in the course of a struggle that lasted for years. His love for her and for his children was deep and sincere and he was only happy in their company. It must indeed have been intolerable for Francis Ferdinand to have to fulfil the conditions imposed upon him by the Emperor as the price of his consent to the Archduke's marriage with the Countess Chotek—the renunciation for his children of all claim or right to the throne as children of a morganatic marriage. This renunciation made it necessary for Francis Ferdinand to provide for his wife and children out of his own purse while the need to save in its turn made him penurious. Francis Ferdinand, like Francis Joseph, was a devout son of the Catholic Church and indeed probably at heart more deeply religious than his uncle. He looked on the Church as one of the great pillars of the State and was always ready to do all he could to strengthen it. Bnt he was no less determined than his uncle not to permit ecclesiastical interference in State affairs. He was strongly opposed to the movement ("Los von Rom") that sought to free the Catholic Church outside Italy from Vatican domination and he was an enemy both of Freemasonry and of the Jews. Nor had he any sympathy with Liberalism or Socialism. Everyone who knew Francis Ferdinand, and this is also true of his personal and political enemies, agreed that he possessed very considerable intellectual abilities. He easily grasped the fundamental factors in a problem and never allowed himself to get lost in a maze of details. He possessed an excellent judgment and wide knowledge and understanding of men. He sought to make good the defects in his education less by reading than by intercourse with scholars and specialists. He was a typical professional soldier who placed the Army and its needs in men and weapons before everything else, and who also lent his powerful support for all schemes for the strengthening of the Navy. Unlike Francis Joseph, Francis Ferdinand was deeply interested in architecture, and especially in the lay-out of gardens, and was also a collector of *objets d'arts*.

Francis Ferdinand was convinced that the inert and submissive policy in domestic and foreign affairs pursued by the Emperor and his advisers would ultimately lead to the downfall of the Empire. He insistently urged that the Government should act and wage a relentless war against those who opposed the reforms that he looked upon as indispensable for the internal pacification of the Empire and also for the maintenance of its position as a European Great Power. Francis Ferdinand believed that the Dual Monarchy must be reconstructed and reorganized if it was to survive. But he frequently changed his views as to how this was to be done. At one time he favoured a trialist solution and at another he thought federation offered better chances of success. He never finally made up his mind. But he entertained no doubts whatsoever that the Southern Slav Question must be solved and that it was imperative to overcome the opposition of the Hungarian aristocracy to the granting of equal rights to the non-Magyar races living in Hungary. He envisaged a reconstructed and revivified Austro-Hungarian Empire of which the strongest supports would be a common culture, an Army and Navy with a uniform organization, a common foreign and tariff policy, and with German as its official language.

Francis Ferdinand was resolutely opposed to an aggressive foreign policy because he believed that an empire rent by such critical internal dissensions as was Austria-Hungary could not risk a war. It is therefore untrue to say, as has often been said, that Francis Ferdinand wanted to wage war with Servia.

"Hands off Servia!" he said. "For God's sake don't touch an inch of Servian soil or even a single Servian plum-tree!" He wanted Austria-Hungary to remain Germany's ally, and to avoid any new quarrels with Russia, because he thought that friendly relations between the Central Empires and Russia would be in the general interest of Austria-Hungary and would serve above all else as a bulwark against revolution and the downfall of the Empire. He was no lover of France. On the other hand he stressed the importance of good relations with Great Britain for Austria-Hungary's position as a European Great Power. On his return from a visit to England in 1913 Francis Ferdinand declared that no differences existed between Great Britain and Austria-Hungary that could occasion a serious dispute, and that he had satisfied himself that both Great Powers were ready to forget the petty differences that had arisen between them.

Francis Ferdinand disliked Italy and did not believe in the sincerity of her protestations of friendship for her Austro-Hungarian ally. Nevertheless he did not want to go to war with Italy, and on this issue he supported the Emperor and Aehrenthal in their opposition to Conrad von Hötzendorff, who wanted to wage a preventive war against Italy.

EDWARD VII

Edward VII was already a man of sixty when he ascended the throne. He had been strictly brought up and even in her old age his mother, Queen Victoria, refused to allow him to have any part in the conduct of affairs. Hence Edward VII, as Prince of Wales, finding any serious occupation denied to him, devoted himself to a brilliant social life for which his inborn tact, unfailing memory, and knowledge of men—and women—eminently fitted him. He travelled widely and was what would be called in modern jargon "a good mixer". For Edward VII never allowed his love of pomp and ceremonial, and his lively sense of his own dignity, to stand in the way of his coming into contact with all sorts and conditions of men. He was as well-known and popular a figure in the theatre as on the race-course. Many of his closest friends were actors and actresses, and few men in England excelled him as a judge of a horse. He was a born *raconteur* and dearly loved a good story. His innumerable friends knew him as a warmhearted and loyal man who was always ready to mediate between them in order to bring about an amicable settlement of their differences. They also knew him as an outstanding man of the world whose immense knowledge of men and affairs had been gained less from books than from personal contact with men of many countries and very different pursuits as well as from daily perusal of the leading European newspapers. Their affection for him was deepened by his willingness to forgive and to forget slights or injuries inflicted upon him. Edward VII was indeed the least vindictive of men. He loved and championed peace and order in personal as in international relations. After he became King in 1901 Edward VII quickly won the esteem and affection of his people. He retained and strengthened the good qualities that had distinguished him as Prince of Wales, and at the same time gave up habits that had brought a measure of disrepute upon his name. He chose his friends with greater care and became more reserved in conversation. While among his intimate friends he still continued to enjoy the free interplay of ideas and of speech, Edward VII knew how to uphold his regal dignity and to show his displeasure with any person who presumed to take a liberty. He also kept his temper under control and his public utterances were models of propriety and moderation. Edward II showed himself throughout his reign meticulously mindful of the limitations placed by the English Constitution upon the royal prerogative. But he was no mere figurehead. He insisted upon being fully informed about everything, read all important political documents, and was certainly not content to play a passive rôle in public life. He formed his own independent opinions upon all important questions and did not hesitate to advise his Ministers. Nevertheless Edward VII understood and accepted the fact that it was for his Ministers as representatives of the majority of the nation— and for them alone—to formulate policy.

It is therefore false to say that King Edward VII formulated and directed British foreign policy. Balfour and Lansdowne both declared that the King never made "an important suggestion regarding great questions of policy" and Grey supported this statement. "A legend," Grey wrote, "arose in his lifetime . . . that British foreign policy was due to his initiative, instigation and control. That was not so in my experience. He not only accepted the constitutional practice that policy must be that of his ministers, but he preferred that it should be so." At the same time Edward VII was always ready to support his Government's policy abroad with his great authority and influence. He was in truth England's best ambassador. His personal charm, tact, and cleverness in the handling of men played no small part in overcoming the difficulties that stood in the way of a Franco-British *Entente Cordiale*. His meeting with the Tsar in Reval in 1908 greatly contributed to the promotion of friendly relations between Russia and Great Britain. It is indeed as absurd as it is wholly lacking in foundation in fact for German writers and historians to portray Edward VII as a warmonger. On the contrary. Edward VII did all that it lay in his power to do to keep the peace. Naturally he strove at the same time to ensure that in event of war England would not stand alone against her enemies. This was his bounden duty as England's King and the fact that his endeavours were crowned with success was recognized in political circles and earned for him the affection and admiration of his people. "He had," Morley writes, "just the character that Englishmen, at any rate, thoroughly understand, thoroughly like, and make any quantity of allowance for."

GEORGE V

George V came to the throne in 1910 on the death of his father, Edward VII. He was a sincere, honourable, warm-hearted man and a much simpler personality than his father. He was also much less of a Society man and did not share his father's love of pomp and ceremony. On the other hand he inherited his father's phenomenal memory, orderliness, and sporting instincts. He was a cooler thinker than his father and also a far better judge of men. He was gifted with a sense of humour and keenly appreciated a good story. Unlike his father, he was a lover of books; especially of those dealing with sport, natural history, and seamanship. Art and science also interested him. His lifelong and greatest love, however, was for the Royal Navy in which he had himself served as a young man. Although George V was imbued with a strong sense of duty, his predominant characteristic was his intuitive under-standing of and sympathy with other people's feelings and pre-judices and his sincere love for "humanity". He understood

the common man and the common man understood him,
and loved him, because he knew that George V's whole life
was devoted to the welfare of his subjects.

George V held very definite opinions upon his rights and
duties as a monarch and voiced them in unmistakable terms.
He once said to the American Ambassador, Mr. Page, that
"knowing the difficulties of a limited monarch, I thank heaven
I am spared being an absolute one." For a quarter of a
century George V reigned as a strictly constitutional monarch
who regarded it as his chief duty to be the representative of
his people—representative, that is to say, of *all* his subjects
because not being elected he did not represent merely a
majority. Although he was intensely interested in politics,
George V always kept himself as far as possible in the background of political life; yet at the same time he did not hesitate
to make his influence felt in innumerable questions of domestic
and foreign policy. He felt himself called upon to act as
mediator between the political parties for the purpose of
smoothing out their differences and of countering the danger
to the commonweal that might arise from some great political
crisis. It was because he held this conception of his kingly
duty that George V himself always declared that the constitutional crisis arising out of the conflict between the House
of Commons and the House of Lords at the outset of his reign
was the worst and most anxious time in his life. It speaks
volumes for his upright character that "what he specially
resented was the promise extracted from him in November
1911 that he would tell no one" what was happening behind
the scenes. "I have never," he said, "in my life done anything
I was ashamed to confess and I have never been accustomed
to conceal things." George V, like his father before him, was
a peacemaker who did all that it lay in his power to do to keep
the peace. When, on 26 July 1914 King George V said to
Prince Henry of Prussia, "We shall try all we can to keep out
of the war and shall remain neutral," there can be no doubt
that he meant what he said. But William II and his advisers
forgot that an English King "reigns but does not govern,"
and therefore that King George V had to follow his Ministers'
advice when they told him that they looked upon the entry
of Great Britain into the war on the side of France and Russia
as the unavoidable fulfilment of a moral obligation and also
as in the interest of his Empire and the Commonwealth.

THE AUSTRO-HUNGARIAN MINISTERS FOR FOREIGN AFFAIRS

COUNT AEHRENTHAL

Aehrenthal must certainly be regarded as one of the ablest of the men who after the deaths of Metternich and Schwarzenberg were called upon to direct Austro-Hungarian foreign policy. He was the second son of Baron Johann Baptist Lexa von Aehrenthal and the Countess Maria von Thun-Hohenstein. His father was leader of a party composed of great landowners in Bohemia who were German by origin and were constitutionalists. Aehrenthal inherited a strain of Jewish blood from his great-grandfather. He married late in life a daughter of one of the greatest and most famous Hungarian noble families, Countess Pauline Széchényi. The fact that he was thus related to great Bohemian and Hungarian noble families left its mark upon Aehrenthal's character. Throughout his life he was a rigid Conservative who demanded a privileged position in the State for the nobility and who wished to see the Government as free as possible from the influence of the masses and their parliamentary representatives. He was an opponent of universal suffrage.

Aehrenthal led a gay life as a young man and entered the Diplomatic Service at an early age. After spending a short time in Paris, Aehrenthal was sent in 1878 to the Austro-Hungarian Embassy at St. Petersburg where he remained for five years. In 1883 his friend Count Kalnocky, who was then Foreign Minister and was idolized by Aehrenthal, summoned him to the Foreign Ministry in Vienna where under Kalnocky's guidance Aehrenthal learnt much about diplomacy and where he distinguished himself by hard work, quickness of apprehension, a capacity for orderly and logical thinking, and by his rigorous sense of duty. Five years later in 1888 he returned to St. Petersburg as Councillor of Embassy. In 1894 he left St. Petersburg for a second time to become Minister at Bucharest only to return to St. Petersburg for a third time in 1899 as Ambassador. Aehrenthal speedily won for himself an exceptional position in the strongly conservative Russian Society and Court where he was regarded by the Tsar with special favour. In 1906 the Emperor Francis Joseph appointed him Minister for Foreign Affairs. Aehrenthal was a big broad-shouldered man with regular features and a reserved manner.

He was very shortsighted. He kept his choleric temperament under such iron control that he outwardly appeared calm and collected. Aehrenthal was a strong-willed and imposing personality whose faultless memory and great knowledge of history and constitutional law stood him in good stead in working-out his plans. While he was a brilliant diplomatist, Aehrenthal's most striking quality was the extraordinary command of logic that he displayed in expounding his political thought. At the same time whenever a situation demanded it he never hesitated to use his mastery of dialectic to conceal his real meaning or to put his interlocutor on a false scent. One who knew him more intimately than the majority of his acquaintances once said of Aehrenthal that when he found himself in an awkward or perilous situation it was his wont "to spin a web of words around some fact of which the existence could not be denied or to conceal it in an aside spoken in a toneless and casual manner." Aehrenthal was a good hater and never shrank from making use of the most brutal and ruthless means to force his enemies to their knees. When he had once made up his mind about anything, Aehrenthal never altered it and he shunned no fight no matter how hard in order to achieve his purpose. His personal conflicts with Isvolsky and Conrad von Hötzendorff bear witness to his fighting qualities. Indeed he always preferred to be respected and feared rather than loved by his contemporaries. Aehrenthal was indeed faithful to his family motto, "Do not rejoice at good fortune. Do not falter in evil days."

Aehrenthal was very ambitious and at the same time not in the least vain. He devoted his whole mental and physical energy to the service of his Emperor and country and demanded in return that his achievements should receive public recognition by the conferment upon him of honorific distinctions. After the Bosnian Crisis Francis Joseph conferred the title of Count upon Aehrenthal who regarded the honour as no more than a well-earned and just reward for his work. Aehrenthal held strong and individual views upon Austro-Hungarian foreign policy. In contrast to his predecessor, Count Goluchowsky, who thought that Austria-Hungary should play a passive rôle in international affairs and make the preservation of peace her main objective, Aehrenthal wanted Austria-Hungary by means of a forcible policy to regain her former status as a Great Power, and therewith to wield once more her former dominant influence in European affairs. Although Aehrenthal was a convinced supporter of the alliance between the Central Empires, he wanted Austria-Hungary to be treated by Germany as a full partner and not as a subordinate. When he became Foreign Minister, Aehrenthal was determined to maintain the good relations between Austria-Hungary and Russia that he himself had done so much to promote, and he would have welcomed a pacific solution of the problems that still stood in the way of a lasting friendship between the two countries. But he insisted that Russia should recognize Austria-Hungary's right to a sphere of influence similar to that of Russia in Balkan affairs. Aehrenthal was successful in achieving his twofold objective. For not only was Austria-Hungary's independence of action in foreign affairs preserved but many people abroad, and also many in Germany, to their chagrin, discovered that the centre of gravity of the Triple Alliance had shifted from Berlin to Vienna. The prestige of the Danubian Monarchy in the Balkans was also enormously strengthened by Aehrenthal's successful and peaceful annexation of Bosnia-Herzogovina. In those days Aehrenthal was widely esteemed as an outstanding statesman, and only a minority of influential politicians and publicists was to be found condemning Aehrenthal's Balkan policy on the ground that his success had been too dearly bought at the price of the danger that must arise for the Triple Alliance, and therefore for the Danubian Monarchy, out of Russia's lasting resentment and enmity and out of the friendship steadily growing up between Russia and the Western Powers. Aehrenthal did not live to see the day on which these fears were realized. He died in February 1912, mourned by his Imperial master who had pointed out his path to him and repeatedly assured him that he was fully satisfied with his conduct of affairs.

COUNT BERCHTOLD

The Emperor Francis Joseph was called upon to make a fateful decision when Aehrenthal's serious illness rendered it necessary for him to appoint his successor. The name of the Austro-Hungarian Ambassador at Constantinople, Count Pallavicini, was frequently mentioned among others in this connection and he was certainly an outstanding diplomatist.

Nevertheless Francis Joseph finally decided to appoint Aehrenthal's nominee, Count Leopold Berchtold, who had served for many years in succession to Aehrenthal as Austro-Hungarian Ambassador at St. Petersburg where he acquired a thorough knowledge of Russian statesmen and their policy and showed much ability in the conduct of his mission at a time when relations between Russia and Austria-Hungary were strained almost to breaking-point. At the moment when Francis Joseph made his decision Austria-Hungary's relations with Russia were the chief concern of the Austro-Hungarian Foreign Ministry because of the unstable state of the Balkans. It was doubtless this consideration that caused the Emperor's choice to fall upon Berchtold rather than Pallavicini. Berchtold for his part never wanted to be Foreign Minister because he did not feel himself fitted for this onerous and responsible post, and he repeatedly begged the Emperor not to appoint him. He finally yielded to the Emperor's insistent demand simply out of a feeling of loyalty to his ageing monarch. Berchtold was certainly not a place-hunter and was not very ambitious. He was a wealthy *grand seigneur* who loved hunting and similar pastimes, and was popular in society by reason of his tact and discretion as well as his personal charm and readiness to help in any difficulty. He was also interested in scientific studies. Although Berchtold was not an outstandingly able man, he was at least as intelligent as many of the men who in those days occupied similar positions throughout Europe; the portrait that was often drawn of him as a political dilettante who neglected his ministerial duties for the pursuit of his pleasures and private affairs is most certainly false. Anyone who reads his dispatches from St. Petersburg or the instructions he sent as Foreign Minister to the Austro-Hungarian diplomatic representatives abroad will quickly discover for himself that Berchtold took his work very seriously and was very industrious. He was a gifted writer who was able to give lucid and cogent expression to his ideas.

Berchtold was lacking in two qualities invaluable for a statesman. He had not got the passionate determination to have his own way that enables a man to see that what he wants done is done despite all difficulties and opposition. He lacked the certitude and conviction that would have given him an unshakable belief in the essential rightness of the policy which he was carrying out. Moreover, Berchtold's incertitude and want of determination compelled him to rely very greatly upon his subordinates, and, above all, upon Count Forgach who was an exceptionally clever, ambitious, and forceful man. It is not true that Berchtold was a war-monger. He would have greatly preferred not to go to war. But he was determined to maintain Austria-Hungary's position and prestige in the Balkans and it was not until he was com-pelled to recognize the impossibility of a peaceful understanding with Servia, even at the cost of far-reaching concessions, that he came to the conclusion that the issue must—if necessary—be decided by force of arms. Twice he was forced to abandon his plan for an arbitrament by arms by the refusal of Germany and Italy to participate. It was not until after the assassination of the Archduke Francis Ferdinand that Germany expressed her readiness to take part in Berchtold's projected punitive expedition against Servia, although Italy declared that there was no *casus foederis* that would justify her participation in the war. In the ensuing negotiations that had for their object the participation of Italy in the war on the side of the Central Empires, and, in event of her non-participation, at least for her benevolent neutrality, Italy continually increased her demands to the point at which Berchtold in complete agree-ment with the Emperor definitely refused to concede them. His refusal led to his resignation in January 1915, and in the following year the Emperor appointed him Lord High Steward. Subsequently Emperor Karl appointed him Lord Chamberlain. Berchtold was one of the very few Ministers who were able to fulfil the duties of their offices in full agree-ment with the old Emperor Francis Joseph and at the same time enjoy the friendship and approval of the Heir-Apparent Archduke Francis Ferdinand.

THE HUNGARIAN PRIME MINISTER

COUNT TISZA

Among the men who in the years immediately preceding the outbreak of World War I decisively influenced Austro-Hungarian domestic and foreign policy Count Stephen Tisza must be given a foremost place. He was unquestionably the ablest and most outstanding statesman in the Dual Monarchy, and a man endowed with a first-rate intellect and a strength of character that was rock-like in its unyielding quality. He did not know fear and was ready at all times to defend his honour with his sword. He was intensely proud of being a Magyar and a member of the landed gentry to whom above all else Hungary owed its rise to power and prosperity. An exceptionally good education was given to him by his father, Koloman Tisza, who as Prime Minister ruled Hungary for many years. Even as a young man Tisza had already acquired much diversified knowledge, had travelled widely with observant eyes and thus learnt much about many countries and races, and had formed definite opinions from which he never subsequently departed on the subject of the best form of government for Hungary. Tisza was a lifelong believer in parliamentary government after the British model. "Parliaentary government," Tisza wrote in 1912, "is the form assumed by national public life in the modern world that in the fullest manner unites freedom and order, individual liberty and organized national force."

Tisza was a proud and upright man with a will of iron who was as relentless towards himself as towards others. He passionately and stubbornly pursued his aims and refused to be diverted from them by the fierce opposition which he often met with. It is not therefore surprising that he should have had many enemies in public life who hated him bitterly while at the same time his supporters adored him and remained loyal to him. He was not popular and did not want to be popular. It would have been contrary to his whole character to have flattered the mob. Although not a coiner of memorable phrases, Tisza was an impressive speaker who held his audience by the stern logic of his thought and by the suggestive force of his personality at moments when his political feelings were brought into play.

The Hungarian Constitution was born of the Compromise (*Ausgleich*) of 1867 and found in Tisza an enthusiastic champion. He believed that it would be a great political mistake to alter the character of the Dual Monarchy, and energetically opposed those political parties that sought to loosen the tie that bound Hungary to Austria not only because he feared Francis Joseph's unyielding antagonism to any such proposal but also because he was convinced that the best way of securing Hungary's future was for Hungary in union with Austria to constitute a Great Power in alliance with the German Empire.

If his vision was clear and farsighted in regard to the future of Austria-Hungary, Tisza's eyes lost their keenness and clarity when he surveyed the problem arising out of the presence of non-Magyar races within the Hungarian frontiers. Here his single-track mind came into play. He underestimated the strength of the nationalist movement among the non-Magyar peoples of Hungary and until the end of his life he obstinately refused to change or moderate his opinion that these non-Magyar races must never be granted their desire for independence and a share in the government proportionate to their numbers. For this reason Tisza also opposed the introduction of universal suffrage which would have destroyed the supremacy of the Magyars in Parliament and the Government. He did not want to see any increase in the Slav population of the Dual Monarchy and therefore he was a fierce opponent of every plan for the incorporation of portions of Servia into the Austro-Hungarian Empire. For a long time he was a steadfast opponent of war with Servia on the ground that such a war would be waged under adverse conditions. He was almost alone in the Council of Ministers, and in the many memoranda which he sent to the Emperor, in protesting against an aggressive policy that would have the effect of increasing the tension between Austria-Hungary and Servia, and he expressly declared that he could not assume the responsibility for any policy deliberately designed to provoke war. Nevertheless he finally abandoned his opposition to the war party chiefly because of the German Emperor's assurance that he would fully carry out his obligations as an ally. At the same time Tisza insisted that it should be explicitly stated that Austria-Hungary did not seek territorial aggrandizement at Servia's expense.

Tisza's conduct when disaster overtook the Austro-Hungarian Empire revealed his innermost personality. He was reviled as a warmonger and made responsible for the catastrophe. But he never once raised his voice in his own defence to point out that it was he alone who for a long time had resolutely opposed war with Servia. After the outbreak of war Tisza refused his consent for concessions to Italy and also subsequently for the conclusion of a separate peace with the Allied and Associated Powers that would have involved Austria-Hungary's desertion of her German ally. Up to the last day of the war he would not hear of making concessions to the Southern Slavs and Rumanians even though many people deemed them vitally necessary in the interest of the Empire's survival.

Count Stephen Tisza was shot dead in his own house on 30 October 1918 by political assassins and thus ended his life as a martyr for his own beliefs.

THE BRITISH PRIME MINISTER

ASQUITH

During the years 1908-1914 the British Prime Minister, Herbert Henry Asquith, did not play a decisive part in foreign policy. He was an intimate friend of Grey in whose hands he left the control of foreign policy and with whom he worked in perfect understanding. Grey never did anything without first informing Asquith and asking his advice. He had no secrets that he concealed from him. Asquith almost invariably shared Grey's opinion and was always ready to give him his support. In those momentous days in 1914 when the decision had to be taken as to the part Great Britain was to play in the World War, Asquith stood shoulder to shoulder with Grey and made no secret of the fact that he intended to stand or fall with him.

Asquith came of a middle-class family and therefore from a very different social environment to that into which Grey had been born. He, like Grey, was at Balliol College in Oxford where he distinguished himself by his energy and intellectual qualities and acquired a great and varied fund of knowledge. After his election to the House of Commons in 1886 Asquith speedily won a name for himself in influential political circles. He was Home Secretary from 1892 to 1895 when he became Chancellor of the Exchequer, and from 1908 to 1916 he was Prime Minister. All who came into contact with him admired his quick grasp of a situation or problem, his effortless understanding, unfailing memory, and thorough knowledge of many and widely different subjects. He was energetic, resolute, and a fighter. His second wife, Margot Tennant, declares in her memoirs that her husband was, above all else, a man of action. Early in his life Asquith had formed very definite views about his attitude to men and things, and from these views he never departed throughout his long life. He possessed to a remarkable degree the philosophic temperament that confronts Fortune in her good and evil moods alike with an inalterable serenity. He loved life and the society of his fellowmen. He was a warm-hearted and faithful friend of those whom he admired and liked. But he hated and despised mean and vulgar minds and never hesitated to show his dislike. Asquith indeed was not a man of the people. On the other hand few Prime Ministers have rivalled Asquith in authority over Parliament. He was a brilliant debater whose wit and readiness in repartee were accompanied by a complete mastery of whatever subject he spoke upon that earned for him the respectful attention of his audience and enabled him to win them for his views. Grey said of Asquith that he was "far the biggest figure in the House of Commons."

At Cabinet meetings Asquith kept himself in the background and spoke as seldom as possible. But he knew better than anyone how to sum up the discussions. He thought of his task as Prime Minister as that of a judge or arbitrator rather than a Party politician, and he spared no pains and displayed much cleverness in composing differences and in achieving unanimity for Cabinet decisions. His outstanding intellect, farsightedness, and sagacity, as well as his courage and skill in handling men, made Asquith a truly great peacetime Prime Minister. In the difficult years immediately preceding and succeeding to the outbreak of war, however, Asquith failed to show himself a leader and in the British Government the motive force no longer came from him.

THE BRITISH SECRETARY OF STATE FOR FOREIGN AFFAIRS

GREY OF FALLODON

Lord Castlereagh has been called the most European of British statesmen. It would be equally true to say of Edward Grey that he was the most insular. He was born into one of those English county families that have contributed so much to making England great. Many of his ancestors had distinguished themselves in home and foreign affairs. Grey was educated in accordance with family tradition, and went to Oxford where he was known as a keen sportsman and took his full share in undergraduate life. Although he entered politics at an early age, Grey always said that even then, and indeed throughout his life, he had no real interest in politics.

He once said of foreign affairs that it was a dirtier game than any in which he had hitherto been forced to take part. By temperament and inclination alike Grey would have preferred the life of a country gentleman. He was a lover of Nature and all her works, a keen fisherman, and a famous and unequalled birdwatcher. He hated to leave England for even a day. In his youth he visited India and the West Indies. Of Europe he knew virtually nothing. It was 1914 before he saw Paris for the first time. He had little or no knowledge of foreign languages and of the political systems of the European States. All who knew him—many of them were outspoken critics of his foreign policy—agree that Grey was a man of high and noble character—sincere, generous, selfless, and unassuming. Nobody has ever questioned the purity of his motives. Dignified and handsome, Grey was a fine speaker with a remarkably pleasing voice. He was tactful, well-mannered, and inspired by a high sense of duty and responsibility. But those who knew him intimately differ widely in their judgements of his intellectual qualities. Nevertheless Grey may not unfairly be described as a man with a good average brain, commonsense, and great skill in handling men. He was a logical thinker who detested any form of pose or pretence and shunned the chicanery by which many statesmen seek to attain their ends. Although Grey was not an orator, his speeches, wholly lacking in passion and imagination though they were, impressed his hearers by their sincerity and matter-of-factness. One seeks in vain in his printed speeches for an illuminating flash of genius or the brilliant epigram that impresses itself upon the memory of an audience. On the other hand, Grey never sought to conceal his real meaning behind a cleverly spun web of colourful phraseology. He never sought to change an audience's opinions by verbal suasion. On the contrary, he said what he thought about the subject and then left it to his audience to form their own judgements. Of the humour and wit to be found in the speeches of many of the great British statesmen and parliamentary orators there is no trace in Grey's speeches. Nevertheless Grey gained for himself to an ever-increasing degree the confidence and support of Parliament and public opinion because both Parliament and the nation were convinced that Grey worked solely for England's welfare and never gave a thought to his own personal position or advantage.

Grey certainly cannot be called a great statesman. For that he lacked farsightedness, daring, self-confidence and unfailing energy. He did indeed remain tenaciously faithful to political principles that he had adopted after much reflection. But he hesitated or retreated in the face of difficulties that stood in the way of the carrying out of his plans and preferred to allow events to take their own course. Moreover, Grey was often in doubt about the method to be employed in the carrying-out of his policy, and therefore sought and acted upon the advice of his immediate subordinates—Hardinge, Nicolson, Crowe—who were his intellectual superiors and far more energetic. Hardinge and Nicolson also excelled him in diplomacy. In the Cabinet discussions—Winston Churchill says—Grey was in the habit of putting forward proposals or suggestions that he deemed important and of defending them against his critics with much skill. But he never acted upon them without first obtaining the assent of the Cabinet and of Parliament. Frank by nature and a lover of frankness in others, Grey as a statesman found himself compelled from time to time to keep silent about matters that he should have made public or to return evasive answers to parliamentary questions. But Grey only resorted to secrecy or dissimulation when his conscience told him that he was acting in the national interest.

Since the publication of the British diplomatic documents relating to the outbreak of the First World War no unprejudiced person will ever again believe that Grey was a warmonger who for years sought to bring about war with Germany. Grey was in truth a convinced lover of peace who detested war. Although he certainly did not like the Germans, Grey was not a Germanophobe. He wanted England and Germany to live peaceably side by side and he was ready to do his utmost to remove possible causes of conflict between them. Nevertheless he held firmly to his resolve never to do anything that would loosen the ties binding Great Britain to France and Russia (he himself had done much to bring about the Anglo-Russian agreement) and never to assume obligations towards Germany that could have a prejudicial effect upon Anglo-Franco-Russian relations. Although he always declared that he was not a believer in the doctrine of the European Balance of Power, Grey deemed it vitally important that Great Britain should be able to count upon the support of the

Entente Powers in the event of Germany's seeking to upset the *status quo* and to gain hegemony over Europe. One of Grey's guiding principles was the upholding of the sanctity of treaties. He regarded this as indispensable for the progress of civilization and as constituting the necessary basis for trust between the nations as compared with a state of lawlessness and armed force. For this reason alone Grey was always loath to promise more than he could perform. It was for this reason too that Grey refused to give an undertaking to the Entente Powers that England would become their comrade-in-arms in a war with Germany, and he was careful not to include any such undertaking in treaties or agreements with them. Grey was compelled to adopt this hesitant policy because the majority of the Cabinet, and also very largely public opinion in England, did not share his belief that war was inevitable and therefore demanded that in event of war Great Britain should remain neutral. But Grey held firmly to his own opinion and was eventually successful in gaining support for it not only from the King and the Prime Minister, Mr. Asquith, but also from the majority of the Cabinet, by declaring that he would have nothing to do with a policy of neutrality and in event of its adoption would resign. It is in the highest degree characteristic of Grey that after the war, and under the influence of the enormous loss of human life that it had cost the nations, Grey asked himself and his friends if he had done rightly and whether or not he might possibly have prevented the war. He obstinately held to his theory of the inevitability of war in order to quieten his conscience. In Oxford in 1929 I myself had a conversation with Grey in the course of which I pointed out to him that the published British diplomatic documents clearly showed that until just before the war he himself had believed that it was possible to prevent it and that he had acted in this belief. Grey was deeply moved and retorted passionately that the war was inevitable. He then refused to join in any further discussion of the subject.

THE FOREIGN OFFICE

Hardinge—Nicolson—Crowe

Among the officials at the Foreign Office whose duty it was to advise the Secretary of State for Foreign Affairs and to keep

British diplomatic representatives abroad informed of the British Government's policy as well as to negotiate with the foreign ambassadors and ministers accredited to the Court of St. James's, the Permanent Under-Secretary of State wielded the greatest influence over the Secretary of State for Foreign Affairs and thereby over the course of events. This responsible post during the years 1908 to 1914 was successively held by Sir Charles Hardinge (1908-1910) and Sir Arthur Nicolson (1910-1914). Second only to them, but less well-known, Sir Eyre Alexander Crowe as Senior Clerk, and from 1912 as Assistant Under-Secretary of State, decisively influenced the attitude adopted by the British Government towards the Central Empires.

HARDINGE OF PENSHURST

When in 1906 he became Permanent Under-Secretary of State, Sir Charles Hardinge (afterwards Viscount Hardinge of Penshurst) already had a long career as a diplomatist behind him. After acting temporarily as Assistant Under-Secretary in 1903 Hardinge was sent as Ambassador to St. Petersburg from 1904 to 1906 when he was recalled to become Permanent Under-Secretary at the Foreign Office. He held this post until 1910 when he became Viceroy of India where he remained until 1916. On his return from India, Hardinge was again appointed to his former post of Permanent Under-Secretary in which he remained until in 1920 he was sent to Paris as Ambassador—a post that he held for two years. Hardinge was an exceptionally gifted man inspired by a strong sense of duty. Cool and deliberate in his judgement of men and events, he possessed great physical and moral courage and was a tireless worker. Sober and realistic in his political thinking and outlook Hardinge pursued his aims with dogged tenacity and inexhaustible patience. He was adored by his friends and feared by his enemies. King Edward VII thought so highly of his ability and character that he took Hardinge with him in his journeys abroad and left negotiations with foreign statesmen in his hands. Hardinge liked to go his own way and did not hesitate frankly to express his opinions to Sir Edward Grey who, as the British Diplomatic Documents make clear, generally agreed with his views and approved his suggestions and actions. Hardinge disliked and distrusted

Germany and feared her endeavours to gain mastery over
Europe. He did not, however, share Crowe's embittered
feelings on the subject of German policy. It is true that in the
negotiations which he carried on from 1908 to 1910 with
Count Mensdorff, and also in his instructions to the British
Ambassador in Vienna, Hardinge was strongly opposed to
Aehrenthal's policy in the Bosnian Crisis. At the same time
he appreciated the difficulties created for Austria-Hungary
by Servia's attitude.

SIR ARTHUR NICOLSON

Arthur Nicolson, first Lord Carnock, was far above the
average in intellect and character. Quick to grasp the
essentials in a situation or problem, letting nothing escape his
observation, unerring in his judgements of men and events,
Nicolson was the possessor of a first-rate brain and exceptionally gifted in giving clear expression to his thoughts. He was
a brilliant diplomatist who pursued a policy with unflinching
tenacity. Nicolson was unselfish, honourable, generous, and
abhorrent of pettiness. He was a realist who was always ready
to accept conditions as he found them and to conform his
actions within the limitations imposed by a situation. Notwithstanding his delicate constitution Nicolson had trained
himself by the exercise of an iron will and self-discipline to
withstand the strain of decades of nerve-racking work. It is
not therefore surprising that Nicolson should have held that
the most indispensable and inestimable quality with which a
man could be endowed at birth was energy. Nicolson was a
devoted son of his native country whose every thought and
action was inspired by a desire to promote England's greatness.
He was a well-read man who knew a great deal about a great
many subjects, and who during the years he had spent as a
diplomatist both in European and non-European countries
had gained an understanding of the idiosyncrasies of their
inhabitants that stood him in good stead as Permanent Under-
Secretary at the Foreign Office and very greatly increased his
influence over the course of affairs. Nicolson believed that
national self-interest should take precedence of all other
considerations in the minds of those charged with formulating
national policy. For many years he held that "splendid
isolation" best served British interests and he therefore sup-

ported the non-committal policy of the British Government towards France and Russia throughout the last decade of the nineteenth century. Subsequently Nicolson became convinced that Germany was Great Britain's most dangerous enemy, and the sharper the rivalry between them, and the greater the increase in strength of the German Army and Navy, the more energetically did Nicolson demand the abandonment of isolation and the enlargement of the Franco-Russian Alliance to include Great Britain.

At the time of the Algeciras Conference in 1906 Nicolson was British Ambassador at Madrid and effectively supported Germany's opponents. Subsequently he became Ambassador at St. Petersburg where he was largely instrumental in achieving a close understanding between Great Britain and Russia. Even when he was at St. Petersburg Nicolson was of the opinion that every sacrifice must be made to make ready for the threatened German onslaught. After the Bosnian Crisis in which Russia was forced to retreat before the Central Empires, Nicolson demanded the transformation of the Entente with France and Russia into a formal alliance, and emphasized the dangerous possibility that if France and Russia were to find themselves abandoned by Great Britain they might be compelled to come to an agreement with Germany. He continued to express this opinion in the strongest possible terms after he became Under-Secretary and thus came into conflict with Grey whose vacillating policy met with his outspoken disapproval. Nicolson did not want a war and would have welcomed an Anglo-German agreement on the condition that it was not purchased at the price of a rupture of Great Britain's friendly relations with the Entente Powers. On this point Nicolson and Grey were in complete agreement. The conviction, however, gradually became stronger and stronger in Nicolson's mind that peace could not be maintained and that war was inevitable. The stronger this belief grew the more emphatic became his demands that Great Britain should declare publicly that she would fight on the side of France and Russia in event of war. Nicolson was certainly never unfriendly towards Austria-Hungary whose demands on Servia after the murder of the Archduke Francis Ferdinand he deemed just. At the same time he condemned Austria-Hungary's want of frankness and moderation and he thought Berchtold (whom he liked personally) was not the man to cope with such a crisis. After World War I Nicolson voiced his disapproval of the severity of the Treaty of Versailles and especially of the fact that the whole responsibility for the war had been placed by the victorious Allied and Associated Powers upon Germany and her allies.

SIR EYRE CROWE

The vast influence exercised by Sir Eyre Crowe upon British policy between 1908 and 1914 only became generally known outside the Foreign Office, and especially abroad, in recent years. As Senior Clerk in the Foreign Office, and from 1912 as Assistant Under-Secretary, Crowe was chiefly responsible, together with Grey and Nicolson, for the course followed by British policy in those years. Crowe owed his advancement in the Foreign Office to his outstanding qualities as a civil servant and administrator. Highly educated, experienced, gifted with tireless energy and an acute understanding, Crowe was animated by a strong sense of responsibility. His personal integrity and charm of manner won him many friends. Crowe worked long and late and made heavy demands upon his subordinates whose affection and respect he nevertheless gained by his unfailing consideration for their welfare. He detested men who dabbled in foreign affairs and whom he contemptuously styled "amateur" diplomatists. In Crowe's ideal Foreign Office everything that was said or done would have been scrupulously placed on record. He never for a moment doubted the essential morality of British policy and was convinced that it lay in Britain's interest to support the weak as against the strong among the nations. Crowe was widely looked upon as a great authority upon German affairs. He had one idiosyncrasy that distinguished him from many of his contemporaries. Crowe never permitted anything that appeared in the newspapers to influence either his opinions or judgements.

Crowe was born in Leipzig where his father—a distinguished writer on art—was serving as British Consul-General before he was transferred to Berlin as Commercial attaché. He was a friend of the Prince Consort's brother, Duke Ernest II of Coburg, and also of the German Crown Prince Frederick and his wife, Victoria, who was Queen Victoria's daughter. Crowe's mother was a German and he himself married a

German. After receiving his early education in Germany, Crowe, at the age of eighteen, arrived in England where he devoted himself to the study of law. He entered the Foreign Office in 1885 and for many years worked as a specialist in legal questions. He was one of the British representatives at the Second Hague Conference in 1907 and in the following year at the Naval Conference in London. From 1906 onwards Crowe was Grey's chief adviser on all questions concerning Western Europe and Germany. His complete mastery of the German language as well as the fact that he made an invariable practice of studying the German Press, and also his constant intercourse with his German relations and friends, among whom the head of Bleichröder's Bank, Paul von Schwabach, occupied a special place, enabled Crowe to acquire a very accurate insight into German political life and to understand the motives that inspired German politicians. Crowe was not a Germanophobe. Indeed he acknowledged and admired the great achievements of the German nation in art and science. So long as Germany—Crowe once wrote—in reliance on her own individual strength and capacity seeks to achieve the intellectual and moral leadership of the world England can only applaud her effort and compete with her. Nevertheless nobody knew better than Crowe that beside this ideal Germany there existed another Germany in which force ruled and might triumphed over right. His youth had been passed in Bismarckian Germany at a time when it was generally believed that Bismarck was striving with might and main to make Germany the master of Europe. How far his youthful impressions influenced Crowe in his belief that Germany's endeavour to win the mastery over Europe constituted a threat to peace can never be known with certainty any more than the degree of truth contained in the suggestion made in some quarters that Crowe laid great emphasis upon his anti-German policy simply because he himself was partly German in origin. All that is certain is that from the moment at which Crowe took charge at the Foreign Office of Anglo-German relations his attitude openly became anti-German. After the Algeciras Conference in 1906 Crowe formed the opinion that Germany was not to be trusted and he refused to listen to men like Goschen and Lascelles who reported from Berlin that the German Government was not harbouring inimical intentions. In the celebrated Memorandum which he drew up in 1907 Crowe sought to prove that Germany was striving for the mastery of the world by every possible means and that by adopting a conciliatory attitude towards her the Great Powers only strengthened her conviction that she would achieve her ambition. In succeeding years Crowe frequently repeated his warning. If it be true that he did not succeed in convincing every influential person and that criticisms of his policy came from many sides, and also that Grey hesitated to adopt such an avowedly anti-German policy, it is no less true that Crowe's warnings did not fall on deaf ears. Nicolson gave Crowe his powerful support. After the failure in July 1914 of all his attempts to preserve the peace Grey himself admitted that Crowe had been right in his insistence that the real issue at stake was not Servia but the conflict between Germany's bid for world domination and the resolve of the other Powers to defend their individual freedom. At the Paris Peace Conference after the war Crowe played an important part in the drafting of the peace treaties.

THE AMBASSADORS

During the years 1908-1914 Great Britain was represented in Vienna by three Ambassadors in swift succession while Austria-Hungary was represented in London by the same Ambassador throughout the whole period—Count Mensdorff-Pouilly. An attempt is made in the following pages to draw thumb-nail sketches of these four diplomatists whose dispatches did not fail of effect upon British and Austro-Hungarian policy.

1. THE BRITISH AMBASSADORS AT VIENNA

(a) SIR EDWARD GOSCHEN

Sir Edward Goschen joined the Diplomatic Service in 1869 and served in Pekin, Copenhagen, Lisbon, Washington, and St. Petersburg before in 1898 he was appointed Minister at Belgrade. After two years in Belgrade he was transferred in 1900 to Copenhagen where he remained until in 1905 he was appointed Ambassador at Vienna. In November, 1908, he left Vienna to become Ambassador at Berlin. Hence Goschen only remained in Vienna for a few weeks after the annexation of Bosnia and Herzegovina. His many friends in Vienna remembered him as an honest man who loved fair play and whose amiability and good nature made him a welcome guest at social gatherings. Aehrenthal and Goschen disliked each other and had little in common. Aehrenthal complained of Goschen's ponderous and deliberate way of thinking that rendered negotiations with him wearisome and long-drawn-out. He thought him a stupid man. For his part Goschen distrusted Aehrenthal and believed him to be a double-dealer. Consequently Goschen's transfer to Berlin was welcomed by both men. Goschen remained as Ambassador at Berlin until the declaration of war on 4 August 1914 brought his mission to a close.

(b) Sir Fairfax Cartwright

At the end of December 1908 Sir Fairfax Cartwright arrived in Vienna in succession to Sir Edward Goschen as ambassador. Both his mother and his grandmother were Germans. His father was a member of an old family and was an intimate friend of the German Crown Prince and Princess. Cartwright was a boyhood playfellow of the future German Emperor William II and resumed his friendship with him in the early eighteen eighties when he (Cartwright) was attached to the British Embassy in Berlin. When, however, differences arose between William II and his parents Cartwright, like his father, took the parents' side and some caustic remarks on the behaviour of the fashionable world in Berlin which he set down on paper at the time, and which became widely known, aroused resentment and were not forgotten. At the time of the Algeciras Conference in 1906 Cartwright was Counsellor at the British Embassy in Madrid and he took an active part in the proceedings of the Conference. Subsequently he became British Minister at Munich and at Stuttgart whence he sent to the Foreign Office extremely interesting and well-written dispatches that attracted the notice of King Edward VII who looked upon him as an exceptionally able diplomatist and advised his appointment as Ambassador at Vienna.

Cartwright was an unusually gifted man. He had a first-rate memory, quick understanding, unfailing energy in the pursuit of his aims, and that rare quality—farsightedness. His wealth rendered Cartwright completely independent of material considerations and consequently he never hesitated to express his opinions with an almost brutal frankness. His strength of character enabled him to gain such complete mastery over a serious physical disability that he was not only able to carry on his work but also to have energy and time left over in which to pursue his artistic interests and brilliantly to fulfil his exacting social duties. Although Cartwright was not predisposed to be unfriendly towards Austria-Hungary, he arrived in Vienna from Munich in the midst of the Bosnian Crisis and believed that the Austro-Hungarian Government harboured warlike designs. He had not been long in Vienna, however, before he realized that Aehrenthal wanted to attain his ends by peaceful means. Once he had attained to this conviction Cartwright devoted himself to bringing about an improvement in the relations between Aehrenthal and Grey, and the success that ultimately crowned his efforts was very largely due to the remarkable skill which he displayed in handling Aehrenthal who was notoriously difficult to manage. Personal differences subsequently arose between Cartwright and Aethrenthal that caused the latter, like his successor Berchtold, to let it be known in London that Cartwright's removal from Vienna would be welcome. Nevertheless it was not until 1913 that Cartwright finally left Vienna.

(c) Sir Maurice de Bunsen

The last British Ambassador in Vienna before the outbreak of the First World War was Sir Maurice de Bunsen, who at the end of November 1913 arrived in Vienna in succession to Sir Fairfax Cartwright. He belonged to a German family. His grandfather was a personal friend of Frederick William IV of Prussia and was sent by him at the beginning of the eighteen forties to London as Prussian Minister. His dispatches to his Royal friend were models of their kind. The Minister and also his son Ernest—the father of Sir Maurice—married English women. Sir Maurice was born in 1852 and after a good early education went up to Oxford. On leaving Oxford he travelled for many years and did not enter the Diplomatic Service until 1887 when he once more resumed his travels by serving at many British Legations and Embassies in Europe, Asia, and America. De Bunsen was a well-educated and intellectual man who through his wide travels had acquired great experience of the world. His judgement in political matters was reasoned and impartial. As Ambassador in Vienna de Bunsen spared no pains to acquaint himself with the exceedingly complex internal political conditions in the Danubian Monarchy and he voiced the opinion that it was a marvel that the Austro-Hungarian Empire held together because—logically speaking—it ought to fall to pieces yet it continued to exist. At the outset of his mission de Bunsen was largely forced to rely for his knowledge of Austro-Hungarian foreign policy upon what he was told by his diplomatic colleagues among whom the French Ambassador was his closest adviser. He was on friendly—though not confidential—terms with Berchtold, and he much preferred to conduct business with one of Berchtold's immediate subordinates, Count Forgach, who was more talkative than the reticent Foreign Minister. Although he condemned the conduct of the Austro-Hungarian Government in the days immediately preceding the outbreak of war in 1914, de Bunsen was not an enemy of Austria-Hungary. He returned to the Foreign Office in 1915, and retired from the Diplomatic Service in 1918, when he once again resumed his travels and also occupied himself in scientific studies and as an active member of philanthropic, political, and economic organizations.

2. THE AUSTO-HUNGARIAN AMBASSADOR IN LONDON

COUNT ALBERT MENSDORFF-POUILLY

The Austro-Hungarian Ambassador at the Court of St. James's from 1904 until the outbreak of the First World War was a most attractive, unassuming, tactful man, Count Albert Mensdorff-Pouilly, who was a son of the former Austrian Cabinet Minister, Count Alexander Mensdorff-Pouilly, and who as a distant relative of King Edward VII enjoyed *vis-à-vis* the English Royal Family an unusual degree of intimacy not accorded to any other member of the Diplomatic Corps. Count Mensdorff was deservedly popular in London Society by reason of his social gifts, frank and open character that abhorred intrigue and cunning, and *flair* for entertaining. Although Mensdorff was of a lethargic disposition, he devoted himself to his work with great concentration and seriousness and displayed considerable diplomatic skill in carrying out his Government's instructions. He was pacific by nature and always sought to compose differences before they led to a serious conflict. Mensdorff did his utmost to promote and maintain friendly relations between Great Britain and Austria-Hungary, and during the Bosnian Crisis he constantly impressed upon Aehrenthal his conviction that Austria-Hungary had nothing to fear from British policy.

Mensdorff was deeply distressed by the cold reception accorded to him by King Edward VII when he handed to the King the letter in which the Emperor Francis Joseph announced the annexation of Bosnia-Herzegovina. The Permanent Under-Secretary of State, Sir Charles Hardinge, remarked at the time: "You have never seen such a woebegone appearance as Mensdorff has now. He thoroughly realizes that his Government have behaved in a very underhand manner and the poor little man has had this well rubbed into him during his stay at Balmoral. I really feel quite sorry for him. He is not a fitting representative of a policy of duplicity such as Aehrenthal's." Nevertheless, despite his frigid manner on this occasion, King Edward VII greatly admired Mensdorff and would have been glad to have seen him replace Aehrenthal as Austro-Hungarian Foreign Minister. Although Mensdorff worked hard to prevent an outbreak of hostilities, he warned the Austro-Hungarian Foreign Ministry on many occasions that in event of war Great Britain would fight on the side of France and Russia against the Triple Alliance. In Mensdorff's opinion the only possible cause of war lay in the Anglo-German rivalry and therefore he strove to mediate between British and German statesmen. His well-intentioned efforts failed of any permanent success. Moreover, Mensdorff himself met with the fate that overtakes many honest go-betweens in that he was suspected in Berlin of intriguing in London against Germany—a suspicion wholly devoid of any foundation. Anyone who knew Mensdorff's sincere and open character would realize the impossibility of his playing such a part while his unshakable conviction that an alliance between the Central Empires was a vital necessity for each of them would of itself have prevented him from intriguing against Germany.

The outbreak of the First World War in August 1914 struck Mensdorff like a tidal wave and left him a shattered man. In 1917 Mensdorff was sent by the Emperor Karl to

Switzerland to discuss with General Smuts, as representative of the Allied and Associated Powers, the possibility and the conditions of peace. The negotiations proved fruitless because Mensdorff was forbidden by the instructions given to him by the Austro-Hungarian Foreign Minister, Count Ottokar Czernin, to discuss the question of a separate peace between Austria-Hungary and the Allies that would have had the effect of dissolving the alliance of the Central Empires and leaving Germany to continue the war alone. After the war Mensdorff represented the new Austrian Republic at the meetings of the League of Nations in Geneva.

Chapter Three

THE BOSNIAN CRISIS, 1908-1909

IN the secret agreement made at Reichsstadt on 8 July 1876 Russia and Austria-Hungary decided that the largest portion—small portions were reserved for Servia and Montenegro—of Bosnia-Herzegovina should be annexed by Austria-Hungary and this decision was confirmed in an Additional Convention appended to the Treaty of Budapest of 15 January 1877 while in a secret treaty concluded in June 1878 Great Britain declared her willingness to support Austria-Hungary's claims to these territories. It cannot be doubted that had Great Britain proposed at the Congress of Berlin that Austria-Hungary should annex Bosnia-Herzegovina the proposal would have been accepted by all the Great Powers with the sole exception of Turkey. The Austro-Hungarian Foreign Minister, Count Julius Andrassy, was nevertheless content with an Austro-Hungarian occupation of these districts partly in order to overcome Turkish opposition and partly because he feared that the Germans and Magyars in the Dual Monarchy would resist "the formal incorporation" within it of more than one and a half millions of Slavs. The Turkish delegates to the Congress had refused to agree to the occupation in the form proposed to them and their assent had only been secured at the eleventh hour in a compromise by which the Austro-Hungarians agreed to place their signatures to a declaration "that the rights of sovereignty of His Majesty the Sultan over the provinces of Bosnia and Herzegovina shall not be affected by the fact of occupation . . . that the occupation shall be considered provisional and that a previous agreement on the details of the occupation shall be made by the two Governments immediately after the closing of the Congress."[1] A Convention to this effect was in fact subsequently signed on 21 April 1879 in Constantinople.

In the First Article of the Protocol attached to the Triple Alliance Treaty that was signed on 18 June 1881 it was stated that Austria-Hungary "reserves the right to annex these provinces at whatever moment she shall deem opportune," and in the Second Article formal recognition was accorded to

Austria-Hungary's right to garrison the Sandjak of Novibazar. This alliance lasted until 1887, and in 1897 the Austro-Hungarian Government gave a more precise definition to its interpretation of these arrangements. In a secret dispatch, dated 8 May to Prince Lichtenstein, who was then Austro-Hungarian Ambassador at St. Petersburg, it was stated that as a result of discussions at St. Petersburg "the territorial advantages accorded to Austria-Hungary by the Treaty of Berlin are and remain acquired by her. In consequence the possession of Bosnia, of Herzegovina, and of the Sandjak of Novibazar may not be made the object of any discussion whatsoever, the Government of His Imperial and Royal Apostolic Majesty reserving to itself the right of substituting, when the moment arrives, for the present status of occupation and the right of garrisoning that of annexation." In his reply to this declaration the Russian Foreign Minister, Count Mouravieff, emphasized that the Treaty of Berlin had only dealt with the military occupation of Bosnia-Herzegovina. "The annexation of these two provinces," he said, "would raise a more extensive question which would require special scrutiny at the proper time and places." No further discussion of the matter took place.

The Austro-Hungarian Foreign Ministry in the following years often examined and discussed the question of replacing occupation by annexation of the two provinces and also the best means of effecting that transformation. Hundreds of memoranda housed in the State Archives in Vienna testify to the Foreign Ministry's preoccupation with this problem. Nevertheless projects remained projects and no action was ever taken upon them. It fell therefore to Aehrenthal, who had become Foreign Minister in 1906, to substitute deeds for words by annexing the two provinces. He hoped by so doing to make an end to their chronic state of unrest and to confer upon them some form of "representative government". After lengthy preparations and the exchange of notes between the Austro-Hungarian and Russian Governments, and after the outbreak of the Young Turk Revolution, Aehrenthal and the Russian Foreign Minister, Isvolsky, met at Buchlau in Moravia on 15 September 1908 and reached a verbal agreement—no trace of a written agreement has ever been found—"that if Austria-Hungary were forced to proceed to annexation of Bosnia-Herzegovina Russia would assume a friendly and benevolent attitude. In return Isvolsky asked Austria-Hungary to observe the same attitude in case Russia should see herself compelled by her interests to take steps for assuring the free passage through the Dardanelles of individual Russian men-of-war."[2] By the end of September Aehrenthal had made all preparations for carrying-out the annexation. He did not expect that Great Britain would oppose his action.[3]

On 28 September Aehrenthal wrote a private letter to the British Under-Secretary of State, Sir Charles Hardinge, for Count Mensdorff to take to London. Aehrenthal informed Hardinge of Austria-Hungary's intention to annex Bosnia-Herzegovina and to renounce her rights in the Sandjak of Novibazar. He recalled the achievements of Austria-Hungary in the two provinces and emphasized the necessity arising out of the Young Turk Revolution of granting a constitution to the provinces which he declared could only be done after the recognition of Francis Joseph's full sovereignty.[4] Francis Joseph wrote a personal letter on the following day to King Edward VII in which he announced his resolve to annex the provinces and drew the King's attention to what Austria-Hungary had done for them. He added that it was on Great Britain's initiative at the Congress of Berlin that Austria-Hungary was entrusted with the task of setting-up a strong and permanent administration in the provinces. The Emperor ended by saying that he would continue in the future to pursue the conservative policy which he had followed in the past.[5]

On 3 October Mensdorff handed Aehrenthal's letter to Hardinge and explained to him the reasons that led the Austro-Hungarian Government to take this step. The Foreign Office was not taken by surprise. On 30 September the British Minister in Belgrade had reported that the Servian Foreign Minister, Milovanovic, had told him that he was certain from what was said during his conversations with Isvolsky and Aehrenthal that the Austro-Hungarian Government would shortly proclaim—he thought the proclamation might be delayed to coincide with the sixtieth anniversary of Francis Joseph's accession to the throne—the annexation of Bosnia-Herzegovina and that all preparations had already been made.[6] On 1 October Goschen reported from Vienna that the newspapers were hinting at the possibility of an annexation to which—they declared—all the Powers, excepting only Great Britain, had already given their assent.

Goschen added that his information led him to believe that the Austro-Hungarian Government wanted to annex the provinces immediately but that the Hungarian Government was opposed to any change in the *status quo*. Nevertheless he thought that something would happen before the meeting of the Delegations.[7] Two days later on 3 October it was reported from Paris that the Austro-Hungarian Ambassador had informed the French Government of his own Government's decision to annex Bosnia-Herzegovina.[8]

Hardinge did not discuss with Mensdorff the possible consequences of annexation and merely laid stress upon the dangers that might arise for Turkey as a consequence of Austria-Hungary's action and the simultaneous declaration of Bulgarian independence. He feared that Greece, Servia, and possibly Italy, might seek compensation. Great Britain had become Turcophil since the Young Turk Revolution, and the British Government had lately advised the Turkish Government in the event of territorial changes to remain calm and in no circumstances to start a war and to bring all questions arising out of the Treaty of Berlin before the Powers.[9] In conclusion Hardinge said that it would have been better if Austria-Hungary had postponed the annexation until the existing crisis in Turkey had been overcome.

After he had read Aehrenthal's letter to Hardinge, Sir Edward Grey frankly expressed his views. He instructed the British Ambassador in Vienna to remind Aehrenthal of the Protocol of 17 January 1871 attached to the Treaty of London, of which Austria-Hungary was a signatory, which declared that no Power could break or alter treaty obligations "except by friendly agreement" and with the assent of the other signatories to the treaty. The British Government could not sanction an open violation of the Treaty of Berlin, or even an alteration in its stipulations, unless the other signatory Powers, and in this case especially Turkey, had been consulted.[10] Goschen therefore should protest to the Austro-Hungarian Government "and urge strongly upon them the necessity of reconsidering their decision to annex the two occupied provinces."[11] On Grey's instructions Goschen, on 4 October, had already requested Aehrenthal to advise Prince Ferdinand of Bulgaria to abandon the projected declaration of Bulgarian independence. Aehrenthal replied that he could not do this before he knew for certain that Ferdinand did in fact intend to proclaim Bulgaria's independence. He had indeed warned Ferdinand only a short time before against embarking on an adventurous policy and Ferdinand had taken his advice in good part.[12] He therefore doubted the truth of the rumour about an imminent declaration of Bulgarian independence. For his part Goschen gravely doubted the truth of Aehrenthal's statement.[13] Grey agreed with him as to Aehrenthal's insincerity and added that "you and we cannot but feel justly aggrieved at being treated with such bad faith."[14] A few days later when the Bulgarian declaration of independence was an accomplished fact Aehrenthal gave his word of honour that he and the Austro-Hungarian Government had had no idea that it would take place so quickly. Goschen commented to Grey that if a man gave his word of honour one had to accept it but that he was convinced "that this word of honour only extended perhaps to the precise date."[15]

King Edward VII and Grey were still more outspoken. They said that they could never again trust Aehrenthal because he had deceived them. On 5 October Aehrenthal and Goschen met to discuss the annexation. After he had listened to Goschen's statement of Grey's views (which was based on Grey's instructions to Goschen) Aehrenthal expressed his astonishment that Grey should regard the annexation as a violation of the Treaty of Berlin because this Treaty said nothing about sovereignty and only mentioned Austria-Hungary's rights without placing any "restrictions on her actions". He was therefore disagreeably surprised at this protest on the part of Great Britain whose representatives at the Congress of Berlin had proposed that Austria-Hungary should be given the mandate and who had "notoriously been in favour of placing her in definitive possession of the two provinces". Nevertheless Great Britain now took up the standpoint that the fact that at the Congress of Berlin she had given her full support to Austria-Hungary in the question of the occupation of Bosnia-Herzegovina did not justify Aehrenthal's expectation that she would also condone Austria-Hungary's unilateral annexation of those provinces. It was said that the change that had taken place in Great Britain's attitude was primarily due to the change that had taken place in Anglo-Russian relations as a result of which the British Government had assumed obligations that conflicted with the

Austro-Hungarian annexation of Bosnia-Herzegovina. Turkey was in a different position. The Convention of 1879 gave her the right to protest. Aehrenthal then went on to emphasize the sacrifices in men and money made by Austria-Hungary in bringing peace and order to the two provinces—the purpose for which the mandate had been given to her. Annexation now offered the only means by which she could continue to carry-out her mandate since it was imperative that the provinces should be given a constitution and this could not be done under the former conditions. Aehrenthal therefore made a pressing request to Grey not to make difficulties because the decision to annex the provinces was irrevocable as the Emperor had already signed the necessary documents. In reply to a question of Goschen's as to why Turkey had not been consulted beforehand in view of the fact that Aehrenthal admitted her right of protest, Aehrenthal said that Turkey would certainly have refused her consent and her refusal would only have increased the tension without bringing about any change in Austria-Hungary's resolve to annex the provinces.[16]

On 7 October the Foreign Office received the formal announcement of the annexation. Hardinge pointed out that the Treaty of Berlin only spoke of "occupation" and that the word "annexation" did not appear in its text, and, moreover, that the preamble to the Convention of 17 April 1879 between Austria-Hungary and Turkey categorically stated that the fact of an Austro-Hungarian occupation of Bosnia-Herzegovina "does not affect the rights of sovereignty of the Sultan."[17] Now that the annexation was an accomplished fact Great Britain was forced to decide what was to be her attitude in regard to it. Grey and his advisers decided to hold fast to their opinion that the annexation constituted a violation of the obligations agreed to by Austria-Hungary in 1871 and 1878, and that therefore Great Britain must refuse her assent to the annexation until the other signatories to the Treaty of Berlin had given their assent.[18]

The revolution in Turkey had made the Young Turks masters of the country. Great Britain wished to strengthen their position and to help them to retain the government. She therefore adopted a policy towards Turkey in the annexation crisis that was as accommodating and conciliatory as was possible. It was for this reason that as early as 5 October

Grey had stressed in conversation with the Turkish Ambassador Great Britain's sympathy for the Young Turk Government, and given him the promise that if Turkey protested against Austria-Hungary's action and asked for compensation Great Britain would support any proposal "which seemed fair consideration for her [Turkey]". But he strongly advised Turkey not to go to war and to accept a monetary compensation of which she stood in urgent need.[19] Hence it is the more necessary to emphasize here the falsity of the allegations made by Aehrenthal, and also by many enemies of Great Britain, that Grey had incited Turkey to make war on Austria-Hungary. From the very outset, and indeed throughout the entire course of the Bosnian Crisis, Grey never concealed, even from Austria-Hungary, his sympathy with the Young Turk movement. Turkey certainly did not suffer material loss through the annexation of Bosnia-Herzegovina and the declaration of Bulgarian independence. But the injury to her prestige was very great and she deserved the compensation which Grey demanded for her.

Another consideration that weighed heavily with Grey and his advisers during the Bosnian Crisis was their desire to meet Russia's wishes and thereby to maintain and to strengthen the ties of friendship that had grown up between the two countries since the agreements of 1907 and 1908. Thus British statesmen in their negotiations with the Austro-Hungarian Government were powerfully influenced by their regard for Russia and Turkey.

In the conversations between Grey and Mensdorff which took place on 9 and 10 October the British Secretary of State for Foreign Affairs condemned Aehrenthal's action. Mensdorff gained the impression that Grey would not change his opinion and that the Austro-Hungarian Government would find Grey's condemnation of their violation of the Treaty of Berlin "standing like a stone wall before them in any future discussions".[20] Mensdorff in his talks with King Edward VII received a like impression. As soon as he had read the private letter from the Emperor Francis Joseph which Mensdorff handed to him King Edward VII at once described the coincidence between the declaration of Bulgarian independence and the Austro-Hungarian annexation of Bosnia-Herzegovina as regrettable. Although his displeasure was chiefly directed against Ferdinand of Bulgaria, King Edward to the accompaniment of expressions of friendship and admiration for Francis Joseph emphasized the dangers that could arise out of Austria-Hungary's action and expressed his hope that the Austro-Hungarian Government would couch its announcement of the annexation to Turkey in the most friendly terms possible.[21] Mensdorff received the impression from the King's words that the British Government feared for the future of the Young Turk regime whom they wished to maintain in power and that at Balmoral it was thought probable that there would be sharp attacks in Parliament and the Press.[22] But when on 7 October King Edward was informed that the annexation had taken place his misgivings were given forcible expression. He deplored the fact that no attempt had been made prior to the annexation to consult and to negotiate with the signatory Powers to the Treaty of Berlin, and he feared that Bulgaria's and Austria-Hungary's actions were tantamount to a severe blow to the Young Turks and would have serious consequences for Great Britain, since the Sultan had now had it demonstrated to him that as long as he was the friend of Germany he would be protected against such attacks. The King also laid stress on the fact that it was essential to learn what Russia's attitude would be in this crisis. A conference would have to be held because the all-important thing was to avoid war. Lord Redesdale recorded the impression made on King Edward VII by Francis Joseph's letter: "No one who was there can forget how terribly the King was upset. Never did I see him so moved. He had paid the Emperor of Austria a visit at Ischl less than two months before. The meeting had been friendly and affectionate, ending with a hearty 'auf baldiges Wiedersehen'. The two sovereigns and their two statesmen (Aehrenthal and Hardinge) had discussed the Eastern Question, especially the Balkan difficulties, with the utmost apparent intimacy and the King left Ischl with full assurance that there was no cloud on the horizon. Now, without a word of warning all was changed!" The King looked upon the Emperor's silence as a "breach of faith".[23] Nothing more is known of what passed between the two monarchs. Wickham Steed relates that King Edward said to him that nothing was said in his talks with Francis Joseph about the projected annexation of Bosnia-Herzegovina.[24] And that is doubtless true. But did Francis Joseph's silence in fact constitute an act of bad faith? It must be admitted that nothing was said in the conversations between the two monarchs about the projected annexation. Francis Joseph's silence on this subject would only have amounted to an act of bad faith if King Edward had asked him how matters stood in regard to Bosnia-Herzegovina. It must also be borne in mind that on the day on which these conversations took place—12 August 1908—no definite decision had been taken in regard to annexation. It would be too much to expect of Francis Joseph that when the subject was not even raised between them he should have informed the King of plans whose execution had not yet been decided upon. Moreover, it was certain that if the British Government had got wind of the proposed annexation it would have exerted itself with might and main to prevent it. If, without the subject being raised, Francis Joseph had communicated to King Edward the proposal to annex Bosnia-Herzegovina, he would have spoilt the plan that had been drawn up by his Foreign Minister with his approval.[25]

King Edward VII replied on 11 October to the Emperor's letter merely expressing his regret at the decision that had been taken and stating that he believed in the principle laid down in the Protocol of 17 January 1871 by which the Treaty of Berlin could not be altered without the consent of its signatories.[26] When he was handed the King's letter Francis Joseph remarked that the King was evidently "not at all pleased. I am very sorry for it, but really annexation was inevitable and had to take place." On Goschen's observing that the fact that the Bulgarian declaration of independence was made simultaneously with the annexation was, as the Emperor had conjectured, one of the main reasons for the bad feeling prevailing in England, Francis Joseph declared that there had been no connection between the two events. Neither he nor his Government had had the slightest idea that Ferdinand of Bulgaria would act so precipitately and throughout his stay in Budapest the Prince had not given even a hint of his intention either to him or to his Government.[27]

Anyone who has any knowledge of Francis Joseph's character cannot doubt that he was speaking the truth. Moreover, it is very improbable that Aehrenthal would have withheld from the Emperor any information that Ferdinand had given him of his intention to proclaim Bulgaria's independence in the immediate future. Hence it is permissable to question the justice of Goschen's accusation against Aehrenthal that he (Aehrenthal) had lied when he told Goschen that the declaration of Bulgarian independence came as a complete surprise to him, and also of the severe judgement passed by Edward VII and Grey on Aehrenthal's character. The most likely explanation is that Ferdinand told Aehrenthal of his intention (Aehrenthal did not deny this) without at the same time telling him the exact date on which it was to be carried out.[28]

The negotiations carried on between the Austro-Hungarian and British Governments after the annexation of Bosnia-Herzegovina—these negotiations alone form the subject of the present enquiry—as a consequence of the British Government's inalterable determination only to recognize the annexation after it had been approved by the signatories of the Treaty of Berlin were concerned with three questions. First: Under what conditions and in what form should the signatory Powers express their assent. Second: What compensation should Turkey receive. Third: To what extent were Montenegro and Servia entitled to compensation. At the very outset of the negotiations it became clear that it would be exceptionally difficult to come to an agreement over these questions and the idea was mooted of a conference between the signatory Powers to the Treaty of Berlin.[29] But this idea met with opposition from different quarters. Grey feared lest Russia might bring up the Dardanelles Question (which he wished to avoid at all costs) and Turkey shared in his misgivings.[30] For his part Aehrenthal at once declared that he could not allow the annexation issue to be discussed in a conference because that would be tantamount to bringing Austria-Hungary before the judgement-seat and would imply doubts about the annexation. He did not object to a conference on principle, but he must first reach an understanding with Turkey that would then be submitted to the conference which would accept it without debate and would then abrogate Article 25 of the Treaty of Berlin.[31] The German Ambassador in London expressed his Government's sympathy for the Young Turks and at the same time declared that Germany must stand by her ally, Austria-Hungary, who would not take part in any conference at which the Bosnian Question was to be discussed. Austria-Hungary—he said—wanted peace. This remark drew from Grey the reply that he did not doubt the sincerity of Austria-Hungary's desire for peace. "Most countries wished to get all they desired without having the trouble of going to war, but an attempt of this kind was often the cause of war, however little it might be desired."[32] Italy favoured a conference at which—she stated—she would demand an alteration in Article 29 of the Treaty of Berlin which placed limitations upon Montenegro's sovereign rights.[33] The Russian Government agreed to a conference at which it hoped Great Britain and Russia would work hand in hand.[34] The Foreign Office was from the outset determined to reject Russia's proposals. Hardinge declared that one must first be certain that the conference would not be used to exert pressure on Turkey, while Grey remarked that before the conference met an agreement must be reached both upon its agenda and upon the manner in which the questions upon the agenda were to be discussed, and also upon the best way and form in which Turkey could draw profit from it.[35]

An agenda for the conference was drafted by Isvolsky and the French Ambassador in London, M. Paul Cambon, which contained nine subjects for discussion. These subjects were:

1. The international legal position of Bulgaria and her obligations to Turkey.
2. Bosnia-Herzegovina.
3. Sandjak of Novibazar.
4. The stipulations of Article 23 of the Treaty of Berlin regarding Turkey's European provinces.
5. Article 61 of the Treaty of Berlin regarding the districts in Turkey inhabited by Armenians.
6. The conditions laid down in Article 29 of the Treaty of Berlin limiting the sovereign rights of Montenegro.
7. Rectifications of frontier in favour of Servia and Montenegro on that part of the territory of Bosnia-Herzegovina bordering on the Sandjak of Novibazar.
8. The Balkan States and the Danube.
9. The Capitulations and the foreign postal service in Turkey.

The French Foreign Minister, M. Pichon, and Grey objected to the wording of Article 7 of this draft and Grey was successful in having it altered to "Advantages to be obtained for Servia and Montenegro."[36]

The German Ambassador in London, Count Metternich, informed Mensdorff of the existence of this draft agenda and on the next day gave him a copy for his personal information.

The draft was not at that time officially communicated to the Vienna Foreign Ministry.[37] Aehrenthal at once said that in no circumstances could he accept the original wording of Article 7, and even in its revised form he thought the Article objectionable, because it opened the door to a demand for territorial compensation at Austria-Hungary's expense that Austria-Hungary would be compelled to refuse. Moreover, it was likely to arouse delusive hopes in Servia and Montenegro and thus add to the tension.[38] Aehrenthal believed that he was fully warranted in warning Great Britain against lending her support for far-reaching demands on the part of these two Balkan States because the menacing attitude of the Servian Government and the fierce attacks on the Dual Monarchy that were appearing in the Servian Press, as well as the reports from Belgrade of mobilization, made possible the danger of an armed intervention by Austria-Hungary.

As a matter of fact there was at this time in Vienna a war party headed by the Chief of the General Staff, Conrad von Hötzendorff, that wanted war with Servia because its members believed that the Servian Question could only be solved by the sword. Their views were not shared either by the Emperor, who was strongly opposed to war, or by Aehrenthal, who was convinced that he could attain his objective without recourse to armed intervention. Even the Heir Apparent, Archduke Francis Ferdinand, who in many quarters in England was thought to be a warmonger, was at this time firmly opposed to war with Servia. In a private letter written on 20 October the Archduke said that he fully agreed with Aehrenthal that Austria-Hungary must in no circumstances embark on a war with Servia. He added that it seemed to him as if these "Balkan curs" were being roused to precipitate action by Great Britain and possibly Italy. His opinion was that Austria-Hungary should use very firm language in Belgrade and Cettinje while at the same time no preparations should be made for war and a damper put upon Conrad's bellicosity. Compensation for Servia and Montenegro was quite impossible.[39]

The Turkish Question formed the chief topic of conversation between Mensdorff and Grey and Hardinge after Mensdorff had received his instructions from Vienna. Turkey had protested against the annexation and had forbidden the import of Austro-Hungarian goods. She then stated in London that she thought her interests would best be served by letting the matter rest and not by bringing the Bosnian Question before a conference. Turkey wished to avoid the recognition of the annexation by the signatory Powers which she knew to be a foregone conclusion, and wated the whole matter to be left to the future.[40] The Foreign Office refused to listen to this suggestion. In any event the conference could see that Turkey retained the Sandjak of Novibazar which Austria-Hungary could then receive back after a solution had been found to the annexation problem.[41] British statesmen also refused to give serious consideration to a plan put forward by the Grand Vizier simultaneously with a renewed demand that the conference should not concern itself with the Bosnian Question. According to this scheme Bosnia-Herzegovina was to be made an autonomous principality ruled over by a Protestant prince from a State not involved in the dispute who was to be chosen by the Great Powers, and whose task it would be to give the new principality the constitution that had been promised by the Austro-Hungarian Government. The Grand Vizier visualized an alliance between the new principality and Servia and Montenegro, and eventually even with Bulgaria. When the Grand Vizier explained his plan to the British Ambassador at Constantinople the Ambassador at once remarked that it would meet with opposition from Austria-Hungary and Germany. The Grand Vizier replied that he could count on the support of Russia, Great Britain, France, and Italy. The Turks—said Hardinge—are like children: they keep coming with new requests that cannot be granted. Nevertheless Grey and his advisers held firmly to their opinion that Turkey deserved suitable compensation.

This question of compensation was brought up time and again by Grey and his immediate subordinates in their conversations with Mensdorff, who invariably replied that Turkey had suffered no material damage through the annexation and that the return of the Sandjak of Novibazar was sufficient compensation for any loss of prestige that she might have sustained. It has already been mentioned above that from the very outset of the crisis Great Britain had warned Turkey that there could be no question of territorial compensation and had advised her to ask for a money payment, and it was for this reason that the British Government now proposed to the Austro-Hungarian Government that it should take over part of the Turkish State debt.[42] In answer to the accusation that was appearing in the Vienna Press that Great Britain had advised Turkey to refrain from direct negotiations with the Austro-Hungarian Government for the purpose of reaching a settlement, and also to Mensdorff's request that Great Britain would counsel Turkey to negotiate directly with Vienna, Grey truthfully replied that he had never advised Turkey to abstain from direct negotiation with Vienna and that on the contrary he had from the outset advised Turkey to examine every proposal that came from Vienna and to decide for herself whether or not it afforded her sufficient satisfaction. Since, however, he did not know what proposals Austria-Hungary had made to Turkey it was not immediately possible for him to accede to Aehrenthal's request and to advise the Turkish Government to enter into direct negotiation with the Vienna Government, or indeed to exert pressure upon the Turkish Government to induce them to accept the compensation offered to them by Austria-Hungary. Hardinge used the same arguments in recommending that Austria-Hungary should take over a part of the Turkish State debt.[43] But Aehrenthal rejected this proposal not only because he deemed it unjustifiable but also because of the bad impression that such a concession would make at home and abroad.[44]

Aehrenthal's rejection of Great Britain's proposals in regard to Turkey aroused ill-feeling in London that was further increased by his refusal to make any concession whatsoever to Servia or Montenegro in response to a Russian demand supported by Great Britain. It was recalled in London how often at the desire of the Austro-Hungarian Government the British Government had warned Servia to refrain from any provocation of Austria-Hungary, to moderate her demands, and, above all, to abandon any hope of territorial compensation. Something had certainly to be done to prevent a revolution in Servia.[45] Mensdorff himself would have welcomed a conciliatory gesture on Aehrenthal's part because he believed that it would be right and also that the occasion called for it. But he was compelled by his knowledge of Aehrenthal's character to be very cautious as to what he said in his dispatches. On 3 November he wrote to Aehrenthal that recently one of his friends who was closely associated with the King and the Government had said to him that he did not think that he (Mensdorff) perhaps fully appreciated how angry the British

Government, and also to a certain degree the King, was with Vienna, and that he would not like to prophecy what Great Britain's policy would be in the event of a serious conflict between Austria-Hungary and Turkey. The desire to sustain the new Turkish Government in power at all costs and to retain the sympathy (which she had lately regained) of the Mohammedan world was of greater importance to Great Britain than an alliance and was so strong that it was sufficiently powerful to turn British policy into courses that ran entirely contrary to British traditions.[46]

Aehrenthal paid little or no attention to Mensdorff's statement.[47] He thanked the British Government for exercising a moderating influence in Belgrade which was all the more necessary since Servia had adopted a bellicose attitude and was making preparations for war.[48] He also instructed Mensdorff to complain to the British Government of the manner in which the British Press was so outspokenly expressing its sympathy with Servia, and to draw attention to the dangers that might arise from toleration of this type of journalism. Aehrenthal then went on to explain in detail the attitude that the Vienna Government would be prepared to adopt in the event of a conference. He emphasized the fact that the conference could only decide the various issues that had arisen out of recent events in the Balkans after the signatories of the Treaty of Berlin had reached a preliminary agreement. Aehrenthal approved in general of the draft agenda for the conference that had been sent to him in confidence by the Austro-Hungarian Ambassador at St. Petersburg, Count Berchtold, and he was ready to take part in an exchange of views. His own views on the individual items of the agenda were as follows:

1. Bulgaria. With regard to Bulgaria's legal status and its financial liabilities to Turkey the Austro-Hungarian Government was prepared to recognize the new state of affairs that had arisen in Bulgaria, and shared the conviction that the conference would not sanction the independence of Bulgaria until a settlement had been reached of the financial questions and especially of the question of the eastern railway.

2. Bosnia and Herzegovina. Sandjak of Novibazar. These questions could appear on the agenda provided that there was no discussion of the extension of the Emperor's

sovereign rights to Bosnia-Herzegovina and of the evacuation of the Sandjak of Novibazar.[49] The Vienna Government wished to reach an agreement with the Porte on this matter after which the conference would deal with the question of the abrogation of Article 25 of the Treaty of Berlin.

3. Turkey's European Provinces and the Turkish districts inhabited by Armenians. Aehrenthal was of the opinion that a discussion of Articles 23 and 61 of the Treaty of Berlin would be useful for the purpose of bringing the text of the Articles into line with the new constitutional regime in Turkey.

4. Montenegro. He would not offer any opposition to an alteration of Article 29 that limited Montenegro's sovereignty, but the Austro-Hungarian Government must retain the right in agreement with Montenegro to construct a railway along the Montenegrin coast and must insist that Montenegro abided by her undertaking not to fortify the coast or to construct a naval base at Antivari.

5. Advantages to be given to Servia and Montenegro. The wording of Article VII of the draft agenda— "avantages à procurer à la Serbie et au Montenegro"— might occasion misunderstandings and therefore Aehrenthal would prefer that it should read "avantages économiques à procurer à la Serbie et au Montenegro."

6. The Balkan States and the Danube. The Austro-Hungarian Government was prepared to concede greater rights to Rumania and Bulgaria as riverain states.

7. The Capitulations and Foreign Postal Service in Turkey. The Austro-Hungarian Government was ready to negotiate an agreement with the Powers on the subject of the necessary modifications to be introduced into the regime of Capitulations and foreign postal service in Turkey.[50]

Evidently Aehrenthal was not prepared to make any changes in the conditions that he had laid down as a *sine qua non* for Austria-Hungary's participation in a conference. An agreement therefore seemed unlikely in these circumstances. Anglo-Austrian relations became strained in the succeeding weeks.[51] The Turkish boycott of Austro-Hungarian goods continued and the British Government anxious though it invariably was to promote the interests of the Young Turks nevertheless refused to support Aehrenthal's demands at Constantinople for a resumption of the—temporarily suspended—negotiations over the question of compensation for Turkey—a resumption that Aehrenthal wished to make conditional upon a previous lifting of the boycott.[52] In London opinion hardened on the subject of Turkey's right to compensation and the British Government again suggested that Austria-Hungary should take over part of Turkey's State debt. Mensdorff exerted himself to the utmost in trying to convince British statesmen that his Government's relinquishment of its rights in the Sandjak of Novibazar was sufficient compensation for Turkey, and that the demand for monetary compensation was unjustified because Turkey had not suffered any material loss through the annexation whereas Austria-Hungary had expended vast sums in improving the administration and promoting the cultural life of Bosnia-Herzegovina. All his arguments and efforts nevertheless did not effect any change in the British Government's attitude.[53] Towards the end of November Mensdorff summed up the impression left upon him by his conversations with British statesmen in saying that the insinuations appearing in the German and Austrian Press that Great Britain was trying to ignite a conflagration in the Balkans were without foundation,[54] and that on the contrary British statesmen were doing all in their power to bring about a pacification and the summoning of a conference. Sympathy with the Young Turks was given public expression in London and Mensdorff declared that he was convinced that Great Britain would stand beside Turkey in event of an Austro-Hungarian-Turkish war.[55] Although Grey could not adopt Aehrenthal's standpoint that as a matter of principle all discussion of the annexation should be forbidden in the conference, he thought that a secret agreement could be arrived at by which no discussion of this subject would in fact take place. Hardinge showed that he shared Grey's views by saying that it was impossible to demand that five Great Powers who had declared the annexation to be a violation of the Treaty of Berlin, and Turkey who felt herself the injured party, should assemble in conference without being able to mention the event that had occasioned the summoning of the conference.[56] Aehrenthal's attitude towards Servia also met with British disapproval. Great Britain undoubtedly did not approve of the provocative behaviour of the Serbs and their unceasing preparations for war. Indeed she warned Servia to be more moderate in her demands and to slow down her military preparations.[57] Nevertheless Great Britain out of regard for Russia, who had agreed not to raise the Dardanelles Question at the conference, specially wanted Aehrenthal to show himself more conciliatory in regard to Servia. But Aehrenthal still refused to consider territorial compensation for Servia and Montenegro, and reiterated his demand for the introduction of the word "economic" in the text of Article 7 of the draft agenda for the conference.

Irascibility was a well-known trait in Aehrenthal's character. It was now aroused without any justification by some words that Hardinge let fall in conversation with the Councillor of the Austro-Hungarian Embassy in London, Count Széchényi, when informing him that Great Britain had again issued a warning to Servia. Hardinge went on to add that there really must be a spirit of compromise "de part ou d'autre". Aehrenthal instructed Széchényi to tell Hardinge in a friendly but firm manner that the Austro-Hungarian Government had never approached any Power, and certainly not Great Britain, with any suggestion for intervention at Belgrade. He did not doubt that continued warnings to the Servian Government to moderate its policy and actions were in the interests of peace. But he felt that he must state in advance that he refused to accept any advice that might be forthcoming as to what the attitude of the Austro-Hungarian Government should be. When it was recalled what unexampled patience Vienna had displayed in face of Servian provocations he had to confess the lively indignation aroused in him by Hardinge's words, "de part ou d'autre", which seemed to place Austria-Hungary more or less on the same plane as Servia as regards her actions.[58] Hardinge was not disturbed by Aehrenthal's outburst and merely said that he had never thought of proffering advice to the Austro-Hungarian Government, and that he knew perfectly well that Aehrenthal had never asked for Great Britain's intervention. He had only intended to convey to Count Széchényi what the British Government had in contemplation, repeating its warning to Belgrade to act with circumspection.[59]

A private letter from Aehrenthal to Mensdorff written on 30 November 1908, in which Aehrenthal frankly disclosed

what was passing in his mind, reveals very clearly that he was
not inclined to believe in the pacific intentions of British
statesmen or in their protestations of friendship for Austria-
Hungary. He wrote that he had declared in his speech to the
Delegations that his policy in regard to Turkey was directed
towards the same end as British policy towards that country.[60]
The answer to his speech was the thwarting by Great Britain
of direct negotiations between Vienna and the Sublime Porte,
and the intensification, at British instigation, of the Turkish
boycott of Austrian goods. Despite official British denials he
was certain that British intrigues were responsible for Turkey's
attitude. The British Press was inciting Russia and Servia
against Austria-Hungary in an utterly irresponsible manner.
Everyone in Vienna was asking whether Great Britain was
trying to provoke a conflict between Austria-Hungary and
Turkey over Bosnia. If this was really true then war between
Austria-Hungary and at any rate Servia would almost certainly
be the result, and upon Great Britain would fall a share of
the responsibility for its occurrence. As to Russia he still
remained convinced that she would be careful not to pick a
quarrel with Austria-Hungary because that would be tantamount to quarrelling with Germany. British statesmen
seemed to think that he (Aehrenthal) was a mere tool in
German hands. This was completely untrue. On the contrary
his whole energy was devoted to the pursuit of a policy that
was as independent as was possible. He had explained this
last summer to King Edward and Hardinge. Nevertheless
Great Britain continued to believe that his policy was dictated
to him by Germany and therefore ruthlessly attacked Vienna
because she wanted to strike at Berlin.[61] King Edward's
behaviour, and especially his political boycott of Mensdorff,
were looked upon in Great Britain as a proof that the King
approved of his Government's policy towards Austria-Hungary.
He (Aehrenthal) therefore asked Mensdorff to lay emphasis
in London upon the fact that the Emperor Francis Joseph
was seriously and painfully disturbed by Great Britain's
incitement of Turkey, Russia, Servia, and indeed of all
Powers, against Austria-Hungary. The Emperor remained
faithful to his pacific policy only it must be made possible for
him to carry it out. The provocations that Austria-Hungary
had endured in recent years would certainly not have been
suffered by Great Britain with a like patience. Nonetheless

the Dual Monarchy's patience had its limits. Unless the in-
flammatory campaign in the British Press ceased, the Serbs
would be led astray and under the illusion that they would be
supported by certain Great Powers they would bring punishment upon themselves.[62] Aehrenthal also instructed Mensdorff
to tell King Edward VII that he (Aehrenthal) sincerely
wanted to see the Young Turk regime established upon solid
foundations and that he was in favour of a conference. But
he could not accept Russia's suggestion that the Bosnian
Question should be openly debated at the conference.
Aehrenthal concluded by saying that he looked with perfect
confidence towards the future development of events, did not
fear any very serious complications, and was even beginning to
believe that it would not be necessary to take punitive measures
against Servia provided that Great Britain speedily gave up her
irresponsible campaign of incitement that was only inspired by
hatred.[63]

Mensdorff in his reply to Aehrenthal's letter said that British
policy now as formerly was inspired by the desire to assist the
Young Turk regime and to uphold the principle of the sanctity
of treaties. Nothing would induce Grey to depart from this
policy. He himself still did not believe that Great Britain was
inciting other Powers against Austria-Hungary and was trying
to get Turkey to go to war. Moreover, he would hold to this
opinion despite what might appear in a perverted Press or
what might be said by a few irresponsible British travellers
abroad. He was certain that the British Government would
only be glad if Aehrenthal came to an agreement with Turkey.[64]
Hardinge had definitely confirmed this, and also urgently
recommended a legalization of the status of Bosnia-Herzegovina
either by a conference or by an exchange of notes, because as
long as this question was left open there was the risk of grave
dangers especially in view of the Pan-Slav movement in Russia.
Mensdorff went on to explain to Aehrenthal that with regard
to the discussion by the conference of the Bosnian Question the
difference between the British and Austro-Hungarian attitudes
might best be defined by saying that while Austria-Hungary
said "Bosnia must not be discussed", Great Britain was ready
to agree to the formula "Bosnia will not be discussed".[65]

Mensdorff's arguments had little effect upon Aehrenthal
who in a strictly confidential letter to Mensdorff on 17 December again gave vent to his views on Britain's anti-Austrian

policy. British policy towards Austria-Hungary—he wrote—
can only be understood when it is accepted as a premiss that
the chief motive inspiring it is the desire indirectly to attack
Germany. It is obvious that Aehrenthal simply did not believe
Grey's assurances that he had never sought to sow seeds of
discord between the members of the Triple Alliance and that
in fact he looked upon the division of the Great Powers into
two groups as conducive to the maintenance of the Balance of
Power in Europe. Aehrenthal may possibly have been right
in holding this point of view in so far as British politicians saw
in Austria-Hungary the ally of Great Britain's rival, Germany,
who was steadily becoming more powerful and dangerous, and
therefore deplored the fact that Francis Joseph had refused to
use his influence in Berlin to bring about a compromise in the
naval issue. Nevertheless it was his desire to support the Young
Turks and to retain Russia's friendship as well as to uphold
the doctrine of the sanctity of treaties that determined Grey's
attitude in the Bosnian Crisis. Aehrenthal would not listen to
this explanation. He believed that the British Government,
Press, and also individual British travellers in the Balkans,
while working with different methods and means, pursued the
same end in complete harmony and unity of purpose. After
fiercely criticizing British policy which—he said—had not
always been so Turkophil, Aehrenthal attacked Grey for the
zeal with which he championed the sanctity of treaties. He
recalled British policy in former times in regard to the problem
of the neutralization of the sea and went on to express his
astonishment that a responsible British politician could become
so roused over the principle of the sanctity of treaties that he
would be ready to defend it by force of arms. Such zealotry
was hardly in accord with British tradition and the history of
Great Britain. Aehrenthal also attacked King Edward VII.
He admitted that he was ignorant of the King's attitude to his
Government's policy and the attacks on Austria-Hungary
appearing in the British Press. But Count Khevenhüller had
reported from Paris that the President of the Young Turk
Committee, Ahmed Riza Bey, who had been received in
audience by the King about a fortnight ago, had said that
King Edward VII had greeted him with the words: "Capital
trick your boycott. Go on." Aehrenthal also said that he
understood that King Edward made no secret of his dislike for
him, and had even declared that he would look on it as a great

piece of good fortune if Mensdorff were to replace Aehrenthal as Foreign Minister, because he would then be certain that Austria-Hungary would pursue a policy consonant with British interests. Aehrenthal brought this portion of his letter to a conclusion by saying that there could be no possible doubt that Great Britain was striving to conclude a formal alliance with France and Russia.[66]

This outburst did not exhaust Aehrenthal's wrath. He went on to say that British policy was the product either of an inexplicable bad-tempered mood or of ignorance and stupidity for which Goschen's incapacity was greatly to blame. Ignorance and stupidity nevertheless had their limits. He himself felt that they could no longer be regarded as an excuse for the conduct and policy of British statesmen.

Mensdorff found himself in an exceedingly awkward quandary in replying to Aehrenthal's letter. He nevertheless extricated himself very skilfully by reporting to Aehrenthal statements made by the German Ambassador in London that sharply conflicted with Aehrenthal's own statements. Count Metternich said that he did not believe that Great Britain in attacking Vienna really intended the blow to strike Berlin. Metternich was of Mensdorff's opinion that friendship for the Young Turks and the upholding of the sanctity of treaties were the guiding motives in British policy. Grey had told him that he would welcome an arrangment between Aehrenthal and the Turks and that he (Grey) would advise the Turks to be moderate in their demands. Hardinge had said the same thing, only adding that up to the present Aehrenthal's offers had been insufficient and that there could be no satisfactory settlement with Turkey unless the Austro-Hungarian Government gave financial compensation.[67] Mensdorff then went on to say that —speaking for himself—he could not share Aehrenthal's belief that Great Britain sought an alliance with France and Russia. Such an idea had hitherto been unpopular in England and certainly that of an alliance that would involve the upkeep of a much larger army. The King's Private Secretary, Lord Knollys, had assured Mensdorff that the King had never given an audience to any Young Turk leader, and therefore not to Ahmed Riza Bey, whose story about the King's having said to him "Capital trick your boycott. Go on." was consequently untrue. Anyone who knew the King, wrote Mensdorff, who knew him well, in ending his letter to Aehrenthal, knew that it was utterly impossible that he would have said such a thing.[68] Knollys' statement certainly cannot be doubted, because even Khevenhüller in writing to Aehrenthal described Ahmed Riza Bey as an idle gossip.[69] It is, however, true that immediately after the Bosnian Crisis certain officials—Nicolson among them—at the Foreign Office wanted to see the Entente with France and Russia turned into an alliance. But Grey was strongly opposed to the idea.[70]

Obviously Aehrenthal's Anglophobia rendered negotiations between London and Vienna difficult. Sir Fairfax Cartwright experienced this when in December 1908 he succeeded Goschen as British Ambassador at Vienna. On his way to Vienna, Cartwright had long talks in Paris with the French Prime Minister, Clémenceau, and the Foreign Minister, Pichon. Clémenceau advised Cartwright to tell the Emperor Francis Joseph, as well as Aehrenthal, that the situation was dangerous and to counsel them to give speedy satisfaction to the Turks. Although Hardinge agreed with this suggestion, he thought a proposal made by Cartwright that a secret agent should be sent from Vienna to Constantinople to find out what conditions the Turks would lay down for their recognition of the annexation and the ending of the boycott would meet with as little success as Clémenceau's suggestion that an Austrian Archduke be sent to St. Petersburg with friendly proposals to the Tsar so long as there was no change in the present "irreconcilable attitude" of Aehrenthal.[71] Very shortly after his arrival in Vienna, Cartwright was able to convince himself that there was in fact no change. Aehrenthal told him that the attitude of Great Britain to the Austro-Hungarian Empire "was at the bottom of the present trouble". The British Press must shoulder at least half the blame for the Servian "trouble". Great Britain incited Servia and Turkey "to resist Austria".[72] Unless Great Britain changed her attitude the traditionally friendly relations between Great Britain and Austria-Hungary would come to an end and very serious conflicts might arise. Aehrenthal would not hear of concessions to the Serbs and Montenegrins. Austria-Hungary could no longer suffer Servian provocations. He would not allow any foreign Power or Powers to demand a reduction in the strength of the Austro-Hungarian troops stationed on the Servian frontier. Cartwright said that as far as he knew the British Government did not contemplate any action in this matter. At the same time—he added—it was obvious that the stronger the troop concentrations the greater became the danger of a conflict. Aehrenthal replied that that was true. If a conflict were to take place, however, it would be provoked by the Serbs and not by the Austro-Hungarian troops. Cartwright thereupon asked if Russia would not intervene in such an eventuality and Aehrenthal replied that his impression was that Russia was not in a situation to wage war. Aehrenthal was ready to accept a conference on condition that he could be certain that there would not be any "inconvenient discussion" of the annexation. Indeed the only satisfactory result of this conversation between Cartwright and Aehrenthal was the latter's assurance that he intended to be very conciliatory with the Turks. When Cartwright suggested a money payment for Turkey, Aehrenthal said that in that event the money that Austria-Hungary had expended on Bosnia-Herzegovina should be deducted from the amount payable to the Turks as compensation. At the same time he did not on this occasion wholly reject the notion of a monetary compensation.[73]

The Foreign Office interpreted Aehrenthal's words as meaning that he was not in principle disinclined to give Turkey monetary compensation, and in expressing its satisfaction at this intimation instructed Cartwright to spare no effort in endeavouring to secure that Aehrenthal changed his words into deeds. On the margin of Cartwright's dispatch reporting his conversation with Aehrenthal King Edward wrote: "Baron Aehrenthal knowing that he is in the wrong uses offensive language towards England which however does not strengthen his case."[74] The Foreign Office also let it be known with regard to Aehrenthal's refusal to make concessions to Montenegro and Servia that Great Britain had promised her diplomatic support to Russia in her endeavour to overcome the difficulties arising out of Servian and Montenegrin demands. Aehrenthal could not therefore expect that Great Britain would support him in his "stiff attitude of resistance" to concessions in other matters even though he had come to an agreement with Turkey.[75] In conversation with Mensdorff on the subject of Aehrenthal's complaints about the British Press, Grey remarked that Great Britain had a far better right to complain of the Austrian Press than Aehrenthal had to complain of the British Press. He also observed in alluding to Aehrenthal's deceitful behaviour at the time of the Bulgarian declaration of independence "that he felt much irritation with Baron Aehrenthal, but, however, I agree that foreign affairs must be conducted without reference to personal feelings and as far as I was concerned I could assure him that I kept any personal feelings I might feel about the Press or anything else in a separate compartment."[76] Grey and Hardinge both assured Mensdorff that they had no objection to the conclusion before the meeting of the conference of an agreement laying down the bounds within which the conference would carry on its discussions. France and Great Britain would place no obstacle in the way of Austria-Hungary's reaching an agreement with the Italian, Russian, and Turkish Governments for that purpose. Agreement between Turkey and Austria-Hungary and between Austria-Hungary and Russia was what mattered most of all.[77]

When Cartwright resumed his discussion with Aehrenthal on this basis he was told that the negotiations that had been in progress between Austria-Hungary and Russia had reached a temporary conclusion. The brusque tone that had been adopted by both sides at the outset had been abandoned and an agreement had been reached that the conference should not meet until the Powers were in agreement upon its agenda. No definite understanding had nevertheless been come to as to whether and within what bounds the conference might discuss the annexation issue. Aehrenthal no longer held to his standpoint of 8 November that no discussion of the annexation must take place in the conference. On the contrary, he merely expressed the hope in his *aide-mémoire* of 8 December 1908 that inasmuch as Russia had agreed to the annexation in previous treaties she would not raise her voice against it in the conference.[78] Isvolsky, too, adopted a milder tone in his *aide-mémoire* of 17 December 1908 and no longer declared, as in his statement of 22 November, that no limitations must be placed upon the discussion by the conference of the annexation issue. Nevertheless he remained of the opinion which he had always held that the annexation problem could only be solved by general agreement. In conclusion he noted with relief that the Austro-Hungarian Government no longer insisted that the conference should not discuss the annexation.[79] Five days later, on 22 December, Aehrenthal told Cartwright that he was not at all pleased with the Russian Note and that it was so phrased that it was difficult "to seize on any definite proposal made by Russia". His impression was that Russia did not want a conference. Austria-Hungary's attitude was by contrast perfectly clear. She wanted and hoped soon to achieve an agreement with Turkey and at the same time was not opposed to a conference. He was also prepared to negotiate in a very conciliatory manner with Servia and Montenegro on the subject of economic advantages for those two countries. Moreover, he was insisting that the Notes exchanged between Vienna and St. Petersburg, and the accompanying correspondence, should be placed before the British Government in order that it might see that the Austro-Hungarian Government was in fact sympathetic to the idea of a conference.[80]

Grey and Hardinge welcomed the prospect of a speedy agreement between Austria-Hungary and Turkey.[81] But when Mensdorff remarked that he hoped that after a settlement with Turkey, Great Britain would not support "the claims of Servia and Montenegro", Grey replied that one must not forget Russian Slavism.[82] Grey, in fact, highly valued Russia's friendship and to retain it was willing to meet Russian wishes in regard to compensation for Servia and Montenegro. The fierce personal dispute between Aehrenthal and Isvolsky in the course of which Aehrenthal threatened to publish the correspondence exchanged between them was deplored by British statesmen who sought to relieve Isvolsky of his anxiety that Great Britain might leave Russia in the lurch. Grey instructed the British Ambassador in St. Petersburg, Sir Arthur Nicolson, to tell Isvolsky that he had no intention of going back on his promise to Russia of diplomatic support in the question of compensation for Servia and Montenegro.[83]

The question of how best to achieve a compromise between Servian and Montenegrin demands and the concessions Austria-Hungary was prepared to make in order to meet them called for immediate consideration because a definite step forward towards an agreement between Austria-Hungary and Turkey had just been taken. On the afternoon of 11 January 1909 Mensdorff handed to Hardinge an *aide-mémoire* in which it was stated that the Austro-Hungarian Government had decided to offer the Turkish Government as compensation for its—admittedly purely formal—sovereign rights over Bosnia-Herzegovina the sum of two and a half million Turkish pounds (T£2,500,000) as purchase money for the Turkish State lands in Bosnia and Herzegovina on the sole—purely formal—condition that these lands should be legally certified to be in fact State property.[84] Aehrenthal hoped that Great Britain would fully appreciate the extent of the sacrifice Austria-Hungary had made to achieve a settlement and his message was, in fact, received by Grey and Hardinge with sincere pleasure as being likely to result in a friendly understanding with Turkey.[85] A provisional settlement of the conflict between Austria-Hungary and Turkey shone like a rainbow in the dark international sky. For it was at this very moment that the campaign of mutual recrimination in the Vienna and London Press reached its climax. On 6 January 1909 the *Neue Freie Presse* published an article filled with violent accusations against Great Britain who was roundly delcared to be the author of all the evils that had befallen Austria-Hungary. Great Britain's conduct—the article went on—was clearly intended to show that any nation that followed in Germany's footsteps would injure its own best interests. Neither Russia nor France wanted war. "Who can it then be who instils the poison into the Servian Cabinet?[86] Who constantly lays snares for us at Constantinople and incites Turkey to boycott our goods? If a referendum could be taken throughout the Dual Monarchy on this question the unanimous answer would be—England."[87] On the following day Cartwright reported to the Foreign Office that Aehrenthal was violently angry. He accused Great Britain of arming the Serbs and of supplying them with money to be used for anti-Austrian propaganda in the Balkans. Great Britain had obviously promised the Serbs something more than moral support. Cartwright, who was no friend of Germany, maintained that "all the trouble comes from Berlin", where everything possible was being done to prevent public opinion in Austria-Hungary from learning the truth about Great Britain's friendship for that country.[88]

In a conversation with Grey at this time when Mensdorff alluded to the suspicion prevalent in Vienna that the reason for Great Britain's unfriendly attitude towards Austria-Hungary was to be found in the friendship between Berlin and Vienna, Grey, as on former occasions, emphatically repudiated the notion, which he characterized as absurd and declared that he had "carefully abstained" from any attempt to make "mischief" between Austria-Hungary and Germany. He added that he certainly did not contemplate upsetting the existing balance of power in Europe. And King Edward wrote on the margin of Cartwright's dispatch reporting his conversation with Aehrenthal, in which Aehrenthal had so violently abused Great Britain: "Aehrenthal's language about England and his conduct towards us savours of 'The Bull in the China Shop' style." British statesmen also complained of the angry out-pourings of the Vienna Press. Aehrenthal replied that these attacks were merely the answer to attacks in the British Press, and that he could not foresee any improvement in the situation before British newspaper correspondents in Vienna such as the correspondent of *The Times* and of the *Morning Post* ceased to send their papers excitatory and untruthful reports.[89] There was, in fact, no cessation of the journalistic warfare. Hardinge drew Mensdorff's attention to an article in the *Wiener Mittag-blatt*, in which King Edward was attacked in gross terms and styled an *agent provocateur*. Mensdorff said that he profoundly regretted that such an article should have been published, even though it appeared in a newspaper of no importance, and at the same time drew Hardinge's attention to the frequent attacks on the Emperor Francis Joseph that were being made in the British Press.[90] Aehrenthal expressed his approval of Mensdorff's statement and in its support cited the *Illustrated London News* which had coupled Francis Joseph with Ferdinand of Bulgaria as the two monarchs "who tricked Europe". He added that a monthly review called *The Near East* had pub-lished an unprecedentedly violent attack on Francis Joseph.[91] Mensdorff brought these facts to the notice of Hardinge who expressed his disgust and indignation at the attacks on Francis Joseph, while at the same time he emphasized to Mensdorff that the chief British complaint was that the Vienna news-papers published false reports of intervention by the British Ambassador at Constantinople for the purpose of preventing the conclusion of an agreement between Austria-Hungary and Turkey, and also alleged the boycott of Austrian goods was organized by the Balkan Committee under the leadership of Noel Buxton.[92] Hardinge added that he had used his influence with the British Press, whose attitude towards Vienna had consequently become more friendly.[93] Mensdorff had already advised his Government to exert pressure upon the Vienna Press and after this had been done an end came to mutual recriminations.[94]

Aehrenthal continued to do all that he could to remove the obstacles that still stood in the way of a final settlement with Turkey, and since at the same time there were hopes of settling the Bulgaro-Turkish dispute with the assistance of Russia, the negotiations between London and Vienna now turned chiefly upon the problem of finding an answer to the Austro-Servian question. British statesmen in demanding that Servia and Montenegro should receive some compensation were doing so less out of sympathy for those two States than out of regard for the wishes of their Russian champion. Isvolsky at St. Petersburg and the Russian Ambassador in London, Count Benckendorff, strongly supported Servian and Montenegrin interests. But British statesmen regarded it as quite impossible to obtain the territorial compensation that Russia demanded for these two countries. Moreover, they were extremely doubtful of Aehrenthal's entertaining the notion of uniting the two into a single autonomous state under Turkish sovereignty.[95] None the less, they continued to assure Russia that they would leave no stone unturned to secure Servia and Montengro the largest possible compensation. They did their utmost to allay Isvolsky's fears that France would join Austria-Hungary, and Great Britain follow her example,[96] and also that Austria-Hungary, after sending an ultimatum to Servia, would attack her, thus involving Russia in the hostilities.[97]   They also simultaneously negotiated with the Austro-Hungarian Government over the question of what compensation that Government was prepared to grant to Servia and Montenegro. Aehrenthal brusquely refused to consider the question and instructed Mensdorff to tell Grey that for Austria-Hungary there had never been any Servian or Montnegrin question in connection with the annexation and that no such questions existed at the present time. When agreement had been reached between Vienna and the Sublime Porte, as well as between the Sublime Porte and Sofia, there would then only remain the Cretan Question and the modification of Article 29 of the Treaty of Berlin (which the Austro-Hungarian Government had already accepted in principle) for the present crisis to reach its end.[98] Aehrenthal complained once more of Servia's conduct and of her continued military preparations and provocations.[99] These threatened to exhaust the patience of Austria-Hungary and even that of the peace-loving Emperor.[100]

Grey was rendered anxious by Aehrenthal's veiled intimation of the possibility of forcible measures against Servia and sought for some way of obviating this danger. On 19 February 1909 he telegraphed to Cartwright:

"We are very seriously disturbed by report that Austria feels she may be compelled to take active measures against Servia in the near future and is already contemplating them. We doubt whether any assurances could induce Russia to regard such a situation with equanimity and the consequence of war between Austria and Servia might therefore be so far-reaching as to disturb the peace of Europe and involve other Powers . . . To secure peace it seems undesirable to delay any longer discussion among the Powers of what settlement can be arrived at with regard to Servian and Montenegrin interests. To initiate this discussion we would suggest that Austria should state confidentially to us what concessions she is prepared to make for we have always understood that she is prepared to make concessions about Article XXIX of the Treaty of Berlin and to offer some advantage in addition."[101]

But Grey found no way open before him. In a talk which Hardinge (who accompanied King Edward to Berlin) had with the Imperial Chancellor, Prince von Bülow, he asked Bülow whether it was believed in Berlin that Austria-Hungary would grant Servia a rectification of her frontiers and make economic concessions to her. Bülow unhesitatingly declared that there could be no rectification of frontiers, but, on the other hand, that there was a possibility that Servia would be given a more advantageous commercial treaty and better export facilities by means of a railway to the Adriatic. None the less, there must be agreement between the Powers prior to the meeting of a conference.[102] Grey supported this plan. He proposed that the British, French, Italian, and German Ambassadors at Vienna should make a joint *démarche* for the purpose of finding out from the Vienna Foreign Ministry whether or not Servia had taken any fresh step that had given the Austro-Hungarian Government cause for complaint, and also whether or not the Austro-Hungarian Government had reason for expecting any such action in the immediate future. If it were to prove to be the case that Servia had taken, or was about to take, such an action the Powers would act, as they had formerly acted, by endeavouring to remove any occasion for complaint by the Austro-Hungarian Government, since it was their common desire to obviate anything that could give Austria-Hungary cause to take punitive measures against Servia. The ambassadors should also endeavour to ascertain what compensation Austria-Hungary had in mind in order that the Powers might negotiate in Belgrade for a settlement.[103]

The French, German, and Italian Ambassadors in Vienna, however, on being informed of this plan immediately declared that any such action would be fruitless.[104] A few days later the German Government refused to participate in the proposed *démarche*, and took up its stand wholeheartedly beside its Austro-Hungarian ally by repeating all the charges that Aehrenthal had brought against Servia and by declaring that Servia's conduct was intolerable. The German Government urged that all the Powers, including Russia, should make strong representations at Belgrade on this subject.[105]

The British Minister at Belgrade meanwhile reported that his Austro-Hungarian colleague had stated that Austro-Hungarian policy would undergo a radical change unless Servia abandoned her military preparations and gave a guarantee that there would be an end to her intrigues and propaganda in Bosnia-Herzegovina. The Minister went on to say that he personally did not believe that any Servian Government would yield to this demand unless it was supported by all the Powers, including Russia.[106] British statesmen found themselves in a very difficult situation as a consequence of the German rejection of the proposed *démarche*, and they too thought that it would be fruitless to confront the Servian Government with a demand such as the British Minister in Belgrade had reported to them unless Russia supported it. On the other hand they found it necessary not only to abandon the idea of a *démarche*, but also to explain to the Austro-Hungarian Government that there had been no intention of exercising pressure upon Austria-Hungary and that the purpose of the *démarche* would have been to prepare the ground for fruitful negotiations in Belgrade.[107] In conversation with Mensdorff, who had said that it was impossible to talk of economic concessions to a country in which every influential person and organization pursued will-of-the-wisps like territorial compensation or even autonomy, Grey declared that he saw no other way of bringing pressure to bear upon Servia than to tell the Servian Government and leaders of public opinion that Servia would certainly receive economic advantages if she remained peaceful. But Servia must also be told that the Powers would not support her far-reaching ambitions. Of course—Grey added—it would be useless to attempt anything at Belgrade without Russia's co-operation, because in the last resort it was upon Russian support that the Serbs counted.[108] Aehrenthal was gratified to learn that France and Great Britain had decided to abstain from any *démarche* in Vienna and he told the French and British Ambassadors in Vienna—the former in exact terms, the latter in less precise terms, though their meaning did not greatly differ—that he hoped on the next day —26 February—that a Protocol would be signed in Constantinople. He added that with the signing of this Protocol his task, in so far as it lay in his power, would have been fulfilled and the formal changes brought about in treaty stipulations by the annexation of Bosnia-Herzegovina and the abrogation of the Convention of 1879 would have received their legal sanction. He did not doubt that the Powers would accept this announcement. Aehrenthal also told the Ambassadors that now, as before, he must refuse any mediation on the part of the Powers between Austria-Hungary and Servia. The situation was that the Serbs coolly refused to accept the annexation notwithstanding its recognition by Turkey, and continued to protest against it from some purely imaginary nationalistic legal standpoint and to demand certain territorial concessions for themselves. Servia's ambitions constituted a threat to the territorial integrity of the empire. It was obvious that such a state of affairs could no longer be tolerated—more especially since Servia continued her military preparations.[109]

Aehrenthal was not content with this statement. He sent Mensdorff a memorandum in which he justified his attitude towards Servia and instructed him in conversation with King Edward VII and Grey to afford them proof that the reports they were receiving did not do justice to his policy. Servia had forfeited all claim to the economic compensation held out to her by Aehrenthal by her conduct since the annexation.[110] Aehrenthal's statements, and that of the German Government, forced British statesmen to the conclusion that Russia would have to be made to realize that there could be no question of territorial compensation for Servia.[111] By the time, however, that a declaration to this effect had been made in St. Petersburg the Russian Government had already decided to inform the Serbs that there could be no question of their receiving the support of the Great Powers for their demand for territorial compensation. The Servian Government was advised to abandon its claim and to inform the Powers that it would submit to their decisions in all outstanding questions.[112] The Russian Government by advising the Servian Government to accept the arbitration of the Powers was seeking to place an obstacle in the way of the acceptance of Aehrenthal's proposal that Vienna should negotiate directly with Belgrade—a proposal that had also been put forward in a memorandum drawn up by French and British statesmen.[113] But while the Servian Government discussed the reply to be given to St. Petersburg, and negotiated with the Russian Government over its proposal, Aehrenthal took the initiative.

On 26 February 1909 a Protocol was signed by the Austro-Hungarian and Turkish Governments by which the Austro-Hungarian Government undertook to pay the Turkish Government two and a half million Turkish pounds as compensation for the estates owned by the Turkish State in Bosnia-Herzegovina and in return Turkey withdrew her protest against the annexation of the two provinces. On the following day, Aehrenthal informed Grey that Servia must accept the Protocol and afford guarantees "of a correct and peaceful policy", after which the Austro-Hungarian Government would enter into direct negotiations with Servia over economic questions.[114] The British Government, however, strongly disapproved of Aehrenthal's action and considered that, as Russia had shown herself so conciliatory, Austria-Hungary should follow her example. But when Grey spoke to Mensdorff in this sense, Mensdorff stated as his personal opinion that Austria-Hungary must insist upon obtaining guarantees direct from Servia that Servia would renounce her territorial and political pretensions, live on friendly terms with Austria-Hungary, recognize the annexation and not, after a few months, stir up fresh agitation on the Austro-Hungarian frontier. Only when these guarantees had been given and fulfilled would Austria-Hungary be prepared to embark on direct—and only on direct—negotiations with Servia over economic questions. Grey replied that he would profoundly regret any such procedure on Austria-Hungary's part. Aehrenthal himself—Grey went on—had stated in Article 7 of his draft agenda for a conference that the conference should discuss the "economic advantages to be obtained by Bosnia and Herzegovina" and if he now went back on this proposal he (Grey) would despair of European politics.[115] Grey also complained of Aehrenthal's conduct to the German Ambassador, who told him that his Government fully supported Aehrenthal's policy. Notwithstanding Grey's criticisms, Aehrenthal refused to alter his course and stressed the fact that economic issues between two States could only be decided by the two States themselves.[116] Nor did he alter his opinion even after Grey had told Mensdorff that the economic issues in question "belonged to the whole complex of Balkan questions" which the Powers had to decide.[117]

Moreover, Aehrenthal denied Russia's right to play the rôle of protector of Servia and by so doing to delay the solution of the Austro-Servian question.[118] He now took a further step. He informed the Servian Government that as a consequence of its present attitude towards Austria-Hungary he did not propose to ask the Austrian and Hungarian Parliaments to renew the commercial treaty concluded the previous year that expired on 31 March, and he added that the Austro-Hungarian Government hoped the Servian Government would follow the Powers' advice to change its policy in regard to Bosnia-Herzegovina and would also announce its deliberate intention to resume neighbourly relations with Austria-Hungary. In that case the Austro-Hungarian Government would be ready to open negotiations over the economic relations between the two countries "and the transit between the Monarchy and the kingdom of Servia".[119] Meanwhile, negotiations had been in progress between the Servian Government and the Great Powers over the form and content of the declaration to be given by Servia, and the Servian Government had resolved not to accept Aehrenthal's demand for direct negotiations between Belgrade and Vienna, but instead to address themselves to the signatory Powers of the Treaty of Berlin in a circular note. Great Britain supported Servia in this resolve and in repeated conversations with Mensdorff and the German Ambassador, Grey contended that Article 7 of Aehrenthal's draft agenda conceded the right of the signatory Powers to a voice in the settlement of the question of Servia's compensation.[120] Grey also indicated that he thought it possible that Servia felt herself too weak to engage in direct negotiation with her powerful neighbour. He was, therefore, very satisfied with the declaration made in London by the new Servian Government that it was determined to pursue the vital interest of Servia along peaceful paths and to abstain from any further military measures on the Austro-Servian frontier.[121] But he was less satisfied with the draft of the circular note which Servia proposed to send to the signatory Powers and joined with Isvolsky (who was equally displeased with the draft) in demanding that the Servian Government should prepare a new draft. The Servian Government was advised to draw up its circular note to the signatory Powers in the sense of the agreement reached by the Powers that Servia should declare that she was ready to live on friendly terms with Austria-Hungary, would not demand any territorial, political or economic compensation, and would leave her fate in the hands of the Powers. At this juncture Russia decided to advise the Servian Government to express its willingness to negotiate direct with the Austro-Hungarian Government over economic questions and a new commercial treaty. There can be no doubt that the Russian Government was induced to make this concession by influential Russian statesmen who were of the opinion that Russia was neither financially nor militarily in a condition to wage the war that they feared would be the outcome of continued opposition to Aehrenthal's demands.[122] This opinion was further strengthened by the fact that the German Government's declaration made it clear that Germany would certainly be found at her ally's side in event of war,[123] while Great Britain was not prepared to wage war solely to satisfy Servian ambitions. Grey had repeatedly told the Russian Government that now, as formerly, he was prepared to give diplomatic support to Russian demands, but that he wished to avoid war at all costs.

The Declaration that was handed on 10 March 1909 by the Servian Government to the signatory Powers of the Treaty of Berlin read as follows:[124]

"Considering that from a legal point of view her situation in regard to Austria-Hungary has remained normal since the annexation of Bosnia-Herzegovina, Serbia has no intention whatever of provoking a war against the neighbouring monarchy, and in no sense desires to modify the legal relations with that Power, while continuing to fulfil on a basis of reciprocity her obligations of good neighbourliness and to maintain with Austria-Hungary, as in the past, relations involving interests of a material order. Though having always put forward the view that the question of Bosnia-Herzegovina is a European question and that it appertains to the Powers signatory of the Treaty of Berlin to come to a decision with reference to the annexation and the new text of Article XXV of the Treaty of Berlin, Serbia, trusting in the wisdom and sense of justice of the Powers, leaves her cause in their hands without reservation as to the competent tribunal and in consequence without claiming from Austria-Hungary any compensation whether territorial, political, or economic."[125]

The Declaration was certainly drafted with great skill and ingenuity. At first sight it would seem to fulfil almost completely the wishes that had been expressed by the Powers to the Servian Government. When, however, it is closely examined it will be seen that it fell far short of fulfilling Aehrenthal's demands. The Servian Government paid no heed to Isvolsky's advice "to examine with the Cabinet in Vienna those questions which relate to the economic relations between the two countries". It was also asking much of the recipient of the Declaration to ask him to recognize as a fact that the relations between Austria-Hungary and Servia had been normal since the annexation. But what was most wounding to Aehrenthal was Servia's refusal to negotiate direct with Vienna and her placing of the decision in the hands of the Powers as the competent tribunal. Aehrenthal's demand that Servia should reduce her military strength was passed over in silence. None the less, Aehrenthal showed no signs of irritation on receiving the circular note and even described it as "a step in the right direction". But he immediately took exception to that portion of the note which declared that Servia entrusted her cause to the Powers, without clearly stating what was implied by these words, because he feared that it might give rise to grave misunderstandings. He also said that he would not reply to the note, which was of little interest to him, and added that what would be important would be the Servian reply to the Austro-Hungarian note of 6 March.[126]

In London Mensdorff spoke even more plainly to Grey about the anxieties occasioned in Vienna by the Servian Declaration, and said that public opinion protested against the placing of the Servian cause in the hands of the Powers as the "competent tribunal". Aehrenthal considered that the annexation issue had been settled once and for all by the Protocol of 26 February, and that the material aspect of the matter was no longer open to discussion, while the formal legal aspect was a question for the Powers and not for Servia. The Servian Declaration opened the door to a discussion of the annexation by the conference and so made it possible for Servia to bring forward her demands. Aehrenthal also objected to the wording of the circular note where it stated that Servia wished to continue ("continuant à remplir") her good neighbourly relations with the Danubian Monarchy. In view of what Servia's conduct had been, and still was, it was hardly a question of continuing friendly relations, but rather of a change in Servia's attitude. Grey replied to Mensdorff's criticisms by attempting to justify the Servian Declaration. Since any alteration in the Treaty of Berlin was a subject for consideration by the signatory Powers, Servia had the right to leave the decision to them. Servia could not be expected to recognize the annexation merely because of the conclusion of the agreement between Austria-Hungary and Turkey and before it had been recognized by the signatory Powers. He could not understand what was meant by distinguishing between the material and the formal legal aspects. Austria-Hungary could not maintain that she could alter the Treaty of Berlin without the assent of the signatory Powers. The signatory Powers must surely have the right to discuss the conditions for their assent to an alteration. Grey again emphasized, as he had done so often before, that preliminary agreement as to the agenda of the conference was indispensable before it could meet.[127]

The Servian Government replied on 15 March to the Austro-Hungarian note of 6 March, and referred to its circular note of 10 March, in which it had set out its point of view in the annexation question. Once more it emphasized its intention on the basis of reciprocity of continuing good neighbourly relations with the Danubian Monarchy and of maintaining the economic ties that bound the two States to their mutual interest and advantage. For this reason the Servian Government thought that the existing Commercial Treaty between Austria-Hungary and Servia might be laid before the Parliaments in Vienna and Budapest for renewal. If this were done, it would be seen whether or not the Parliaments wanted to abrogate or to prolong the treaty and, in event of no decision having been reached by the end of March when the Treaty expired, the Servian Government proposed that it should be provisionally prolonged until the end of the year.[128] Aehrenthal found this new Servian note wholly unsatisfactory and his opinion was shared by the French, German, Italian and British Ministers in Belgrade.[129] The British Minister advised his Government that the time had come for very plain speaking in Belgrade and the Foreign Office agreed with him. Indeed, Tyrrell described the note as silly, and said he could only explain its extraordinary phraseology by the fact that King Peter wanted to retain his throne and acted on the assumption that the Powers would exert such pressure in Belgrade that he

(Peter) would be able to say that he was forced to give way.[130] Parker called the note "an insolent reply". Maxwell made the comment: "I am afraid Servia has put herself in the wrong by the tone of this reply." Mallet observed: "This reply does not meet the Austrian requirements in any particular and is impertinent in substance." And Grey expressed his judgement in the words: "Nothing to be done but to wait for the effect of this upon Austria."[131]

Grey, indeed, found Servia's behaviour all the more embarrassing because he was engaged with Mensdorff at the time in talking over the agenda for a conference and the manner in which the various items on it should be discussed. These conversations arose out of the note addressed by the Foreign Office to Mensdorff in which the British Government with much satisfaction acknowledged the receipt of the Protocol signed by the Turkish and Austro-Hungarian Governments and stated that in as much as the Protocol involved an alteration in the Treaty of Berlin it would require to be brought to the notice of the signatory Powers. The note added that the British Government was prepared to enter into a discussion over the summoning of a conference that should deal with this and other questions.[132] In reply to Mensdorff, who had asked what questions the British Government had in mind for discussion at the conference, Grey stated the following:[133]

1. The annexation of Bosnia-Herzegovina as arising out of the Protocol of February 26.
2. The independence of Bulgaria about which an agreement was about to be concluded between the Bulgarian and Turkish Governments.
3. Economic compensation for Servia. Grey said he presumed that Servia would engage in direct negotiations with Austria-Hungary for the renewal of the commercial treaty.
4. Alteration of Article XXIX of the Treaty of Berlin regarding Montenegro.

Grey was nevertheless convinced that the Austro-Hungarian Government would prevent the summoning of a conference unless the Austro-Servian dispute was first cleared up, and consequently he decided to draft a note for Servia to send to Austria-Hungary and to lay the draft before Aehrenthal for his acceptance or refusal. The text of the draft read as follows:[134]

"La Serbie pourrait fournir des assurances, qu'elle ne ferait aucune démarche qui créerait des difficultés, ou directement ou indirectement, sur territoire autrichien: qu'elle observait toutes les obligations d'amitié et de bon voisinage, tout en conservant son indépendance et son intégrité: qu'elle serait contente de profiter de l'offre faite par l'Autriche d'entrer en négociations directes pour la conclusion d'un traité de commerce et, si l'on le trouvait désirable, elle pourrait ajouter qu'il n'était pas de son ressort d'introduire des changements dans le Traité de Berlin, mais qu'elle serait prête à accepter ce qui aurait été dûment reconnu par les Puissances Signataires de ce Traité."

It is difficult to understand how Grey could have hoped that Aehrenthal would accept this draft when it is recalled how frequently and determinedly Aehrenthal had emphasized that he did not desire mediation by the Powers and that he demanded direct negotiation between Vienna and Belgrade. None the less, Grey thought he should make the attempt. He expressed the hope that, once his draft had been approved by Aehrenthal, Servia would send the Austro-Hungarian Government a note in identical terms and would simultaneously undertake to reduce the strength of the Servian army to the footing on which it stood prior to the Austro-Servian conflict in return for a promise from Austria-Hungary that she would not attack Servia.[135] But when, on 17 March, Cartwright saw Aehrenthal, he was told that Grey's draft was unacceptable for the sole reason that nothing was said in it about Servian disarmament.[136] Cartwright returned the next day bearing a proposal from the British Government that Aehrenthal should himself draft a declaration for Servia to make. The British Government would then do its utmost to have his draft accepted in Belgrade. All that Great Britain asked was Aehrenthal's assurance that for so long as she mediated detween Belgrade and Vienna the Austro-Hungarian Government would not attack Servia. Aehrenthal at once said that he was prepared to give such an assurance because Austria-Hungary and never threatened the independence or integrity of Servia and did not now intend to do her any injury. Nevertheless, it was impossible to stop indispensable defensive military preparations before Servia had made a declaration that removed the necessity for them.[137] But he would be glad to act on Grey's suggestion that he (Aehrenthal) should draft a declaration for Servia to make. And on 19 March the draft was ready. It read as follows:[138]

"La Serbie reconnait qu'elle n'a pas été atteinte dans ses droits par le fait-accompli créé en Bosnie-Herzégovine. Elle déclare, qu'ayant appris l'arrangement survenu à Constantinople entre l'Autriche-Hongrie et l'Empire Ottoman, par lequel le nouvel état de choses se trouve matériellement réglé, elle abandonne l'attitude de protestation et d'opposition qu'elle a observée à l'égard de l'annexion depuis l'automne dernier, et elle s'engage en outre à changer le cours de sa politique actuelle envers l'Autriche-Hongrie pour vivre désormais avec cette dernière sur le pied d'un bon voisinage.

"Conformément à ses déclarations pacifiques, la Serbie ramenera son armée à l'état du printemps de 1908, en ce qui concerne son organisation, sa dislocation et son effectif. Elle désarmera et licenciera ses volontaires et ses bandes, et elle empêchera la formation de nouvelles unités irrégulières aux frontières de l'Autriche-Hongrie et de la Turquie.

"L'Autriche-Hongrie, loin de prétendre imposer des entraves au développement normal de l'armée serbe, se borne à demander la révocation des mesures exceptionnelles qui contiennent une menace à son adresse."

It was now Grey's turn to express dissatisfaction. He thought that it was asking too much of Servia to demand that she should state that she was not injuriously affected by the annexation of Bosnia-Herzegovina and that she should make a declaration that was tantamount to a sort of confession of misconduct. Furthermore, he did not see how the signatory Powers of the Treaty of Berlin could be asked to inform Servia of their attitude towards the annexation before they themselves had declared what was their attitude. He, therefore, once more urged Aehrenthal to accept his draft which had been approved by other Powers.[139] In answer to Cartwright's request on 21 March that he would act on Grey's suggestion, Aehrenthal said that under no circumstances could he accept Grey's draft and that his own draft contained the minimum that Austria-Hungary must demand. Cartwright then handed to Aehrenthal a new draft in which the final words of the first paragraph read: "qu'elle (Serbie) se conformera par conséquent à telle décision que les Puissances prendront par rapport à l'Art. XXV du traité de Berlin."[140] In order to overcome Aehrenthal's opposition, Cartwright asked him whether or not he would accept this version on condition that the signatory Powers individually, and in writing, gave an assurance prior to the conference that at the conference they would agree to the Protocol of 21 February.[141] In a private letter to Grey on

1 April Cartwright wrote that he had given Aehrenthal to understand that an essential preliminary condition for this action on the part of the signatory Powers at the conference must be the termination of the Servian crisis. Aehrenthal told Cartwright that he could not give him an immediate answer. However, he decided after brief reflection to accept the suggested draft as affording a possible way out of a difficulty. On the following day, therefore, he sent Cartwright two drafts which he hoped would meet with the British Government's approval and he also told him that he had informed the Emperor Francis Joseph of the action it was proposed to take. The first was the proposed text of a declaration abrogating Article XXV of the Treaty of Berlin that was to be signed by the signatory Powers at the forthcoming conference. It read:

"L'Autriche-Hongrie a communiqué aux Cabinets le Protocole signé à Constantinople le 26 Février dr. et dans lequel la Turquie reconnait le nouvel état de choses créé en Bosnie-Herzégovine par la Proclamation de Sa Majesté Impériale et Royale Apostolique en date du 5 Octobre 1908. Les Puissances signataires du Traité de Berlin prennant, conformément au principe énoncé à la Conférence de Londres de 1871, acte de cette communication et déclarent aboli l'Article XXV du Traité de Berlin."

The second was still another draft of the declaration to be made by Servia and the changes now made by Aehrenthal only affected the first paragraph of the former draft, while the following two paragraphs remained unaltered because Aehrenthal found nothing to object to in Grey's text. The revised paragraph I now read:

"La Serbie reconnait qu'elle n'a pas été atteinte dans ses droits par le fait accompli créé en Bosnie-Herzégovine et qu'elle se conformera par conséquent à telle décision que les Puissances prendront par rapport à l'article XXV du traité de Berlin. Se rendant aux conseils des Grandes Puissances la Serbie s'engage dès à présent à abandonner l'attitude de protestation et d'opposition qu'elle a observée à l'égard de l'annexion depuis l'automne dernier, et elle s'engage en outre à changer le cours de sa politique actuelle envers l'Autriche-Hongrie pour vivre désormais avec cette dernière sur le pied d'un bon voisinage."[142]

In a private letter to Cartwright accompanying the two drafts Aehrenthal stressed the fact that he must make his acceptance of the draft Servian declaration conditional upon the making by the signatory Powers, individually and in writing, of a declaration corresponding to the enclosed draft. Meanwhile, Grey (who was not in agreement with Aehrenthal's first draft) had decided to make still another proposal. He said to Mensdorff that the phrasing of Aehrenthal's first draft amounted to nothing less than a humiliating apology by Servia for her former conduct, while the demand that Servia should recognize the Protocol of 26 February before the signatory Powers had accorded it recognition implied an indirect humiliation for these Powers and especially for Russia. This —Grey added—he wished to avoid and yet at the same time to concede everything that Aehrenthal wished for. If his draft was accepted—Grey went on—the Servian crisis would be over in a few days and the main questions could be settled, whichever way the Powers chose, either in a conference or by an exchange of notes. If, on the other hand, Aehrenthal refused to accept his draft, then the responsibility would fall upon Aehrenthal in event of an outbreak of war.[143] Grey was, in fact, repeating the warning that Asquith had given to Mensdorff when he dined with him the previous evening that were war to break out European public opinion would be hostile to Austria-Hungary, as it had been hostile to England during the Boer War, because the public in their ignorance saw only a war between a Great Power and a small Power and their sympathies were always on the side of the small Power.[144] Hardinge expressed the view that no Power would question the annexation. None the less he thought that the preliminary assurance demanded of the signatory Powers could not be secured unless Austria-Hungary was prepared to give assurances in advance on the subject of Article XXIX of the Treaty of Berlin regarding Montenegro.[145] Grey shared Hardinge's opinion and added that Austria-Hungary must simultaneously recognize the independence of Bulgaria.[146] Subsequently, Grey declared that the Powers could not bind themselves by a declaration of this nature so long as peace was not assured.[147] The text of the new British draft read:[148]

"La Serbie ne possédant pas de droits légaux sur les provinces annexées de Bosnie et de l'Herzégovine, le Gouvernement Serbe, sur l'invitation des Puissances, déclare reconnaître et accepter formellement toute modification apportée au Traité de Berlin soit par un fait accompli, soit par suite d'un accord matériel intervenu entre l'Autriche-Hongrie et la Turquie, soit d'une autre façon, qui pourra obtenir l'assentiment des Puissances Signataires du dit Traité.

"Le Gouvernement Serbe donne des assurances formelles au Gouvernement Austro-Hongrois qu'il ne prendra pas à son égard de mesures malveillantes lesquelles, soit directement suit indirectement, puissent créer des difficultés ou de désordres en Austriche-Hongrie et en Bosnie-Herzégovine, et que, tout en sauvegardant l'indépendance et l'intégrité du Royaume Serbe, il observera dès à présent et désormais toutes les obligations d'amitié et de bon voisinage qui devraient gouverner les relations existant entre deux Etats amis et limitrophes.

"Se fiant aux assurances formelles du Gouvernement Austro-Hongrois de ne former aucun projet d'agression contre la Serbie et de ne prétendre ni porter atteinte à l'indépendance, à l'intégrité et à la libre évolution de celle-ci ni imposer d'entraves au développement régulier de l'armé serbe, le Gouvernement Serbe, donnant suite àla demande des Puissances, s'engage à ramener dès à présent l'armée serbe à son état normal en temps de paix—c'est à dire, d'il y a un an, —et à révoquer les mesures exceptionnelles qu'il a prises dernièrement. Le Gouvernement Serbe, en outre, désarmera les bandes irrégulières et empêchera la formation de nouvelles unités semblables sur les frontières de l'Autriche-Hongrie et de la Turquie.

"Le Gouvernement Serbe, ayant la certitude que ces asurances amicales rencontretent un espirt de réciprocité auprès du Gouvernement Austro-Hongrois s'empresse de profiter de l'offre qui lui a été faite par ce dernier d'entamer des négociations directes en vue de la conclusion d'un traité de commerce et il est prêt à entrer dès à présent en pourparlers à cet effet."

Aehrenthal, as soon as he had read the new draft, declared "that it was inadmissible". He said that the words used in the second paragraph about Servia's giving Austria-Hungary "formal assurances . . . that it will not take unfriendly measures with respect to the latter" did not satisfy Austria-Hungary's demands, and that he must insist that Servia clearly and publicly declared that she would cease to pursue the inimical policy that she had pursued since 1908 in regard to Austria-Hungary. Moreover, Grey's text left it open to the Serbs to maintain that they had armed solely for defensive reasons. The wording of the third paragraph opened the way to the assumption that in future the Powers would exercise a sort of protectorate over Servia. Aehrenthal added that that was something that he could not permit. He also took exception to the words Austria-Hungary "claims no right to infringe the

independence, integrity and free development" of Servia
because they could be interpreted to mean that Servia reserved
rights to Bosnia for the future.[149] And Aehrenthal went still
further in his criticism of this inacceptable draft. He told
Cartwright that it was so naive in places that it seemed to him
that it had been composed in the Servian Foreign Ministry in
Belgrade rather than in the Foreign Office.[150] He therefore
requested Grey again to examine his (Aehrenthal's) draft
before rejecting it. If the Powers were unsuccessful in their
mediation he would have to try to attain his end by other ways.
But Grey stood his ground. The gulf between the standpoints
of the two men was so broad that it seemed unbridgeable. An
agreement seemed impossible. At this criticial juncture an
event suddenly occurred that quickly changed the attitude of
Grey and his advisers in the Foreign Office. Throughout the
crisis the German Government had frequently expressed its
determination to do all that it could to preserve peace. None
the less it had, at the same time, emphatically declared that it
could never be disloyal to its Austro-Hungarian ally and had
frankly displayed its sympathy with Austro-Hungarian policy.
But now, in the middle of March, the German Government
suddenly decided to use its influence at St. Petersburg for the
purpose of settling the Austro-Servian dispute. After negotiations had been in progress between Berlin and St. Petersburg
for several days, the German Ambassador at St. Petersburg was
instructed, on 21 March, to inform Isvolsky that the German
Government was prepared to propose to the Austro-Hungarian
Government that Austria-Hungary should invite the signatory
Powers on the basis of the Austro-Turkish agreement that had
already been communicated to them to agree to the abrogation of Article XXV of the Treaty of Berlin. It was, nevertheless, necessary before making this proposal in Vienna to be
certain that Russia would accept such an invitation from
Vienna and would give her formal consent to the abrogation
of Article XXV without reservations. The German Government, therefore, asked for a definite answer, "Yes' or "No".
Isvolsky bowed before the storm. He gave the German Government an affirmative answer and informed both Vienna and
London of his decision.[151] There was jubilation in Vienna and
profound resentment and dejection in London.[152] Isvolsky's
acceptance of the German proposal and his statement that he
preferred Aehrenthal's to Grey's draft left Grey no choice but

to give up his own draft and accept Aehrenthal's as the basis for the Servian declaration. But Grey was none the less determined that the abrogation of Article XXV of the Treaty of Berlin by the signatory Powers should not take place before the settlement of the Austro-Servian dispute, and in accepting Aehrenthal's draft he demanded that some minor alterations should be made in the text that had been suggested to him by the Russian Ambassador in London at the Russian Government's request.[153] Accordingly, he instructed Cartwright to demand the following alterations in the text of Aehrenthal's draft: Paragraph I. The words "à abandonner l'attitude de protestation et d'opposition qu'elle a observée à l'égard de l'annexion depuis l'automne dernier" should be replaced by the words "à s'abstenir d'une attitude de protestation et d'opposition dans la question de la Bosnie-Herzégovine." Paragraph II. Grey had not previously criticized the wording of this paragraph. Now he wished the words "Conformément à ses déclarations pacifiques" to be replaced by the words "Se fiant aux assurances pacifiques". And in the final sentence of this paragraph he demanded the substitution of the words "sur son territoire" for the words "aux frontières de l'Autriche-Hongrie et de la Turquie."[154] Paragraph III. Sir Edward Grey suggested that this paragraph of Aehrenthal's draft of 19 March should be omitted from the declaration to be made by the Servian Government and should form the subject-matter of a declaration to be made by the Austro-Hungarian Government.[155] In its altered form the Servian declaration would now read:[156]

"La Serbie reconnait qu'elle n'a pas été atteinte dans ces droits par le fait accompli créé en Bosnie-Herzégovine et qu'elle se conformera par conséquent à telle décision que les Puissances prendront par rapport à l'article XXV du traité de Berlin. Se rendant aux conseils des Grandes Puissances la Serbie s'engage dès à présent à s'abstenir d'une attitude de protestation et d'opposition dans la question de la Bosnie-Herzégovine et s'engage en outre à diriger le cours de sa politique envers l'Autriche-Hongrie de manière à vivre désormais avec cette dernière sur le pied de bon voisinage.

"Se fiant aux assurances pacifiques du Gouvernement Austro-Hongrois, la Serbie ramènera son armée à l'état du printemps de 1908, en ce qui concerne son organisation, sa dislocation et son effectif. Elle désarmera et licenciera ses volontaires et ses bandes, et elle empêchera la formatoin de nouvelles unités irrégulières sur son territoire."

Meanwhile, Aehrenthal had been officially informed that Isvolsky had declared his willingness to give his formal and unreserved assent to the abrogation of Article XXV of the Treaty of Berlin on condition that the other Governments gave their assent and the Austro-Hungarian Government addressed itself to them for this purpose. He had also learnt that Isvolsky would approve any form of declaration for Servia to make that had been agreed upon by Grey and Aehrenthal.[157] Moreover, the German Government was pressing him to continue negotiations with Grey and to agree to the summoning of a conference that should give formal approval to the decisions that had already been taken. It was this knowledge that determined Aehrenthal's attitude on 25 March, when Cartwright handed Grey's new draft to him. He was equally resolved to secure acceptance for his own draft and to continue negotiations with Grey. He refused to accept most of the changes suggested by Grey and said he must insist upon a Servian declaration that made it clear beyond any question that Servia's attitude towards Austria-Hungary since the annexation had not been correct. The only alterations he was prepared to accept were the substitution in Paragraph II of the words "Se fiant aux assurances pacifiques" for "Conformément à ses déclarations pacifiques" and in the concluding sentence of the words "sur son territoire" for "aux frontières de l'Autriche-Hongrie et de la Turquie". Aehrenthal told Cartwright that he had accepted the first of these two alterations in the text because the words admirably expressed the forbearance which Austria-Hungary had hitherto shown Servia, and also revealed a real appreciation of the pacific intentions that would continue to inspire Austro-Hungarian policy towards Servia if Servia once again adopted a correct attitude in her relations with Austria-Hungary. The Servian declaration —Aehrenthal emphasized—must be made in a note addressed directly to Austria-Hungary and not in the form of a circular note addressed to the signatory Powers.[158] Aehrenthal also instructed Mensdorff to inform the British Government that he (Aehrenthal) had impressed upon Cartwright that the statement made by him that Austria-Hungary did not wish to place any obstacle in the way of the normal development of the Servian army—a statement that was incorporated at Cartwright's suggestion in the first draft of the declaration to be made by Servia—must not be communicated to the Servian

Government, since it was only intended for the British Government's information. Mensdorff was also instructed to tell Grey that Aehrenthal was prepared to make this statement in a more formal manner.[159] Aehrenthal's revised draft embodying Grey's suggested alterations was described by its author as his last word on the subject.[160] Paragraph I was exactly similar to Paragraph I of Aehrenthal's first draft of 19 March.[161] But Paragraph II now read:

> "Conformément à ces déclarations et confiante dans les intentions pacifiques de l'Autriche-Hongrie la Serbie ramenera son armée à l'état du printemps de 1908, en ce qui concerne son organisation, sa dislocation et son effectif. Elle désarmera et licenciera ses volontaires et ses bandes, et elle empêchera la formation de nouvelles unités irrégulières sur son territoire."

Aehrenthal requested a speedy and affirmative reply for which he was prepared to wait until Sunday 28 March when —if the reply was unsatisfactory—he would regard the Powers' intervention as having failed and on the following day— 29 March—would dispatch Austria-Hungary's reply to the last Servian note. Before Aehrenthal's draft reached him, however, Grey had been asked by the German Government whether or not he was prepared to give a similar unconditional assent as Russia to the abrogation of Article XXV of the Treaty of Berlin in event of Austria-Hungary demanding it. Grey answered in the negative. The British Government—he explained—could not give such an assurance before the Servian Question had been settled in a manner satisfactory to all parties. Moreover, the other questions, and especially that concerning Paragraph 29 regarding Montenegro, would first have to find their solution. After he had received Grey's answer the German Ambassador said that this was a very grave decision that might lead to war. Grey replied that the British Government would never give its assurance under such pressure, since that would make it possible for Austria-Hungary, Servia, and Montenegro to do as they liked and would therefore not afford any guarantee of peace.[163] Grey's words aroused fierce resentment in Vienna. Aehrenthal became convinced —Cartwright believed under German influence—that Grey was seeking in this way to postpone the abrogation of Article XXV of the Treaty of Berlin and to make fresh difficulties for

Austria-Hungary in her attempt to settle the Bosnian crisis.[164] As soon as he learnt of Grey's decision, Aehrenthal summoned Cartwright and told him that it was impossible for him (Aehrenthal) to abide by the text of his latest draft in which he only demanded of Servia that she should accept the decision of the Powers on the subject of Article XXV of the Treaty of Berlin without receiving any prior assurance as to what this decision would be. Aehrenthal went on to say that he must now demand that the British Government gave an assurance similar to that given by Isvolsky to the German Ambassador at St. Petersburg, Count Pourtalès, namely, that Great Britain would formally and unconditionally agree to the abrogation of Article XXV of the Treaty of Berlin if Austria-Hungary should demand its abrogation. Aehrenthal added that he wished this assurance to be given either to himself or to the German Imperial Chancellor, Prince von Bülow. But when Cartwright explained that for Grey to make such a statement to Bülow would be tantamount to the British Government's yielding to German pressure, and that that was something which he wished to avoid, Aehrenthal consented to leave out Bülow's name. Aehrenthal also told Cartwright that he expected to receive Grey's answer by Sunday 28 March or at the latest by Monday 29 March, and that if he was not by that time in possession, at any rate, of a verbal assurance from the British Government—a course that Cartwright advised—regarding their agreement to the abrogation of Article XXV of the Treaty of Berlin, he would be forced to consider the negotiations with the British Government as broken off. He concluded by saying that he was compelled to fix this time limit because it was necessary for him in the interest of Austro-Hungarian tariff policy to make a communication to the Servian Government on 29 or 30 March.[165]

But Grey had already beaten a retreat before Cartwright's dispatch reporting this conversation with Aehrenthal reached him. He had decided to accept Aehrenthal's second draft[166] and on the day following his decision—26 March—he communicated it to the British Ambassadors at St. Petersburg, Paris, and Rome, with the justification that "it is hardly worth while to risk the cause of general peace by splitting hairs upon the interpretation to be placed upon certain words which in any case cannot make the Note palatable to the Serbian Government, although no doubt they will accept it under the collective pressure of the Powers whatever its ultimate form may be". He added that he would gladly have secured a more satisfactory text and that he only accepted the text which Cartwright had drawn up with Aehrenthal because he deemed it more politic to "cut the ground from under the feet of those who wish to force an ultimatum to be followed by an attack on Serbia".[167] The concluding words reveal that, despite Aehrenthal's frequent protestations that he wanted to avoid war if at all possible, Grey still believed that the Austro-Hungarian Government was seriously contemplating military intervention.[168] When, on 27 March, Grey was handed Aehrenthal's latest draft, he accepted it on the condition that Austria-Hungary made a suitable reply to Servia on receiving her declaration and that the Powers at whose insistence Servia was making the declaration would not be exposed to a rebuff.[169] Some hours after Grey's acceptance had been dispatched to Cartwright, a telegram reached the Foreign Office from Cartwright that contained Aehrenthal's demand that Great Britain should now, at any rate verbally (which was Cartwright's suggestion), give her unconditional assent under the conditions already agreed upon to the abrogation of Article XXV of the Treaty of Berlin. That same evening Grey telegraphed his agreement and his readiness to give by way of Cartwright the required assurance. On 28 March Cartwright handed Aehrenthal an *aide-mémoire* containing Grey's assurance as follows:[170]

"Après que la Serbie aura adressé à l'Autriche-Hongrie la note dans les termes rédigés entre le Baron d'Aehrenthal et l'Ambassadeur d'Angleterre et que l'Autriche-Hongrie l'aura acceptée comme satisfaisante, le Gouvernement de Sa Majesté sera prêt à donner son assentiment sans réserves à l'abrogation de l'article XXV du traité de Berlin, si le Baron d'Aehrenthal en fait la demande directe. Si par hasard la Serbie refuserait d'adresser à l'Autriche-Hongrie la note que le Gouvernement de Sa Majesté, de concert avec les autres Puissances, va recommander à la Serbie, le Gouvernement de Sa Majesté serait également prêt à donner son assentiment à l'abrogation de l'article XXV, si toutes les autres Puissances Signataires, comme il a toute raison de croire, sont prêtes à en faire de même. A condition que la réponse serbe en les termes convenus sera favorablement acceptée comme satisfaisante, et à condition que le Baron d'Aehrenthal n'adressera sa demande pour l'abrogation de l'article XXV qu'après que la médiation des Puissances à Belgrade aura été efficace ou sera restée sans résultat, l'Ambassadeur d'Angleterre est autorisé à donner

à Son Excellence les assurances verbales qu'Elle lui a demandées. Il
est bien entendu que tout ce qui précède dépend de l'assurance verbale
que le Baron d'Aehrenthal a donnée récemmant à l'Ambassadeur
d'Angleterre au sujet des changements que le Gouvernement austro-
hongrois sera prêt à admettre dans l'article XXIX."

Subsequently Aehrenthal declared that it was Cartwright
who had requested that this form should be chosen for the
declaration and that he (Aehrenthal) had given his assent as
a mark of conciliation. Aehrenthal gratefully accepted Grey's
two declarations and renewed his own promises that Austria-
Hungary would not attack Servia if Servia disarmed, and that
he would not approach the Powers on the subject of the
abrogation of Article XXV of the Treaty of Berlin before the
mediation of the Powers in Belgrade had met with either
success or failure.[171] Aehrenthal said that an agreement would
very shortly be concluded with Italy on the subject of the
alteration of Article XXIX and that he had given the Italian
Foreign Minister, Signor Tittoni, the necessary assurances. A
preliminary condition for the settlement of this question was
that Montenegro should resume correct good-neighbourly
relations with Austria-Hungary.[172] Full agreement was thus
reached between Vienna and London on the steps to be taken
in Belgrade. On handing his *aide-mémoire* to Aehrenthal,
Cartwright strongly emphasized that the Powers who were
mediating in Belgrade would not permit any discussion of the
text that had been agreed upon for the Servian declaration
and that the Servian Government would be asked simply to
accept or reject the text presented to them. If Servia refused,
she would be left to her fate.[173] As a matter of fact, Servia
accepted the Note presented to her on 30 March 1909 by the
Powers and on the following day it was handed to Aehrenthal
in Vienna.[174] Aehrenthal said that he took cognizance of the
Servian declaration with satisfaction and regarded the Servian
crisis as at an end with friendly relations once more restored
between the two countries.[175]

On the very next day Aehrenthal asked the British Government to take measures to ensure the earliest possible abrogation
of Article XXV of the Treaty of Berlin, since it was already
understood by the Powers that the abrogation would be
effected in an exchange of notes and that there was no longer
any question of summoning a conference.[176] Grey replied that
he must first get into contact with the other Powers[177] and also

await the final arrangements for the alteration of Article XXIX of the Treaty of Berlin regarding Montenegro before he could carry out in the name of the British Government the abrogation of Article XXV by means of an exchange of notes. Although Aehrenthal was impatient at this delay,[178] he was forced to wait until the Italian Ambassador in London was able to inform Grey that the Montenegrin Question had been completely settled. Only then did Grey tell Mensdorff that he was ready to abrogate Article XXV and a few days later Cartwright was instructed to hand Aehrenthal a Note to this effect. On 17 April Cartwright handed the Note to Aehrenthal.[179] His action brought the negotiations between Vienna and London over the Bosnian Question to a close.

In a dispatch on 29 March Cartwright, knowing that there was no longer any danger of the failure of British mediation, surveyed his diplomatic activity in Vienna since the outset of his mission, and gave his opinion of the parts played by the leading Austro-Hungarian statesmen. The most outstanding contribution towards the successful conclusion of a negotiation that had seemed likely to end in failure had been made by the old Emperor who, notwithstanding the pressure brought to bear on him by his military advisers, firmly clung to his belief in the possibility of a peaceful, and also honourable, solution of the Servian Question and who brought his whole influence to bear to achieve this end. There can be no doubt that Cartwright was right. The old Emperor wanted to maintain peace if it were at all possible, and did not share the views of the war-party which, under the leadership of the Chief of the General Staff, Conrad von Hötzendorff, wanted to decide the issue by the sword, because they did not believe that any other method would result in a permanent improvement in Austro-Servian relations.[180] What Cartwright failed to mention in his dispatch, simply because he was ignorant of it, was the fact that the Heir Apparent, Archduke Francis Ferdinand, who in most questions held different views to the Emperor, shared Francis Joseph's views on the Servian Question not necessarily out of a sincere love of peace, but because he wanted to avoid wounding Russian susceptibilities in the interests of the friendly relations with Russia that he wished to maintain. Another reason for the Archduke's reluctance to wage war on Servia was that he feared lest an Austro-Hungarian victory over Servia might result, by means of territorial annexation, in an increase of the Servian population of the Dual Monarchy that would be injurious to the Dual Monarchy's best interests.

Cartwright's opinion of Aehrenthal was higher than might perhaps have been expected and he did not hesitate to say that he believed that Aehrenthal sincerely desired a peaceful solution of the crisis. Here again it is possible to agree with Cartwright, who at this time thought more highly than he subsequently did of Aehrenthal's character. It is certain that Aehrenthal sought to restrain the warlike ambitions of Conrad and his friends, and that he personally believed that even a victorious war against Servia would not repay the loss of life and money that it would involve.[181] But it is no less certain that Aehrenthal was determined to force the Serbs to their knees even at the risk of provoking war. If war should break out, Aehrenthal calculated that it would be short and result in an Austro-Hungarian victory. The information reaching him from St. Petersburg went to prove that Russia was neither militarily nor financially in a position to wage war on Austria-Hungary, and in any case, even if Russia were to attack the Danubian Monarchy, Aehrenthal knew that he could rely with certainty upon German support. His prevision proved correct. Isvolsky bowed to German wishes and Grey accepted Aehrenthal's draft for the Servian declaration. Aehrenthal emerged the victor from the diplomatic duel with St. Petersburg and London. He could indeed say with pride that he had earned the honour done to him by the Emperor Francis Joseph in conferring the title of Count upon him. Aehrenthal was looked upon by many people at that time, both within the Empire and abroad, as one of the most outstanding statesmen of the Austro-Hungarian Empire in recent years. Subsequent events, however, that led to the downfall of the Dual Monarchy have given rise to doubts of the wisdom of Aehrenthal's policy. In the light of those events it may well seem to-day that Aehrenthal's victory was in truth Pyrrhic.[182]

Aehrenthal was certainly in the wrong in the exaggeratedly fierce attacks that he made upon Grey's policy. An impartial verdict based upon the published documents must be that there was no justification whatsoever for Aehrenthal's statement that Grey intrigued at Constantinople and Belgrade with the object of involving Austria-Hungary in war.

Shortly after the outbreak of the Bosnian crisis, Grey clearly defined his standpoint by saying that a violation had been done to a treaty signed by Austria-Hungary with other Powers and that this violation could not be recognized before it had been discussed by the signatory Powers assembled in conference. At the same time he made no secret of his intention to support the newly-established Young Turk Government's claim for compensation for the injury sustained by Turkish prestige through the annexation of Bosnia-Herzegovina. None the less he had from the very outset advised the Young Turk Government not to go to war with Austria-Hungary and to accept monetary compensation. Nor can it be proved that Grey incited the Turkish Government to boycott Austro-Hungarian goods. But he did not restrain them from using this form of economic warfare, and, in reply to complaints from Vienna, he declared that boycott was the weapon used by the weak against the strong. Moreover, Grey never concealed the fact that in the furtherance of the good relations between Great Britain and Russia that had sprung up in the years 1907 and 1908 he was anxious as far as it was possible to fulfil the wishes of the Protector of the Balkan Slavs. It was for these reasons, and not out of sympathy for the Serbs—a sympathy that he did not entertain, that Grey supported their demands, although from the beginning of the crisis he regarded as impossible any territorial compensation on the part of Austria-Hungary for the Serbs. And it was precisely because he realized this fact that Grey so tenaciously fought the diplomatic battle over the phrasing of the Servian declaration that has been described in these pages in order to save them, and with them their protector, from any possible humiliation. Nor did Grey give up the fight until after Isvolsky had lowered his own colours. Isvolsky became convinced that Russia was neither militarily nor financially in a position to wage war on the Central Empires, and that France showed no inclination to go to war with Germany over Servia; especially at a time when she had just concluded an agreement with Germany over Morocco. Great Britain, too, had told him that, while she was willing to afford Russia diplomatic support, she was not prepared to support her by force of arms. It was with these considerations in his mind that Isvolsky yielded to the German demand and declared his willingness to give Russia's unconditional assent to the abrogation of Article XXV of the Treaty of Berlin in the event of Austria-Hungary demanding its abrogation. Only after Isvolsky yielded to Germany's demand did Grey abandon his opposition and accept Aehrenthal's second draft which Isvolsky preferred to Grey's own draft. Nevertheless, Grey at this latest hour still contrived to snatch a victory. Aehrenthal undertook not to ask the signatory Powers to abrogate Article XXV of the Treaty of Berlin until after the Servian Government had either accepted or rejected the Note presented to it by the Powers containing the declaration drafted by Aehrenthal and Grey that Servia was to make to Austria-Hungary.

Grey knew that he had not achieved all that he had striven for. But he could justly claim that it was largely thanks to his efforts that Turkey obtained a large monetary compensation, the Servian Note was drafted in less humiliating phraseology, Montenegro's sovereign rights enlarged, and, above all, that a war was avoided that in his opinion was incompatible with the interests of Servia, Great Britain and the Entente.

Chapter Four

THE BALKAN WARS, 1909-1913

HROUGHOUT the Bosnian Crisis Aehrenthal had repeatedly denied the charge brought against him by
many members of the Foreign Office, and also by many
British newspapers as well as by wide sections of British public
opinion, that he was the tool of German policy. He insistently
protested that the policy which he pursued was an exclusively
Austro-Hungarian policy that demanded above all else that
Austria-Hungary remained inalterably faithful to her alliance
with the German Reich, while at the same time she was free
to be guided in all other important questions by self-interest.
He was indeed grateful for the invaluable support that the
German Government had given him during the Bosnian Crisis,
and he fully realized that his victory over Isvolsky was in no
small measure due to Germany's decisive intervention at St.
Petersburg in March 1909, although even in those days he
had never allowed himself to be put on a German leading-rein
and had successfully managed to maintain Austria-Hungary's
standing as a full and equal partner in the Dual Alliance often
to the extreme annoyance of leading German statesmen.

No conflict had disturbed the friendly relations between
Great Britain and Austria-Hungary for many years. But Great
Britain now began to regard Austria-Hungary chiefly as the
ally of the German Reich and the fiercer the rivalry between
Great Britain and Germany the more necessary did it seem to
British statesmen to keep a watchful eye on Austro-Hungarian
statesmen.[1] It is, therefore, not difficult to understand why
Great Britain should have been made uneasy, and even to some
extent apprehensive, by the news in the Spring of 1909 that
Austria-Hungary planned an enlargement of her fleet and the
construction of dreadnoughts at the very moment when
Germany was devoting all her energies to naval construction
and all attempts by Great Britain to achieve an agreement with
Germany over this question had proved fruitless.

The most energetic advocate of an expansion of the Austro-
Hungarian Navy was the Archduke Francis Ferdinand, who
was tireless in his endeavours to overcome the many obstacles

—not only financial—that stood in the way of the carrying out of his plans. Towards the end of April 1909, shortly after the settlement of the Bosnian Crisis, Cartwright asked Aehrenthal what truth there was in the rumours reaching London of Austro-Hungarian plans for the construction of dreadnoughts. Aehrenthal did not deny that an expansion of the fleet was contemplated, but said that he did not know how many ships would be built or what attitude the Parliaments would adopt towards the proposal. Public opinion in Austria-Hungary in general preferred a strengthening of the Army rather than the Fleet. Nevertheless, Austria-Hungary needed warships to protect her interests in the Mediterranean and, in any case, the Austro-Hungarian Navy was far behind those of the other Great Powers. Aehrenthal said he was astonished that reports "that Austria-Hungary was about to slightly increase the strength of her Navy should have caused so much excitement in England" and he assured Cartwright that the new dreadnoughts "would not be built with an intention of strengthening the German Fleet under any eventualities". In short, he said, "what Austria-Hungary was about to do need cause no alarm whatever in England". But British informed opinion did not agree with Aehrenthal that there was no cause for anxiety. Sir Eyre Crowe—Germany's arch-enemy who never ceased to believe in the inevitability of war between Great Britain and Germany—made the following comment on Cartwright's dispatch:

"In considering the strength of foreign navies it is not sufficient to take into account only the present intentions real or asserted of the governments owning such navies. In this particular case it may be quite true that no hostility to England is contemplated, but in view of the existence of the Triple Alliance it cannot be overlooked that Austria-Hungary may, whether she like it or not, find herself engaged in a war against us. The essence of the doctrine of the two Power standard is, I take it, that it wisely eschews the almost impossible task of determining whether a particular Power may or may not be opposed to us in war and seeks safety in the abstract and general principle of superiority over any numerically possible combination of two Powers."

And to this comment of Crowe's, Grey added the significant words:[1a]

"Whatever Aehrenthal may say, there is jubilation in Germany, where some papers consider the Austrian move as an answer to the offers of our colonies."

Moreover, Great Britain did not change her mind in this matter. In the House of Commons questions were frequently put to the Government on the subject of the strengthening of the Austro-Hungarian Navy and notwithstanding calming assurances from the Government Front Bench the belief continued to be held by large sections of public opinion that the expansion of the Austro-Hungarian Navy indicated an addition to the numbers of Great Britain's enemies.[2]

In his conversations with Hardinge, Mensdorff did his utmost to combat this point of view, while Aehrenthal told Cartwright that he did not wish to take any official action in the matter because the British Government's attitude had been so correct in replying to parliamentary questions. But he added that he could not understand the lively interest shown by the British public in the very restricted strengthening of the Austro-Hungarian Navy. The insinuation—Aehrenthal concluded—that another Power was behind the naval construction programme was ridiculous.[3] Aehrenthal's statement fell upon deaf ears. British public opinion continued to be gravely disturbed by the strengthening of the Austro-Hungarian Navy. Notwithstanding this anxiety, however, there was a real desire both in Vienna and London to put the relations between Great Britain and Austria-Hungary on a friendlier footing. At the beginning of July, Cartwright reported Aehrenthal as saying that he now realized that his policy during the Bosnian Crisis had created a state of tension in the relations between Austria-Hungary and Great Britain, France, Russia, and Italy, and that he now wished to improve those relations in order to make Austria-Hungary less dependant on Germany. For this reason the Austro-Hungarian Government hoped that King Edward VII would break his journey to Marienbad in order to visit the Emperor Francis Joseph at Ischl as a proof (Aehrenthal put it) that the past was forgotten and that Great Britain had resumed her old traditional friendship with the Habsburgs.[4] According to the report of Aehrenthal's audience with Francis Joseph on 16 July, it was Cartwright who put the "confidential and personal" question to Aehrenthal whether or not a short unofficial visit by King Edward VII to Ischl would be agreeable to the Emperor Francis Joseph. Aehrenthal answered the question by saying that he had not yet spoken to the Emperor on the subject, but that he was personally convinced that the Emperor would extend a cordial welcome to the King if the

latter wanted to visit him in Ischl. At the same time—
Aehrenthal added—he was equally certain that the Emperor
would not be offended if King Edward only went to Marienbad.
Cartwright suggested that Mensdorff should be instructed to
ask if the King wished to visit the Emperor—a proposal that
if acted upon would have been tantamount to an invitation.
But Aehrenthal did not respond to the suggestion and at his
audience of the Emperor he said that he was not in favour of it.[5]
King Edward told Mensdorff that on this occasion he could
not ask for an invitation as he had formerly done, because it
was very important at this time that the Emperor should at
least indicate that his visit would be welcome.[6] Since the
Emperor did not move in the matter King Edward did not
pay him a visit in Ischl and instead sent a special messenger
to Ischl for the Emperor's birthday on 18 August, bearing a
personal letter to Francis Joseph in which the King offered
him his warmest congratulations and good wishes. The King's
action gave much pleasure in Vienna and Aehrenthal told
Cartwright that it would help to disprove the story that when
the King was last in Ischl in 1908 the relations between the
two monarchs had become less cordial.[7]

Soon afterwards another minor difference between Austria-
Hungary and Great Britain was settled in a friendly manner.
In a speech in the House of Commons on 22 July 1909 Sir
Edward Grey had quoted from a letter written by Gladstone
to the then Austro-Hungarian Ambassador, Count Karolyi, in
which Gladstone said: "Your Excellency is now good enough
to assure us that your Government has no desire whatever to
extend or add to the rights acquired under the Treaty of Berlin
and that any such extension would be actually prejudicial to
Austria-Hungary." .Grey had expressly added that this remark
had no connection with the existing obligations of Austria-
Hungary.[8] Aehrenthal nevertheless felt bound to demand
clarification of the exact meaning of Gladstone's letter to
Karolyi inasmuch as the latter had declared at that time that
Austria-Hungary was not contemplating any movement
towards Mitrowitza and Salonica. Nothing had been said
about Bosnia-Herzegovina.[9] Grey at once assented to Aehrenthal's request and agreed to his telling the Delegations that
Grey had not interpreted Karolyi's letter to Gladstone as
referring to Bosnia-Herzegovina, "but only to an advance
beyond these provinces".[10] These minor disputes were thus

settled in a spirit of compromise as were others in the succeeding years.

In his speeches in the House of Commons, Grey frequently expressed his pleasure at the good relations that existed between the Danubian Monarchy and Great Britain, and also instructed Cartwright (who was by now an extremely popular figure in Viennese society) to tell Aehrenthal how sincerely he admired and appreciated Austro-Hungarian policy. Early in 1909, when Cartwright reported that Aehrenthal's position as Foreign Minister was endangered by the attacks of German and many Austrian enemies, Grey said that he hoped that Aehrenthal would not lose his post.[11] Aehrenthal, too, told Cartwright, and instructed Mensdorff to let it be known in London, how glad he was that the ill-feeling that had existed at the time of the annexation crisis had been completely and permanently overcome.[12] In every question that arose between Austria-Hungary and Great Britain from the autumn of 1909 to the autumn of 1911 Grey and Aehrenthal displayed a spirit of friendly accommodation without abandoning the standpoint that each deemed to be imposed upon him by the interests of his country.

For the most part these were questions that arose out of the relations between Austria-Hungary and Russia and out of conditions in the Balkans. After the Bosnian Crisis, Aehrenthal was willing to improve Austro-Russian relations. But his personal quarrel with Isvolsky outlived the Bosnian Crisis and placed an obstacle in the way of improved Austro-Russian relations. This quarrel also found an echo in the British Press. The idea of inviting British mediation in this quarrel was in Aehrenthal's mind, because in June 1909 Cartwright reported from Vienna that, after the failure of a German endeavour to bring Vienna and St. Petersburg together, Aehrenthal wanted France and Great Britain to make the attempt. But Grey had his doubts. He said that he certainly wanted to see better relations between Austria-Hungary and Russia, yet at the same time he feared that mediation would not earn the mediator the gratitude of either party and would be regarded by Germany as an intrigue for the purpose of isolating her. He wanted the friendliest relations between Great Britain and Austria-Hungary, "but without entangling ourselves".[13] Hardinge shared this opinion. He also thought a compromise between St. Petersburg and Vienna was essential in order to prevent the danger of war between the two countries and he believed that this could only be accomplised by the pursuit by the two statesmen of a policy of "self-abrogation". He knew and mistrusted both Isvolsky and Aehrenthal. But he placed more trust in Aehrenthal than in Isvolsky because Aehrenthal was the cleverer.[14] Consequently, when normal relations were restored between St. Petersburg and Vienna at the beginning of 1910 and both Powers had agreed to maintain the *status quo* in the Balkans, Russia proposed that the other Great Powers should be asked to make a similar declaration. Grey welcomed this proposal.[15] Aehrenthal rejected it. No new agreement had been concluded between Vienna and St. Petersburg—he said— and all that had happened was the restoration of normal relations.[16] He was not prepared to take any further step. Cartwright believed that Aehrenthal's attitude was occasioned by an intensification of his personal quarrel with Isvolsky—it was at this time that the *Fortnightly Review* published an article attacking Aehrenthal—as well as by the visit of Ferdinand of Bulgaria and the forthcoming visit of King Peter of Servia to St. Petersburg.[17] An improvement in the relations between St. Petersburg and Vienna only took place after Isvolsky's resignation in the autumn of 1910.

Another question that was frequently discussed by the British and Austro-Hungarian Governments during these years was the attitude to be adopted by them towards the conflicts that arose between Turkey and Greece over Crete and Macedonia. Grey and Aehrenthal were as one in their desire to preserve peace and both used their influence at Athens and Constantinople for this purpose. But they differed in their views as to their countries' obligations. Aehrenthal thought that Austria-Hungary was not one of the four Powers exercising a sort of protectorate over Greece, whose duty it therefore was to settle the Cretan Question. He believed that Austria-Hungary took second place and therefore should maintain an attitude of reserve. Hence he refused an invitation at the close of 1909 from the four protecting Powers to collaborate in drafting a definitive statute for Crete which had already been handed over to Turkey. According to a declaration made by the former Austro-Hungarian Foreign Minister, Count Goluchowski, Austria-Hungary could only participate in negotiations over Crete when the object of the negotiations was a fundamental change in the status of the island. At the same time, Austria-Hungary would agree to any change in the Cretan administrative system that met with the approval of Turkey and the protecting Powers.[18] In February 1910, Aehrenthal suggested that the best way of solving the Turco-Greek dispute that had been heightened by the summoning of the Greek National Assembly would be for the four protecting Powers to re-occupy Crete.[19] But he said nothing about Austria-Hungary participating in any such action. When, in the summer of 1910, the protecting Powers succeeded in obtaining satisfaction for Turkey from the Cretan Government, and when, notwithstanding their action, Turkey continued to boycott Greek goods, Great Britain proposed to the Austro-Hungarian Government that the six signatory Powers, through their ambassadors at Constantinople, should bring pressure to bear on the Turkish Government in order to put an end to a dangerous situation. Aehrenthal rejected this proposal on the ground that it might lead to the fall of the Turkish Government, which he wished to prevent. In any case, he did not believe in war between Greece and Turkey and, even were it to break out, the Great Powers would easily be able to restore order in the Balkans.[20] Grey was dissatisfied with Aehrenthal's attitude. He believed that Austria-Hungary had a greater stake than Great Britain in the maintenance of peace in the Balkans and should therefore support the protecting Powers in their endeavours to make Turkey "moderate and reasonable". He was prepared, together with the three other protecting Powers, "to hold Crete in trust for the Porte" and, in event of the Cretans not observing the conditions laid down for them, to collaborate with the other three Powers in "carrying out a military reoccupation of the island in order to fulfil our obligations to Turkey". But he was not prepared to go beyond the fulfilment of these obligations in regard to Crete and to accept responsibility—unless it were in common with the other five signatory Powers—for whatever Turkey might do elsewhere. If Turkey attacked Greece he would not move unless all the other Great Powers were ready to intervene.[21]

Aehrenthal answered Grey's statement by saying that he would continue to maintain his attitude of detachment in regard to Cretan affairs. Moreover, he denied that he thereby delayed a settlement of the Cretan Question and pointed out that he had repeatedly urged moderation upon the Turkish Government. Austria-Hungary could not accept responsibility for the policy pursued by the High Commissioner in Crete, Prince George, who had been appointed by the protecting Powers. It was true that the Austro-Hungarian Foreign Minister did not have the world-wide responsibilities that, as Grey had rightly pointed out, weighed upon the shoulders of the British Secretary of State for Foreign Affairs. None the less, his responsibilities were no less burdensome and close proximity to the Near East imposed upon the Austro-Hungarian Government the pursuit of an especially cautious and carefully calculated policy.[22] He did not believe that Turkey would go to war in the existing circumstances, and in the event he was proved right. Indeed, Aehrenthal maintained an extremely reserved attitude towards the many questions, both in and outside Europe, that came up for discussion during the year 1909 between the British and Austro-Hungarian Governments. But he made it perfectly clear to the British Government that he intended to hold fast to the alliance with Germany, while at the same time he pursued an independent policy solely serving the interests of the Habsburg Monarchy, the preservation of peace, and correct relations with other States. Hence Aehrenthal was anxious about the tension in Anglo-German relations, and was sincerely relieved whenever he heard of any improvement in those relations, because it was in Austria-Hungary's interest that Great Britain and Germany should be on friendly terms.

Aehrenthal expressed these views in conversation in February 1910 with the German Emperor, William II, and the German Imperial Chancellor, Herr von Bethmann-Hollweg. He said that as Austria-Hungary was not a colonial Power she had no overseas interests to fight for. Germany was a world Power and, therefore, in a different position. Consequently, Austria-Hungary would be glad if Germany and Great Britain could achieve a settlement of their differences.[23] On the other hand, he was extremely reserved in his conversations with the British Ambassador and avoided saying anything that could arouse the British Government's displeasure. He maintained the same reserve in 1911 when the conflict between Germany and France over Morocco increased the tension between Germany and Great Britain to a dangerous degree. He held, nevertheless, that the Act of Algeciras of 1906 should be maintained in force. At the same time—he said—he understood that Great Britain was bound by her treaty with France of

8 April 1904 to pay special regard to French interests in Morocco.[24]

At the end of September 1911 war broke out between Italy and Turkey over Italy's claims to Tripoli and gave rise to a constant and lively exchange of views between the British and Austro-Hungarian Governments. Grey and Aehrenthal both found themselves in difficult situations. Grey's difficulty was that although Italy was formally a member of the Triple Alliance she was, in fact, bent on maintaining friendly relations with Great Britain—a wish that was reciprocated by the British Government. King George V strongly sympathized with Italy and her monarch.[25] Moreover, the British Government had already declared in 1902 that it would bear in mind Italian wishes in regard to Tripoli.[26] On the other hand, Great Britain had to consider the feelings of the many millions of her Mohammedan subjects, and therefore did not wish to pursue an anti-Turkish policy that would also have resulted in the weakening of her influence at Constantinople from which Germany would have derived the benefit. Aehrenthal found himself in a very similar situation, though for different reasons. Italy was indeed a member of the Triple Alliance, but she was an ally who for years past had not been trusted by the two other members of the alliance and who was only suffered to retain her membership in order to prevent her open defection to the opposing camp. Italy and Austria-Hungary were permanently in conflict. In the Italian Parliament and Press vociferous expression was given to Italy's longing to reincorporate in the Italian State her "unrecovered lands" in Austria, irredentist propaganda and subversive movements within the Dual Monarchy were actively encouraged and supported from Italy, and the rivalry between Italy and Austria-Hungary in Albania became steadily keener. Many Italians openly said that Italy had only one enemy in Europe and that was her Austro-Hungarian ally. In Vienna, on the other hand, it was widely held that one must be either the friend or the enemy of Italy, and since friendship was impossible there was nothing left except open enmity. The war party was led by the Chief of the General Staff, Conrad von Hötzendorff, who was in this instance supported by the Heir-Apparent, Archduke Francis Ferdinand.[27] Conrad bombarded Aehrenthal and the old Emperor with demands that Austria-Hungary should make preventive war on Italy. Neither would listen to him, because each was equally determined not to unleash the dogs of war. The conflict was finally ended by the removal of Conrad from his post.

Aehrenthal nevertheless did not approve of Italian action in Tripoli and, out of regard for the Dual Monarchy's interests in the Balkans, wanted to maintain good relations with Turkey, upon whom he counted in event of a conflict between any of the Balkan States and Austria-Hungary. Grey and Aehrenthal were, therefore, animated by a common desire to avoid giving offence in any quarter. They were unable to prevent the war because Italy had begun it without approaching them in the matter beforehand. They also hesitated to intervene, notwithstanding Turkey's appeal to them to do so, when it appeared that Italy would not be content with anything less than complete sovereignty over Tripoli. Aehrenthal was of opinion that only united action by Austria-Hungary, Germany, Russia, Great Britain and France held out any hope of success, and he asked whether or not they would agree to mediate on the basis of an Italian annexation of Tripoli.[28] Grey agreed to this proposal on condition that the ambassadors of these Powers at Constantinople should first be instructed to ask for the Turkish Government's views.[29] It at once became clear that at this juncture mediation on the lines of Aehrenthal's proposal would have no chance of success. The British and Austro-Hungarian Ambassadors at Constantinople were both of this opinion.[30] Grey agreed with them; more expecially since he wanted to avoid doing anything that might give the impression in Italy that he was seeking to exert pressure.[31] Even when, on 6 November 1911 Italy announced that she had annexed Tripoli the Powers still hesitated to intervene in a decisive fashion. Aehrenthal censured Italy for her action and said that the Powers could not sanction it since they had declared themselves neutral. Nevertheless, nothing was done. Nor did Great Britain make any move in the matter, despite the fact that it was thought in London that Italy's action violated treaty obligations. It seemed, both in London and Vienna, to be useless to attempt mediation and the efforts of both Governments were henceforth directed to preventing any extension of the conflict that might give rise to further complications affecting their respective interests. Great Britain and Austria-Hungary in their attitude to the Straits (Bosphorus and Dardanelles) Question were actuated by similar political and economic considerations. Both Powers wanted to prevent an Italian attack on the Dardanelles and in co-operation with the other Great Powers they successfully averted this danger. But Russia met with no success in her simultaneous attempt to induce Turkey to open the Straits to Russian men-of-war in return for a Russian promise to make the Balkan States enter into friendly relations with Turkey. In replying to the Russian suggestion, Turkey stated that no change of such importance in the régime of the Straits could take place without the previous assent of the signatory Powers to the Treaty of Berlin. The Western Powers, moreover, said that they could not bring pressure to bear upon Turkey in event of a Turkish refusal of the Russian offer. Austria-Hungary and Germany refused to consider the Russian proposal. Hence Turkey rejected it.

Another danger arising out of the Italo-Turkish conflict that especially threatened Austria-Hungary was the possible extension of military operations to the Balkans. Austria-Hungary was resolved to offer determined resistance to any attempt on the part of Italy to extend her influence to the Balkans or to obtain a foothold on the peninsula. The negotiations that were carried on for this purpose by Aehrenthal and his successor as Foreign Minister, Count Berchtold, do not come within the scope of the present study. But negotiations still went on between London and Vienna over the question of mediation between Italy and Turkey, in which it was constantly reiterated that only common action by the Great Powers held out any prospect of success. Great Britain, for her part, continued to insist that the time for mediation had not yet come inasmuch as Turkey was determined to carry on the war.[32] Towards the end of February 1912 Great Britain proposed that Italy should be asked to declare that she would abstain from any military or naval action in the Dardanelles "et dans ces parages" in order that Turkey might then be requested to refrain from the mine-laying that was causing serious losses to international shipping.[33] Although he was not hopeful of success, Berchtold was willing to join with the other Powers in making a *démarche* in Rome for this purpose. The proposal had to be dropped, however, because all the Powers with the sole exception of France held aloof.[34] On the other hand, Great Britain and France adopted Russia's proposal that Italy and Turkey should be asked to state their conditions for peace.[35] While he did not believe that anything would come of it, and the event proved him right, Berchtold nevertheless gave his assent. But what specially pleased the Austro-Hungarian Government was the success that rewarded British efforts to induce Turkey to re-open the Straits to international traffic—they had been closed to traffic by the Turkish Government towards the end of April for a short time—because Austro-Hungarian commerce had been seriously affected by the closure.[36] There was, nevertheless, still no prospect of successful mediation between Turkey and Italy. British and Austrian interests in Italy and Turkey alike forbade energetic intervention.

At the beginning of June 1912, at a diplomatic reception in Vienna the question of summoning a conference to settle the Italo-Turkish dispute came under discussion. Berchtold remarked that the question was not actual because hitherto no Power had come forward with a proposal for a conference. In saying this, Berchtold meant that no conference would be likely to produce results unless some formula embodying a compromise between the opposing standpoints of Turkey and Italy had been agreed upon before its meeting. This, however, was never done. The war, therefore, went on. An Italian occupation of islands in the Aegean was bitterly resented in Vienna and led to fierce recriminations that nevertheless did not produce any change in Italian policy. There was no longer any question of intervention or mediation. But, when the Balkan War broke out, Turkey hastily concluded a peace with Italy that left Italy in possession of Tripoli without settling the question raised by the Italian occupation of the Aegean islands. All that was agreed was that certain islands should continue in Italian occupation until Turkey had fulfilled the stipulations of the treaty, when Italy promised to restore them to their former sovereignty.

At the outset of the Italo-Turkish war the Austro-Hungarian Government asked itself what would be the effect of this conflict upon the Balkans and upon Austro-Hungarian interests in those countries. In the negotiations which he instructed Mensdorff to carry on in London, as well as in his own conversations with Cartwright in Vienna, Aehrenthal stressed the necessity for Austria-Hungary to keep a watchful eye upon Balkan developments. Any serious weakening of Turkish power must unquestionably be prevented, because it would lead to a disturbance of the Balkan balance of power. For the Austro-Hungarian Government still looked upon Turkey as a Power that constituted a valuable counterweight to the annexationist ambitions of the Balkan States. Although the British Government shared Aehrenthal's views, it did not want to be entangled in Balkan affairs. At the beginning of December 1911, Cartwright reported that while Aehrenthal wanted the maintenance of the Balkan *status quo* he was making preparations for the eventuality of Turkey's downfall, in order to be able to protect the interests of the Dual Monarchy and to be in a position to decide the fate of the Balkan States. Cartwright then asked: "Would it not be well for Great Britain, France and Russia to exchange views with regard to these matters and either come to terms with Aehrenthal as to a possible joint action of the Powers in the Balkans in the event of trouble arising there, or to form a plan of action of their own to oppose that which will be pursued by Austria-Hungary in the event of a Near Eastern crisis?" Grey answered Cartwright's question by saying that it would be a mistake to take the initiative "in opposing Austria in the Balkans." Russia must first make up her own mind and then approach Great Britain. To take the initiative by making suggestions to Russia would involve Great Britain far too deeply in Balkan affairs.[37] Nor did the British Government express any other opinion whenever Aehrenthal pointed to the dangers threatening European peace from the Balkans. The Foreign Office did not even change its attitude when it learnt of the treaties concluded by Servia and Bulgaria in March 1912 under Russian guidance.[38] Officials there certainly were astonished by what they considered to be the shortsighted and mistaken policy of Ferdinand of Bulgaria, but they were, nevertheless, careful to guard against any knowledge of these treaties reaching the Austro-Hungarian Government and to maintain their attitude of reserve.

Aehrenthal's death on 17 February 1912, and the appointment of Count Berchtold as his successor, did not produce any change in Anglo-Austrian relations. Berchtold continued Aehrenthal's policy, while the Foreign Office maintained its reserve. In July 1912, Grey said to Mensdorff that Great Britain wished to maintain the Balkan *status quo* and thought that the only threat to it was to be found in the internal situation in Turkey. If there should be any change in the Balkans—Grey continued—he hoped that the Powers would stand together. In seeking to dissipate Mensdorff's anxiety as to Russia's attitude, Grey recalled the failure of Tscharikoff's mission to Constantinople and emphasized the fact that Russia gave no sign of wishing to bring up the Straits Question.[39] Berchtold was of a different opinion, to which he gave expression on 20 July in his instructions to Mensdorff that were intended primarily for Mensdorff's guidance, though Berchtold gave him permission to make use of the information as he thought fit. Berchtold pointed out to Mensdorff that within the past two years the attitude of the Powers to the maintenance of the *status quo* in the Near East had undergone a change. Up to that time the Triple Alliance, and especially Germany, had regarded the maintenance of the *status quo* in the Balkans as axiomatic, and even Russia, notwithstanding her traditional aspirations, believed herself, as a consequence of her defeat by Japan, to be too weak to play an active rôle in Balkan affairs. Now everything was changed. Turkey was no longer Germany's pet, Russia was once more active in the Near East, Italy was at war with Turkey, Austria-Hungary alone had not altered her policy and still wished to maintain the *status quo*. Although Great Britain was nowadays more friendly towards Russia than in earlier times, she was compelled to consider the interests of Egypt and India and of millions of Mohammedan subjects, and could not therefore stand aside and calmly watch the destruction of Turkey. Great Britain and Austria-Hungary had identical interests and therefore it seemed indicated that they should act in common. Nonetheless, they must work together as equal partners and no doubt must be entertained that Austria-Hungary would not change her place in the existing system of alliances.[40]

In August 1912, after the Turkish Government had made concessions to Albania, Berchtold proposed to the Powers that they should take joint action at Constantinople in order to obtain similar concessions from Turkey for the Christian inhabitants of the Balkan States. The British Government accepted the proposal. But it recommended that the Powers should act individually at Constantinople in order to avoid giving the impression to the Turks that the Powers were seeking to exert pressure upon them.[41] Berchtold took great pains in replying to the British suggestion to allay possible suspicions that the Austro-Hungarian Government was solely animated by self-interest. He said that he was opposed to a conference and to any action at Constantinople that could be interpreted as pressure, as well as to any collective action at Constantinople or in the Balkan capitals. On learning this Grey remarked: "All this I cordially reciprocate and I think it shows a very just appreciation of the situation." Berchtold, moreover, suggested that the Turkish Government should be reminded of its declared intention to grant the Christian inhabitants of the Balkan States similar concessions to those granted to the Albanians. The Turks must be made to understand—he continued—that Europe was at one in her endeavour to maintain peace, contentment, and the *status quo* in the Balkans. He added that his previous actions had already shown good results. On this Grey observed: "I can't endorse this altogether, but nothing could be said on this point and that the present *démarche* had its origin in his proposals." He agreed with Berchtold that the electoral system in Macedonia could be improved and the *conseils généraux* restored in the vilayets.[42] Nothing further came of these suggestions.

On 11 September Berchtold said he was extremely satisfied with Grey's statement and in reply to a question by Cartwright declared that he did not desire the continuance of the discussions and would prefer to wait upon events in the Balkans. He was content to know—he added—that the Powers were ready to consult together whenever events in the Near East demanded it. This point of view was shared by Grey, who said: "We do not want the conversation to advance."[43] But Berchtold, who for some time had been aware of the Serbo-Bulgarian and Greek-Bulgarian treaties, felt obliged to summon a Council of Ministers on 14 September for the purpose of discussing what policy should be followed by Austria-Hungary in event of these States uniting in making war on Turkey. Two courses seemed open to Austria-Hungary: (a) to forbid any alteration in the *status quo* without her assent, (b) to warn Servia that Austria-Hungary would not permit any violation of the Turkish frontier. No decision was, however, taken. The Council of Ministers merely resolved to continue in association with the other Powers its endeavour to maintain peace. Towards the end of September the Chief of the General Staff, Schemua, sent the Emperor a memorandum setting forth the aims that ought to be pursued by Austro-Hungarian policy in the light of the general European situation. It was his opinion that Turkey had neither the strength nor the will to carry out the reforms required by the Powers and, therefore, that the maintenance of the *status quo* in the Balkans could no longer be regarded as axiomatic. For the same reason it was imperative that Austria-Hungary should define her aims. Schemua proposed that Austria-Hungary should at once take up arms in event of the outbreak of a Balkan war. But Berchtold opposed Schemua just as Aehrenthal had opposed Conrad in 1911, and declared that Russia and Italy would not tolerate any such policy. To mobilize before consultation with the other Great Powers would provoke counter-action on the part of Russia and Italy. Berchtold preferred that Austria-Hungary should continue to work with the Powers to prevent an outbreak of war and should indicate her disapproval of any mobilization by the Balkan States. A declaration should be publicly made at a suitable moment that any alteration in the *status quo* could not take place without Austria-Hungary's consent. Military preparations should only be made at first on the south-eastern frontier, while at the same time careful watch should be kept on Russian military movements on the Austro-Hungarian and Rumanian frontiers.[44]

Shortly afterwards, on 8 October, at Poincaré's suggestion, a Note that had already been approved by Grey and Berchtold was handed in the name of the Powers to the Balkan States in which the Powers announced their disapproval for any action that might lead to war. They also declared that they proposed, by virtue of Article 23 of the Treaty of Berlin, to concern themselves with administrative reforms in European Turkey without interfering with the Sultan's sovereignty or the integrity of his dominions. Above all, the Note stated that in event of war no change in the *status quo* could take place.[45] On the very day on which this Note was delivered in the capitals of the Balkan States, Montenegro declared war on Turkey, and her example was soon followed by Bulgaria, Servia and Greece. Surprised by the outbreak of war, the Great Powers at first united in an attempt to localize it and to maintain the *status quo*, despite whatever might be the outcome of the war. This standpoint was adopted by Russia in the interest of the Balkan States and by Austria-Hungary in the interest of Turkey. In a very short time these two Great Powers differed in their interpretations of this policy. Berchtold said Austria-Hungary could not allow Salonica to become the property of a victorious Balkan State, and especially not if that State were Bulgaria, while she must also refuse to let Servia take the Sandjak of Novibazar. Russia feared lest

Austria-Hungary would reoccupy the Sandjak and was therefore disposed to support Servia. At the very outset of the war
the British Government tried to get the Powers to agree on a
common policy.[46] But when the French Government made the
proposal in London and Vienna that the Powers should come
to an agreement over the question of mediation at some future
date Grey, in accepting the proposal, said that it would be
necessary to await a favourable opportunity.[47] For the present
he wanted Russia, Austria-Hungary, and Italy, as the Powers
primarily concerned, to take the lead and he suggested to them
that they should agree as to their plans.[48]

A conference was held between 25 and 30 October at the
Ministry of Foreign Affairs in Vienna, at which discussions
took place over Austro-Hungarian policy. Albania loomed
large on the Austro-Hungarian horizon. In the memorandum
summing up the results of these discussions, Albania is given
pride of place and great emphasis is laid on the fact that the
most important question for Austria-Hungary—a question that
must in case of necessity be decided by the sword—was to
prevent any Great Power, or for that matter even a small
Power like Servia, gaining a foothold on the east coast of the
Adriatic or the Ionian Sea. An autonomous, or in the event of
the abolition of Turkish sovereignty an independent, Albania
would serve this purpose. This new State should be given as
much territory as possible in order that it might be viable and
capable of development. None the less, it was obviously impossible at this stage to delimit its frontiers. When, however,
this came to be done it would be desirable that the new
Albania should comprise part of the province of Janina and in
the vilayet of Monastir the western part of the Sandjak of
Koritza, up to the mountains lying to the east of the town of
Koritza. It should also comprise Monastir, up to the water-
shed between Lake Ochrida and Lake Presba, as well as the
whole of the Sandjak of Elbassa, and the greater portion of the
Sandjak of Dibra. The Albanian Sandjaks of Prizren and
Ipek should be separated from the vilayet of Kossova and
given to Albania, and also from the same vilayet the districts
of Luma, Hassi and Djakova, together with the town of that
name. Lastly, it would be desirable that in the purely Albanian
vilayet of Scutari Montenegrin settlements should be restricted
as far as possible. Another question that came up for discussion was whether or not Austria-Hungary should consent

to the creation of a smaller Albania or to a partition of the country with Italy. The conference decided against the latter alternative as impracticable, and also rejected a condominium as likely to prove the cause of friction between the two Powers. Hence it seemed preferable to be content with a small Albania.[49]

While this conference was sitting in Vienna, the Balkan States were winning victory after victory. Their success produced immediate repercussions. The Chief of the Austro-Hungarian General Staff, Schemua, wanted to restore the *status quo* by force. Berchtold said this was impossible. He thought that Austria-Hungary, with or without the assistance of the Powers, should endeavour to guide the course of events in such a manner as would safeguard her political and economic Balkan interests.[50] By the end of October opinion in London no longer entertained hopes of maintaining the Balkan *status quo* and Grey was reported as saying: "The victor cannot be deprived of what he has won by his sword."[51] Nicolson did not think the Turks could hold the Chataldja Line and asked Mensdorff what the Austro-Hungarian Government would do if the Bulgarians entered Constantinople or the Greeks captured Salonica. Mensdorff answered by asking Nicolson what he thought Russia would do in event of the Bulgarians capturing Constantinople, to which Nicolson replied that he personally thought Russia would raise a protest in a conference and would prefer that Constantinople should remain in Turkish hands. On the other hand, he thought that if Russia were faced with a *fait accompli* she would hesitate to chase a Slav Power like Bulgaria out of Constantinople and hand it back to the Sultan.[52] Indeed, Grey's attitude was that it was a matter of indifference for the British Government how the victors divided up their Turkish booty and that the only important thing was that events did not lead to an European war in which Great Britain would be forced to take sides.[53] Asquith held the same language. Newspapers like *The Times* and the *Westminster Gazette* stressed the calm and correct attitude of Austria-Hungary and declared that Austria-Hungary's wishes were justifiable and capable of fulfilment.[54] Grey thought it would be of the greatest service if Austria-Hungary and Russia were to agree as to the conditions on which they must make a stand. The antagonism between the two States nevertheless became steadily greater. Berchtold refused a French suggestion (which he rightly suspected was inspired by Russia) that Austria-Hungary should sign a protocol declaring her *désintessement* in the Balkans. Austria-Hungary, he told Cartwright, looked upon herself as a Balkan State and would never cease to do so.[55]

The Austro-Hungarian Government was shortly afterwards given an opportunity of informing the British Government of its attitude towards territorial changes in the Balkans. This opportunity arose out of Turkey's request to the Powers that they would intervene to bring the war between Turkey and her enemies to a close and to initiate peace negotiations.[56] Grey said that he would have to consult the other Powers before taking any definite step. His own opinion—he added— was that all that could be done was to ask the Balkan States for the conditions on which they would agree to an armistice.[57] On 4 November Grey and Mensdorff discussed the whole situation. Mensdorff said that in the event of a partition of European Turkey, or the territorial aggrandizement of neighbouring States, Austria-Hungary would be compelled to safeguard her vital interests and to demand that any territorial enlargement, or any aggrandizement of the might, of a neighbouring State must be accompanied by a guarantee that this State would not pursue an inimical policy directed against the Habsburg Monarchy. Guarantees would therefore be asked for that Servia would maintain good-neighbourly relations with Austria-Hungary. Fine words and promises were not of themselves sufficient: improved economic relations were necessary that would also profit Servia. In reply to a suggestion by Grey that Austria-Hungary contemplated annexation, Mensdorff declared that the Austro-Hungarian Government did not harbour any such design. He added, however, that any demand by Servia for territory on the Adriatic would be rejected *a limine*. Mensdorff went on to say that Albania must be free to pursue her own development and that Rumania's justifiable demands ought to be granted. Austria-Hungary did not ask for any frontier rectifications. Markets in European Turkey that had hitherto absorbed Austro-Hungarian industrial products must remain open for such goods even in the event that such markets passed into other ownership. Austro-Hungarian interests in Salonica must also be protected and this could be done by making Salonica a free harbour with certain safeguards for Austro-Hungarian commerce.[58] When, however, Grey mentioned Servia's desire to obtain San

Giovanni di Medua, Mensdorff pointed out to him on a map that Servia could only gain access to San Giovanni across Albanian and Mohammedan districts.[59]

Two days later, on 6 November, Mensdorff met King George V at a shoot and had a long conversation with him. The King highly praised the bravery of the Balkan troops and said that they fully deserved to enjoy the fruits of their victory. Public opinion in England would not tolerate any attempt to deprive them of it. The King said that if the Bulgarians were to occupy Constantinople—according to him they had promised not to remain in the city—he feared a massacre of the Christian population and the destruction of mosques. The Turks should be left in possession of Constantinople and the surrounding district. In the King's opinion, Adrianople should be given to the Bulgars "despite the fact that Russia is opposed to it." He thought it would be very difficult to concede Russia's demands. Although she had not fired a shot she was asking that a victorious Bulgaria should cede territory to her. It seemed to him that this was a matter that could best be left to Austria-Hungary to deal with. King George then went on to discuss Servian demands. While he acknowledged the force of Mensdorff's objections to any acquisition by Servia of territory on the Adriatic, the King reminded him that the Austro-Hungarian Government must recognize the fact that Russia would support—at any rate to a certain degree— Servia's demands. Finally, King George said that he thought very definitely that Montenegro should be given Scutari.[60]

In the course of further conversations with Mensdorff, Grey made it clear that he thought it useless to discuss the question of access to the sea for Albania or Servia so long as the war went on, and that it would be time enough to discuss this question when the war was over. Mensdorff also gained the impression that Grey understood Austria-Hungary's views in regard to Albanian autonomy, while at the same time he wanted Servia to gain access to the sea by some means or other.[61] Berchtold's comment on this information was that Servia's demand for access to the Adriatic was unjustifiable and could only be granted at the expense of other more legitimate interests.[62] Furthermore, he did not share Grey's opinion that discussion of the questions affecting Austria-Hungary should be postponed until the time came when Europe would find herself faced with a number of *faits accomplis.* The creation of an autonomous Albania, for example, which Rome and Vienna desired and on which Grey certainly counted, should not be prejudiced by the occupation of a part of Albania by Servian troops without previous notification. Berchtold also rightly said that it was France and Russia, and not Austria-Hungary, who had initiated the discussions.[63] Grey was impressed by Berchtold's statement. He recognized the necessity of creating a viable Albania without, at the same time, being willing to define or to admit the territorial extent of the new Albania. He merely voiced his belief that agreement would be reached over this question as well as over the question of Servia's economic outlets to the Adriatic.[64] Two days later he read to Mensdorff the instructions that were being sent to the British Minister at Belgrade to inform the Servian Government that the British Government understood Servia's economic needs, but that there was more than one way of fulfilling them. If Servia were to refuse to adopt any other way than the one she had herself proposed, she would forfeit the sympathy of those who wished to support her.[65] The warning was indeed both timely and necessary, since the Servian Government increased its demands by leaps and bounds. Cartwright wrote to Nicolson on November 8 that Servia at first hoped only for the vilayet of Kossovo, but after her initial victories she demanded Uskub and Monastir, and now she was already talking of partitioning Albania with Greece. Tomorrow Servia would demand that she should be allowed to annex Bosnia-Herzegovina. Influential circles in Vienna—Cartwright went on—were of the opinion that a dam must be erected against Servian ambitions. Austria-Hungary was not prepared to concede Servian demands for large slices of Turkish territory, and in Vienna it was thought that Albania should be made an integral autonomous or independent State, probably ruled over by a Mohammedan prince. Austria-Hungary and Italy were agreed upon this plan and were supported by Germany. But Russia was supporting the French Press in its campaign for furthering Servian endeavours to gain a foothold on the Adriatic. Cartwright concluded by saying that the differences between St. Petersburg and Vienna that were steadily becoming more obvious constituted the greatest danger for the peace of Europe.[66]

Throughout November the situation steadily grew more tense. Servian troops advanced towards the Adriatic. On

6 November Berchtold told the Delegations that he was willing to take the allies' victories into account and only to demand that Austria-Hungary's vital interests should be safeguarded. He unsuccessfully endeavoured to win over Servia by far-reaching concessions. He was even prepared to grant Servia an economic outlet to the sea. He would not, however, consent to Servia's acquiring any territorial access to the Adriatic that would injure Albania's ethnical rights. But he was ready to afford Servia access through Bosnia or Albania or by the acquisition of a port on the Aegean.[67] The Servians, nevertheless, persisted in their demand for direct access to the Adriatic and Russia energetically supported them. The Albanians were roused to fever-heat by Servia's demands. They had not joined in the war because, on the one hand, they feared that the victory of the Balkan allies would mean the partition of their country and, on the other, they did not wish to see any strengthening of Turkish power. Now they decided, at Valona on 28 November, to proclaim their independence. Berchtold approved their action. Exaggerated rumours of excesses committed by Serbs on Austro-Hungarian consular officials heightened the nervousness prevailing in Vienna and Budapest. Berchtold, nevertheless, remained calm and did not abandon hope that war would be avoided—a war that once begun might take on unforeseeable dimensions.[68] He informed the British Government of the limits within which he was prepared to meet Servian and Montenegrin demands, while at the same time he insisted that he must protect Austria-Hungary's vital interests. The Austro-Hungarian Foreign Minister's calmness and prudence met with warm appreciation in London, where the Prime Minister, Mr. Asquith, said it was fortunate for Europe that Berchtold displayed so much cleverness, discretion, and patience.[69] In order to meet Russia's wishes the British Government, nevertheless, did its utmost to find a solution to the problem of affording Servia a port on the Adriatic.[70] Indeed, Grey asked Mensdorff what the Austro-Hungarian Government would say to giving Servia a narrow strip of land not through Albania but along the Montenegrin frontier that could be neutralized and on which the Powers would guarantee that no naval base should be constructed.[71] Obviously, San Giovanni di Medua was what Grey had in mind. But Mensdorff rejected Grey's proposal and said that Berchtold had no intention of allowing

San Giovanni de Medua to fall into Servian hands.[72] Nor was
the Foreign Office any more successful in its subsequent
endeavour to induce Berchtold to agree to a compromise in
this matter. An improvement was, however, brought about
in the situation by a conversation which the Austro-Hungarian
Ambassador at St. Petersburg had with the Tsar Nicholas II
in the course of which the Tsar declared that, while he thought
Servia ought to be given concessions in regard to outlets to the
Adriatic for her commerce, he would not regard an Austro-
Hungarian rejection of such demands as a ground for a
Russian declaration of war on Austria-Hungary.[73]

The Servian Government, nevertheless, maintained its uncompromising attitude and both Austria-Hungary and Russia
continued their preparations for war. The question of the
Austro-Hungarian consulates in Servia gave rise to renewed
anxiety in Vienna and Budapest, and nobody could foretell
whether or not it would be possible to avoid war. Such was
the situation when the two Great Powers—Great Britain and
Germany—who were not directly concerned in Balkan affairs,
started discussions in London for the purpose of seeing what
they could do to effect a settlement of the crisis. Grey told the
new German Ambassador in London, Prince Lichnowsky, that
Great Britain was wholly disinterested in the Adriatic Question
and that her sole desire was to prevent the outbreak of war
between the Great Powers, because it was impossible to foresee
the consequences of such a war or to know who would take
part in it.[74] His remark was an answer to the wish expressed
by Lichnowsky that Great Britain and Germany should work
together to preserve peace. Neither Great Britain nor Germany
had any reason either to demand or to oppose Servia's acquisition of a harbour on the Adriatic and both were agreed that
such an issue was no ground for a European war. Hence Grey
sounded the German Government as to its opinion of a proposal made some time previously that the ambassadors of the
six Great Powers in any European capital—Grey proposed
Paris—should meet in conference and answer three questions
which their Governments would pose to them: (1) To what
extent are the Balkan allies at liberty to alter the map of
Europe without the Great Powers being able to impose conditions upon them? (2) Upon what questions must the Great
Powers reserve their right to be heard? (Grey indicated as
questions upon which the Great Powers must be consulted—

Albania, Aegean Islands, Servia's access to the Adriatic. He assumed that the Balkan States would not lay claim to Constantinople and the Straits.) (3) Of these three questions— Albania, Aegean Islands, Servia's access to the Adriatic— which would meet with the agreement and support of all the six Great Powers? Grey said that Great Britain was not making formal proposals and merely wanted to know what the German Government thought of these suggestions. He also asked if the German Government shared his belief that the other Great Powers would give their assent.[75] In order to obviate any disagreeable conflict of opinion at the conference between the Austro-Hungarian and Russian ambassadors it should be given as "informal" a character as possible.[76] On 30 November Cartwright communicated these suggestions to Berchtold, who received them in a friendly manner. He said that if the discussions were in fact "informal" and only for the purpose of bringing about agreement between the Powers over matters arising out of the war, and also agreement only on "certain incontrovertible points", he would give Grey's suggestion his sympathetic consideration and would presently instruct Mensdorff to inform Grey of his definite answer. Berchtold said he would prefer London to Paris as the scene of the conference, because Great Britain had displayed praiseworthy impartiality throughout the crisis and also because the choice of London would prevent Isvolsky (who was now Russian Ambassador in Paris) from being Russia's representative.[77]

A few days later Mensdorff informed the Foreign Office that Berchtold gave his assent to the holding of these "noncommittal" conversations. At the same time he pointed out that Italy and Austria-Hungary had signed a treaty by which they pledged themselves to establish an autonomous Albania and each had handed a declaration to the Servian, Greek, and Montenegrin Governments on the subject of the Albanian coastline. Consequently, Austria-Hungary's representative at the conference would be instructed not to take part in discussions over the question of Servia's access to the Adriatic except in so far as these were restricted to the securing of economic outlets to the Adriatic for Servia. He would also be instructed not to participate under any circumstances in discussions concerning the extension of Servian territory to the shore of the Adriatic. Grey replied that he was well acquainted with Berchtold's views and yet saw no necessity to announce them at the present time. It would be time enough for Mensdorff to make a declaration to this effect once the "non-committal" conversations had begun. Great Britain herself had no reason for raising the question of a port for Servia on the Adriatic in the conference and was solely concerned to effect a compromise between the conflicting interests of the two chief protagonists—Russia and Austria-Hungary.[78] Berchtold strongly advocated Rumania's participation in the conference. Grey, however, while not objecting to it on principle, thought it should be postponed to a later date.[79]

The summoning of a conference of this nature seemed all the more necessary because recent events gave rise to fresh fears for the preservation of peace. Conrad von Hötzendorff had again become Chief of the Austro-Hungarian General Staff and had renewed his campaign for forcible action against Servia, the re-occupation of the Sandjak of Novibazar, and the expulsion of Servian troops from Albania. Again the old Emperor refused his consent for Conrad's warlike plans and Berchtold continued his task of seeking to maintain peace. The German Imperial Chancellor, Herr von Bethmann-Hollweg, came to his assistance. In a speech which he delivered on the occasion of the renewal of the Triple Alliance, the Imperial Chancellor declared that Germany would only come to the aid of Austria-Hungary in a conflict in which her ally was the victim of an unprovoked attack. This speech undoubtedly strengthened the peace party in Vienna in its efforts to avert a bloody conflict by every possible means. Its members could also hope that their endeavours would be advanced by the conclusion on 4 December of an armistice between Turkey and the allied Balkan States with the exception of Greece. These gains for the cause of peace were, however, offset by Russia's attitude. The Russian Foreign Minister, M. Sazonov, rejected Grey's suggestion that Russia should induce the Serbs and Montenegrins to content themselves with the acquisition of the Sandjak of Novibazar and to abandon their Adriatic ambitions. On 9 December Sazonov declared that Russia's aim was nothing less than the political and economic emancipation of Servia, who should be given direct communication across Albania with the Adriatic and guaranteed freedom of transport for all classes of goods, inclusive of munitions of war.[80]

None the less, Berchtold was determined not to abandon his point of view in the question of Servia's access to the Adriatic. He informed Grey of his resolve and declined to receive a visit from the Servian Prime Minister, M. Pašić, who wanted to come to Vienna to negotiate directly with the Austro-Hungarian Government the conditions under which Austria-Hungary would concede Servia a port on the Adriatic connected by a small corridor to Servia that would give the Serbs their economic independence. Berchtold declared with great emphasis that this question would be dealt with by the conference of ambassadors. Indeed, Cartwright gained the impression that Berchtold deemed it of the greatest importance that the conference should be opposed to Servia's acquisition of a port on the Adriatic, because he would then be able to bring pressure to bear on the Servian Government to abandon this demand.[81] On 15 December Mensdorff was sent instructions that should serve as a guide for him in the discussions at the conference. Briefly summarized, these ran: No decisions were to be taken by the conference. Each ambassador would inform his Government of the results of the discussions. The ambassadors themselves should lay down the programme for the conference. Mensdorff was instructed to keep in touch with his German and Italian colleagues and as far as possible form a common front with them. No protocols of the discussions were to be drawn up. On the subject of Albania the instructions said that Austria-Hungary was chiefly concerned to see that the balance of power in the Adriatic was not upset either at the present time or in the future. For this reason Albania's frontiers must be delimited in such a manner that the Albanian State was rendered viable and its internal organization was protected from any interference by individual foreign countries. No districts exclusively inhabited by Albanians were to be ceded to other Powers. (Berchtold was under no illusion that this principle could be upheld in its fullest extent. Although the towns of Ipek, Prisren, and Ochrida could hardly be saved for Albania, they could afford an excuse for Albania's receiving compensation.) In the strongest possible fashion Mensdorff was told not to take part in discussions that had for their subject the territorial expansion of Servia to the Adriatic or the acquisition by Servia of territory on its coast. Austria-Hungary was ready to meet Servian wishes in all other matters. Servia could reach the sea by constructing a short railway line on her own territory that could be connected with the railway across Bosnia to the coast. Alternatively, it would be possible to build a railway across Montenegro or to enlarge the Danube-Adriatic Railway to serve the same purpose. Aegean Islands: Mensdorff was instructed to wait and see which Powers brought up this matter and what were their proposals. Above all, he was to avoid giving the impression that he wanted to engage in any discussion of the future of the islands in Italian occupation. Macedonia: Austria-Hungary was chiefly interested in the future of Salonica where, as Mensdorff knew, she hoped to see a free port established while any rectifications of frontiers would be settled between Austria-Hungary, Turkey, Servia and Montenegro.[82]

On 17 December the Conference of Ambassadors met for the first time. After the customary formalities had been completed, Mensdorff was invited to address the Conference on the subject of the creation of an Albanian State. He emphasized that it was essential that Albania should be an autonomous viable State capable of development. The Russian Ambassador, Count Benckendorff, said that in principle he agreed with Count Mensdorff, but that he thought an autonomous Albania should be guaranteed by the Powers and placed under the sovereignty or suzerainty of the Sultan, who should appoint, or confirm the appointment of, a Governor to direct its administration.[83] Mensdorff and the Italian Ambassador, Marquis Imperiali, were then requested to express their views on the organization of the new Albanian State and, after they had done so, the Conference resolved to neutralize Albania. The next question for discussion was the frontiers to be given to the new State. It was agreed that Albania should extend to the Montenegrin frontier on the north and in the south to the Greek frontier. But differences of opinion between Mensdorff and Benckendorff, who represented respectively Albanian and Serbo-Montenegrin interests, prevented the Conference from arriving at any definitive recommendation. The Conference, having thus disposed of Albania, now turned its attention to the thorny question of access to the sea for Servia without, however, discussing the question of territorial access. After prolonged discussion, and at Benckendorff's suggestion, the Conference finally recommended that Servia should be given economic union with a neutral Albanian free port, which should be connected with Servia by an international railway under European control and guarded by a special international force. This railway was to be permitted to carry all classes of goods, inclusive of munitions of war.[84]

In giving an account of these discussions to Cartwright, Grey said that he thought that Austria-Hungary was prepared to resist Russia's demand that Scutari should be given to Montenegro.[85] The abandonment of the demand for the territorial expansion of Servia to the Adriatic—Grey continued —was unquestionably a triumph for the Austro-Hungarian Government and therefore he thought, and Prince Lichnowsky was of the same opinion, that for that reason Russia's particular wishes should be met.[86] On the following day—18 December— Grey invited Mensdorff to explain to the Conference Austria-Hungary's views on Albania's frontiers. Mensdorff was in possession of a map that had been sent to him from Vienna on which the towns of Ipek, Prisren, and Ochrida were marked as lying outside Albania, yet it was these districts that Austria-Hungary thought should be incorporated in the new State. Hence, Mensdorff did not produce this map in the Conference and instead asked the Austrian Foreign Ministry to allow him to prepare new maps for the next meeting of the Conference on which these towns would be shown within Albania's frontier.[87] At this meeting of the Conference, Grey told its members that the Servian delegate had informed him that his Government had instructed him to abandon the demand for direct territorial access to the Adriatic and therefore he (Grey) wanted the Governments represented in the Conference to authorize him to inform the Servian Government that the Conference had recommended that Servia be accorded an economic outlet to the Adriatic.[88] The question of the Aegean Islands also came up for discussion at this meeting. The Russian Ambassador thought that only Turkey should possess the islands of Tenedos, Imbros, Lemnos, and Samothrace. After lengthy discussion the Conference resolved unanimously that the islands must, under all circumstances, be declared neutral and placed under the guarantee of the Powers. The Conference was also unanimously agreed that Crete should go to Greece in full sovereignty and unconditionally. Mensdorff demanded in regard to Salonica that the Conference should find a solution compatible with Austria-Hungary's commercial interests. The French Ambassador's proposal that Constantinople should remain Turkish under all circumstances did not encounter any opposition.[89]

On 19 December Mensdorff discussed with Grey Austria-Hungary's relations with Servia and laid emphasis on the fact that his Government did not desire to place any obstacle in the path of Servia's political existence or economic prosperity. Austria-Hungary wished to live in friendship with her neighbour and not continually to be forced to take military measures against the aggressions of an inimical neighbour. Guaranties would have to be asked for, but it was difficult to define them. A commercial treaty that offered Servia solid advantages would be the best means of achieving this end. Grey had no objections to raise so long as the principle of the "open door" was upheld. "I observed", Grey reported to Cartwright, "that I understood Count Mensdorff not to make any special demand on any given point. The objection to guarantees was that they might not be consistent with Serbia's political independence, and I gathered from what he said that this objection was the reason why he did not suggest actual guarantees. This he confirmed." Grey also told Mensdorff that if Austria-Hungary did not, as had been feared, dispatch an ultimatum to Servia, and refrained from making demands incompatible with Servia's national independence, he would use all the influence he possessed to induce the Serbs to maintain friendly relations with Austria-Hungary.[90]

On 20 December the Conference of Ambassadors held its third meeting at which the question of a harbour for Servia on the Adriatic was discussed in great detail. The Conference resolved that its previous resolutions, which had now been approved by the different Governments, should be communicated to the Servian Minister, and it adopted proposals by the Russian Ambassador designed to safeguard Servia's rights in regard to the railway and terminal port by which she would have access to the Adriatic. Grey was of opinion that these concessions did not conflict with the resolutions already taken. The French, Italian, and German Ambassadors raised no objections to the Russian proposals, of which they said they would inform their respective Governments, while Mensdorff, who took no part in the discussion, declared that he would report to his Government what had taken place. A discussion then followed over the question of Albania's frontiers. The Conference came to the conclusion that the ethnical principle inspiring Austria-Hungary's attitude would not of itself win the support of all its members and therefore resolved that the Ambassadors of Austria-Hungary and Russia should each lay before the Conference at its next meeting on 2 January 1913 a map on which would be marked the frontiers proposed by his Government.[91]

Berchtold expressed his satisfaction with the resolutions passed by the Conference in regard to Albanian autonomy and a commercial outlet for Servia on the Adriatic. As to the Albanian frontier question, Berchtold said that Albania must be big enough to be able to remain independent and that it was essential that Albania's coastline joined that of Greece in the south and that of Montenegro in the north. He also remained firmly convinced that in delimiting the internal frontiers the ethnical principle should be the sole guide. Protests had been made by influential circles in Albania against the cession of Janina to Greece and of Scutari to Montenegro. Berchtold was not interested in Janina's future, but Scutari must remain Albanian. As to the Aegean Islands he thought those near to the Dardanelles and the coast of Asia Minor should belong to Turkey, while for all he cared the remainder might be given to Greece, only he thought the Powers should declare that these islands might not serve as naval bases. On learning of Berchtold's remarks, Grey said that the Conference was undoubtedly in agreement that all the Aegean Islands should be declared neutral and that Albania's frontiers should extend in the south as far as Greece and in the north as far as Montenegro, but nothing was decided about the Greek and Montenegrin frontiers remaining unaltered.[92] Cartwright at this juncture spared no pains in seeking to justify Austria-Hungary's conduct. He said that Austria-Hungary had to make a display of force and to act energetically because the Serbs would not otherwise have moderated their demands.[93] Nor did he think that Austria-Hungary would disarm before the Serbs had left the vicinity of the Adriatic.[94] Austro-Hungarian military movements aroused much anxiety in London, where King George V, who had expressed to Mensdorff his satisfaction at the progress made by the Conference of Ambassadors, complained of Austria-Hungary's vast military preparations and said that he feared lest a world war might be the outcome. The King was also strongly in favour of Montenegro's retaining Scutari. It was in vain that Mensdorff

tried to point out that the purely Albanian population of
Scutari and the surrounding district did not want to be
Montenegrin subjects. The King then told Mensdorff of a
conversation he had had with the German Emperor's brother,
Prince Henry of Prussia, who had recently been on a visit to
England. (The King asked Mensdorff not to report what he
told him to Vienna. Mensdorff reported the King's remark
in a telegram that same day!) Prince Henry asked the King
whether or not England would fight on the side of France and
Russia in event of a war between those Powers and Austria-
Hungary and Germany. The King replied: "Under certain
circumstances quite certainly." When Prince Henry, on receiving this answer, became very angry, the King said to him:
"Do you think we are less honourable than you are? You have
formal signed alliances. We have only drafts without signatures. Nevertheless, we could not allow either France or
Russia to be defeated." The King told Mensdorff that Grey
had approved of his reply and added that neither he nor his
Government wanted any such eventuality to occur.[95]

Since Grey's hopes that Austria-Hungary and Russia would
reach an agreement as to Albania's frontiers during the interval
between the third and fourth meetings of the Conference of
Ambassadors were disappointed, the Conference at its fourth
meeting on 2 January 1913 decided not to discuss this question and instead to deal with the problem of the Aegean
Islands. Here again unanimity was lacking. The French
Ambassador, M. Cambon, and Grey supported Benckendorff's
new proposal that the four islands lying off the Dardanelles,
which Russia had previously suggested should be given to
Turkey, should now be given to Greece under special guarantees. The Triple Alliance delegates, however, having no
instructions in this matter, maintained an attitude of reserve.
An attempt that had been in progress in London since 16
December 1912 with Grey as intermediary to bring about
agreement between the allied Balkan States and Turkey also
ended in failure because Turkey refused their demands for
Adrianople and the Aegean Islands. On 6 January 1913 the
negotiations were broken off. Meanwhile, the Conference of
Ambassadors had been debating what was to be done in event
of a failure of these negotiations and had also failed to reach
agreement. Grey proposed that the Powers should take common action at Constantinople, and it was also suggested that

a joint naval demonstration off Constantinople might be necessary to show that the Powers meant what they said. While Berchtold approved of common action by the Powers, he told Cartwright that he thought a naval demonstration might have serious consequences and for that reason he was opposed to it.[96] Nevertheless—he added—Austria-Hungary would not separate herself from the other Powers in this question. The proposal was soon afterwards abandoned. Meanwhile it became steadily more and more obvious that fighting would shortly be resumed between Turkey and the allied Balkan States.

Negotiations meanwhile proceeded over the question of Albania's frontiers and internal organization. Berchtold was opposed to an idea mooted in the Conference of Ambassadors that the delimitation of the frontiers should be entrusted to an international delimitation commission that would carry out its task on the spot. He thought this would prove a tedious and unnecessary way of dealing with the problem. In his opinion it was for the Conference to lay down the frontiers on broad lines and leave only details to be decided on the spot. He told Mensdorff that he should make it very clear to those of his colleagues at the Conference who supported Servian demands for the districts of Ipek, Djakova, Prisren and Dibra that were wholly, or almost wholly, inhabited by Albanians that the Serbs ruthlessly oppressed their Catholic and non-Slav subjects.[97] On the following day, however, he telegraphed to Mensdorff that in event of Russia's agreeing to the incorporation of Scutari in Albania on condition that the regulation of the River Bojana was undertaken, he (Mensdorff) was not in any discussion of Albania's frontiers to make use of the new map drawn by Giesl and Ippen (which he had already placed before the Conference), but that he was to refer to the map that had been sent to him from Vienna with his original instructions.[98] Berchtold also sent Mensdorff a new project for the organization of the Albanian State. Albania was to be an autonomous State under the Sultan's suzerainty. This would be purely nominal and, in fact, all ties between Turkey and Albania were to be cut. The new State would be declared neutral and placed under the guarantee of the six Great Powers. Order would be maintained in the country by an international gendarmerie composed of foreign soldiers who were not subjects of any of the Great Powers. Austria-Hungary and Italy would jointly propose the name of a prince to the other Powers as ruler of Albania.[99] Berchtold was indeed specially concerned to collaborate with Italy and not to afford her any ground for a quarrel. When the rumour was spread abroad in Rome, for example, that negotiations were in progress between the Austro-Hungarian and Montenegrin Governments for the cession of the Lovcen Mountain to Austria-Hungary—a cession that Italy could under no circumstances permit because, once master of the Lovcen, Austria-Hungary would be master of the whole of Montenegro—Berchtold hastened to describe the rumour as a pure invention and instructed Mensdorff to inform Grey of this fact.[100] Simultaneously, Mensdorff was ordered to tell Grey that Austria-Hungary could not yield on the question of the inclusion of Scutari in Albania. At the outset of the Conference, Italy had seemed not unwilling to give Scutari to Montenegro, but she now joined with Austria-Hungary in insisting upon its incorporation with Albania and the Italian Ambassador assisted Mensdorff in his efforts to achieve this end. Mensdorff, for his part, let it be understood that in event of a satisfactory solution of this problem, Berchtold was willing to consider Montenegro's wish for fertile territory and he mentioned the possibility of regulating the course of the River Bojana. Grey said that his wish was to see the question settled in a manner that would leave no resentment in anybody's mind. He was, however, afraid of the feeling in Russia over this question.

The Conference of Ambassadors resolved to discuss the Albanian Question at its meeting on 22 January, and on learning of this Berchtold instructed Mensdorff to declare that the Albanian frontiers, as defined in his instructions of 15 December 1912, must be regarded as Austria-Hungary's minimum demand. But Mensdorff was also told for his personal information only that in event of a favourable solution of the Scutari question Berchtold would be prepared to discuss the cession of Janina and the sources of the River Vogussa to Greece on the understanding that Janina had meanwhile been captured by the Greeks, and the possibility had arisen of a frontier delimitation by which the Kutzow-Wallachian district round the Pindus and Grammos Mountains maintained an economic connection with Albania.[101] The Foreign Office anxiously awaited the Conference's handling of the Albanian Question, because it realized only too well that both Berchtold and

Sazonov found themselves in difficult situations. Nicolson said that Russia was in a dangerous state of excitement and that there was a risk of demonstrations in the event of Sazonov's giving way over Scutari. Russia was very different to-day from what she had been in 1908-9 and was still smarting from the humiliation she had then suffered at Austria-Hungary's hands. For that reason—Nicolson told Cartwright—it would be difficult to bring about a compromise between Vienna and St. Petersburg.[102] The standpoints of the Russian and Austro-Hungarian Governments were as a matter of fact sharply opposed to one another. The Russian Ambassador told the Conference on 22 January 1913 that the King of Montenegro risked losing his throne if he was forced to give up his claim to Scutari after Montenegro had made such sacrifices. Mensdorff retorted that, politically, culturally, and economically, Scutari was an Albanian town which the northern Albanians regarded as their capital. Without Scutari Albania would not be viable. Montenegro's claims were wholly lacking in foundation. Count Benckendorff then endeavoured to refute Mensdorff's arguments. The German and Italian Ambassadors sided with Mensdorff and Grey, and the French Ambassador with Benckendorff. At this juncture the Conference was adjourned until its members had had time to consult their Governments.[103]

In reporting this discussion to his Government, Mensdorff said that on this occasion only the *town* of Scutari was spoken of and, therefore, that it was to be expected that if Russia gave way in this matter she would fight all the more determinedly to secure for Montenegro the districts outside the town itself. Mensdorff thought that he should, therefore, take the next opportunity of showing his opposition to any such course. And, in fact, Grey did suggest in a conversation with Mensdorff on 25 January that if Russia could be persuaded to agree to the incorporation of Scutari in Albania the surrounding districts might be given to Montenegro as compensation. Mensdorff bluntly replied that such a concession was impossible. But he went on to say that—speaking personally—he could draw Grey's attention to Ipek as a possible compensation in the event—and only in the event—that the remaining Austro-Hungarian proposals regarding the frontier between Albania and Montenegro were agreed to. He added that at the Conference he obviously could not mention the possibility of any such concession.[104] King George V said that he thought the Austro-Hungarian Government ought to make a concession to Russian wishes. His Government had supported Austria-Hungary in the Adriatic Question and must now respect Russia's demands in regard to Scutari. The King spoke of the agitated state of St. Petersburg society and of the difficulties in which Benckendorff and Sazonov found themselves. He said account must be taken of Russian public opinion, which still looked upon the events of 1908-9 as a Russian humiliation. Mensdorff justly retorted that the Austro-Hungarian Government had also to consider public opinion and could not allow the impression to become widespread that it was taking no thought for Austro-Hungarian interests.[105]

At the Conference on 25 January the discussion once more turned on the question of Scutari's future. Benckendorff and Mensdorff again opposed one another. Mensdorff declared it was impossible to separate Scutari from its hinterland. Although he rejected the French proposal that both banks of the River Bojana should be given to Montenegro on the ground that this would deprive Albania of the fertile soil she sorely needed, Mensdorff said it was quite possible to regulate the flow of the river so as to benefit both States. Benckendorff then stated that his instructions were to demand that the River Drina should be the frontier and that Scutari should be given to Montenegro. Mensdorff returned to the attack by suggesting the possibility of giving Montenegro territory taken from the Sandjak of Novibazar. This suggestion Benckendorff indignantly rejected on the ground that it was a matter for Servia and Montenegro to settle between themselves, since it had been agreed that the victors should themselves delimit the frontiers of conquered territories. Thus the Conference again failed to reach agreement. Both Benckendorff and Mensdorff wanted their Governments to arrange a compromise.[106] At Germany's instigation, Lichnowsky and Grey set to work to persuade the Austro-Hungarian and Russian Governments to come to an agreement. Berchtold warmly welcomed the idea.[107] It was proposed that Scutari and a portion of Lake Scutari should be retained by Albania to the accompaniment of certain guarantees for the control of the Bojana and the draining of the lake. The northern frontier of Albania would run from a point that was to be fixed later along the eastern shore of Lake Scutari in an easterly direction until it met the River Drina. Notwithstanding the fact that he had many objections to it, Berchtold decided to accept this compromise.[108] But when, before the opening of the Conference on 29 January, Mensdorff informed Grey of the concessions that Berchtold was prepared to make, Grey replied that they were still a long way away from a real compromise. Indeed, it appeared that both Grey and Lichnowsky expected Austria-Hungary to make still greater concessions. Consequently, Mensdorff told his Government that he feared that nothing would be achieved by the present concessions.[109] The Conference, therefore, decided to discontinue its discussion of the Albanian Question for the time being.

On the following day the German Emperor, William II, told the Austro-Hungarian Ambassasor in Berlin that, while Germany would fulfil its treaty obligations to its ally, it would be difficult for him to convince his people of the necessity for fighting merely because Scutari or Lake Scutari should belong to Montenegro rather than Albania.[110] Under the impression made upon him by the Emperor William II's statement, and also by the news from London, Berchtold decided upon further concessions, which he communicated to Mensdorff to be used in his negotiations with Grey. These were the cession of the Orthodox monastery of Visoki-Decani to Montenegro and, as a final gesture in case of absolute necessity, the cession of Prisren to Servia.[111] When, however, Mensdorff again talked with Grey on 31 January on the subject of a compromise, it became clear that Russia, with French support, was asking far more in the way of compensation for Albania's retention of Scutari than Austria-Hungary was ready to concede. Russia was now demanding the cession to Montenegro of the Malissori tribes, as well as territory on both banks of the Bojana, and was also upholding her original demand for the Drina frontier and the separation from Albania of the towns of Ipek, Prisren and Djakova. (According to Mensdorff, Russia was irrevocably resolved upon the cession of Djakova.) Mensdorff thereupon declared that upon this basis a compromise was impossible. At the same time he asked his own Government to consider whether further concessions should not be made. Ipek and Prisren obviously would not suffice. Moreover, he was not in a position to say whether or not Russia would abandon her opposition in regard to Scutari, etc., in return for Djakova.[112] All that was certain—Mensdorff told Berchtold—was that Benckendorff was supported by Cambon, and to a certain degree by Grey, who nevertheless endeavoured to appear impartial, and against them Lichnowsky and Imperiali constituted no real counterweight.[113] Berchtold received the news of Russia's demand for Djakova with unconcealed annoyance. He said that he regarded this town as the political and economic capital of the Mohammedan Malissori, whose welfare was a matter of the greatest importance for him, because they seemed to be destined to form Albania's natural bulwark against the Slavs. Moreover, Djakova was the place in northern Albania where Albanian nationalism was strongest.[114] Since the British and German Governments considered that Berchtold's previous offers were insufficient to satisfy Russia's demands, they renewed their efforts to induce him to make even greater concessions. Berchtold replied that he was quite willing to make further small concessions to Montenegro, but that he must insist on Albania's retaining Djakova.

On 3 February the Conference of Ambassadors resumed its discussion of Albania's frontiers. On the same day hostilities again broke out between Turkey and the allied Balkan States. The peace conference had proved unsuccessful because Turkey was only prepared to cede a portion of the city of Adrianople, and was unwilling to make any definite statement regarding the Aegean Islands, while the Balkan States refused to make peace on these terms. The negotiations between Rumania and Bulgaria had also ended in failure. In both instances, while Berchtold had acted in accord with Grey, he had also endeavoured as far as possible to further Turkish interests. About this time Prince Hohenlohe's visit to St. Petersburg contributed to lessen the tension in Austro-Russian relations. Each Empire showed a welcome tendency to cease from regarding the other as a potential aggressor. Nevertheless, Hohenlohe's mission failed to achieve its principal objective—mutual reduction in armaments. Discussions took place over Scutari in which Sazonov stressed the great danger that would threaten the Montenegrin dynasty from failure to secure Scutari for Montenegro, while Hohenlohe emphasized the necessity for having a viable Albania.[115] All this did not augur well for the success of the Conference of Ambassadors, which resumed its discussions on 6 February with a report from Grey on a proposal for a compromise made by Lichnowsky after consultation with Grey and Mensdorff. This plan foreshadowed certain concessions to Montenegro. The Visoki-Decani Ortho-

dox monastery, Ipek, and Prisren, excepting the district of
Luma, were to remain outside the Albanian frontier, while
Djakova and Dibra were to be incorporated with Albania.[116]
While the Italian Ambassador supported the proposal,
Benckendorff gave no indication that he would accept it.
Under these circumstances Grey thought the best way of
resolving the differences would be to send an international
commission to delimit Albania's frontiers "on the basis of
ethnography, geography and customs of the locality." Mensdorff opposed this suggestion.[117] Since Benckendorff said that
Russia would not give up Djakova and Dibra, he arranged
with Mensdorff for a conference between the Austro-Hungarian
specialist on Albanian affairs, Theodore Ippen, and a Russian
expert named Petragoff. Their meeting, however, produced
no result. Petragoff maintained that Montenegro's claim to
Djakova and Dibra was well founded, while Ippen was no less
convinced that they belonged to Albania.[118] True to his rôle
as mediator, Grey continued to seek a solution to these highly
controversial problems despite Mensdorff's rejection of his
proposal for an international delimitation commission. When
Grey pointed out to Mensdorff that it was hardly to be
expected that the Conference would agree to the Austro-
Hungarian demand for Scutari, Djakova and Dibra after
Russia had given way in the Adriatic Question, Mensdorff
retorted that the Conference had deprived Albania of Ipek
and Prisren at Russia's demand.[119]

At Benckendorff's suggestion Grey made a fresh proposal
at the Conference on 14 February regarding Albania's frontiers.
The new suggestion was that Mount Tarabos should be
included in Montenegro and that Albania should lose Djakova,
Dibra and Luma. Mensdorff voiced his profound disappointment and declared that, while Austria-Hungary would not
surrender Djakova and Dibra, the inclusion of Mount Tarabos
in Montenegro would make the possession of Scutari by Albania
purely illusory.[120] Mensdorff was supported by the German
and Italian Ambassadors who, nevertheless, said that the
Austro-Hungarian Government would have to give up one of
these towns.[121] In conversation with Mensdorff, Grey said that
he was doing all he could to change Russia's attitude, but that
he did not think she would beat a retreat in regard to Djakova
and Dibra. Nevertheless, the last word had not yet been
spoken. But—Grey added—he had no desire to have his voice

used to speak that last word. That must be done either by Mensdorff or Benckendorff at the Conference, or directly by either the Russian or Austro-Hungarian Government. In that eventuality he would again propose the dispatch of an international delimitation commission.[122] Berchtold, like Mensdorff, was strongly opposed to the sending of a commission, so he decided, in the hope of bringing about a speedy solution of the question, to make yet another offer. He now proposed the cession of the district of Rekatol, inclusive of the town of Dibra, on the understanding that the Conference would then adopt the frontier demarcated by Austria-Hungary in its entirety. Berchtold thought that he had thus struck a balance between Russian and Austro-Hungarian concessions—Prisren, Ipek and Dibra against Scutari and Djakova.[123] But Grey was still not satisfied. He had pressed the Russian Government to agree to a compromise if Berchtold gave up Djakova, and therefore all he could do was simply to transmit Berchtold's new proposal to St. Petersburg without comment. He instructed Cartwright to inform Berchtold of his attitude, and once more to advise the Austro-Hungarian Government to abandon Djakova and Dibra, while at the same time he told Mensdorff for transmission to Vienna that before the news of Berchtold's latest offer had reached St. Petersburg the Russian Government had decided to give up Mount Tarabos and Luma if the Austro-Hungarian Government gave up Djakova and Dibra.[124]

In his conversations with Berchtold, Cartwright did his utmost to induce him to accept the Russian compromise and stressed the fact that Grey had met with no success in St. Petersburg because Servia refused to allow Djakova and Dibra to remain Albanian, and also could not be persuaded by friendly means to withdraw her troops from this town. Moreover, Russia could not stand aside and watch the Servian troops being expelled by force. Grey's single-handed efforts had therefore been in vain. None the less, Berchtold insisted that Albania must retain Djakova. He also rejected as useless and impracticable Cartwright's proposal that either the decision should be left to an international commission as proposed by Grey, or else Djakova and the surrounding district should be created an autonomous enclave under supervision by the Great Powers.[125] A suggestion emanating from the Foreign Office that Servia should buy Djakova from Albania and assure the Albanians the use of its market did nothing to bridge the gulf between Austria-Hungary and Russia. In a long memorandum handed to Grey on 26 February, Mensdorff set down all the reasons that made it impossible for Berchtold to allow Servia to take Djakova or to adopt any of the proposals that had been made.[126] Grey was in despair. He saw no possibility of bringing Russia and Austria-Hungary into agreement, yet it was obviously absurd that the Great Powers should go to war over a town like Djakova with only six thousand inhabitants.[127] Indeed it is difficult for anyone who studies the negotiations between the Russian and Austro-Hungarian statesmen and ambassadors not to gain the impression that in reality they were less concerned about this or that town and this or that tiny strip of territory than about the preservation of their prestige in the Balkans. The obstinacy with which they maintained their opposing points of view can only be understood on the basis of this supposition.[128]

Nevertheless, Berchtold undoubtedly desired a speedy and permanent settlement of the Albanian frontier question, because he feared that the King of Montenegro, whose troops were besieging Scutari with Servian assistance, would not again surrender the town after he had captured it. Yet Berchtold would not give up Djakova. In order to show his readiness to compromise, however, Berchtold said he was willing to agree to the sending of an international commission for the purpose of deciding to which State Djakova should belong. In return he would expect Russia to accept the Austro-Hungarian standpoint in regard to the left bank of the Bojana and Lake Scutari. Nor was this all. Berchtold went on to demand that, before any decision was taken in the matter of Djakova, the resolutions of the Conference of Ambassadors on other matters should be communicated to the Servian and Montenegrin Governments with the observation that the Powers intended them to be put into effect, and that a demand should also be simultaneously sent to these two Governments to withdraw their troops from the districts already assigned to Albania. In thanking Grey for what he had already done, Berchtold asked him to bring the Albanian frontier question once more before the Conference and expressed the hope that Grey would be able to arrange "something" with regard to Scutari as well as to speed up the ambassadors' deliberations.[129] Grey was all the more willing to accede to Berchtold's request because he had learnt from St. Petersburg that if Austria-Hungary gave up Djakova Russia would undertake to keep the Montenegrins out of Scutari and to order Servia to withdraw her troops from the districts assigned to Albania.[130]

At its meeting on 6 March the Conference of Ambassadors did, in fact, pass a resolution recommending the various Governments represented in it to make a renewed *démarche* in Belgrade and a *démarche* in Cettinje in the terms of the communication made by Grey on 23 January to the Servian Minister in London on the subject of the evacuation by Servian troops of the districts assigned to Albania.[131] After a lengthy discussion the Conference also resolved that a general agreement was possible once an understanding had been reached in the Djakova question.[132] Berchtold expressed great satisfaction at these resolutions, because he wholeheartedly desired the permanent delimitation of Albania's frontiers in order to place an obstacle in the way of further Servian advances and to prevent the capture of Scutari by the Montenegrins. For this reason he deemed it specially important that Russia should formally declare that she would prevent the Montenegrins from entering Scutari and compel the withdrawal of Servian troops from the districts assigned to Albania in event of an Austro-Hungarian renunciation of Djakova. Berchtold, nevertheless, did not wish to bind himself to give up Djakova and he suggested to Grey that he should try to secure the desired undertaking from Russia in return for Berchtold's agreement to leave the fate of Djakova to be decided by an international commission.[133] Berchtold also spoke in the same sense to Cartwright, to whom he suggested that the Conference of Ambassadors should declare that the question of Albania's northern and north-eastern frontiers was now settled, Scutari was Albanian, and that the future of Djakova should be decided by a local commission. Djakova should remain in Servian hands until the commission gave its decision.[134]

Notwithstanding these further Austro-Hungarian concessions Russia continued to insist that Servia must have Djakova. Berchtold was forced to recognize, from the accounts that Grey gave to him of his neogtiations with Russia, that the Russian Government was not prepared to induce Montenegro to raise the siege of Scutari, or to force Servia to withdraw her troops from the districts that were to be given to Albania, unless Servia obtained Djakova. As a further proof of his readiness to compromise, Sazonov said he would be content with an assurance—a verbal assurance to Grey would suffice—on the part of the Austro-Hungarian Government that it recognized as a matter of principle that Djakova should be Servian. An international commission could subsequently investigate the economic problems of the district.[135] Berchtold categorically rejected this proposal. He said with some justification that while on paper the Conference of Ambassadors undoubtedly passed resolutions in favour of the rigorous execution of its decisions in practice it shrank back affrighted before the prospect of employing the necessary forcible measures. When Sazonov said that Servia would not give way, then—Mensdorff could tell this to Grey—it was useless to continue to take part in what were no more than theoretical discussions, so long as Servia and Montenegro were not compelled to carry out the unanimous resolutions of the Powers regarding the military evacuation of the territory given to Albania and the cessation of military operations.[136] Berchtold's rebuke was wholly un-justified in so far as it was directed at Grey, who had spared no pains in seeking to achieve agreement between Vienna and St. Petersburg, even though he did support the Russian demand for Djakova. Grey replied to Berchtold's charges by saying that there was nothing more he could do and that he intended to say so in the House of Commons. There was no longer any object to be served by the Conference of Ambassadors con-tinuing its discussions.[137]

It was at this time, too, that Grey learnt by experience how hard it was effectively to influence small States in their policy and actions. Grey had requested the Servian Government to refrain from supporting Montenegro in her siege of Scutari. He received the reply that Servia was bound by treaty to render assistance to Montenegro at her demand and, therefore, a refusal to come to Montenegro's aid would be tantamount to a violation of the alliance between the two countries. For this reason Servia could only stop sending troops when Mon-tenegro said she no longer needed them or that she was placing the future of Scutari in the hands of the Powers.[138] This almost unbelievable behaviour on the part of Servia and Montenegro is only to be explained by the presence in Belgrade of Russian advisers, especially the Russian Minister, M. Hartwig, who stiffened the backs of the leading statesmen in Belgrade and Cettinje, and also by the fact that these statesmen had heard from St. Petersburg that Russia would not yield in the Djakova question.[139] It was the knowledge of these facts that induced Mensdorff (who never wearied in seeking to justify Grey's attitude to the Austro-Hungarian Government) to ask Berchtold whether or not any useful purpose was being served by continuing to pursue the policy that had hitherto been pursued by Austria-Hungary in regard to Albania.[140] As a matter of fact, Berchtold did abandon his opposition to Servia's retention of Djakova out of regard for the danger threatening the settlement of the whole Albanian Question in the event of Montenegro's capturing Scutari. Berchtold himself declared that his change of policy was due to sympathy for the desperate plight of the besieged civil population of Scutari and to his desire to save the Roman Catholics and Mohammedans from the brutalities that might be inflicted upon them by the victorious Montenegrins. In truth his decision was more probably animated by his fear that Scutari might fall to the Montenegrins, and therewith the plan for an independent Albania become unrealizable, unless an agreement was speedily concluded with Russia.[141] He nevertheless made his surrender of Djakova depend upon what was in his eyes a self-evident condition: the agreement on principle of the Powers to take those measures that had already been drawn up for the safety of the inhabitants of the districts that were to be ceded to Servia and Montenegro, and to recognize the line already laid down as Albania's northern and north-eastern frontier, inclusive of the Bojana river and Scutari.[142]

Grey breathed a sigh of relief. The Conference of Ambassadors, at his suggestion, at once resolved to take the security measures necessary for the protection of the Roman Catholic and Mohammedan inhabitants of the districts that were to be handed over to Servia and Montenegro, and also to demand of the Servian and Montenegrin Governments the raising of the siege of Scutari, cessation of hostile acts in the districts that were to become Albanian, and the evacuation of those districts.[143] Berchtold pressed for immediate action and Grey did his utmost to give effect to his wishes. A joint *démarche* by the Powers was to be made in Cettinje. The war party in Vienna demanded the landing of Austro-Hungarian troops. On Berchtold's advice this was postponed for the time being lest it should arouse Italy's jealousy.[144] Grey, too, was opposed to any unilateral action by Austria-Hungary, because it would arouse anxiety in Russia and Italy.[145] In event of Montenegro proving recalcitrant Grey thought it might be necessary to stage a naval demonstration, but it would have to be a joint demonstration by the Powers, since Russia would certainly not agree to give a mandate to Italy and Austria-Hungary for this purpose.[146] At its sitting on 28 March the Conference of Ambassadors passed a resolution to this effect after Sazonov had agreed to an united naval demonstration in which Russia would, nevertheless, not participate. The British Admiralty received orders to prepare for this demonstration.[147] Berchtold urged all possible speed in making the preparations, because Russia's attitude was such as to make these Balkan States doubt the seriousness of the Conference's decisions. He said that Servia was pursuing a policy of obstruction and wanted to send fresh troops into Albania. If Montenegro were to resume the bombardment of Scutari the naval demonstration should take place at once. Berchtold disagreed with the idea of a joint *démarche* by the Powers at Belgrade and Cettinje on the ground that stronger action was called for, and he drew attention to the subterfuges, and at times blunt refusals, of the Servian Prime Minister.[148]

On 30 March Vienna received news of the renewed bombardment of Scutari, which was at once transmitted to London with the request that coercive measures should be taken against Montenegro.[149] On the following day all the members of the Conference of Ambassadors stated that their Governments would take part in a naval demonstration. The Russian Ambassador explained that, while his Government certainly approved of the demonstration, it could not take part in it because Russia had no warships in the Mediterranean.[150] The carrying-out of the coercive measures that had been planned was, nevertheless, so dilatory that what was actually done did not suffice to compel Montenegro to raise the siege of Scutari.[151] On 22 April Berchtold said that the situation was more critical than it had ever been. The international blockade of Montenegro had signally failed to produce any effect, and it was now imperative that an international force should be landed in order to occupy Antivari and Dulcigno under cover of the guns of the fleet. While Italy and Germany supported this proposal, France's decision depended upon Great Britain's action. Nicolson observed that France was against the landing of troops. If Scutari falls, Berchtold retorted, the

Austro-Hungarian Government will not leave Montenegro in possession of the town. On the contrary, Austria-Hungary will drive the Montenegrins out of it either—if possible—in conjunction with other Powers or otherwise by herself or with Italian help.[152] Berchtold's forebodings were justified in the event. On that day—22 April—Scutari fell.[153] Montenegro's action—Mensdorff said in London—in the face of the declarations by the Powers and the international squadron of warships anchored in Montenegrin waters made patent to the whole world that Montenegro simply ignored the wishes of the European Great Powers. Berchtold demanded that coercive measures should at once be put into effect—either the occupation of the Montenegrin ports or their bombardment. If the Powers were unwilling to do this—Berchtold added—Austria-Hungary would herself drive the Montenegrins out of Scutari.[154]

At the Conference of Ambassadors on 28 April it proved impossible to achieve agreement on what was to be done. Mensdorff's demand for coercive measures was supported by the Italian and German Ambassadors, while the French Ambassador said he did not believe that his Government would agree to such measures and instead would prefer that certain promises should be made to Montenegro on the condition that she submitted to the Great Powers' behests. Even Grey himself said that, while he was prepared to suggest military action to the Cabinet, he did not believe that the Cabinet would sanction it. He, too, would prefer to persuade the King of Montenegro to evacuate Scutari by means of promises.[155] This unsatisfactory state of affairs induced Berchtold to inform the British Government that Austria-Hungary would take action against Montenegro and that he still hoped that some of the Powers would join with her. He added that it would be specially gratifying were Grey in a position to inform the Conference that Austria-Hungary could count at least upon Great Britain's naval assistance.[156] The Conference, none the less, still hesitated to resort to force. Grey told the Conference that Montenegro had enquired, through Nicolson, whether or not the Powers would be prepared, in event of a Montenegrin abandonment of Scutari, to grant Montenegro territorial compensation and financial assistance. The Foreign Secretary proposed that the Conference should return the answer that Montenegro would receive financial assistance if she peacefully withdrew her forces from Scutari, and that if she did not do so, she would be expelled by force and would receive no financial assistance. All the members of the Conference expressed their readiness to bring this proposal to the notice of their Governments.[157] These resolutions did not satisfy Berchtold, who said that he could find no trace of definite coercive measures nor of a time limit for the evacuation of Scutari. Besides— Berchtold continued—he had asked for the unconditional submission of Montenegro to the will of Europe and therefore was opposed to any promise of financial support before Montenegro had acted upon the Powers' orders to hand over Scutari. It would, therefore, be impossible for Austria-Hungary to take part in a *démarche* containing a formal promise of financial help, although she would gladly see the other Powers make a *démarche* on these lines.[158]

A meeting was held in Vienna, on 2 May, of the Council of Ministers for Joint Affairs, to discuss the situation. The minutes that were kept of its discussions clearly reveal the firmness with which Austro-Hungarian statesmen were resolved to break Montenegro's resistance, if necessary by force, and to risk not only war with Servia, but also possibly with Russia. After he had given the assembled Ministers a bird's eye view of the whole situation, and had demonstrated to them that Albania could not be viable without Scutari, Berchtold pointed to the dangers that would in future threaten the Dual Monarchy from Servia and Montenegro unless their steadily-growing ambitions were nipped in the bud. This task of curbing their ambitions was all the more perilous not only because it would lessen the influence wielded by important persons in Russian Government circles who disapproved of Servia's presumptuous policy, and would also detrimentally affect French public opinion, but because it might result in an unwelcome change in the attitude of the Austrophil British Cabinet which might be forced to alter its policy out of regard for the other Entente Powers and for British public opinion that was peculiarly susceptible to foreign influences. It was for this reason— Berchtold continued—that he had informed the Conference of Ambassadors that he must reserve for Austria-Hungary the right to take at the given moment coercive measures to enforce obedience to their—Europe's—decisions. Italy was prepared, under certain conditions, to join in a war against Montenegro. After Berchtold had ended his *exposé* the Ministers, almost without exception, expressed themselves as strongly in favour of forcible measures, even though these should result in war, and voted the necessary financial credits.[159]

Meanwhile, Grey was doing his utmost in the Conference of Ambassadors to find a solution that would prevent Austria-Hungary from taking coercive measures and enable the Powers to act in common—an endeavour that encountered opposition on the part of Russia and France. It was at this juncture that the news reached London and Vienna that Montenegro had decided to offer, unconditionally, to evacuate Scutari and that she asked the Austro-Hungarian Government to postpone any military action for forty-eight hours.[160] Berchtold told Mensdorff that he did not intend to answer this request or to send Montenegro a short-term ultimatum. The Conference of Ambadsadors took cognizance of Montenegro's decision with much satisfaction and advised the European Governments represented in the Conference to take the necessary measures for the evacuation of Scutari.[161] On 14 May detachments were landed from the international fleet and the control of Scutari passed into the hands of the European Great Powers. Berchtold could congratulate himself on the victory won for him by his tenacity in refusing to alter his decisions. Nevertheless, it was unquestionably Grey whom Europe had to thank for the fact that this success had been achieved without bloodshed.[162]

The settlement of the Scutari Question did not bring to an end either Grey's or the Conference's labours. Three questions still awaited solution: (1) The administration of Albania. (2) The demarcation of the southern and south-eastern frontiers of Albania. (3) The future of the Aegean Islands. Above all, it was essential to restore peace between Turkey and the four allied Balkan States. The conditions for peace laid down by the Powers had been rejected by both sides. Notwithstanding the fact that she had now lost Janina and Adrianople, Turkey refused to make the required concessions, while the Balkan States increased their demands. They were now asking for a voice in the discussion of the Albanian Question and in that of the Aegean Islands. On 5 May Grey placed before the Conference the project of a preliminary peace that had been drafted by Cambon, in which Berchtold would have liked to make certain alterations. He refrained from suggesting them in order to avoid further dissension between the Powers. The delegates of the Balkan States, and especially the Greek delegate, Venizelos, who demanded to be heard on all questions affecting Albania and the Aegean Islands, sought to drag out the negotiations. But Grey lost patience with them and demanded that the representatives of the belligerent States should sign the peace preliminaries that had been laid before them. In event of a refusal—he said—they could leave London. After having received the assent of their Governments they signed on 30 May 1913 the preliminary treaty of peace. The signatories undertook to leave to the Powers the decision in the Albanian frontier question as well as in all other questions affecting Albania, and also in regard to the future of the Turkish islands in the Aegean with the exception of Crete and the peninsula of Mount Athos.

The division of the spoils among the victors produced yet another war in which Bulgaria was confronted by the united forces of Servia, Greece, and Montenegro, to which were subsequently added those of Turkey and Rumania. Bulgaria was heavily defeated and was forced to sign on 10 August in Bucharest a peace treaty which involved her in large territorial losses. The Conference of Ambassadors in London was meanwhile wrestling with the three questions still awaiting solution. The longer the negotiations were drawn out the clearer became the differences between France and Russia on the one side and on the other side the Triple Alliance. Austria-Hungary and Italy sought a speedy and permanent administrative organization of Albania and also that there should no longer be any question of the Sultan's suzerainty. They wanted a European prince to be chosen as ruler and the succession established in accordance with the law of primogeniture. Their proposals met with opposition from France and Russia. The Conference postponed taking any decision regarding the legal relationship between the Sultan and Albania. Cambon and Benckendorff were opposed to any immediate setting up of a permanent organization and instead wanted to establish only a provisional system of government. Cambon, indeed, would not hear of a prince as ruler and said that France would prefer the appointment of a High Commissioner.[163] Towards the middle of June the Austro-Hungarian and Italian Ambassadors placed before the Conference a draft of a plan for the future organization of Albania by which Albania should become an independent State ruled over by a Prince appointed by the six Great Powers with the right of succession secured to his family in accordance with the law of primogeniture.

Albania was to be declared neutral and placed under the guarantee of the six Great Powers. After the foreign troops at present in occupation of the country had left, an international commission composed of one representative from each of the six Great Powers, and a single Albanian representative, should be appointed for the purpose of organizing the entire administration and ordered to report on their work at the end of six months. The appointments of the commissioners should be for five years with the possibility of renewal.[164]

Cambon and Benckendorff again raised objections. They were opposed—they said—to the choice of a Prince and to the setting up of a permanent administration. A deadlock now ensued because Austria-Hungary and Italy refused to give up their proposal. All Grey's efforts to overcome it were at first unsuccessful and it was only very gradually that he succeeded in bringing the opposing standpoints closer together.[165] The Conference resolved to abandon the idea of the Sultan's suzerainty over Albania and to advise the Governments represented in it that Albania should be declared a completely independent State.[166] But for a long time it proved impossible to reach agreement over the date for the election of a Prince and also as to whether or not there should be a provisional or permanent administration. When Grey approached the Austro-Hungarian Government with the suggestion that it should assent to a provisional administration since there was no hope of securing agreement for a permanent administration before the Conference adjourned for its summer recess, Berchtold not only rejected the proposal, but said that Austria-Hungary and Italy must reserve the right to act independently in the event that no decision was taken by the Conference in the matter of a permanent administration.[167]

Grey took Berchtold's remark more seriously than it was meant and strongly advised him against any such action, since in certain quarters it would be taken to mean that Austria-Hungary and Italy intended to partition Albania.[168] Throughout July negotiations were, as a matter of fact, carried on intensively under the impulsion of Grey's repeated threats to adjourn the Conference, and on 15 July Mensdorff and Imperiali brought forward a revised plan that satisfied the demands of the French and Russian Ambassadors in certain particulars while providing for the election of a Prince within six months. The duration of the Control Commission was

fixed at five years with the possibility of prolongation—a
provision to which the Russian Ambassador in particular
raised objections.[169] Since he had secured for Albania the
status of an independent neutral sovereign State ruled over by
a Prince chosen by the Great Powers, Berchtold felt that he
could make a concession to Russia's wishes on this point and
therefore gave his assent to the prolongation of the Control
Commission's mandate to ten years.[170] This concession speeded
up the negotiations, and after minor difficulties had been
overcome, the Conference on 29 July adopted the Statute for
Albania, of which the principal provisions were as follows:

1. Albania is an autonomous sovereign hereditary princi-
    pality under the guarantee of the six Powers. The Prince
    is to be chosen by the six Powers.

2. All ties of suzerainty between Turkey and Albania are
    broken.

3. Albania is neutral. Its neutrality is guaranteed by the
    six Powers.

4. The control of the civil administration and the finances
    will be entrusted to an international commission com-
    posed of a delegate from each of the six Powers and an
    Albanian delegate.

5. The duration of the powers of this commission will be for
    ten years and may be prolonged in case of necessity.

6. This commission will be given the task of drawing up a
    a plan for the organization of all branches of the
    Albanian administration and will report within six
    months.

7. The Prince will be appointed at the latest within six
    months. Until his appointment, and until the formation
    of a definitive national government, the international
    commission will control the existing native authorities
    ["autorités indigènes existantes"] and the gendar-
    merie.[171]

There followed provisions for the appointment of a com-
mandant and officers for the gendarmerie who would be
responsible for the maintenance of order in the country.[172]
    The work of the Conference of Ambassadors, nevertheless,
did not end with the delimitation of the northern and north-
eastern frontiers of Albania and the administrative organization
of the new State. A number of other questions remained to be
settled, of which the most important were the delimitation of

the southern and south-eastern frontier of Albania and the
future of the Aegean Islands. Now it was the turn of Greece
to make far-reaching demands, and in her fight to secure their
fulfilment Greece was supported by France, and also to some
extent by the German Emperor, William II, who was brother-
in-law of King Constantine I of Greece. It quickly became
evident that the problem of the delimitation of Albania's
southern and south-eastern frontiers could not be solved unless
a solution was simultaneously found to the problem of the
future ownership of the Aegean Islands. Agreement over either
question proved impossible. Under Venizelos' leadership
Greece put forward extensive demands. She was, indeed,
willing to give up Valona. On the other hand, she demanded
Janina (which she had not yet captured) and the neighbouring
harbour of Santi Quaranta, as well as the district of Argyrocastro and Koritza.[173] Austria-Hungary and Italy were determined to reject these demands. All kinds of proposals were
made in regard to the ownership of the Aegean Islands, and it
was even suggested that, with the exception of the four islands
of Tenedos, Imbros, Lemnos and Samothrace lying off the
Dardanelles, which should go to Turkey, all the islands should
be given to Greece. This, like other proposals, met with
opposition. Grey strove in vain to achieve a compromise in
regard to the questions of the Albanian frontier and the
Aegean Islands. Indeed, matters reached such a pass that
Germany asked whether the Aegean Question should not be
excluded from the discussions and left for decision by the
belligerent Powers.[174] Berchtold refused this suggestion. A few
weeks later he said that he would leave the initiative in the
matter of Albania's southern and south-eastern frontiers to
Italy, since he was less interested in these frontiers than in
Albania's northern and north-eastern frontiers.[175] Italy did,
in fact, take the initiative, and on 19 March proposed to the
Conference a frontier exceedingly advantageous for Albania,
although Italy herself did not believe that it would meet with
acceptance. But, whatever the decision, Italy and Berchtold
were resolved that Koritza must under all circumstances be
retained for Albania.[176] The Conference took cognisance of
the proposal without discussing it.

The Conference found far heavier and more serious obstacles
in its path when France and Russia demanded that Greece
should be given the coast opposite Corfu as far as Cape Kefalu.

Austria-Hungary and Italy protested strongly, because they feared it was the prelude to the construction of a powerful naval base. In addition, Russia claimed Koritza for Greece, while France said that Austria-Hungary's project for an Albanian southern and south-eastern frontier was unacceptable.[177] The longer the negotiations dragged on, the wider became the gulf between the opposing points of view. At the beginning of May Mensdorff reported that it was impossible to foresee how things would turn out. The French Ambassador enthusiastically supported Greek claims and in the question of the Aegean Islands agreement seemed impossible. Grey spared no pains to achieve a compromise. Moreover, he was not to be shaken in his conviction that the question of the Aegean Islands could not be separated from that of the delimitation of Albania's southern and south-eastern frontier.[178] He made an attempt to induce Italy to compromise over the islands. But Imperiali stressed the fact that Italy was bound by the Treaty of Lausanne to return the islands in Italian occupation to Turkey after the latter Power had fulfilled her obligations in regard to the withdrawal of her troops from Tripoli. At the same time he hinted that his Government might give its assent to a compromise in the event of a formula being found that would safeguard both certain interests and the *amour propre* of Turkey, and also if concessions were made in regard to Albania's southern and south-eastern frontier in conformity with Austro-Hungarian and Italian views. Imperiali then indicated Cape Stylos and Koritza as the two places over which Austria-Hungary and Italy were not prepared to bargain. Grey thereupon asked the Ambassadors to enquire of their Governments if a compromise was possible on this basis.[179] Benckendorff at once said that he had never been empowered to give up Koritza. And, indeed, it quickly proved that no compromise was, in fact, possible on this basis. For, on 11 June, the Italian Ambassador declared that his Government was unable by reason of its treaty obligations to take part in discussions for the purpose of inducing Turkey to accept these proposals. Since it was in the interest of the Powers to protect Turkish interests, and to assure the safety of Turkey's Asiatic provinces, the Italian Government—Imperiali continued—did not doubt that, when the Powers came to decide the fate of the Aegean Islands, they would share Italy's views and would safeguard the interests and prestige of Turkey.

Simultaneously with this statement Mensdorff and Imperiali informed the Conference that they must abide by their declarations on the subject of Albania's southern and south-eastern frontiers. Cambon at once retorted that his instructions did not permit him to assent to the Austro-Hungarian and Italian proposals for the delimitation of these frontiers, especially with regard to Koritza. Finally, Grey said that in this difficult situation he could not "become a party to any agreement without being prepared to join in imposing it or to see it imposed upon Greece by force". He added that this was a very serious decision to have to take and that he must first consult with the Prime Minister and the Cabinet.[180]

On 1 July Mensdorff handed Grey a memorandum setting forth the conditions on which Austria-Hungary was prepared to allow an international commission to decide certain questions in connection with Albania's southern and south-eastern frontier. These conditions were: The Albanian coast must extend as far as Phtelia. Koritza and the surrounding district must be Albanian. A delegate from Rumania must be admitted to the Conference in order to take part in the discussions over the future of the Wallachians living around Mount Pindus. The international commission should be left free to delimit the rest of the frontier on condition that for every concession made to Greece at the expense of the minimum proposals made by Italy and Austria-Hungary, Greece was to make a corresponding concession in regard to the Aegean Islands. Greece should only obtain districts inhabited by a Greek majority and in determining the nationality of the inhabitants their mother tongue should be taken as furnishing the best evidence. Before the commission began its labours the Greeks must evacuate Koritza, the coastal district to the north of Thalia, and the island of Sasseno. All districts assigned by the commission to Albania must immediately be evacuated by the Greeks.

Grey at once said that these proposals were inacceptable. If Phtelia and Koritza were in principle to be regarded as Albanian, it must also be recognized in principle that the area inhabited by the Wallachians should become Greek to the accompaniment of safeguards for religion, language, and education. Furthermore, it would have in principle to be admitted that all the Aegean Islands where Greeks were in the majority (Tenedos, Imbros and Thasos would be exceptions) would have to go to Greece, while those on which the Greeks were in the minority would become Turkish. In event of Koritza and Stylos being given to Albania the fate of the Aegean Islands should not depend upon any decision taken by the international commission in regard to southern and south-eastern Albania.[181] Grey promised to discuss the matter with the French and Russian Ambassadors, and also not to bring Mensdorff's proposal before the Conference, unless it seemed probable that it would be accepted. The war between Bulgaria and the other Balkan States, as well as with Turkey, had meanwhile broken out and was preoccupying both the Powers and the Conference to the virtual exclusion of other matters. None the less, negotiations proceeded over Albania's southern and south-eastern frontiers. Grey was finally successful in overcoming French and Russian opposition to Albania's retention of Koritza, because Bulgaria's defeat made possible a common frontier between Greece and Servia in Macedonia, the lack of which had been the chief reason for the demand that Koritza should be incorporated with Greece.[182] Grey also redoubled his efforts to bring about a general agreement. At Italy's insistence Austria-Hungary demanded the neutralization of the Corfu channel as a condition for her agreement to the appointment of an international commission for the delimitation of Albania's southern and south-eastern frontiers.[183] In addition, Italy demanded that the fate of the Italian-occupied Aegean Islands should be excluded from the international commission's field of decision because by the Treaty of Lausanne these islands must be returned to Turkey. On the other hand, Italy was prepared in event of no other solution being found to agree that the question of the incorporation into Greece of the Greek-occupied islands, excepting Imbros and Tenedos, should be settled at the same time as the question of Albania's southern and south-eastern frontier.[184]

On 31 July Grey summoned the Austro-Hungarian and Italian Ambassadors to the Foreign Office and informed them that after the end of the following week he would not summon the Conference to meet again. Since it was desirable that before that date there should be agreement over the instructions to be given to the international commission, he proposed that the Ambassadors obtained the consent of their Governments to the inclusion of Koritza and Stylos in Albania. Mensdorff and Imperiali at once said that the inclusion of the island of Sasseno in Albania and the neutralization of the Corfu channel must also be included in the instructions, and to this demand Grey raised no objection. On the other hand, he demanded in return that Greece should obtain the Greek-occupied Aegean Islands with the exception of Tenedos, Imbros and Thasos. Mensdorff and Imperiali, in their turn, made no objections. When, however, Grey said that the question of Koritza and Stylos could not be settled unless the Italian-occupied Aegean Islands were simultaneously returned to Turkey, Imperiali replied that his Government would not remain in office for twenty-four hours if it were to accept this proposal. Grey thereupon observed that since Turkey had never completely carried out the stipulations of any treaty Italy would doubtless remain in occupation of the islands *ad infinitum.* Grey little knew what a true prophet he was to prove.[185] On 1 August Grey laid these proposals before the Conference and said that no decision should be taken in regard to the islands in Italian occupation until after they had been returned to Turkey.[186] Grey thought that he had thereby overcome the obstacle placed by Cambon in the way of a solution to the problem when he said that these islands should at once be given to Greece. Grey also asked Mensdorff to withdraw his suggestion that Russia should be represented in the discussions over the future of the Wallachians inhabiting the neighbourhood of Mount Pindus, because it would only create fresh difficulties.[187]

On 5 August the Conference discussed these proposals. The French Ambassador demanded that the Aegean Islands, excepting only those already assigned to Turkey, should be given to Greece after the occupying troops had left. The Italian Ambassador said that he found nothing to alter in his previous declaration that the islands at present occupied by Italian troops would be restored to Turkey after Turkey had fulfilled the obligations laid upon her in the Treaty of Lausanne, and that as soon as these obligations were carried out Italy was ready to negotiate with the Powers over the ultimate fate of these islands provided that regard was paid to the general interests of Europe and to the safety and integrity of Asiatic Turkey. The German and Austro-Hungarian Ambassadors supported the Italian proposal. Benckendorff said that he would vote for these resolutions if the other Ambassadors followed his example. In regard to the island of Sasseno, however, which in his opinion ought to be given to Greece, he said that he reserved the right in the event that this island was given to Albania to demand compensation for Greece. The Italian, German and Austro-Hungarian Ambassadors contested Greece's claim to this island on the ground that it should share the destiny assigned to the Bay of Valona with which it was in close proximity.[188] Mensdorff said that the Austro-Hungarian Government wanted to see the frontier between Stylos and Koritza demarcated more accurately, and also that Rumania should be afforded the opportunity of safeguarding the rights and interests of the Wallachians in Epirus. The Austro-Hungarian Government also wanted definite dates to be fixed for the beginning and ending of the work of the international commission, and that regulations governing its work should be laid down that would take into consideration the needs of the districts with which it would have to deal.[189] All difficulties were, nevertheless, still not overcome. France demanded Argyrocastros for Greece if Albania got Koritza. Although Grey managed to get Cambon to abandon this demand, Cambon continued to insist that the Italian-occupied Aegean Islands should be given to Greece without any further delay. Grey was again successful in having this proposal dropped, and in inducing the French Government to be content with an arrangement by which Italy left the final decision to the six Powers and agreed not to raise objections to their united verdict.[190] No sooner had these obstacles been overcome than Mensdorff again rose up in the Conference to declare that his assent to the appointment of an international commission was dependent upon the fulfilment of a number of new demands. Above all, he demanded that the delimitation of the southern and south-eastern Albanian frontiers in the instructions to be given to the commission should be more accurate, and he produced draft instructions which laid down precisely the frontiers desired by Austria-Hungary for Albania.[191] The Commission was to be required to begin its task on 1 September 1913 and to complete it by 30 November of that year, and it was to be guided in its work of demarcation by ethnical and geographical considerations.[192] In regard to the districts inhabited by Wallachians the Commission's task was simply to be the determination of the nationality of the inhabitants, and the decision as to whether the districts in question were to become Greek or Albanian was subsequently to be taken by

Greece and Albania. The Greek troops in occupation of the districts assigned by the Commission to Albania were to be withdrawn within a month after the Commission had ended its labours. At Grey's suggestion it was left to the Powers to decide the fate of the Wallachians. Finally, Berchtold drew attention to the fact that in the final draft instructions Thasos was not named among the islands that were to become Turkish and that this should not be interpreted to mean that Thasos *ipso facto* became Greek. Grey replied that in December 1912 Thasos was given to Bulgaria, but that now when it was proposed that Kavallas might be given to Bulgaria the question of the ownership of this island could again come up for discussion.[193]

On 11 August the Conference of Ambassadors met for the last time. No decision was taken with regard to the remaining disputed issues. After a long discussion over the future of the islands in Italian occupation, Grey proposed a resolution by which Italy expressed her readiness to return to Turkey the islands still in Greek occupation after Turkey had withdrawn from Cyrenaica, while at the same time the Powers reserved to themselves the right to dispose of these islands by common accord. The French and Italian Ambassadors, after consulting their Governments, agreed to this proposal on the following day. Mensdorff put before the Conference certain regulations designed to secure the international character of the inhabitants of Mount Athos. It was resolved that Mount Athos "should have an independent and neutral autonomy". Further regulations were agreed upon regarding the form of government for Albania, its police, and the retention of land to serve for newly-established religious institutions.[194] Grey expressed his regrets that so far only the Austro-Hungarian, Italian, and British Ministers in Belgrade had received instructions to demand of the Servian Government to the accompaniment of a renewed assurance of economic access for Servia to the Adriatic that Servia withdraw her troops from the districts given to Albania—a matter that had been the subject of prolonged negotiations, especially between the Austro-Hungarian and Russian Ambassadors.[195] The Ambassadors were also requested to urge upon their Governments the desirability of carrying out the measures recommended by the Conference for the protection of the minorities in the Balkan States.

What then were the results of the discussions and negotiations carried on by the Conference of Ambassadors for nearly eight months? First: The creation of an independent Albania, ruled over by a Prince, of which the frontiers were indeed as yet not finally demarcated, but to which Scutari, Koritza, Stylos and the island of Sasseno were to belong. Second: Greece was to be given permanent possession, under certain neutrality conditions, of the islands in the Aegean already in Greek occupation and on which the majority of the inhabitants were Greeks. Turkey was to regain possession of Tenedos and Imbros. Italy undertook to return to Turkey the islands in her occupation after the Turks had withdrawn from Cyrenaica, and it was left to the Powers to decide the ultimate ownership of these islands. Third: An international commission was set up with a limited duration and given instructions that must be followed in carrying out its task. Many matters in dispute were indeed left for the future to decide.[196] The most important and welcome result of the Conference was the maintenance of peace between the Great Powers, which had been threatened time and again during these months. And it was undoubtedly Grey whom Europe had to thank for this immense service. As chairman of the Conference, Grey had revealed his possession of inexhaustible patience and complete impartiality, great understanding of and still greater skill in calming the often passionate feelings of the delegates, and remarkable inventiveness in the contriving of compromises that frequently met with general acceptance. Although he was under no illusion that the results achieved were perfect, he could regard with justified satisfaction what was, after all, the greatest achievement of the Conference—the maintenance of peace between the European Great Powers. The words which he subsequently used in writing of the labours and achievements of the Conference deserve quotation here.[197]

"There was no formal finish, the ambassadors were not photographed in a group, there were no votes of thanks, no valedictory speeches, they just stopped meeting. The conference had not settled anything, not even the details of the Albanian boundaries, but it had served a useful purpose. It had been something to which point after point could be referred, it had been a means of keeping all the six Powers in direct and friendly touch. The mere fact that it was in existence, and that it would have to be broken before peace was broken, was in itself an appreciable barrier against war. It was a means of gaining time, and the longer it remained in being, the more reluctance there was for it to disperse, the governments concerned got used to it, and to the habit of making it useful. When the Conference ceased to meet, the danger to the peace of Europe was over, the things that it did not settle were not threatening that peace, the things that had threatened the relations between the Great Powers in 1912-1913 it had deprived of their dangerous features."

Among the resolutions passed by the Conference was one demanding that Servia should withdraw her troops from the districts assigned to Albania. At the meeting of the Conference on 29 July Grey had proposed an united *démarche* by the Ministers of the six Powers in Belgrade in which Servia, in return for an immediate withdrawal of her troops, would be again promised, and in writing, an economic outlet to the Adriatic.[198] This *démarche* was made on 17 August and the Servian Prime Minister, Pašić, promised the withdrawal of Servian troops from Albania.[199] But nothing happened. A warning by Berchtold at the beginning of September proved equally fruitless. Fighting broke out between Serbs and Albanians, and the Serbs were driven back. Negotiations between Berchtold and Pašić in Vienna at the beginning of October produced no results because no one believed in Pašić's word.[200] The Austro-Hungarian Government informed the British Government that the blame for the intolerable state of affairs in Albania was to be found in the fact that Servia had been given towns such as Ipek, Prisren, Dibra and Djakova that were of the utmost importance for Albania.[201] At a Council of Ministers on 3 October, Tisza, Conrad and other Ministers spoke in favour of adopting coercive measures.[202] When news reached Vienna of fresh Servian advances it was stated that the Austro-Hungarian Government would take all possible measures to enforce the decisions of the Conference of Ambassadors, and Berchtold sought, with the assistance of Germany, who approved of the Austro-Hungarian Government's decision, to induce the British Government to support their action. But when Lichnowsky made a statement to this effect Crowe expressed disapproval in the sharpest terms of Austria-Hungary's action in seeking to carry out a decision of the Conference of Ambassadors by force, without previously consulting, or at the very least notifying, the British Government. Crowe said: "This is tantamount to breaking up the concert without any warning." He thought it was quite understandable that Servia should not wish to withdraw her troops from strategically important places on the frontier in

view of the unrest in Albania and the lack of a proper government in that country.[203] Nevertheless, Austria-Hungary
refused to go back on her decision. The Austro-Hungarian
Government was, moreover, not satisfied with Pašić's declaration in reply to the Austro-Hungarian *démarche* that, while
Servia would forbid her troops in Albania to make any further
advance, she must make their complete withdrawal dependent
upon developments in Albania. On 17 October Berchtold
addressed a Note to the Servian Government in which he
demanded the withdrawal of all Servian troops from Albania
and threatened forcible measures in event of a refusal.[204] This
Note, which was delivered in Belgrade on 18 October, produced the desired results.

On 20 October the Servian Government announced its
readiness to comply with the Austro-Hungarian demand and
on 25 October Servia withdrew her troops from Albania. Not
one of the Great Powers made any attempt to persuade Servia
to oppose the Austro-Hungarian demand. But the Western
Powers, including Great Britain, protested against Austria-
Hungary's unilateral action and failure to inform the Powers
until 18 October of the Note she had already sent to Servia.[205]
None the less, they accepted the accomplished fact without
further demur. It was at this time, too, that the Austro-
Hungarian Government renewed its request for the recall from
Vienna of Cartwright, whose political outlook, and especially
his strong anti-German feelings, had aroused Aehrenthal's
animosity during the last months of his life.[206] Berchtold had
earlier expressed a wish for his recall and, while agreeing to it
in principle, the British Government had continually postponed
his recall until it now at last gave its assent. At the beginning
of November 1913, Cartwright left Vienna and on 24 November his successor, Sir Maurice de Bunsen, arrived to take
up his post.

The two Commissions set up in conformity with the resolutions of the Conference of Ambassadors had meanwhile begun
their work. The International Commission for the delimitation
of the northern and north-eastern frontiers of Albania, and for
the internal organization of the country, should have begun
its work on 1 August, but in fact it was not until 23 September
that the Commission held its first sitting in Scutari whence, on
14 October, it transferred itself to Lake Ochrida. The withdrawal of the Servian troops from Albania greatly eased the

Commission's task. It is not necessary to examine the Commission's work in detail here, and it will suffice to say that the work was greatly hampered by differences of opinion between the members.[207] The Commission found itself involved in conflicts with the Servian authorities, who complained of the want of impartiality displayed by the British Delegate, and also with the Servian frontier guards. In December the Commission adjourned its meetings for the winter months and only resumed them in May 1914, after which its labours came to a quick and unexpected end with the outbreak of the First World War.

The activities of the second International Commission appointed to delimit the southern and south-eastern frontiers of Albania, and to solve the question of the Aegean Islands, can also only be commented upon here in so far as they affected Anglo-Austrian relations.[208] In the peace treaty signed in London on 30 May 1913 Greece and Turkey agreed that the fate of the Aegean Islands should be decided by the Great Powers and, in as far as the islands occupied by Italy came into question, the Conference of Ambassadors had resolved that no final decision should be taken about their future ownership until after Turkey had received them back from Italy. With regard to the islands occupied by the Greeks, no formal decision had been come to, but it was generally accepted that, with the exception of Tenedos and Imbros, they would be given to Greece. No engagement was, however, made with Greece to this effect.[209] The Commission, within whose purview this question also came, was supposed to start work on 1 September, and to finish by 3 November, yet in fact its first sitting was not held until 4 October in Monastir and no sooner had it begun its work than very sharp differences of opinion arose between the Italian and Austro-Hungarian delegates on the one hand and on the other the French and Russian delegates. The former sought to advance Albanian interests, while the latter supported Greek claims. While Germany took sides with Austria-Hungary and Italy she was also concerned to meet Greek wishes as far as possible. Great Britain served as intermediary between both parties. In London, discontent was expressed with the early results of the Commission's labours. Towards the end of October, Grey observed to Cambon that the aim of Austro-Hungarian policy "obviously was to turn the international control of Albania into an Austrian control. This policy might result in an absolute deadlock on the commission of control and the commission for delimiting the southern frontier." He added that he wondered if it would not perhaps be better to stay in the background and leave to Italy and Austria-Hungary the settlement of the Albanian Question.[210] Nicolson also had little hope of a successful issue to the Commission's deliberations and did not believe that the artificial structure that was Albania would survive. It was difficult to delimit the southern frontier, and still more difficult to drive the Greeks out of the occupied districts, while the future of the Aegean Islands was wholly uncertain.[211]

The Greeks certainly did all that lay in their power to enhance the difficulties attendant upon the Commission's work. It quickly became obvious that the language spoken by the inhabitants would not suffice as a guide in delimiting the frontier. The progress made by the Commission became steadily slower until, in the hope of making some advance, the British representative on the Commission, supported by his Austro-Hungarian and Italian colleagues, drafted a delimitation of the southern and south-eastern frontiers that Grey placed before the Powers in December for their approval.[212] It largely met the wishes of the Triple Alliance Powers, and was finally approved by the different Governments, after which it was adopted by the Commission, which had been transferred on 13 December from Monastir to Florence where, on 19 December, was signed the so-called Protocol of Florence that laid down the southern and south-eastern frontiers of Albania. The frontier ran in a general south-west—north-east direction from Phtelia, near Cape Stylos, to Lake Prespa, passing about twenty-five miles from Janina. Koritza and Argyrocastro—the two principal prizes for which the long struggle had been waged—were given to Albania.[213] No word was said about the Aegean Islands. Grey, therefore, declared that the solution of the one question was bound up with the solution of the other, "for it was on the understanding that Greece would keep the islands in her occupation, except Tenedos and Imbros, that an agreement to assign Koritza and Stylos to Albania was reached". The Triple Alliance representatives stated that it was certainly not the intention of their Governments to postpone a decision in the question of the islands *ad calendas graecas*, but that the question of evacuation by Greece seemed to them so urgent that a decision had to be taken. Simultaneously they stated that they were prepared to postpone the date for the evacuation by Greece of the occupied Albanian districts from 31 December 1913 to 18 January 1914. The negotiations with the Triple Alliance representatives had been conducted by Crowe, who now indicated his acceptance of this statement while, at the same time, declaring that Grey must abide by his decision that the two questions must be discussed jointly.[214]

Another subject that came up for discussion at this time was how the expenses of the princely establishment in Albania— Prince William of Wied had been appointed Prince of Albania by the six guarantor Powers—were to be met. Prince William had asked for three million pounds sterling, of which he was to be paid 800,000 at once.[215] Austria-Hungary and Italy had said that they were prepared to foot this bill in the event that the other Powers refused to be responsible for a share of it. The attitude adopted by Crowe to this problem was very interesting. In a Minute that he wrote at this time he began by saying that Great Britain should not support the selfish policy pursued by Austria-Hungary and Italy in regard to Albania. "The whole position of Great Britain in the world," he continued, "rests largely on the confidence she has earned that at least with questions not touching her own vital interests she deals strictly on their merits according to the generally accepted standard of right and wrong." Great Britain—he said—must remain true to this principle in this question also and, therefore, Great Britain must unceasingly oppose Austria-Hungary and Italy whose policy was to make Albania "a private preserve of their own and whose methods and dealings are strangely discordant with our views and practice". He foresaw friction with the Triple Alliance were Great Britain to champion the creation of a free and truly independent Albanian State. Nevertheless, Great Britain could not be a mere looker-on so long as she continued to be represented on the Commission. The question was, therefore, one either of retiring from the Commission and leaving the fate of Albania in Austrian and Italian hands or of co-operating in the establishment of a really free and independent State.

There can be no question as to which course Crowe preferred to adopt. He wanted to see the establishment of a free and independent Albania. And Grey agreed with him. "I would come to that decision," Grey declared, "and act upon it at once, if Russia and France had not to be considered."[216] On 6 January 1914 he proposed to the Cabinet that the British Government should "join in the guarantee of the loan" if each of the other five Powers took its share.[217]

Meanwhile, Grey was strenuously striving to achieve a compromise between the rival demands of Greece and Turkey, which they steadfastly clung to, despite the treaty signed on 14 November 1913 in Athens. For this purpose Grey, on 12 December, sent a memorandum to the Powers suggesting that the Greek and Turkish Governments should be informed that the Powers had decided that the islands in the Aegean in Greek occupation should be given to Greece and that the islands in Italian occupation should be restored to Turkey after that Power had fulfilled the stipulations of the Treaty of Lausanne.[218] The Turkish Government learnt at once of this secret proposal and protested against the retention by Greece of the islands in her occupation, while Italy was greatly irritated by Grey's demand that a date should be fixed for the return to Turkey of the islands now in Italian occupation.[219] Replying to British charges that Austria-Hungary was placing obstacles in the way of the compromise sought by Grey, and that she was also affording Italy much support in the matter of the Aegean Islands, Berchtold stated that he only regarded a decision in the evacuation issue as urgent because of the threat to European peace that further delay might bring in its train, and that he agreed in general with the British proposals in regard to the islands in Greek occupation. He added that he was advising his Italian ally in this sense. As regards the evacuation by Italy of the islands she was at present occupying, it was obvious that the Austro-Hungarian Government must support its ally and could not be expected to demand of that ally that she should evacuate the islands which she had so frequently promised to restore to Turkey.[220] The Austro-Hungarian Government was, in fact, at this time carrying on negotiations with its partners in the Triple Alliance for the purpose of synchronizing their policies in regard to Grey's demands,[221] and after agreement had been reached among themselves, the Austro-Hungarian Government transmitted on 14 January 1914 to the British Government its reply. The Austro-Hungarian Government stated that it agreed that the islands occupied by Greece, with the exception

of Tenedos, Imbros, and Castellerizo, which were to become
Turkish, should be promised to Greece on condition—and only
on condition—that the Greek forces occupying the districts
that were to become Albanian, inclusive of the island of
Sasseno, should have been withdrawn by 18 January and,
furthermore, that Greece undertook to abandon every form of
opposition to the organization laid down by the Powers for
Albania as well as to agree to the other guarantees demanded
by Great Britain, and especially those for the protection of the
Mohammedan minorities. In regard to the Aegean Islands the
Austro-Hungarian Government gave its full approval for
Italy's declaration that she would restore the islands to Turkey
as soon as Turkey had fulfilled the stipulations of the Treaty
of Lausanne. The actual date and detailed conditions for the
transfer of the islands was a matter that should be left to the
two Governments to settle by mutual agreement.[222]

Since it was impossible for the Greeks to withdraw from
Albania by 18 January Austria-Hungary and Italy said they
were prepared to prolong the time limit to 31 January, while
at the same time they asked for definite particulars about the
time limit for the withdrawal of troops and immediate evacuation of Koritza, the coastal district in the neighbourhood of
Phtelia, and the island of Sasseno. Grey said he was in agreement with the declaration of the Triple Alliance on all
important points, and he drafted Notes containing the terms of
the declaration which were to be sent to Italy and Turkey,
after they had received the approval of the Powers, who were
also to be responsible for seeing that the conditions were
carried out.[223] But he observed in regard to Italy's attitude to
the question of the Aegean Islands: "I would, however, point
out that as long as one of the Great Powers remains in occupation of these Aegean Islands the situation will remain
abnormal, and that while it is primarily a matter for Italy and
Turkey to arrange the return of these islands to the latter in
accordance with the provisions of the Treaty of Lausanne, yet
all the Powers with whom by the subsequent agreement of
last August it rested to decide the ultimate destination of the
islands have an interest in their fate."[224] Grey was successful
in securing the assent of France and Russia to these arrangements. Meanwhile, negotiations with Venizelos had resulted
in agreement that the evacuation should begin on 1 March
and be completed by the last day of that month. On the other

hand, Berchtold refused to consider Venizelos' proposals for certain frontier rectifications.[225] The British Government was prepared to communicate the Protocol of Florence to the Greek and Turkish Governments. Fears were, however, expressed that it would be difficult to persuade Greece to submit to the dictates of the Powers unless it was protected against attack by Turkey, and therefore it was recommended that such protection should be afforded the islands that were to become Greek possessions.[226] Grey also proposed to the Austro-Hungarian Government that an agreement should be arrived at to provide for the eventuality that Greece refused the conditions laid down by the Powers, and he asked whether or not, after the communication to the Greek Government of the declaration of the Powers (Protocol of Florence), it would be possible for the Austro-Hungarian, Italian, and Greek Governments to arrive at a voluntary agreement for the rectification of the southern Albanian frontier. Berchtold was disinclined to entertain Grey's proposal. He thought that the proposed action to be taken in Athens and Constantinople should not be delayed any longer. Venizelos had promised to withdraw all Greek troops by 31 March and there was, therefore, at present no reason for using threatening language at Constantinople. Upon hearing Berchtold's views Grey said that if all the other Powers did the same he would dispatch the declarations to Athens and Constantinople, but that he reserved to himself full freedom of action in the event of a refusal by the Turkish and Greek Governments to accept the conditions, because his proposals for a prior understanding between the Powers on the method of carrying out their decisions had not met with acceptance.

The declarations by the Powers were handed to the Greek and Turkish Governments on 13 and 14 February and what Grey and Nicolson had feared took place.[227] The Turkish Government voiced its regret that the Powers had not paid sufficient regard to Turkey's vital interests. The Greek Government, indeed, promised to complete the withdrawal of Greek troops by 31 March, but demanded a rectification of the frontier by Koritza and in the valley of Argyrocastro. In return for the cession of certain towns in the neighbourhood of Argyrocastro the Greek Government offered Albania a small strip of coast and a monetary compensation while, at the same time, repeating its demand that the Powers should guarantee the neutrality of the districts to be ceded to Albania and also the property and religious and linguistic rights of the Greek population.[228] On 8 March the Austro-Hungarian and Italian members of the Commission made verbal replies in the presence of the German Minister at Athens to these Greek demands without having first consulted with their British, French or Russian colleagues. The Commission—they said—was looking after the minorities. They refused any rectification of the frontier and merely held out the hope of concessions in regard to one or two districts. No mention was made of the Aegean Islands. The Foreign Office was angered by Austria-Hungary's and Italy's high-handed and unilateral action and seriously discussed the question of Great Britain's withdrawal from the International Commission. Grey was advised to mention this possibility to the ambassadors of the Triple Alliance and to await the effect of such a threat.[229] Mensdorff admitted that the Austro-Hungarian and Italian members of the Commission had acted over-hastily, while from Vienna the occurrence was explained and excused by a statement that the need for haste made it necessary.[230] A declaration to be made by all the Powers was then drafted and on 24 April handed to the Greek Government. There was, indeed, little difference between this and the previous verbal declaration made by the Austro-Hungarian and Italian Governments in Athens except that greater emphasis was laid on the protection of the Greek minorities on Imbros, Tenedos and Castelloritza. This declaration, nevertheless, did not mean that the questions of Albania's southern and south-eastern frontiers and of the Aegean Islands had found their solutions. Revolts in Epirus and Central Albania in which Greece, and certainly also Turkey, had a hand, prevented the final delimitation of the southern and south-eastern frontiers. The International Commission did, indeed, on 18 May in Corfu reach an agreement with the leaders of the Epirote rebellion which conceded the Epirotes a measure of autonomy within Albania for which the Powers subsequently gave their assent. The Epirotes, nevertheless, did not prove submissive. Even at the outbreak of the First World War the Greeks had still not completely withdrawn from Albania.[231]

Nor did the question of the Aegean Islands meet with any better fate. Greece and Turkey continued to quarrel with unabated zest and to accuse each other of barbarous misdeeds.

All attempts to mediate, in some of which the German Emperor, William II, and King Carl of Rumania took part, failed of success. Even Dr. Dillon's final attempt that at the outset seemed likely to succeed ended in failure. The outbreak of the First World War made an end to these negotiations and disorder reigned triumphant on the Balkan peninsula. Berchtold could not be satisfied even with what had been achieved. He had succeeded in establishing Albania as an independent State. But he had been forced to surrender large portions of northern Albania to the Serbs while, in the south, Albania's frontier was not secure. The Prince of Albania was not master of his own country, his life was in peril, and the viability of Albania was certainly a matter for doubt. Moreover, Austria-Hungary had to reckon with Italy's rivalry which steadily became more obvious.

Above all else, Austro-Hungarian policy in the Balkans had failed to achieve its chief aim. Servia emerged from the Balkan Wars much more powerful and with large territorial gains, and she redoubled her machinations against the Dual Monarchy.

Grey, too, could not be wholly content with the final results of his patient labours. The Balkans were still in a state of unrest and in the Spring of 1914 the conflict between Turkey and Greece seemed likely to end in war. As in August 1913, so in the Spring of 1914 Grey could, nevertheless, comfort himself with the thought that in large measure Europe owed it to his unremitting efforts that war between the Great Powers, which had so often threatened to break out, had always been averted. Finally, Grey could hope, in view of the improved relations between Great Britain and Germany that had come about in the Spring of 1914, that peace might be preserved for a long time to come.

Chapter Five

AUSTRIA-HUNGARY, GREAT BRITAIN, AND THE OUTBREAK OF THE FIRST WORLD WAR

IN the early months of 1914 Anglo-Austrian diplomatic relations might fairly be described as not unfriendly. True, both States stood in opposite camps. Austria-Hungary was the ally of Germany and, at least formally, of Italy. Great Britain, on the other hand, stood beside Russia and France in the *Entente Cordiale*.[1] The interests of Great Britain and Austria-Hungary, nevertheless, did not cross one another and, therefore, did not form a barrier to friendly relations. Friendly relations had succeeded the coolness that had arisen out of the Bosnian Crisis and that had persisted for several years afterwards. Again and again Count Berchtold told the British Ambassador in Vienna, and instructed the Austro-Hungarian Ambassador in London, Count Mensdorff, to express himself in similar terms, how sincerely he desired to avoid any cause of friction and to work together with Great Britain for the preservation of peace in Europe. The British Government, for its part, reciprocated Berchtold's wish. King George V constantly assured Mensdorff of his veneration for the old Emperor Francis Joseph, while Grey was not tardy in expressing his approval for Berchtold's policy.[2] Austria-Hungary stood apart from the great world problems that preoccupied the British Cabinet, and the British Cabinet had no desire to interfere in Balkan affairs so long as they did not constitute a threat to European peace. The British Delegates on the International Commissions for the delimitation of Albania's frontiers and for the Aegean Islands invariably sought to mediate between their Triple Alliance and their French and Russian colleagues. Moreover, Austria-Hungary and Great Britain worked together to maintain peace when disputes between Greece and Turkey seemed likely to result in war. Another cause for satisfaction was the promise of an improvement in Anglo-German relations as a result of the negotiations that had long been in progress between Berlin and London over the Bagdad Railway and the future of the Portuguese colonies, since any improvement in Anglo-German relations was tantamount to an improvement simultaneously in Austro-British relations. Austro-Hungarian and British interests were, in truth, widely separated in space. The British Government was primarily concerned with Far Eastern affairs, and the Irish independence movement, while the Austro-Hungarian Government was forced in an ever-increasing degree to devote its attention to the Balkans, where the state of affairs increasingly threatened Austria-Hungary's position as a Great Power.[3]

Servia had become more powerful and more presumptuous as a consequence of her victories in the Balkan Wars and was intriguing all the more energetically against the Dual Monarchy. Rumania was allied by treaty with the Central Empires and the King of Rumania (who was a Hohenzollern) was certainly well disposed towards them. There was, however, in Rumania a pro-Russian party, whose influence steadily increased from month to month. It was also well known in Vienna that in Russia itself many influential forces were working to create a powerful anti-Austrian Balkan alliance under Russian leadership. The Austro-Hungarian Government deemed it essential to bring these plans to nought and it looked upon Servia as its most resolute opponent. It was decided to make a renewed attempt to bind Rumania still more closely to the Central Empires, and, in event of its failure, to try and win over Bulgaria. But more than anything else it was imperative to gain Germany for the creation of a Balkan alliance under Austro-Hungarian and German leadership. For a long time the Emperor William II refused his consent for this plan. He disliked the idea of allying himself with Tsar Ferdinand of Bulgaria, whom he hated; he never doubted that he could rely on King Carol of Rumania; and therefore he did his utmost to induce his Austro-Hungarian ally to come to an agreement with Servia. During the year 1914, however, William II's views underwent a change in so far as he recognized that Austria-Hungary had been right in her Balkan policy and, in consequence, he lifted his ban upon an understanding with Bulgaria.

At the end of June 1914, a memorandum was drawn up in Vienna for the purpose of winning over the German Emperor and his Government for the idea of bringing about a Balkan alliance under Austro-German leadership. But before it could

be dispatched to Berlin the news reached Vienna that the
Heir-Apparent, Archduke Francis Ferdinand, and his wife
had been assassinated in Sarajevo by Bosnian Serbs. This
crime aroused in Great Britain, as in virtually all other
countries in the world, horror and indignation and the fiercest
condemnation of the assassins. Grey expressed his deepest
sympathy to Mensdorff and instructed the British Ambassador
in Vienna to convey it to Berchtold.[4] In the House of Commons
the Prime Minister, Mr. Asquith, and the Leader of the
Opposition, and Lords Crewe and Lansdowne in the House of
Lords, voiced the sympathy of the British Parliament and
people with the aged Emperor and his subjects in the heavy
blow that had fallen upon them.[5] The whole British Press, not
even excepting the anti-German newspapers, was unanimous
in its condemnation of the crime. Once, however, political
considerations began to appear, differences of opinion also
manifested themselves.[6] The Northcliffe Press and the
Morning Post put part of the responsibility for the assassination on Austria-Hungary's mistaken policy in regard to
Bosnia-Herzegovina. Other newspapers defended the Austro-
Hungarian Government and spoke highly of what Austria-
Hungary had accomplished in Bosnia-Herzegovina in the
course of thirty years. *The Observer*, notwithstanding its anti-
German tone, was very outspoken on the subject of the Great
Servia movement which threatened both to destroy the
territorial integrity of Austria-Hungary and to upset the
existing European order inasmuch as it was undermining one
of the pillars on which rested the balance of power—a pillar
which it was inconceivable could be replaced by anything else.
The *Daily Graphic* wrote on 1 July that sympathy for Austria-
Hungary was politically important. Austria-Hungary and
Great Britain were, it was true, in different and opposing
groups of Powers; but, nevertheless, they stood much nearer
to each other than did any of their allies, because their interests
did not conflict anywhere and because in their inalterable
attachment to peace—an outstanding trait in the Emperor
Francis Joseph's statecraft—they possessed a common tradition
and a common aim. Other newspapers were more reserved in
their utterances. Hence it would be untrue to say of the
British Press in this connection that it presented an united
front. Nor was it any different in Austria-Hungary, where
certain Vienna newspapers such as the *Reichspost* and the

Militärische Rundschau, and also indeed the *Neue Wiener Journal,* advocated strong coercive measures. Provincial newspapers like the *Innsbrucker Post* sounded the same note. From the very outset *Die Zeit* championed Servia's cause, while the Socialist *Arbeiterzeitung* fiercely attacked the Austro-Hungarian Government, and the more moderate newspapers like the *Neue Freie Presse* in Vienna and the *Pester Lloyd* in Budapest maintained an attitude of reserve, although at the same time they stressed Austria-Hungary's right to demand adequate expiation for the crime. But they kept silence on the subject of the possibility of serious European conflicts.

Opinion in influenctial political circles was also far from unanimous. A small yet very influential group within the Foreign Ministry, led by Count Forgach[7] and Count Hoyos,[8] favoured, like most of the Army officers, swift punitive action. At first Berchtold would not hear of such forcible measures. Public opinion—he said—was not sufficiently prepared for such measures. Bunsen believed he was drawing an accurate picture of the situation when, on 3 July, he wrote:

"The *Reichspost* and some few papers of that colour are insisting strongly to an attack on Servia and severe suppression of the Southern Slavs within the Dual Monarchy. The official *Fremdenblatt,* however, and most of the more reasonable papers, take the line that it would not be politic to take Servia as a whole to account for the crime of a small band of degenerates who draw their inspiration from the Pan-Serb headquarters at Belgrade. The Army, I hear, are very bitter and straining at the lead. I can hardly believe they will be let slip . . . I must say I think the Servian Press is behaving shamefully."[9]

Two days later Bunsen's views had already undergone a change. He said that the Russian Ambassador in Vienna had told him that a straight fight between Servia and Austria-Hungary alone was an impossibility, and that Russia would be forced to take up arms for Servia's sake. Bunsen also said in his dispatch that virtually the entire population of the Dual Monarchy was "just now blindly incensed against the Servians and I have heard on good authority that many persons holding usually quite moderate and sensible views on foreign affairs are expressing themselves now in the sense that Austria will at last be compelled to give evidence of her strength by settling once and for all her long-standing accounts with Servia and by striking such a blow as will reduce that country to impotence for the future."[10] London received the news from Vienna with calmness and there was little or no evidence of sympathy with Servia. It was also taken for granted that Great Britain's task must be to prevent the occurrence of serious European complications.

Grey and Nicolson both held this view. On 9 July Nicolson wrote: "I have my doubts whether Austria will take any action of a serious character and I expect the storm will blow over."[11] And Grey told the German Ambassador that in the event that Austria-Hungary put forward reasonable demands on Servia it would not be difficult for him (Grey) to advise moderation at St. Petersburg. If, on the other hand, Slav emotions were aroused in Russia through Austria-Hungary making exaggerated demands on Servia, he would hardly be able to achieve anything at St. Petersburg. In any event he would do all that was possible, as he had done at the time of the Balkan Wars, to prevent the outbreak of war between the Great Powers.[12] A further and more determined step, however, had in the meanwhile been taken in Vienna along the path that led to war. Influenced by statements made by the German Emperor and the Imperial Chancellor von Bethmann-Hollweg that Austria-Hungary could count upon the full support of the German Empire, Berchtold told the Council of Ministers on 7 July that the moment had come in which to make Servia for ever powerless to injure the Dual Monarchy. The only determined opposition that Berchtold met with in the Council came from the Hungarian Prime Minister, Count Stephen Tisza, who as early as 1 July in a memorandum which he sent to the Emperor Francis Joseph had opposed an attack on Servia and now forcibly repeated his objections to Berchtold's proposals. He told the Council *inter alia* that in order to assure herself of Great Britain's sympathy and to enable Russia to remain a spectator of the war (between Servia and Austria-Hungary) Austria-Hungary must declare that she had no intention of destroying—and still less of annexing—Servia.[13] Nothing was known in London of the Austro-Hungarian Government's decision. In a speech in the House of Commons on 10 July on the vote for the Foreign Office, Grey never even mentioned what had been happening in Vienna. True, Bunsen had reported on 5 July that it was difficult to get a precise statement from Berchtold of his views on international questions. "One is left to conjecture . . .

from a few vague remarks made by Count Berchtold, from newspaper articles, and from conversations with other persons more or less intimately connected with public affairs."[14] Even as late as 11 July he could only report that rumours were flying around but that he knew nothing certain.[15] Two days later he reported that Berchtold was credited with pacific intentions, yet that there were influential officials in the Foreign Ministry who were pressing for strong action against Servia. And he wrote: "The *Reichspost* and other more or less independent organs of the Vienna Press are conducting a vigorous campaign on these lines. The *Neue Freie Presse* has distinguished itself in clamouring for vengeance against Servia." Regret was expressed—Bunsen continued—that the opportunity was not taken in 1908, and again at the time of the Balkan Wars, of making Servia incapable of waging war for a generation. He added that it was believed in Vienna that not only Great Britain, but also Russia, would approve of punitive action by Austria-Hungary against Servia.[16]

The hopes entertained in Vienna that in event of war Great Britain would not fight against the Central Powers were strengthened by a dispatch from the Austro-Hungarian Ambassador in Berlin, Count Szögenyi, who reported that the German Government had reasons for believing that Great Britain would not go to war over a Balkan State, even if Russia, or indeed even France, were involved in the struggle. Anglo-German relations had improved to such an extent that Germany no longer feared that Great Britain would adopt an inimical attitude towards her, and above all else, Great Britain was at the present time disinclined for war and certainly unwilling for Servia's, or in the ultimate resort Russia's, sake to pull the chestnuts out of the fire.[17] Since 7 July the number of British newspapers which had adopted an anti-Austrian attitude had risen and on instructions from the Ministry of Foreign Affairs in Vienna Mensdorff approached Lord Lansdowne and Lord Rosebery with the request that they would use their influence to induce the British Press to change to a more friendly tone in writing of Austro-Hungarian affairs. Both statesmen promised to do so.[18] At the same time, Baron Franckenstein (now Sir George Franckenstein), who was on the staff of the Austro-Hungarian Embassy in London, approached the Editor of the *Westminster Gazette*, Mr. J. A. Spender, with a similar request.[19] An attempt to influence

The Times was less successful. For, on 16 July, *The Times* published a leader which reported Austria-Hungary's projected demands on Servia as communicated by the Austrian Press and then, after condemning the campaign waged against Austria-Hungary by the Servian Press, continued by strongly advising the Servian Government to lose no time in bringing the assassins to trial "fairly and openly" and in communicating the results of the trial to the Powers. *The Times* went on to say that the Austro-Hungarian Government should bear in mind that nothing was to be gained and everything was risked "by adoption of the kind of policy for which the military organs clamour". After giving this piece of advice, *The Times* praised the Austro-Hungarian Government for having hitherto acted "with self-possession and with restraint" and expressed the hope that it would continue to do so until the end of the crisis. "Her [Austria's] own history," *The Times* continued, "since the middle of the last century contains some very impressive warnings of the irreparable mischief which a sudden fit of impatience may do to a policy that has been long and carefully followed under difficult conditions. These warnings, we believe, she has taken to heart."[20]

Franckenstein's efforts produced better results. On 17 July the *Westminster Gazette* wrote *inter alia*:

"After the crime of Sarajevo we cannot deny that Austria-Hungary has a *prima-facie* case for desiring to clarify her relations with Servia. There is strong indignation in the Empire, and it is widely believed that the anti-Austrian conspiracy which struck at the Archduke had its origins in Servia. The case has not been improved by the Press campaign which has gone on in Servia since the assassination and it is suspected in Vienna and Budapest that a deliberate attempt is being made to work on the population of Servian nationality in the Empire in order to prepare their separation from the Monarchy should an opportunity present itself. In such circumstances the Government cannot be expected to remain inactive, and Servia will be well advised if she realizes the reasonableness of her great neighbour's anxiety and does whatever may be in her power to allay it without waiting for a pressure which might involve what Count Tisza calls 'warlike complications'."[21]

This leading article (which was reproduced by the Vienna newspapers) made a profound sensation, because the relations between the *Westminster Gazette* and the Foreign Office were known, and therefore its pronouncements were regarded a

expressing the British Government's views. The Russian Ambassador in Vienna characterized the article as a British
warning to Servia and as an encouragement to the Austro-
Hungarian Government to take strong action against Servia.[22]
Grey, indeed, strongly repudiated the notion that the Foreign
Office had inspired the article.[23] But he could do nothing about
it and all the more so because more trustworthy information
about the proposed Austro-Hungarian demands on Servia had
just become known for the first time. On 16 July Bunsen
reported that he had been told by a well-informed friend—he
wrote the next day that his informant was the former Austro-
Hungarian Ambassador in Rome, Count Lützow[24]—who had
spoken with Berchtold and officials of the Foreign Ministry
that the Ministry regarded the situation as serious "and that
a kind of indictment is being prepared against the Servian
Government for alleged complicity in the conspiracy which
led to the assassination of the Archduke. Accusation will be
founded on the proceedings in the Sarajevo Court. My
informant states that the Servian Government will be required
to adopt certain definite measures in restraint of nationalist
and anarchist propaganda, and the Austro-Hungarian Government are in no mood to parley with Servia and will insist on
immediate unconditional compliance, failing which, force will
be used."[25]

It had also become known that Count Tisza, who had
spoken in the Hungarian Parliament on 8 July in a non-
committal manner, changed his tune somewhat in a speech
delivered on 15 July to the same audience.[26] Of the reasons
that induced Tisza to abandon his opposition to Berchtold's
proposals nothing was known.[27] Nor was it known that the
Emperor Francis Joseph had also become convinced that
Austria-Hungary could not now beat a retreat. On 19 July
the Council of Ministers held its fateful sitting at which the
text of the Note to be sent to Servia was approved and a time
limit of forty-eight hours was fixed within which Servia must
accept or reject the Austro-Hungarian ultimatum. No voice
was raised against the decision. Tisza abandoned his opposition in principle and contented himself with making his assent
dependent "on a decision to take no Servian territory apart
from small frontier modifications". The Protocol of this
meeting of the Council of Ministers closes with the words:
"The contents of the Note to Belgrade agreed on to-day are

such that we must reckon with the probability of war. If, nevertheless, Servia gives way and accepts our demands, it would not only be a profound humiliation for her and *pari passu* a blow to Russian prestige in the Balkans, but would secure certain guarantees for the limitation of Great Servian intrigues on our soil."[28]

The news that had meanwhile reached London from various sources of the Servian crisis did not fail to produce a sensation. Unanimity of opinion was still lacking in the British Press and a number of newspapers defended Austria-Hungary and approved her conduct, while others condemned it. The principal change that had come over the British Press was the violence with which the opposing points of view were now given expression. The *Morning Post* occupied a leading position among the anti-Austrian newspapers and on 23 July it drew attention to the reactions that would be produced in Europe by an attempt on the part of Austria-Hungary to annex Servia. The Russian Government would not play the rôle of a passive onlooker, Italy would dislike it, and, if Germany did not remain neutral, Russia's ally, France, would become involved in the embroilment. It was on the cards that the long-dreaded European War might break out under circumstances unfavourable for the Triple Alliance.[29]

While following the course of events with anxiety, Grey kept himself in the background. When Mensdorff complained of the unbridled attacks on Austria-Hungary in the Servian Press, which were aimed at stirring up revolutionary movements in districts that formed an integral part of the Dual Monarchy— attacks that no State, however pacific, could permit, Grey merely took cognizance of the complaints without discussing them.[30] Grey still hoped for a peaceful solution of the crisis and desired it the more ardently because he was forced to recognize that the majority of British newspapers, whether they supported Austria-Hungary or Servia, did not contemplate Great Britain's active participation in an eventual war or else were decidedly opposed to it.[31] He knew that bankers, merchants and industrialists in so far as they concerned themselves at all with the Servian Question, regarded the outbreak of a war in which Great Britain would take part as an inconceivable catastrophe. Moreover, Grey was aware that the majority in the Cabinet were opposed in principle to Great Britain's active participation in continental conflicts and that their views were shared by most Members of Parliament.[32] In addition, the Irish Question was daily becoming more serious and might lead to the fall of the Government. All these considerations impressed upon Grey the need for caution.[33] And his endeavours were, in fact, directed towards impressing moderation upon all parties and to finding a peaceful solution to the crisis.

It was with this pacific object in mind that Grey negotiated with the foreign Ambassadors in London and instructed the British Ambassadors and Ministers. Thus Buchanan in St. Petersburg was ordered to state that "if Austrian demands in Servia are kept within reasonable limits, and if Austria can produce justification for making them, I hope every attempt will be made to prevent any breach of the peace."[34] He expressed the same hope to the German Ambassador in London and added: "I hated the idea of a war between any of the Great Powers, and that any of them should be dragged into a war by Servia would be detestable."[35] He also hoped that the conflict could be settled without it being necessary for Great Britain to play a prominent part, and it was for this reason that he proposed to the Russian Government that, in the event of differences arising between Vienna and St. Petersburg, they should be discussed and settled by the two Governments in direct negotiations. This proposal (which he subsequently renewed) accorded with his sincere desire to maintain peace, and also with his fervent efforts to avoid offending Russia, with whom Great Britain had now maintained friendly relations for many years—Grey himself was chiefly responsible for the existence of these improved relations—since the differences still arising between them in many questions, and especially in regard to Asiatic affairs, called for a cautious and—if possible—accommodating British policy towards Russia. For Grey was firmly resolved that come what might the Entente with France[36] and Russia must be maintained under any circumstances.[37] In holding this opinion, Grey was in full accord with his advisers in the Foreign Office, where Nicolson observed at this time that "Russia is a formidable Power and will become increasingly strong. Let us hope our relations with her will continue to be friendly."[38]

The suggestions made by Grey to the Russian Government —suggestions that could hardly be said to amount to an attempt at mediation—met in St. Petersburg with a cold reception. The French Prime Minister, M. Poincaré, who was then on a visit to St. Petersburg and to whom Sir George Buchanan had communicated Grey's suggestions, was strongly opposed to them. Discussions à deux at this moment between Russia and Austria-Hungary would be highly dangerous. He preferred that the British, French and Russian Ambassadors at Vienna should exert their influence with the Austro-Hungarian Government. Sazonov agreed with him.[39] The most influential officials of the Foreign Office were, nevertheless, unanimous in their disapproval of any such action which—they thought—could do no good and might possibly do harm.[40] The idea was therefore let drop. Grey now waited upon events and did not comment upon a statement by the German Government that Austria-Hungary's demands on Servia were justifiable, and that in the German Government's opinion the dispute ought to be settled by the two Governments themselves without outside assistance or mediation.[41] He wanted first to speak with Mensdorff, because the news from Vienna seemed alarming. The newspapers were stating that Austria-Hungary would shortly dispatch a Note to Servia in which she made heavy demands and required an answer within forty-eight hours. According to the Neue Freie Presse these demands were: (1) the pursuit and punishment of the conspirators and all who were in any way connected with the assassination of the Archduke and his wife; (2) the suppression of the Great Servian organizations; (3) the tightening-up of frontier control; (4) the complete revision of Servian policy in regard to Austria-Hungary.[42] Grey's conversation with Mensdorff took place on 23 July and made it unnecessary to reply to Rumbold's telegram, since Grey was already in possession of the contents of the Austro-Hungarian Note to Servia.[43]

It does not come within the scope of this study of Anglo-Austrian relations to submit the text of the Note to close and critical examination or to pass judgement upon the action of the Austro-Hungarian Government in delivering this ultimatum to Servia. The Note was exceptionally severe. It condemned the conduct of the Servian Government for having, contrary to its promise of 3 March 1909, attacked the Dual Monarchy by all the means in its power and ultimately sought to separate from the Monarchy portions of its territory. The Note demanded the publication on the front page of the Journal officiel of an official declaration condemning the propaganda directed against Austria-Hungary that in the final resort had for its aim the detachment from the Monarchy of portions of its territory. This official declaration must also express regret that Servian officers and officials should have taken part in this propaganda, and should state that the Servian Government regarded it as its duty to summon the entire population of the Servian kingdom to treat persons guilty of such actions with the greatest severity. The Note contained ten further demands of which the more important were: (1) an undertaking to suppress any publication that taught hatred and contempt for the Dual Monarchy and strove to disrupt its territorial integrity; (2) the immediate dissolution of all associations for anti-Austrian propaganda; (3) the dismissal of all officers and Civil Servants guilty of propaganda against the Dual Monarchy. It was, however, the fifth and sixth demands that weighed heaviest upon, and were most humiliating for, the Serbs, in that they required that Austro-Hungarian officials should be permitted to assist the Servian authorities in their task of suppressing subversive movements that had as their aim the destruction of the territorial integrity of the Dual Monarchy, and also at the trial of those persons within Servia who had participated in the assassinations on 28 June at Sarajevo. The Note stated that the delay of forty-eight hours given to the Servian Government for its reply would expire on 25 July at six o'clock in the evening.

There can be no question that these terms were extremely harsh and that they were deliberately meant to be harsh. It was neither expected nor desired in Vienna that the Servian Government would accept them. The Austro-Hungarian Government was, in fact, determined that this time Austria-Hungary's quarrel with her small neighbour should be settled for all time.[44] In official circles it was clearly realized that war with Servia might also involve Austria-Hungary in war with Russia. Yet even this prospect did not daunt Austro-Hungarian statesmen who, relying on the might of their German ally, were prepared to wage war even if the participation of Russia were also to mean France's participation at Russia's side. It is tempting to condemn the decision of the Austro-Hungarian Government in the light of what followed and with the knowledge that it led to Austria-Hungary's downfall. But it must not be forgotten that in the opinion of everyone holding a position of authority in the Empire the very existence of

Austria-Hungary was this time at stake, as well as her position as a Great Power, which they believed to be seriously threatened by Servia. Nor can it be denied that the strong opposition to the Governments in Vienna and Budapest manifested by the peoples of the Dual Monarchy was to a very large degree due to the methods of government employed, especially by the Magyar ruling classes in Hungary in their government of the non-Magyar population. Whether, however, in face of the steady growth in power of the nationalist movements, the pursuit of another and more conciliatory policy would have brought about the complete pacification of the different races within the Dual Monarchy is a question that will never receive a definite answer. Opinions on this subject are too sharply divided. Innumerable politicians and historians, both then and now, have adopted the standpoint that had Austria-Hungary continued along the path on which her feet were set by the *Reichstag* in Kremsier in 1849 she would have been led to a federalization of the Empire and the fulfilment of the nationalist aspirations of the different peoples, and therewith to the permanent establishment of the Dual Monarchy as a Great Power. On the other hand, there are others who believe that even the most far-reaching concessions to the national movements, as a consequence of the strength of the national idea in every country in the world, would only have resulted in an even speedier separation of the individual nationalities from the centralized Austro-Hungarian Empire.

There can be no doubt that this latter point of view finds support in the fact that in Hungary, where the Apostolic King had in the *Ausgleich* of 1867 done so much to satisfy national aspirations, a large number of Magyars continued to work for the complete severance of Hungary from Austria, and that in Bohemia concessions to the Czechs only occasioned fresh demands, while even the Poles who held a special place in the Austrian half of the Dual Monarchy, and were accorded special rights and privileges, remained faithful to their ideal of a restoration of their ancient independent Polish kingdom. Nationalism had also become a mighty force among the Southern Slavs, who bitterly resented the harshness with which the Magyars endeavoured to repress their aspirations to independence. And it was precisely the Serbs in the Dual Monarchy, whose numbers had been considerably increased by the annexation of Bosnia-Herzegovina, who fought with every means available to them against the Austro-Hungarian Government's policy and were powerfully supported in their struggle by vast numbers of Serbs in Servia. The submission forced upon the Servian Government on 31 March 1909 was illusory. The fight against Austria-Hungary continued unabated and, indeed, increased in vigour after Servia's victories in the Balkan Wars. On many occasions wide circles of public opinion in the Dual Monarchy had demanded armed intervention and twice troops were drawn up on the frontier ready to invade Servia. The old Emperor's and his Foreign Minister's desire for peace induced them to hold the bellicose Army officers on the leash. Now, however, after the murder of the Heir-Apparent, Government and people were at one in demanding the destruction of the enemy even at the risk of their own defeat. "Better a fearful end than endless fears" exclaimed a leading Viennese statesman.[45]

The Austro-Hungarian Government instructed Mensdorff on 23 July to inform Grey in the strictest confidence of the contents of the Note to be delivered that evening in Belgrade and to hand the Note itself to him on the following day.[46] Since it was believed in Vienna that of the Entente Powers Great Britain was the likeliest to judge the action of the Austro-Hungarian Government objectively, Mensdorff was also instructed to refer to the mutual confidence once more subsisting between Great Britain and the Dual Monarchy as well as to the understanding shown by British public opinion of Austria-Hungary's importance as a Great Power, and to justify the step that had now been taken. He was to say that this time a vital interest of the Dual Monarchy was at stake. The murders in Sarajevo had shown what was to be expected if Servia was not forced fundamentally to alter her conduct. He was, furthermore, to emphasize strongly that Servia would have taken the edge off the harsh conditions she must now expect from Austria-Hungary if she had voluntarily taken the necessary measures to bring to trial in Servia the Servian participants in the assassination, and to discover with regard to the assassination the lines of communication that it had already been proved led back from Bosnia-Herzegovina to Servia.[47] When, on 23 July, Mensdorff confidentially informed the Foreign Secretary of the contents of the Note to Servia, Grey—Mensdorff reported to Vienna—replied to him in a "cool and objective, yet as always friendly, manner, and not without sympathy for Austria-Hungary". But he regretted the short time allowed to Servia in which to reply, and declared that an ultimatum could have subsequently been sent to Servia if her reply to the Note had not been satisfactory. Everything would depend—Grey added—upon the degree to which the accusations against the Servian nation were justifiable. On this occasion Grey abstained from any critical discussion of the Note, and merely remarked that Russia could only exert a calming influence upon Servia if the Austro-Hungarian demands did not go too far and were not calculated to give rise to the danger of a blazing up of Slav agitation in Russian public opinion. He then painted a picture of the fearful consequences of a war between the Great Powers. Economic bankruptcy would result for Europe, no credit would be obtainable, industrial centres would be in an uproar while, in the majority of European countries, whether victors or vanquished, many existing institutions would be swept away. It was obvious, from Grey's words, that he did not attach any great importance to the Austro-Servian conflict by itself and that what he feared was its effect upon Russia, whose interests he gave Mensdorff clearly to understand he was bound to take into consideration. In conclusion, Grey once again advised an exchange of views directly between Vienna and St. Petersburg.[48]

On the following day—24 July—after he had read the Note, Grey's comments were much sharper. His chief criticism was directed against the brief delay afforded to Servia for her reply, which rendered any mediation by other Powers virtually impossible, and also against the demand for the association of Austro-Hungarian with Servian officials in the investigation that was to be conducted in Servia into the conspiracy that resulted in the assassination.[49] He said that this would be tantamount to a suspension of the independence of Servia as a State. It was on this occasion that Grey used words that were often to be repeated when he said that the Note was the most formidable document that had ever been sent from one State to another State. He also repeated what he had said on the previous day about his anxiety lest the Austro-Hungarian action might have dire repercussions for the peace of Europe. If it were not for this possibility, he added, he would regard the whole business as a matter for Austria-Hungary and Servia alone.[50] Grey used the same language to the German Ambassador who summed up the results of their conversation by saying that Grey wanted to collaborate with Germany to localize the Austro-Servian conflict, but that in event of a quarrel arising between Vienna and St. Petersburg he would propose mediation *à quatre* (Great Britain, Germany, France and Italy).[51] It is worthy of note that at this time Grey did not envisage any mediation in the Austro-Servian dispute because he was not specially interested in Servia's fate.[52] He was, however, vastly interested in that of Russia, and it was her interests that he had in mind when he conceived the plan of a mediation *à quatre* for the eventuality that direct negotiations— negotiations that he desired and had frequently proposed— between Vienna and St. Petersburg failed of success.[53] This, indeed, was the substance of Grey's remarks on 24 July when the German Ambassador handed him a Note from the German Government in which it said that it deemed the Austro-Hungarian demands justifiable, and that it looked on this question as one concerning only Austria-Hungary and Servia and, as such, only to be settled by those two Powers between themselves. The Note also expressed the German Government's urgent desire to see the conflict localized inasmuch as the intervention of another Power must have incalculable consequences.

In the Foreign Office this Note met with an unfavourable reception. Crowe—Germany's outspoken enemy—remarked: "The answer [to the Note] is that owing to the extreme nature of the Austrian demands and the time limit imposed, the localization of the conflict has been made exceedingly difficult, because the Austrian terms bear on their face the character of a design to provoke war. The statement made by Austria and now asserted by Germany concerning Servia's misdeeds rest for the present on no evidence that is available for the Powers whom the Austrian Government has invited to accept those statements. Time ought to be given to allow the Powers to satisfy themselves as to the facts which they are asked to endorse."[54] Here it should be noted that the dossier containing the proofs for the accusations against Servia had not yet been delivered in London and that it was not until 29 July that it was handed to the Foreign Office, where it made no impression.[55] On 24 July an urgent telegram reached the Foreign Office from Buchanan in St. Petersburg in which he reported the agreement between Sazonov and Poincaré, by which

France declared her complete solidarity with Russia and her readiness to fulfil, in case of necessity, all her obligations. Sazonov described Austria-Hungary's conduct as "immoral and provocative". He said he hoped that Great Britain would announce her solidarity with her Entente friends. Buchanan could not, and did not, want to say so much. He suggested instead that Grey "might perhaps point out" that Vienna's aggressive action "would in all probability force Russia to intervene, that this would bring Germany and France into the field, and that if war became general, it would be difficult for England to remain neutral". The impression left upon him by the French Ambassador was "as if France and Russia were determined to make a strong stand even if we declined to join them". Crowe made use of this information to voice his own opinions unreservedly and ruthlessly. They were inspired by the same spirit that had animated his utterances in his celebrated Memorandum of 1 January 1907 which he had often repeated in the intervening years and which were identical with the opinions of the Under-Secretary of State, Nicolson, who on 27 March 1909 had declared that sooner or later England would have to wage the same fight with Germany that in previous centuries she had waged against Spain, Holland and France.[56]

"The moment (Crowe said) has passed when it might have been possible to enlist France's support in an effort to hold back Russia. It is clear that France and Russia are decided to accept the challenge thrown out to them. Whatever we may think of the merits of the Austrian charges against Servia, France and Russia consider that these are pretexts, and that the bigger cause of Triple Alliance versus Triple Entente is definitely engaged."

The sole possibility—Crowe went on—of avoiding war lies in the danger for Germany of finding England on the side of Russia and France. But that could only happen if the whole British Fleet were placed on a war footing at the same moment that either Austria-Hungary or Russia mobilized its forces. In the event of this suggestion meeting with approval, Crowe recommended that Russia and France should immediately be informed as that would be the best way "to prevent a very grave situation arising as between England and Russia". He put forward as grounds for his proposal the consequences that must ensue for England if she were to remain neutral.

"Either Germany and Austria win, crush France and humiliate Russia. With the French Fleet gone, Germany in occupation of the Channel with the willing or unwilling co-operation of Holland and Belgium, what will be the position of a friendless England? Or France and Russia win? What would then be their attitude towards England? What about India and the Mediterranean?"

This, as well as other statements made by Crowe in the succeeding days, reveal that he regarded Great Britain's task as the maintenance of the European Balance of Power and that it was for this reason that he demanded war with the most powerful Continental Great Power—Germany—of whom he believed that she sought hegemony in Europe.[57] Nicolson said that Crowe's observations called for the most careful consideration. "Our attitude", he wrote, "during the crisis will be regarded by Russia as a test and we must be most careful not to alienate her." But Grey was very unwilling to go to such lengths. The influence of his advisers in the Foreign Office has, indeed, often been over-estimated. Grey was no weakling nor a man who did not know his own mind and was therefore easily persuaded to adopt any course that was suggested to him. True, he greatly valued Nicolson's and Crowe's judgement and often followed their advice because he shared their views on most of the chief questions of the day.[58] In the execution of his plans, nevertheless, he acted independently and was not seldom at variance with his advisers over the use of methods. He saw the path before him very clearly and believed that his first and most important task was to prevent the outbreak of war between the Great Powers with all the means that lay at his disposal. But he did not at this moment feel called upon to take any decision as to the rôle of Great Britain in event of an outbreak of war. He was, indeed, determined for his part that Great Britain should fight at the side of the Entente. Nevertheless, he was still doubtful at this stage whether or not he would be successful in inducing the whole Cabinet to follow him along this path because a majority of its members were opposed to active participation by Great Britain in a continental war.

At a meeting of the Cabinet on the evening of 24 July Grey read the Vienna Note and remarked that the situation was dangerous and, therefore, that the Government should watch it closely. He did not voice his own opinions. Moreover, he was still in the dark as to public opinion. In so far as it found its true reflection in the Press, public opinion in Great Britain, even after the delivery of the Note, was by no means unanimous. Undoubtedly, the number of newspapers that considered the tone of the Note too harsh and many of the demands it made virtually incapable of fulfilment steadily increased; but only a few—the *Morning Post* was among them—wholeheartedly took Servia's side and unreservedly condemned the Austro-Hungarain Government's action. Other newspapers, among which was *The Times*, maintained an attitude of reserve notwithstanding their obvious inclination to disapprove of Austria-Hungarys' attitude and action, and demanded the evidence that was still lacking for the complicity of the Servian Government in the assassination.[59] Voices were, nevertheless, heard from both Liberal and Conservative circles supporting Austria-Hungary and declaring her action understandable, sometimes even justifiable, and advising Servia to make far-reaching concessions and Russia to abstain from too active support of the tiny Slav State. The *Daily Chronicle*, for example, found that the Note was no more drastic than "the reasonable self-defence of the Dual Monarchy required it to be," and the *Manchester Guardian* went so far as to declare that Russia's threat of war was "a piece of sheer brutality". Dillon wrote in the *Daily Telegraph* that not only was the prestige of the Dual Monarchy at stake, but that for her it was a matter of life and death which would be dealt with in a manner conformable to that fact. The *Pall Mall Gazette* wrote of the Vienna Note as simultaneously displaying firmness and reserve, and went on to declare that there could be no doubt that Servia was the hatching-place for conspiracies against her Austro-Hungarian neighbour.[60] *John Bull* was alone in its fierce anti-Servian attitude that found no echo in any other quarter of the Press and which it subsequently expressed pithily in the words, "To hell with Servia!"

The best expression of Grey's own views at this time is to be found in the words that he subsequently wrote in his autobiography. He says that at that time he had

"the conviction that a great European war under modern conditions would be a catastrophe for which previous wars afforded no precedent . . . I thought that this must be obvious to everyone else, as it seemed obvious to me, and that if once it became apparent that we were on the edge, all the Great Powers would call a halt and recoil from the abyss. (2) That Germany was so immensely strong and Austria so dependant upon Germany's strength that the word and will of Germany would at the critical moment be decisive with Austria. It was therefore to Germany that we must address ourselves. (3) That, if war came, the interest of Britain required that we should not stand aside, while France fought alone in the West but must support her. I knew it to be very doubtful whether the Cabinet, Parliament and the country would take this view of the outbreak of war, and through the whole of this week I had in view the probable contingency that we should not decide at the critical moment to support France. In that event I should have to resign, but the decision of the country could not be forced and the contingency might not arise, and meanwhile I must go on. (4) A clear view that no pledge must be given, no hope even held out to France and Russia which it was doubtful whether this country would fulfil.

"One danger I saw so hideous that it must be avoided and guarded against at every word. It was that France and Russia might face the ordeal of war with Germany relying upon our support, that this support might not be forthcoming, and that we might then, when it was too late, be held responsible by them for having let them in for a disastrous war. Of course I could resign if I gave them hopes which it turned out that the Cabinet and Parliament would not sanction. But what good would my resignation be to them in their ordeal? This was the vision of possible blood-guilt that I saw and I was resolved that I would have none of it on my head."[61]

Thus Grey still thought caution was the best policy. As a result of the opinions expressed by Nicolson and Crowe, Grey asked the First Lord of the Admiralty, Mr. Winston Churchill, how long it would take to mobilize the British Fleet and received the answer, "Twenty-four hours." Nevertheless, Grey said it was still too soon to make any communication to France and Russia on this subject.[62] Servia had not yet replied to the Vienna Note. All that could be done, therefore, was to await her reply and, in the meanwhile, to do everything possible to prevent an extension of the quarrel. It was for this purpose that Grey advised the Servian Minister in London that the Servian Government should reply to the Vienna Note in a conciliatory and "moderate" tone.[63] He instructed the British Minister at Belgrade to hold the same language and to advise the Servian Government to afford Austria-Hungary full satis-faction in every instance in which an official, even a subordinate official, was implicated in the assassination. But he charac-teristically added that the only thing he could say was that the Servian Government should reply in whatever manner it thought best served Servia's interests.[64] At the same time he was again busied in an endeavour to gain Germany for joint action with England, France and Italy in the event that he feared that Austria-Hungary and Russia should shortly mobilise. The Governments in Vienna and St. Petersburg should be advised to avoid frontier violations and to give the four Great Powers time in which to attempt a peaceful settlement of the quarrel between Vienna and St. Petersburg. Grey again told the German Amdassador that while he did not wish to be involved in the Austro-Servian dispute he would certainly intervene if the conflict was extended to involve Austria-Hungary and Russia. It was for that reason—he said—that he was seeking Germany's co-operation.[65] And Germany agreed in principle to co-operate. At Russia's suggestion the Entente made an attempt in Vienna to get the Austro-Hungarian Government to extend the time limit for the Servian reply. Although their endeavours were backed up by Germany they met with no success. On the day—25 July—on which the attempt was made, Berchtold was with the Emperor at Ischl and his representative at the Foreign Ministry said that it was too late.[66] Grey now pinned his hopes on Berchtold's statement that the Note was not an ultimatum, and that in event of its refusal the diplomatic relations between Austria-Hungary and Servia would be broken off and preparations made for war, but that war itself would not be begun.[67] While his fears were allayed by the news from Berlin that Austria-Hungary did not intend to annex Servian territory they were again aroused by news from St. Petersburg that Russia planned to mobilize 1,100,000 men. This news was, however, accompanied by an assurance that she was not harbouring aggressive intentions.[68]

Meanwhile, Sazonov again asked Buchanan what England's attitude would be in event of war. Buchanan told Sazonov what he had already told the Tsar that Great Britain could play the part of mediator in Vienna and Berlin better as a friend than as Russia's ally.[69] On the same day—25 July—Grey warned the German Ambassador not to underrate the existing danger and said he himself did not believe that the conflict could be localized. If Russia were to mobilize against Austria-Hungary he would like to see Germany bring pressure to bear in Vienna to obtain modification of the demands made upon Servia. He told Lichnowsky that he still believed firmly in his plan for mediation by the four Great Powers not directly involved in an Austro-Russian conflict. Austria-Hungary and Russia should be called upon "not to cross the frontier till there had been time to endeavour to arrange matters between them". It was essential for success that Germany should co-operate. "We could do nothing alone."[70] On the same day, Grey informed the Russian Ambassador of this conversation. But Benckendorff was made uneasy by Grey's statement and pressed him to indicate to Germany that in a general war England would not remain neutral and would join with the Entente Powers. Grey did not want to make this declaration. He told Benckendorff what had passed between him and Lichnowsky, and drew his attention to the fact that his demands on Germany were not easily capable of fulfilment.

"I was afraid, too, [Grey said] that Germany would reply that mobilisation with her was a question of hours, whereas with Russia it was a question of days, and that, as a matter of fact, I had asked that if Russia mobilised against Austria, Germany, instead of mobilising against Russia, should suspend mobilisation and join with us in intervention with Austria, thereby throwing away the advantage of time, for if the diplomatic intervention failed, Russia meanwhile has gained time for her mobilisation."

Grey knew that this statement was incompatible with complete impartiality, while the omission of any warning to Russia not to mobilize clearly reveals that he wanted to avoid exerting pressure on Russia and to further Russian military preparations for the eventuality that it proved impossible to maintain peace. He was also concerned not to give Russia the impression that she could count on Great Britain's assistance in event of war. It was for that reason that he introduced into his statement the words:

"It is true that I had not said anything directly as to whether we would take any part or not if there was a European conflict, and I could not say so, but there was absolutely nothing for Russia to complain of in the suggestion that I had made to the German Government and I was only afraid that there might be difficulty in the acceptance by the German Government. I had made it on my own responsibility, and I had no doubt it was the best proposal to make in the interest of peace."[71]

It is clear from this statement that Grey still held firmly to his conviction that his chief task was the maintenance of peace and that mediation by the four Great Powers not directly concerned in the dispute was the best way of avoiding the outbreak of an European war. But France and Russia rejected this proposal. They did not want mediation between Vienna and St. Petersburg, but instead an international examination of the justification for the Austro-Hungarian demands on Servia, and mediation by the Powers between Vienna and Belgrade, which Berchtold had always refused. Sazonov now made Grey a counter-proposal. He had learnt from the Servian Minister in St. Petersburg that, if attacked by Austria-Hungary, Servia would abandon Belgrade and withdraw her army into the interior of the country. Simultaneously she would appeal to the Powers for help. Sazonov was "in favour of such an appeal. Obligations taken by Servia in 1909, to which reference is made in the Austrian ultimatum, were given to the Powers and not to Austria and he (Sazonov) would like to see the question placed on international footing." In event of the acceptance of this proposal he was prepared to stand aside and leave the decision to the Four Powers.[72] This proposal was tantamount to a complete change-over in the question of mediation since up till now it was mediation in an Austro-Russian dispute by the four Great Powers not directly involved in that dispute that had been in question, while now Russia was proposing mediation between Austria-Hungary and Servia. But before Grey had had time to consider this proposal the news reached London from Vienna that the Servian reply to the Vienna Note had been delivered shortly before the expiry of the time limit and had deen described as unsatisfactory by the Austro-Hungarian Minister, who had thereupon left Belgrade. "War is thought to be imminent," Bunsen added in his report, "Wildest enthusiasm prevails in Vienna."[73]

Servia's answer had been drafted very cleverly. It is impossible to say with any certainty whether, and to what extent, Russia, and perhaps even France, helped in its composition. After emphasizing the pacific and moderate conduct of the Servian Government throughout the Balkan Wars, the reply went on to say that Servia was ready to fulfil nearly all the demands contained in the Vienna Note, and, in the case of those demands to which Servia found it impossible to accede, the refusal was conveyed in a very conciliatory and polite form. Although the Servian Government was unable properly to understand the demand for the co-operation of Austro-

Hungarian officials in the suppression of subversive movements directed against the territorial integrity of the Dual Monarchy, Servia consented to their co-operation "qui répondrait aux principes du droit international et à la procédure criminelle ainsi qu'aux bons rapports de voisinage". Servia only refused the sixth demand in the Vienna Note which asked for the participation of Austro-Hungarian delegates in the proceedings against Serbs suspected of complicity in the assassination who were living within the kingdom of Servia "car ce serait une violation de la Constitution et de la loi sur la procédure criminelle". Nevertheless, Servia expressed her readiness to communicate the results of these proceedings to the Austro-Hungarian "agents". Finally, the Servian Government declared itself willing in event of its reply being regarded in Vienna as insufficient to leave the decision to the International Court of Justice at The Hague or to the Great Powers who had assisted in drafting the Servian Declaration on 31 March 1909.[74]

The Austro-Hungarian Government based its rejection of the Servian reply to the Vienna Note on an assertion that it only simulated acceptance of Austria-Hungary's demands and in reality sought refuge in evasions and reservations such as, for example, those in regard to the participation of Austro-Hungarian delegates in the proceedings against those Serbs living in Servia who had taken part in the assassination of the Heir-Apparent on 28 June.[75] This statement was hardly calculated to impress the outside world. Although the Servian reply did not accept the demands of the Austro-Hungarian Government in their entirety, it certainly afforded a basis for further negotiations. There can be no doubt whatever that the decisive reason for rejecting the Servian reply sprang from the mistrust which the Austro-Hungarian Government felt for every Servian declaration. Servia had time and again broken solemn pledges and now no one believed in her new promises.[76] The decision, moreover, had been taken to destroy Servia as a factor in Balkan power politics and thus, simultaneously, to make an end forever to Servian agitation within the frontiers of the Dual Monarchy. The reception accorded to the Servian reply in all quarters of Europe was very different to what the Austro-Hungarian Government had expected and hoped for. It is now well known that after he had read the Servian reply the German Emperor, William II, exclaimed: "A brilliant

performance for a time-limit of only forty-eight hours! This
is more than one could have expected. A great moral success
for Vienna, but with it every reason for war disappears."[77]
The Foreign Office unhesitatingly condemned the action of the
Austro-Hungarian Government and the Senior Clerk, Mr.
G. R. Clerk, after closely comparing the Austro-Hungarian
Note with the Servian reply, said he got the impression that
the Servian reply was read in Vienna with the firm determination not to find it satisfactory, "for it swallows nearly all the
Austrian demands *en bloc*". He found that the objections raised
by Servia were "reasonable". Crowe shared Clerk's opinion.
"If Austria", he wrote, "demands absolute compliance with
her ultimatum it can only mean that she wants a war. For she
knows perfectly well that some of the demands are such as no
State can accept as they are tantamount to accepting a
protectorate."[78]

Grey was profoundly dissatisfied with Berchtold's conduct.
He told Mensdorff that in Vienna they treated the Servian
reply as if it were a complete refusal, whereas it was, in fact,
the greatest humiliation an independent State had ever undergone.[79] To the German Ambassador he said that if Vienna
was not satisfied with this unexampled humiliation it only
showed that it was a pretext and that Austria-Hungary was
really aiming at the destruction of Servian and Russian influence in the Balkans. The occupation of Servia by Austria-
Hungary would be an over-hasty step that would certainly
give rise to a vast European conflagration.[80] The British Press
was still far from unanimity in its expressions of opinion. Many
Conservative newspapers which had supported Servia, and,
above all others, the *Morning Post*, were the most extreme
advocates of the Servian cause. Even *The Times* said that
Servia had made extraordinary concessions for a sovereign
State though, doubtless, there were secret reservations.
Numerous Liberal newspapers also supported Servia. *The Star*
wrote on 27 July that the Servian reply was so conciliatory that
peace could be preserved if Austria wished to preserve it.
Servia had accepted extremely harsh and humiliating demands
and had made no unreasonable reservations. The *Manchester
Guardian* and *Westminster Gazette* took the same line. There
was, however, a third group of newspapers, like the *Standard*
and *Pall Mall Gazette*, which thought the Servian reply
amounted to a refusal. These newspapers discovered all sorts

of subterfuges in the Servian reply and declared that a permanent settlement could only be achieved on the basis of reparation and justice. To sum up—the British Press was very largely pro-Servian, although there were newspapers that shared Vienna's distrust of Servian honesty.[81]

What was Grey's attitude? How did he behave at this stage in the crisis? We know that he had often declared that he was not interested in the Austro-Servian conflict, did not want to be mixed up in it, and, on the other hand, that it was his task to settle conflicts arising between Russia and Austria-Hungary. It was for this purpose that he had proposed mediation in Vienna and St. Petersburg by the four Great Powers who were not directly involved in the dispute—a proposal that had been rejected by France and Russia. Germany had certainly transmitted this proposal to Vienna without seriously recommending it to the Austro-Hungarian Government's attention. The crisis was meanwhile growing in intensity. It was at this juncture —26 July—that Nicolson seized on a suggestion by Sazonov and urgently advised Grey "to telegraph to Berlin, Paris, Rome, asking that they shall authorize their Ambassadors here to join you in a Conference to endeavour to find an issue to prevent complications and that abstention on all sides from active military operations should be requested of Vienna, Servia and St. Petersburg pending results of conference."[82] He renewed his proposal the same day and emphasized that "it seems to me the only chance of avoiding a conflict—it is, I admit, a very poor chance—but in any case we shall have done our utmost."[83] Nicolson never revealed by a single word that at this Conference the question for discussion would no longer be mediation between Austria-Hungary and Russia, but between Austria-Hungary and Servia. If Grey were now to act upon Sazonov's suggestion that was so warmly supported by Nicolson, it would be the definite abandonment of the attitude he had hitherto adopted during the crisis.[84] That Grey did act upon it was undoubtedly due to the fact that he refused to leave any path untrodden that might lead to the preservation of peace. Hostilities had not yet begun between Servia and Austria-Hungary and, therefore, it was still possible to prevent them. The proposal for a conference in London seemed to hold out prospects of success. Success would, nevertheless, depend in the first instance upon Austria-Hungary, Servia and Russia abstaining from open hostilities, for so long as the conference was engaged on its mediatory work. Grey also knew that the decision lay with Germany. France and Italy would undoubtedly accept the proposal. Everything depended on Germany. The German Ambassador had shortly before informed Grey that his Government was prepared in principle to take part with the three other Great Powers in an attempt to mediate between Austria-Hungary and Russia "reserving, of course, the right as an ally to help Austria if attacked". In the course of their conversation, Grey had stressed the differences in their judgements of Austria-Hungary's rejection of the Servian reply and had pointed to the frightful consequences of a European war. In conclusion he had said that "as long as Germany would work to keep the peace I would keep closely in touch".[85]

To Mensdorff Grey spoke with great seriousness. He repeated that he had been disgusted by Berchtold's refusal to accept Servia's extremely conciliatory declaration and her far-reaching concessions to Austro-Hungarian demands. He said that in consequence he was no longer able to ask the Russian Government to bring further pressure to bear upon Servia. He had taken for granted that the Servian reply furnished the basis for mediation by the four Great Powers not directly involved in the dispute with a view to achieving a peaceful solution. It was the same idea that had inspired his proposal to hold a conference with the French, Italian and German Ambassadors on the understanding that Russia and Austria-Hungary abstained from all military operations for the duration of the conference. When Mensdorff said that it was perhaps now too late for a conference, Grey retorted that if Austria-Hungary was determined, under all circumstances, to wage war in the belief that Russia would remain quiet, she was taking a tremendous risk upon herself. If Berchtold succeeded in persuading Russia to remain quiet, everything would be all right and he had nothing more to say. But he confessed he entertained the gravest doubts. As proof of the anxiety prevailing in London, Grey informed Mensdorff that the British Fleet, which should have retuned to its stations after the summer manoeuvres, would instead remain in readiness.[86] Grey's words about the risk that Vienna was running in not taking the danger from Russia into serious consideration were meant in all sincerity. It was known in London that Austria-Hungary was mobilizing[87] and therefore it was assumed that she had resolved upon war.[88] News coming in from St. Petersburg indicated that Russia was about to mobilize. Crowe made use of these facts in a further attempt to stir up Grey to active and powerful intervention in the crisis. "I am afraid," he wrote, "that the real difficulty to be overcome will be found in the question of mobilization. Austria is already mobilizing. This, if the war does come, is a serious menace to Russia, who cannot be expected to delay her own mobilization which, as it is, can only become effective in something like double the time required by Austria and Germany. If Russia mobilizes, we have been warned, Germany will do the same, and as German mobilization is directed almost entirely against France, the latter cannot possibly delay her own mobilization for even a fraction of a day." He said that Bunsen's reports from Vienna showed that Austria-Hungary would certainly go to war, which he had been of opinion she would do from the very outset of the crisis. Under these circumstances it would be neither right nor wise to stop Russia from mobilizing. "This, however, means that within twenty-four hours H.M.'s Government will be faced with the question whether in a quarrel so imposed by Austria on an unwilling France, Great Britain will stand idle aside or take sides." He did not return any definite answer to his own question. But he pointed to the fate of Prussia who, in 1805, had stayed out of the war only to be compelled, in 1806, to engage in it under very un-favourable circumstances.[89]

Crowe's arguments made a powerful impression upon Grey, as was revealed by his attitude at the meeting of the Cabinet on the same day (27 July). He knew that many of his Cabinet colleagues were opposed to participation in a continental war and in favour of neutrality.[90] Nevertheless, he resolved to speak his mind. He declared that the time had come for Great Britain to decide whether to wage war at the side of the Entente or to stand aside and observe complete neutrality. If the Cabinet decided upon neutrality he was not the man to carry out such a policy.[91] Although no decision was taken, it appeared that the majority of the Cabinet was opposed to Great Britain's participation in an eventual continental war. On the same day Grey described the situation to the House of Commons and informed the House of his plan for a con-ference.[92] This plan, which had been accepted by France and Italy, was firmly rejected by the German Government. The

German Secretary of State for Foreign Affairs, von Jagow, said that Grey's proposed conference "would practically amount to a court of arbitration, and could not in his opinion be called together except at the request of Austria and Russia". He was, therefore, unable to accept the plan because it appeared to be unworkable. "He added that news he had just received from St. Petersburg showed that there was an intention on the part of Mr. Sazonov to exchange views with Count Berchtold. He thought that this method of procedure might lead to a satisfactory result, and that it would be best before doing anything else to await the outcome of the exchange of views between the Austrian and Russian Governments."[93] Grey did his utmost to combat the notion that it was intended to bring Austria-Hungary before a sort of Court of Justice.

"The conference [Grey said] would not be an arbitration, but a private and informal discussion to ascertain what suggestion could be made for a settlement. No suggestion would be put forward that had not previously been ascertained to be acceptable to Austria and Russia, with whom the mediating Powers could easily keep in touch through their respective allies."[94]

The notion that Austria would permit her quarrel with Servia to be decided by a conference was indeed absurd.[95] After the experience gained in 1912-13 the Austro-Hungarian Foreign Ministry was averse in principle to the summoning of another conference, and all the more so because what was known in Vienna of Italy's attitude gave rise to fears that her representative in London would be found at the side of Austria-Hungary's enemies and that Germany would, there-fore, be left alone to contend with the other three Great Powers.[96] In conveying his refusal to Bunsen, Berchtold was careful to appear as friendly as possible. "He spoke," Bunsen reported, "gratefully of Grey's efforts for peace which had been so useful before, but feared that proposed inclusion of Russia among the directly interested Powers would be obstacle to acceptance."[97] The majority of the British Press regretted the Central Powers' rejection of a conference, while at the same time seeing in it nothing more than the refusal of a particular proposal, and not a refusal of every form of mediation, as was evidenced by the German support for direct negotiations between Vienna and St. Petersburg. It was not believed that the situation had worsened nor that this was evidence of

Germany's wish for war. Certain newspapers found it understandable that Austria-Hungary could not consent to appear before a European tribunal and to allow its policy to be influenced by any such Court of Justice. The *Westminster Gazette* wrote, on 29 July, that there was only one way to secure for Austria-Hungary the guarantees she had demanded of Servia, and that was somehow to assure Russia that the balance of power between Slavs and Germans on the Continent would not really be upset by Austria-Hungary's action.[98] From the very outset Berchtold had maintained that he could not permit any interference by foreign Powers in the Austro-Servian conflict, and that it was for this reason also that he had rejected the notion of a conference. Now, however, Sazonov (who changed his views with rapidity) after he had just suggested intervention by Great Britain and Italy in Vienna, came forward at the suggestion of the German Government and proposed to Berchtold direct negotiations between Vienna and St. Petersburg. While not refusing to take part in a conference, Sazonov simultaneously declared that he would prefer an exchange of views directly with Vienna.[99] He had already stated in Vienna that he would use "all his influence at Belgrade to induce Servian Government to go as far as possible in giving satisfaction to Austria, but her territorial integrity must be guaranteed and her rights as a sovereign State respected". He was also ready to take measures in Belgrade to make certain that no revolutionary movement would be centred and supported there that would be directed against the Dual Monarchy.[100] Berchtold said that he was, in principle, willing for conversations to be carried on by the Austro-Hungarian Ambassador at St. Petersburg, Count Szapary, for this purpose.

Although he was embittered by the rejection of his proposed conference, Grey welcomed Sazonov's proposal which conformed to the first suggestion that he had made in Vienna and St. Petersburg even before the delivery of the Austro-Hungarian Note to Servia.[101] Grey at once said that Sazonov's way was the best and that he would await its success. Doubtless, Sazonov's proposal is the explanation for the lack of interest shown by the Foreign Office in an almost simultaneous suggestion emanating from Italy that had for its object to make possible the acceptance by Servia of the Austro-Hungarian demands in their entirety, while, at the same time, affording

Servia a means of escape from the humiliation of having to submit to the dictates of her powerful neighbour. The Italian proposal was that Servia should leave the decision in the hands of the Great Powers and on their advice accept the Austro-Hungarian ultimatum in its entirety. The Great Powers would then bear the responsibility for affording Austria-Hungary the necessary guarantees for the carrying out of her demands and, at the same time, for ensuring that no injury was done to Servia's territorial integrity and sovereignty. The adoption of this plan—Italy claimed—would deprive the Austro-Hungarian Government of every reason for going to war. It is doubtful whether this proposal would have proved practicable. Crowe said it was too vague "for any practical purpose".[102] Hence, Grey did not discuss it and preferred to await the result of the direct negotiations between Vienna and St. Petersburg. Yet he still held firmly to his intention to return to his plan for mediation by the four Great Powers who were not directly involved in the conflict in event of the failure of the direct negotiations, and he strongly commended his idea to the German Government's consideration. The German Government felt compelled to give effect to Grey's wish and, after stressing its rejection of the proposed conference, told Vienna that it found it impossible to reject Great Britain's new proposal. In event of a refusal, Germany would be made responsible before the whole world for the consequences and branded as the true instigator of war. Moreover, Germany in her own interest could not reject this proposal since, in event of war, she would by virtue of its acceptance appear to have been forced to take up arms. The German Government asked for Berchtold's views on Sazonov's and Grey's proposals.[103] These words certainly did not evince either urgency or compulsive suggestion.

On the same day—28 July—that the German message reached Vienna, Bunsen sought to make Grey's standpoint clear to Berchtold. He began by saying that Grey sympathized with Berchtold's point of view, had no liking for Servia, and understood Austria-Hungary's accusations against her. It was purely the desire to prevent the outbreak of a European war that induced Grey to bring forward his proposal for a conference, and at this eleventh hour all his endeavours were bent towards the prevention of an Austro-Servian war. Was it really not possible to avoid a bloody conflict by Servia's beating a retreat and not engaging in hostilities? Grey still thought that an understanding could be reached on the basis of the Servian reply and was ready to use his influence for that purpose. There was, in reality, not the slightest prospect of Grey's proposals meeting with acceptance in Vienna where—and, indeed, throughout the Dual Monarchy—enthusiasm for a war with Servia had reached its height. On 27 July Bunsen had reported that "postponement or prevention of war with Servia would undoubtedly be a great disappointment in this country, which has gone wild with joy at the prospect of war". Public opinion in Vienna held that no mediatory proposals could be considered before Servia had been punished.[104] Hence Berchtold, while thanking Grey for his expressions of sympathy, said that it was now out of the question to stop hostilities, since the declaration of war on Servia had already been made. The news of the declaration of war was greeted throughout Austria-Hungary with wild enthusiasm.[105] With the exception of the *Arbeiterzeitung* the entire Vienna Press emitted paeans of jubilation. Berchtold told Bunsen that he could no longer negotiate on the basis of the Servian reply and that since the prestige of the Dual Monarchy was now at stake nothing could prevent the war from being fought to a finish.[106]

Public opinion in Great Britain underwent little change as a consequence of Austria-Hungary's declaration of war. None of the newspapers that had supported the Dual Monarchy went over to the camp of those who followed the policy of the *Morning Post* and *The Times*, although some papers thought the Austro-Hungarian declaration of war precipitate, while others found it understandable. Many newspapers declared that the chief thing to remember was that the declaration of war did not mean the end of everything nor that the situation had grown worse. The *Manchester Guardian* even said that the Austro-Hungarian action had eased the task of mediation by the Great Powers by clearing the air. A subject that was much discussed at this time was the question of what Great Britain's attitude should be in event of a general war—entry into the war on the side of the Entente or neutrality.[107] Opinions differed. Some papers, like the *Morning Post* and *The Times*, advocated the entry of Great Britain into a general European war at the side of France and Russia, while others were opposed to it. The *Westminster Gazette* disapproved of any attempt to tie Grey's hands and to force him along any previously marked-out path. The sole possibility of saving Europe lay in Grey's position as an impartial mediator between the two groups of Powers. The *Daily Graphic* said that if Austria-Hungary's conduct had been less justifiable than it was it would still be madness to plunge Europe into war merely on that account, and especially since Berchtold had already declared in St. Petersburg that he had no intention of acquiring territory at Servia's expense.[108]

One result of the Austro-Hungarian declaration of war on Servia was the temporary suspension of the direct negotiations between Vienna and St. Petersburg that had hardly begun.[109] These negotiations showed little prospect of succeeding, because Sazonov described many of the Austro-Hungarian demands as being incapable of fulfilment and advocated revision of the Vienna Note—a course that Berchtold never for a moment thought of taking.[110] The situation was thus rendered still more difficult for the British Government and opinion within the Foreign Office became increasingly unfavourable to Austria-Hungary. On 28 July Nicolson wrote to Buchanan in St. Petersburg: "I can quite understand Russia not being able to permit Austria to crush Servia. I think the talk about localizing the war merely means that all the Powers are to hold the ring while Austria quietly strangles Servia. This, to my mind, is quite preposterous, not to say iniquitous. I do not understand, after the very satisfactory way in which Servia has met the Austrian requests, how Austria can with any justification proceed to hostile measures against her. If she deliberately provokes war with Servia with the intention of giving her what she calls a lesson, she is, I think, acting most wrongly, for she must know very well that such action on her part would in all probability lead to a general European conflagration with all its untold disastrous consequences." He criticized Germany's conduct and sought to justify Great Britain's refusal to make any declaration of solidarity with Russia by the dependence of the Government upon public opinion.[111] The concentration of the Fleet had, however, clearly shown in which direction Great Britain's sympathies lay. "There is no doubt whatsoever," Nicolson concluded, "that were we drawn into the conflagration we should be on the side of our friends." Although Grey was less outspoken, his utterances revealed that he, too, would not leave the Entente in the lurch if war came. The difference between Grey and his closest advisers lay in the fact that Grey was still determined to achieve—if at all possible—a peaceful solution both to the existing and the threatening conflicts. At the instance of the Servian *chargé d'affaires* in Rome, the Italian Foreign Minister forwarded Grey a proposal that Austria-Hungary should be invited to make a statement to the Powers about the projected co-operation of Austro-Hungarian officials in the proceedings against the Servians who had taken part in the Archduke's assassination. If this participation by Austro-Hungarian officials was confined solely to the preliminary investigation, and did not extend to judicial or administrative proceedings, then Servia would be prepared to accept the Vienna Note in its entirety.[112] Grey believed that he could not enter into any discussion of this proposal because Austria-Hungary refused to permit any discussion of the Vienna Note.[113] However, he advised the Italian Foreign Minister to explore the ground in Vienna and Berlin, and added that he would be only too pleased when any suggestion that Italy might make to the German and Austro-Hungarian Governments met with a favourable reception.[114]

Another suggestion discussed at this time was whether or not the four Great Powers should make yet another attempt to mediate—a suggestion supported by Russia after the failure of direct negotiations between Vienna and St. Petersburg.[115] Negotiations in Berlin revealed that Germany was willing to work for peace, although the Imperial Chancellor stated that if Russia were to mobilize fourteen Army Corps against Austria-Hungary he would be unable to give the Austro-Hungarian Government counsels of moderation. Bethmann-Hollweg took this opportunity of repeating that the Austro-Servian dispute only concerned those two Powers. The Foreign Office did not believe that Germany had sought in any way to restrain Austria-Hungary.[116] Nevertheless, Grey felt that he was bound to state in Berlin that if Germany were able to persuade Austria-Hungary to give assurances that would satisfy Russia, everyone would be united in gratitude for the preservation of peace.[117] This appeal to Germany seemed to Grey to be all the more urgent because Sazonov had appealed to him for help, and had suggested returning once more to the idea of a conference, or at least an exchange of views, between the four Great Powers with the possible inclusion of Austria-Hungary. Sazonov stated his willingness to accept any arrangement that

France and Great Britain approved of. Haste was, above all, necessary. The Austro-Hungarian ultimatum must, nevertheless, be given a milder tone.[118]   On the same day—29 July— the French Ambassador at Berlin, M. Jules Cambon, asked if an opportunity would not be given to the Powers of avoiding worse complications after Austria-Hungary had invaded Servia and therewith safeguarded her prestige. The German Under-Secretary for Foreign Affairs thought the idea worthy of consideration and it again made its appearance that same day in a conversation between Grey and the German Ambassador.[119]   The Ambassador defended Austria-Hungary's cause, while Grey championed Russia. When Lichnowsky said that Austria-Hungary could be humiliated by force and robbed of her position as a Great Power, Grey replied that he fully agreed with him, but that that was not the question, which was the humiliation of other States at Austria-Hungary's hands. "There must, of course, be some humiliation of Servia, but Austria might press things so far as to involve the humiliation of Russia." On Lichnowsky's remarking that Austria-Hungary did not want a foot of Servian soil Grey said, as he had often said before, that Austria-Hungary could reduce Servia to the status of a vassal State without taking any of her territory and while leaving her nominally independent. This would be a severe blow to Russian prestige in the Balkans.[120]

Lichnowsky and Grey resumed their conversation that afternoon. Grey informed Lichnowsky of Russia's partial mobilization, and the failure of the direct negotiations between Vienna and St. Petersburg, and then repeated the proposal made that morning. It was essential—Grey said—to find some way of saving the peace.

"I pointed out, however [Grey continued], that the Russian Government while desirous of mediation regarded it as a condition that the military operations against Servia should be suspended, as otherwise a mediation would only drag on matters and give Austria time to crush Servia. It was, of course, too late for all military operations against Servia to be suspended. In a short time, I supposed, the Austrian forces would be in Belgrade, and in occupation of some Servian territory. But even then it might be possible to bring some mediation into existence if Austria, while saying she must hold the occupied territory until she had complete satisfaction from Servia, stated that she would not advance further pending an effort of the Powers to mediate between her and Russia."[121]

This was the so-called "Halt in Belgrade" proposal. At this time Belgrade had not been captured and for military reasons the commencement of the campaign had been postponed to a later date. In London, however, it was assumed that the advance on Belgrade would begin at once. In reply to a question in the House of Commons on the same day, Mr. Asquith had stated that the situation was extremely critical, but that the Government was doing everything in its power "to circumscribe the area of possible conflict".[122] Asquith spoke the truth. On the same day came the news that Russia had mobilized against Austria-Hungary.[123] Goschen reported from Berlin that the Imperial Chancellor had said to him that were Russia to attack Austria-Hungary Germany would fulfil her obligations to her ally. That would mean a European war. He (Bethmann-Hollweg) hoped for Great Britain's neutrality and offered in return that, in event of her gaining the victory, Germany would not demand any French territory in Europe. He would not, however, give the same undertaking in regard to the French colonial possessions. Germany was prepared not to violate Dutch neutrality for so long as the other belligerent Powers did the same, while, with regard to Belgium, he could not say to what operations Germany might be forced by French military movements. But "he could state" that provided Belgium did not place herself at the side of Germany's enemies her territorial integrity would be respected at the end of the war. Goschen said at once in reply to Bethmann-Hollweg's question that he thought Grey wished to keep a free hand "and would not care to bind himself to any course of action at this state of events".

At the Foreign Office Bethmann-Hollweg's offers were condemned outright. Crowe said that "the only comment that need be made on these astounding proposals is that they reflect discredit on the statesman who makes them . . . It is clear that Germany is practically determined to go to war and that the one restraining influence so far has been the fear of England joining in the defence of France and Belgium."[124] Grey employed exceptionally strong language in rejecting Germany's suggestion that Great Britain should bind herself to neutrality under such conditions. He said it was completely out of the question that Great Britain would allow France to lose her position as a Great Power and herself to become subject to Germany. A deal of this kind would destroy forever England's good name. He was no less profoundly dissatisfied with Bethmann-Hollweg's statement regarding the neutrality of Belgium. In these circumstances it was superfluous to examine whether or not the prospect of some future general state of neutrality between Great Britain and Germany offered such positive advantages as to compensate for Great Britain's hands being bound at the present time. "My answer must be [Grey went on] that we must preserve our full freedom to act as circumstances may seem to England to require in any development of the present crisis, so unfavourable and regrettable as the Chancellor contemplates."[125]

It now became a question for Grey and all men of goodwill of trying to save the peace. The German Government was, in fact, trying to influence the Austro-Hungarian Government in the sense of the British proposal. But it was questionable whether Vienna was prepared to accept mediation and to communicate her terms after the occupation of Belgrade and a few other places. Jagow voiced the fear that Russian mobilization against Austria-Hungary increased the difficulties that stood in the way of a peaceful settlement of the conflict.[126] While an answer was awaited from Vienna, Sazonov declared in reply to the German Ambassador's question whether he would be satisfied with a declaration by Austria-Hungary that she would not violate the integrity of Servia that such a declaration would not suffice. But when Pourtalès asked under what conditions Russia would stop her military preparations, Sazonov said that if Austria-Hungary, recognizing that the Austro-Servian dispute had become a European question, declared herself ready to eliminate from her ultimatum the demands "portant atteinte" to Servia's sovereign rights, then Russia would undertake to call off her preparations for war.[127] The German Government at once said that this proposal was inacceptable. Austria-Hungary could not suffer such a blow to her prestige in the Balkans. Nor was it believed in London that Berchtold would accept such a proposal, although Grey still continued to hope that Sazonov might be induced to change his attitude if Austria-Hungary accepted the "Halt in Belgrade" proposal.[128] He therefore instructed Buchanan to support a German proposal for renewed direct negotiations between Vienna and St. Petersburg.[129] As was expected, Berchtold rejected Sazonov's proposal, while, at Germany's insistence, declaring his readiness in principle to resume negotiations with Russia. All questions affecting Austro-Russian relations were to be discussed in conversations between Szapary and Sazonov, yet there was no mention of any agreement to the Russian proposal to discuss the Servian Question.[130] Berchtold did, indeed, once again assure the Russian Ambassador in Vienna that Austria-Hungary was not planning any acquisition of territory at Servia's expense, and that after the conclusion of peace Austria-Hungary would only occupy Servian territory temporarily in order to ensure fulfilment of the peace conditions and the creation of good-neighbourly relations for the future. Once this has been accomplished Austria-Hungary would withdraw from Servia. He also reported this undertaking to Berlin and added that he could not give an answer to the "Halt in Belgrade" proposal until after he had spoken with the Emperor and Tisza. Since, however, Russia had stated that the demands contained in the ultimatum, whose fulfilment the "Halt in Belgrade" proposal was intended to force, were inacceptable, this proposal had little likelihood of being accepted in St. Petersburg.[131] For the same reason no better reception would have been accorded to an idea mooted in Vienna on the previous day by the Italian Ambassador "that Russia might be induced to remain quiet if Austro-Hungarian Government would convert into a binding engagement to Europe declaration made at St. Petersburg to the effect that she desires neither to acquire Servian territory nor to destroy independence of Servia." Even if it had been forthcoming the Austro-Hungarian Government's consent to such a step would have made no difference.[132]

Notwithstanding the unfavourable news that reached London from Berlin and St. Petersburg on 29 and 30 July, Grey continued his endeavours to prevent a general war. In lengthy conversations with Mensdorff on 30 July he drew the Ambassador's attention to the difficult situation in which he found himself as a consequence of the breaking off of direct negotiations between Vienna and St. Petersburg. (He knew nothing as yet about the resumption of these negotiations.) Two opposing standpoints confronted him between which he must make a choice. The one was to state publicly that Great Britain stood beside France and Russia, which might prevent the war, or to declare that Great Britain would not under any circumstances take part in a war between the Entente and

Triple Alliance Powers. Grey gave Mensdorff no inkling of what his decision would be. On the contrary, he stressed that he was still endeavouring with all his energies to save the peace, and was seeking to influence Russia in this direction notwithstanding the fact that the German-Russian negotiations did not seem to be making any progress. But he could accomplish nothing at St. Petersburg with empty hands. To demand that Russia should stand aside until Austria-Hungary had finished with Servia could only meet with a refusal. Vienna offered nothing that was of any value to St. Petersburg.

Grey stopped making suggestions. None the less, Berchtold believed that Grey still hoped to prevent the outbreak of a general war if Austria-Hungary would declare that, after occupying Belgrade and a portion of Servia, she would cease operations if Servia fulfilled her demands for the fulfilment of which the Powers would give a guarantee. Mensdorff believed that Grey was sincere in his endeavour to keep the peace, and that he would give his support for any plan designed for that purpose. He also thought that Grey was sincerely anxious to obtain for Austria-Hungary very complete satisfaction and guarantees for the future in regard to Servia if only Austria-Hungary could make—for which, Mensdorff added, it may now be too late—some sort of declaration on the subject of the future of Servia as an independent State that would be in any way acceptable by Russia.[133] If Russia were to reject this proposal, and therewith put herself in the wrong, Grey would be in the position to exert pressure upon her. He had frequently, and again on 29 July, given expression to his personal views on this matter, namely, that Great Britain would not abandon her neutrality to serve Russia's interest, but that the moment France took up arms the whole situation underwent an important change. No British Government could refuse to stand by France in a life and death struggle. It was a fundamental principle of British policy adhered to by all political parties that France must not be allowed to suffer any weakening of her position as a Great Power.[134] He was strengthened in this opinion by Lichnowsky who, in view of the extremely threatening situation, on 30 July through Mensdorff advised the Austro-Hungarian Government to negotiate with St. Petersburg *via* Berlin, and to avoid bringing up again the question of the ultimatum, which could only give rise to "irritating" protests, and instead to put forward new terms.[135] An attempt was also made from Berlin to win over the Austro-Hungarian Government to a compromise.

At the personal request of Tsar Nicholas II, the German Emperor, William II, advised the Emperor Francis Joseph to accept Grey's proposal that Austria-Hungary, after occupying Belgrade and other places in Servia, would state her conditions for peace in order to open the way to negotiations with St. Petersburg.[136] On the evening of the same day—30 July—the German Ambassador in Vienna, von Tschirsky, was again instructed earnestly to advise acceptance of Grey's proposal more especially as Grey was prepared to use this influence in Paris and St. Petersburg to halt mobilization. If Grey was successful, and Vienna rejected all proposals, then the Austro-Hungarian Government would clearly show that it wanted war—a war into which Germany would be dragged while Russia remained guiltless. The result would be that the German Government would find itself in an untenable situation in regard to the German nation.[137] Two hours later, news was received in Berlin that France and Russia were mobilizing, and the Imperial Chancellor therefore stopped the dispatch of the telegram to Tschirsky. This had hardly been done before a telegram reached Berlin from King George V to the Emperor's brother, Prince Henry of Prussia, which ran:

"I am earnestly desirous that such an irreparable disaster as an European war should be averted. My Government is doing its utmost suggesting to Russia and France to suspend future military preparations if Austria will consent to be satisfied with occupation of Belgrade and the neighbouring Servian territory as a hostage for satisfactory settlement of her demands, other countries meanwhile suspending their war preparations."[138]

This telegram helped to increase German pressure on Austria-Hungary. Meanwhile, official information reached Vienna from St. Petersburg that the Tsar had ordered mobilization in all military districts on the Austro-Russian frontier. Austria-Hungary, therefore, on 31 July, ordered general mobilization. The Emperor Francis Joseph communicated this decision to the German Emperor, William II, in the words: "Conscious of my grave responsibilities to my realm I have ordered the mobilization of my entire forces. The operations of my Army against Servia cannot be interrupted by the threatening challenge of Russia. Another rescue of Servia by Russian intervention would involve the most serious consequences for my country and therefore I cannot possibly allow it."[139]

On the same day the Emperor Francis Joseph held a Council of Ministers which adopted decisions reached the previous evening by the Emperor, Berchtold, Conrad von Hötzendorff and Krobatin (Minister for War), which laid down as indispensable preliminary conditions for any negotiation the continuance of the war with Servia, the cessation of Russian mobilization, and the acceptance of the Vienna Note. Any discussion of these conditions would be inadmissible. Berchtold stated that a victory on paper that only saved Austria-Hungary's prestige would be worthless and—even were Russia to allow it—an occupation of Belgrade useless. Russia would appear as the saviour of Servia and the Serbs would again attack Austria-Hungary in two or three years' time under conditions far less favourable for the Dual Monarchy. The Council resolved that Grey should be informed of its decisions.[140] Mensdorff was instructed to inform Grey that Berchtold was prepared to give closer consideration to Grey's proposals for mediation out of regard for Great Britain's efforts to maintain peace. The preliminary conditions were that Austria-Hungary should temporarily carry on the campaign against Servia and that the British Government was able to induce the Russian Government to halt its military preparations against Austria-Hungary. In this event, Austria-Hungary would call a halt to the military measures she had taken in Galicia as a result of the Russian mobilization.[141] Berchtold also informed the British Government that he remained faithful to the promises he had made to Russia and other Powers that Austria-Hungary harboured no intention of interfering with Servia's existence as a sovereign State nor of annexing Servian territory.[142] Even at this late hour Grey was still willing to work for a peaceful solution to the conflict. On 30 July Mensdorff reported that Grey was doing his utmost to secure from Servia the fullest satisfaction for Austria-Hungary's demands and guarantees for the future. A preliminary condition was, however, that Austria-Hungary should make a declaration on the subject of Servia's future existence as an independent State that would be couched in some form that would be acceptable to Russia.[143] Grey's instructions to Goschen followed the same lines. Goschen was told to make an urgent and imperative demand of the German Government to use its influence in Vienna to obtain this declaration. For were Russia to be rebuffed the blame would rest on Austria-Hungary's shoulders.[144] It is significant that Mensdorff was convinced that Grey did everything that lay in his power to preserve peace—all that was necessary was that he should be afforded the possibility of doing so.[145]

The renewed negotiations between Szapary and Sazonov in St. Petersburg afforded Mensdorff new grounds for hope. Sazonov wanted the negotiations to be carried on in London under Grey's chairmanship with the representatives of the other three Powers not directly involved in the dispute, and was willing to alter the text of the recent Russian proposal so that it would now read:[146]

"Si l'Autriche consentira à arrêter marche de ses troupes sur le territoire serbe, si, reconnaissant que le conflit austro-serbe a assumé le caractère d'une question d'intérêt européen, elle admet que les Grandes Puissances examinent la satisfaction que la Serbie pourrait accorder au Gouvernement d'Autriche-Hongrie sans laisser porter atteinte à ses droits d'Etat souverain et à son indépendance, la Russie s'engage à conserver son attitude expectante."

Grey breathed again, for he thought the new text more suitable than the earlier text to serve as the basis for further negotiations. Peace can still be preserved—Grey exclaimed—if only no Power starts a war. The British Government certainly refrained from any step that could precipitate matters.[147] The Austro-Hungarian Government, however, said that the new Russian text was completely inacceptable because Sazonov required Austria-Hungary to cease all military preparations, while Russia was to adopt a "Wait and see" attitude without any cessation of her preparations for war.[148] On 1 August Mensdorff called at the Foreign Office and said that on the previous day Berchtold had informed the Russian Government that Austria-Hungary had by no means "banged the doors" on further negotiations, and had also renewed to the Russian Ambassador in Vienna his assurance that Austria-Hungary did not contemplate the acquisition of a foot of Servian soil nor the placing of any limitation upon Servia's sovereign rights.[149] Mensdorff's statement awakened fresh hopes. The negotiations in St. Petersburg, nevertheless, proved fruitless, because German-Russian relations steadily worsened, until the attitudes of the two Empires to one another became mutually inimical.[150] On 31 July Russia ordered general mobilization against Germany, and, after the expiry of the twelve hours within which Germany had demanded Russia should cease mobilization, Germany on 1 August declared war on Russia and a few days later on France. On 4 August Great Britain entered the war at the side of the Entente.

Germany tried hard to induce Austria-Hungary to declare war on Great Britain and France, because she wanted the Austro-Hungarian Navy to assist the German warships *Goeben* and *Breslau* in their operations in the Mediterranean. The Austro-Hungarian Government hesitated to accede to its ally's request, because it feared by a too precipitate declaration of war to expose the Austro-Hungarian Fleet to complete destruction. Austria-Hungary, therefore, merely promised to enter the war against the Western Powers as soon as her naval preparations had been completed.[151] Great Britain, too, did not contemplate declaring war on Austria-Hungary before she received direct provocation.[152] But it soon became evident that clashes with the Austro-Hungarian Navy could not fail to arise out of the necessity for the British Navy to co-operate with the French Navy in the Atlantic and the Mediterranean. On 12 August Austria-Hungary found herself at war with the Western Powers.[153] Since 6 August she had been at war with Russia. Ever since 1 August Austria-Hungary had played a very minor part in the negotiations leading up to the British declaration of war and the British Press was virtually silent on the subject of Austro-Hungarian affairs.[154] Her fate was, indeed, indissolubly bound up with that of Germany. Grey deeply regretted Mensdorff's departure. He had been on terms of intimate friendship with him and parted from him most cordially. On 7 August Mensdorff wrote:[155]

"Grey is in despair that his efforts to maintain the peace have gone to ruin. Again and again he said of the war, 'I hate it, I hate it.' He recalled all the efforts we have made together in the previous year during the Balkan conferences. He earnestly hoped that, once the present danger were passed, it might be possible to preserve the peace for years. I was quite ready (he said) if ever Russia had been aggressive —in the case of France it was not likely that she should—to stand by Germany, and that we might come to some sort of understanding between the Powers. Now all that was shattered and the universal war with all its horrible and revolting consequences had broken out."

Mensdorff was in despair. The war for him was a personal tragedy.[156] No real enmity existed between Great Britain and Austria-Hungary. True, they belonged to different rival groups of Powers—Austria-Hungary to the Triple Alliance, Great Britain to the Entente. Since, however, their interests did not run parallel to one another, and since each was invariably guided in its policy by regard for the welfare of the State, they became mutually involved in serious conflicts that led to war. The present writer deliberately abstains from expressing any opinion as to whether or not war could have been avoided. It is, however, permissible to draw attention once more to the standpoints adopted by the statesmen of these two Great Powers in formulating and conducting their policy. In the light of the consequences that the war brought in its train to Austria-Hungary it is unquestionable that Austro-Hungarian policy was wrong. A peaceful dissolution of the Dual Monarchy —quite apart from the enormous sacrifice of human life caused by the war—would certainly have been preferable in the interest alike of the culture and economic prosperity of the various races living within the Monarchy's wide-flung frontiers. But no Great Power has ever given up its position as a Great Power without an appeal to arms.[157] Moreover, it must be borne in mind when seeking to arrive at an impartial verdict upon the decisions taken by the rulers of the Dual Monarchy that public opinion throughout the Monarchy was convinced that this time the existence of the Monarchy itself was at stake. Every attempt to call a halt to the assaults of the individual races upon the unity of the Dual Monarchy had proved ineffectual. The attractive force exercised by the races living outside the frontiers of Austria-Hungary upon their co-racials living within those frontiers had become so powerful that the Austro-Hungarian Government became convinced that the Dual Monarchy's fate was sealed unless an end could be made by force of arms to the conspiracies and disruptive intrigues of the most dangerous of the Monarchy's enemies—Servia.

Austria-Hungary's standpoint contrasted sharply with that of Great Britain. Neither Grey not his advisers were greatly interested in the Austro-Servian dispute. In fact, they were not interested in it at all. They could never on its account alone have wanted to summon the British people to arms nor would the nation have responded to such an appeal.[158] The sole consideration that British statesmen kept firmly before their mental vision was the welfare and vital interest of their nation. Great Britain saw her vital interest in the maintenance of her position as a world Power and, therefore, in the repulsion of every attempt to destroy that position. British statesmen were convinced at this time that there was only a single Power that had both the will and the strength to make this attempt— Germany. Neither commercial nor naval rivalry with Germany alone brought Great Britain into the war. The guiding principle of British policy was the unshakable conviction that Germany was striving for the mastery over Europe.[159] That is not to say that war was inevitable. The overwhelming majority of influential men in British public life were opposed to any disturbance of the peace and solely desired that the differences between Great Britain and Germany that were becoming clearer every day should be settled by peaceful means. Nobody desired this more strongly than did Grey himself. But he was no less convinced that if war were to prove inevitable, Great Britain must fight beside the Entente. It has often been said both by Grey's contemporaries and by subsequent critics of his policy that a public statement to this effect would have prevented the outbreak of war. French and Russian statesmen in the years preceding the war certainly pressed Grey to make a statement of this kind, because they were convinced that Germany would beat a retreat if confronted with it. It is possible—if also improbable—that a public declaration of solidarity with the Entente would have produced the desired effect.[160] Might not such a declaration by Great Britain, however, have resulted in France and Russia forcing war upon Germany? France in the hope of regaining Alsace-Lorraine, Russia the possession of Constantinople and an outlet on the Mediterranean. Would Grey have had the nation behind him in the purusit of this policy?[161]

Grey knew that the majority in the Cabinet, the banking world, industrialists and great merchants were outspokenly opposed to a war policy.[162] He had to ask himself whether he could gain the support of a majority in the House of Commons for a public announcement at such an early date of Britain's intention to fight at the side of the Entente; more especially because he was aware that the vast majority of the British people were averse to intimate relations with an autocratic reactionary Russia. It would have been even more difficult for Grey to have entertained Germany's proposal for British neutrality. We have only to recall Crowe's words on 24 July on the subject of the consequences that would follow from British neutrality in a war in which it seemed likely that the Central Empires would smash France to pieces and humble Russia in the dust. "With the French Fleet gone," Crowe wrote, "Germany in occupation of the Channel with the willing or unwilling co-operation of Holland and Belgium, what will be the position of a friendless England? Or France and Russia win? What would then be their attitude towards England? What about India?[163] And the Mediterranean?"[164] Moreover, what about the possibility that a defeated France and humbled Russia might, of necessity, be reconciled with Germany and then join with Germany in an attack upon Great Britain?[165] It was characteristic of Grey that in rejecting the German proposal for British neutrality he emphasized that its acceptance in its present form would leave an indelible stain on British honour. After taking into consideration every reason that must have affected Grey in making his decision it is only possible to say that he chose the only way that seemed to promise to lead him to the fulfilment of his aim. Although he rejected Germany's neutrality proposal as incompatible with Great Britain's engagements to France, Grey would not bind Great Britain to France and Russia until the last possible moment. Grey himself quite early reached the decision that if war proved inevitable Great Britain should fight with the Entente, and he was resolved to resign if Parliament preferred a policy of neutrality. Yet Grey spared no pains in endeavouring to preserve peace and only came out openly on the side of the Entente when he could reasonably expect the Cabinet, Parliament, and public opinion would support him.[166] Germany's declaration of war on France, and, above all, the German violation of Belgian neutrality, gave him the opportunity of rousing the whole British Empire to a frenzy of enthusiasm for war with Germany. It was in the firm belief that Germany intended to achieve the mastery over Europe, no less than in the Empire's own special interest, that Grey decided that Great Britain must fight at the side of France and Russia.

"We felt [Grey subsequently wrote in his autobiography] that to stand aside would mean the domination of Germany, the subordination of France and Russia, the isolation of Britain, the hatred of her by both those who had feared and those who had wished for her intervention in the war, and ultimately that Germany would wield the whole power of the Continent. How would she use it as regards Britain? Could anyone feel comfortable about that question? Could anyone give to it truthfully in his heart any but a sinister and foreboding answer?"[167]

The maintenance of France as a Great Power and regard for Russia whose friendship he valued on account of British interests in Asia, and whose enmity he wished to avoid under all circumstances, were objects that came within the sphere of those British interests whose service was the guiding principle of his policy.[168] Of Austria-Hungary little was heard in the days immediately preceding the outbreak of the First World War. Since, however, Austria-Hungary was Germany's ally, war had to be declared upon her. As is well known, it ended for Austria-Hungary in the break-up of the empire to which Great Britain only gave her assent late in the war as a consequence of engagements taken with her new allies. In view of all that has happened in the years that have succeeded to the First World War, it is at least permissable to question whether that decision served Great Britain's most enduring interests. It may well be that the day will yet come when Palacky's famous saying, "If Austria did not exist, it would be necessary to invent her," will meet with the approval of many who still believe that the struggle for national fulfilment is the noblest occupation of mankind. Happily, it is not the business of the historian, whose gaze is perforce turned upon the past, to act the prophet in seeking to foretell the future. *Qui vivra, verra.*

NOTES

ABBREVIATIONS

The following abbreviations have been used throughout:

A.D.   Oesterreich-Ungarns Aussenpolitik 1908-1914.
Br.D.   British Documents on the Origins of the War 1898-1914.
D.D.F. Documents diplomatiques Françaises, 1871-1914.
G.Pol. Die Grosse Politik der Europäischen Kabinette 1871-1914.

CHAPTER ONE

1. Quoted in Pribram, *England and the International Policy of the European Great Powers, 1871-1914*, p. 2.
2. Cf. Pribram, *op. cit.*, pp. 21 ff.
3. Salisbury wrote to Queen Victoria at this time "that though the entente with Italy left Great Britain free to give or to withdraw material co-operation, it was as close an alliance as the parliamentary character of our Constitution would permit". Quoted in Hammond, J. L., *Life of C. P. Scott*, p. 134.

CHAPTER THREE

1. Fournier, A., *Wie wir zu Bosnien kamen* (Vienna, 1909), p. 64 ff. Carathéodory Pasha, *Le rapport secret sur le congrès de Berlin* (Paris, 1919), p. 164 ff.
2. For a similar plan in 1882 cf. Seton-Watson, R. W., *Russian Commitments in the Bosnian Question and an early project of annexation. Slavonic Review*, VIII, p. 586 f, also quoted in Schmitt, Bernadotte E., *The Annexation of Bosnia, 1908-1909* (Cambridge University Press, 1937), p. 3, n. 2. It is not necessary to enter into the controversy that arose over what actually was said between Isvolsky and Aehrenthal at Buchlau. It is dealt with by Schmitt, *op. cit.* Chapter II, where he also lists a number of publications on the subject.
3. Schmitt, *op. cit.*, p. 12.
4. A.D., I, 91. The numbers refer to the numbering of the documents reproduced in these volumes and not to the page numbers.
5. A.D., I, 93. Also reproduced in Lee, Sir Sidney, *King Edward VII*, Vol. 2, p. 632.
6. Br.D., V, 273. Whitehead to Grey, 30 September 1908. The numbers refer to the numbering of the documents reproduced in these volumes and not to the page numbers.
7. Br.D., V, 276. Goschen to Grey, 1 October 1908.
8. Br.D., V, 281. Bertie to Grey, 3 October 1908.
9. A.D., I, 114 and 115. Mensdorff to Aehrenthal, 3 October 1908. Cf. also Br.D., V, 287, Memorandum respecting an interview between Sir. C. Hardinge and Count Mensdorff, 3 October 1908.

10. A similar declaration was made by Asquith in the House of Commons on 12 October. G.Pol, XXVI/I, 9035. The numbers refer to the numbering of the documents reproduced in these volumes and not to the page numbers.

11. Br.D., V, 302. Grey to Goschen, 5 October 1908. Cf. also Grey of Fallodon, *Twenty-five Years*, I, p. 175, where he describes his attitude to the Annexation. He writes: "A cruel blow it seemed to the budding hopes of better things in Turkey. Besides this, it was the alteration of an European treaty to which other Powers as well as Turkey were parties. To us the territorial changes were indifferent, it mattered not to us that Austria should annex instead of merely occupying Bosnia and Herzegovina, but besides sympathy with the new hope in Turkey we felt that the arbitrary alteration of an European treaty by one Power without the consent of the other Powers who were parties to it struck at the root of all good international order." His instructions to Goschen on 5 October 1908 are also reproduced on this page.

12. Br.D., V, 289. Goschen to Grey, 4 October 1908.

13. *Ibid.*, 291. Goschen to Grey, 4 October 1908.

14. *Ibid.*, 299. Grey to Goschen, 5 October 1908.

15. *Ibid.*, 381. Goschen to Grey, 14 October 1908.

16. *Ibid.*, 318. Goschen to Grey, 6 October 1908.

17. *Ibid.*, 330. Grey to Goschen, 7 October 1908.

18. Grey had already said much the same thing in a speech to his constituents on 7 October. Cf. Gooch, G. P., *History of Modern Europe*, p. 415.

19. Br.D., V, 296. Grey to Lowther, 5 October 1908.

20. A.D., I, 228. Mensdorff to Foreign Ministry, 10 October 1908.

21. *Ibid.*, 140. Telegram from London, 5 October 1908.

22. *Ibid.*, 192. Telegram from London, 8 October 1908.

23. Quoted in Lee, *op. cit.*, Vol. II, p. 633 ff.

24. Steed, Henry Wickham, *Through Thirty Years*, Vol. I, p. 283. Cf. also Br.D., V, Appendix IV, and Lee, *op. cit.* Vol. II, p. 633.

25. This is also Nintchitch's opinion in *La crise bosniaque 1908-1909 et les puissances Européens* (2 vols., 1934), I, p. 346.

26. For the text cf. A.D., I, 244. Emperor William II said: "Pharisee! Look at the Morocco Agreement of 1904 with France in which England threw over the Treaty of Madrid." Cf. G.Pol., XXVI/2, 9213.

27. Br.D., V, 397. Goschen to Grey, 19 October 1908. Goschen also reported the Emperor Francis Joseph as saying: "Servia threatens all sorts of things—but I have taken no military measures whatever—and I do not intend to do so unless insult gives place to direct aggression." When reporting his farewell audience of the Emperor on 5 November Goschen wrote: "His Majesty then said that Servia continued to be the black spot on the horizon. He hoped that all would go well, but the Servians must not push things too far, as Austria-

Hungary had already pushed patience to the verge of imprudence." Cf. Br.D., V, 430, Goschen to Grey, 5 November 1908.

28. Wittrock, G., *Oesterrike-Ungern i Bosniskakrisen 1908-1909*, p. 45 deals vaguely with this question but inclines to think that Aehrenthal was not honest.

29. In reply to a question by Lord Lansdowne on 12 October the Under Secretary said "that no definite arrangement for a conference had yet been made". But on the following day "an official *communiqué* announced that the British and Russian Ministers had agreed to demand a conference". Cf. *Cambridge History of British Foreign Policy*, Vol. III, p. 404.

30. A.D., I, 228. Dispatch from London, 10 October 1908. Also Br.D., V, 338, Lowther to Grey, 8 October 1908.

31. A.D., I, 276. Telegram to London, 14 October 1908.

32. Br.D., V, 350. Grey to Lascelles, 9 October 1908.

33. *Ibid.*, 354. Grey to Egerton, 10 October 1908.

34. *Ibid.*, 303. Nicolson to Grey, 5 October 1908.

35. *Ibid.* On this telegram from Nicolson are important minutes by Hardinge and Grey.

36. Cf. Schmitt, *op. cit.*, p. 56.

37. *Supra.* Note 35.

38. A.D., I, 335. Telegram to London, 19 October 1908.

39. *Ibid.*, 347. A private letter to Aehrenthal from Archduke Francis Ferdinand, 20 October 1908. Cf. Nintchitch, *op. cit.*, Vol. I, p. 161.

40. Br.D., V, 362. Lowther to Grey, 12 October 1908, with Minute by Sir Louis Mallet.

41. *Ibid.*, 404. Lowther to Grey, 26 October 1908.

42. *Ibid.*, 407. Grey to Goschen, 26 October 1908.

43. A.D., I, 408-9-10. Telegrams from London, 26 October 1908.

44. *Ibid.*, 441. Telegram to London, 28 October 1908.

45. *Ibid.*, 453-454. Dispatches from London, 30 October 1908. Throughout October 1908 discussions went on in the Foreign Office over the question of what districts might possibly be given to Servia and Montenegro as compensation. Spizza and the two Turkish enclaves of Suttorina and Klek on the Dalmatian coast were thought of for Montenegro. For Servia Kossovopolye, or at least a part of it, including the famous Field of Sparrows where Servia lost her independence in 1389 and where the Christian armies were annihilated in 1448. But doubts were at once expressed about Aehrenthal's agreeing to this plan. Cf. Br.D., 400. Memorandum of 21 October 1908. Subsequently it was agreed by all the Powers at Great Britain's suggestion that no territorial compensation should be made at Turkey's expense. Cf. Lübbing, H., *Englands Stellung zur bosnischen Krise*, p. 45.

46. *Ibid.*, 489. Dispatch from London, 3 November 1908.

47. A.D., I, 489. Dispatch from London, 3 November 1908. The following incident aptly reveals Aehrenthal's nervousness.

On 3 November Mensdorff wrote from London that he had
received a telegram from the Austro-Hungarian Ambassador
in Rome which said that the Italian Foreign Minister,
Tittoni, had told him that if Austria-Hungary refused to
take part in a conference the British Government would not
hesitate to recall the British Ambassador from Vienna, and
even to send a naval squadron into the Adriatic. Mensdorff
added that he was of the same opinion as the Ambassador in
Rome who thought such a statement was far too pessimistic.
Aehrenthal, however, became extremely excited, took the
matter seriously, and wrote to Rome: "It is unheard of that
England should take upon herself to force a Great Power to
take part in a conference and that for this reason she is ready
to recall her Ambassador. As to the projected naval demonstration in the Adriatic we are certainly not to be placed on
the same footing as the old Turkey whom one was accustomed
to terrify by such methods."

48.   *Ibid.*, 513 and 514. Telegrams to London, 6 November 1908.
On 5 November Goschen took his leave of Aehrenthal and
Francis Joseph. Cf. Br.D., V, 428 and 429. The Emperor
said to him "that he was exceedingly sorry that I (Goschen)
was leaving Vienna just when affairs were in rather an un-
settled state and when there was some difference of opinion on
certain matters between Austria-Hungary and Great Britain.
'But,' His Majesty added, 'we are such old and good friends
that I am sure that any slight misunderstanding that may
now exist will soon pass away, and we shall be as good friends
as ever.' "

49.   Grey spoke in the House of Commons on 10 November 1908,
on the subject of the conference. Cf. Knaplund, Paul,
Speeches on Foreign Affairs by Sir Edward Grey, p. 110.
"We have all an interest in upholding the sanctity of
treaties in Europe and for that reason we hold it necessary
that the consequences of what has happened recently in
the Near East should be discussed by and brought under
the cognizance of the European Powers who are parties
to the Treaty of Berlin, and in that way I hope the consequences will be disposed of peacefully . . . I think that
some progress has been made in the last week, because we
now have evidence that Turkey, the Power whose interests
have been most affected by what had happened, has been
reassured by the action of ourselves and other Powers that
in submitting the questions which had affected her to the
council of Europe she will find there sympathy and fair
play."
On a dispatch from the British Chargé d'affaires in Vienna
to Grey dated 26 November 1908, which reported Aehrenthal's
views on the conference proposals, Hardinge remarked in a
Minute:
"This is simply vebiage and does not advance matters.

It is rather a strong order to expect Turkey and five Great Powers to meet in Conference and simply take act of an illegal proceeding without discussion and presumably without even expressing an opinion (as was done in 1871) upon the character of such proceedings."
Cf. Br.D., V, 466. Also cf. Gall, W., *Sir Charles Hardinge und die englische Vorkriegspolitik*, p. 145. Hardinge held similar language to the Servian Minister in London. Cf. Boghitschewitsch, *Die auswärtige Politik Serbiens 1903-1914*, Vol. I, Number 37.

50. A.D., I, 524. Enclosure 2 to instructions to the Councillor of the Austro-Hungarian Embassy in Berlin, Baron von Flotow, 6 November 1908.

51. Some of Aehrenthal's remarks at this time reveal his standpoint. At the beginning of November he said to Goschen: "You people in England are incurring a great responsibility and the Russians too." When he was warned not to underestimate Great Britain's influence he replied: "What can England do to us?" Cf. Conwell-Evans, *Foreign Policy from a Back Bench*, p. 24. Also cf. Gooch, G. P., *Before the War*, Vol. I, p. 402, and Lee, S., *op. cit.* I, p. 644.

52. A.D., I, 644. Aide-Mémoire for English Chargé d'Affaires in Vienna, 25 November 1908.

53. *Ibid.*, 590. Dispatch from London, 17 November 1908; and 565. Instruction to London, 13 November 1908.

54. That Great Britain during the entire Balkan crisis did not want a war in the Balkans is shown by her attitude when news reached London of a projected alliance between Turkey and Servia. Instructions marked "very confidential" were sent on 1 December 1908 by Sir Edward Grey to the British Minister in Belgrade, Mr. Whitehead, which ran:
"His Majesty's Government could not give official countenance to any Convention specifically directed against any Power or Powers designated by name. We are very anxious to see the establishment of the closest and most friendly relations between the Balkans States and Turkey, as the surest means of promoting peace in the Near East and of preventing any further encroachments, but the Convention as now drafted would defeat that object since it is directed against Bulgaria as well as Austria. Any agreement concluded by Servia with Turkey and the other Balkan States should be of a purely defensive character. I do not see how any agreement can secure the Balkan peninsula against aggression unless Bulgaria is on its side and a combination which forced Bulgaria into alliance with Austria would never secure peace or be strong."
Cf. Br.D., V, 468. Also cf. Boghitschewitsch, *op. cit.* III, p. 92, n. 2.

55. A.D., I, 660-661-662. Dispatches from Mensdorff in London, 27 November 1908.

56. *Ibid.*, 662.

57. Br.D., V, 412 and 416. Grey wrote to Nicolson on 27 October 1908:

> "I have not, myself, much sympathy with the clamour of Servia and Montenegro for territorial compensation. If they are afraid of the Austrian advance, they had better sit still, put their own houses in order, make friends with Turkey, and hope that she will get strong under the new regime."

Boghitschewitsch, *op. cit.* III, p. 85, n. 3, is right in pointing out the discrepancy between this statement and that which a few days later Grey made to Milovanovic (Servian Minister for Foreign Affairs) in which he expressed his sympathy with Servia's case and his readiness to support Servia's territorial demands provided that Russia also supported them. Her regard for Russia's wishes decisively influenced Great Britain's policy in the Servian Question. It was in this spirit that Grey wrote the private letter to Nicolson which has been quoted in part above. For he added: "I do not want to cold-shoulder Isvolsky on the Servian Question, if the Russians are keen about it, and I will do my best to support him."

58. A.D., I, 564. Telegram to Széchényi in London, 13 November, 1908.

59. *Ibid.*, 587. Telegram from London, 16 November 1908.

60. The Austrian and Hungarian Delegations each consisted of sixty members of the Austrian and Hungarian Parliaments chosen by their fellow-members and met annually and alternately in Budapest and Vienna to supervise the work of the joint Austro-Hungarian Ministries for Finance, War, and Foreign Affairs.

61. Aehrenthal frequently protested against the notion (which was widely held and accepted by many historians) that he was the tool of Germany. On this subject cf. Kabisch, Ernst, *England und die Annexionskrise, 1908-1909* in *Berliner Monatshefte* October, 1930, p. 915 ff, and also Wedel, O. H., *Austro-German Diplomatic Relations, 1908-1914*, p. 65, where the sources are cited. Crozier in his essay *L'Autriche et l'avant guerre* in *Revue de Paris*, April-June, 1921, writes on p. 289 that Aehrenthal said to him on the subject of Austria-Hungary's position *vis-à-vis* Germany in the Triple Alliance:

> "J'entend rester scrupuleusement fidèle aux obligations inscrites dans le traité Austro-Allemand, mais je ne cache pas mon intention de profiter avec un sain égoisme de toute la liberté d'action laissée à chacun des contractants en dehors de ces obligations qui sont définies et par là même précises et limitées."

62. Count Forgach reported from Belgrade that the Special Correspondent of *The Times*, Mr. Brown, had told him confidentially that the attacks in the English Press were the result of a "mot d'ordre" from the Foreign Office. Grey

denied that the Foreign Office exerted any influence upon the Press. Moreover, Aehrenthal himself did not believe Forgach's story of the millions which Noel Buxton was supposed to have distributed in Servia for anti-Austrian propaganda.

63. A.D., I, 681. Private letter from Aehrenthal to Mensdorff, 30 November 1908.

64. Br.D., V, 485. Grey to Cartwright, 14 December 1908. Grey answered Aehrenthal's complaints about England's conduct by saying:

> "Baron d'Aehrenthal's views as to England's responsibility for the present situation are on a par with the statements in part of the Austrian press, which writes as if it were England and not Austria which had first disturbed the *status quo*."

And shortly afterwards Grey again wrote to Cartwright and said *inter alia*: "As far as the press was concerned, I considered that we were the injured party." Cf. *ibid.*, 487. Grey to Cartwright, 16 December 1908. Cf. also Schmitt, *op. cit.* p. 77 n. 5.

65. A.D., I, 695. Private letter from Mensdorff to Aehrenthal, 5 December 1908.

66. A.D., I, 768. Private letter from Aehrenthal to Mensdorff, 17 December 1908 marked "Very Confidential" and only to be opened by Mensdorff.

67. Hardinge went so far as to say that if Aehrenthal refused to agree to a compromise with Turkey on the basis of the proposals made by Great Britain—financial compensation— the Emperor would have to dismiss him. Cf. Gall, *op. cit.*, p. 145.

68. A.D., I, 781. Private letter from Mensdorff to Aehrenthal, 20 December 1908.

69. *Ibid.*, 730. Private letter from Count Khevenhüller in Paris, 12 December 1908. Cf. Wittrock, *op. cit.*, p. 218 ff. Wittrock thinks that Edward VII did let fall some such remark, but not at an official audience nor directly to Riza, but to somebody who knew him. Wittrock also thinks Aehrenthal overestimated Edward VII's influence.

70. Br.D., V, 823. Private letter from Grey to Nicolson, 2 April 1909.

71. *Ibid.*, 475. Cartwright's Memorandum of 4 December 1908 enclosed in Bertie's dispatch of 5 December 1908.

72. Grey in a letter to Cartwright on 23 December 1908 said that this accusation was wholly unfounded. Cf. Grey, *Twenty-five Years*, I, p. 190, where he quotes this letter:

> "I can only qualify as preposterous and utterly absurd the Austrian suspicions that H.M.'s Government are desirous of bringing about an European war. Both public opinion here and and the foreign policy of H.M's Government are alike opposed to such a scheme. So far from ever

having encouraged the Governments of Servia, Montenegro, and Turkey in an attitude of opposition to Austria, we might fairly claim that it is to some extent due to our influence that the Ottoman Government has shown itself ready to negotiate with Austria. We have used all our influence in the cause of peace by discouraging impossible claims and demands and by curbing the violence of public feeling, which was outraged by the policy of Baron d'Aehrenthal himself."

73. Br.D., V, 483-484. Telegram and letter from Cartwright to Grey 11 December 1908.
74. *Ibid.*, 484. Minute by King Edward VII on a dispatch from Cartwright to Grey, 11 December 1908.
75. *Ibid.*, 485. Telegram, Grey to Cartwright, 14 December 1908.
76. *Ibid.*, 487. Private letter from Grey to Cartwright, 16 December 1908.
77. A.D., I, 758. Dispatch from London, 16 December 1908.
78. Br.D., V, 491. Enclosure IV in Aide-Mémoire, 25 December 1908.
79. *Ibid.* Enclosure V.
80. A.D., I, 790. Instruction to London, 23 December 1908.
81. *Ibid.*, 830. Telegram from London, 2 January 1909.
82. Br.D., V, 500. Grey to Cartwright, 4 January 1909.
83. *Ibid.*, 500. Ed. Note. Private letter from Hardinge to Nicolson, 4 January 1909. Also cf. No. 528, Grey to Nicolson, 23 January 1909.
84. A.D., I, 868. Telegram to London, 9 January 1909. The aide-mémoire handed to Grey by Mensdorff on 11 January was enclosed in Grey to Cartwright, 16 January 1909, cf. Br.D., V, 516.
85. In his speech in the House of Commons on 22 January 1909, Grey said he was glad that at least in principle an agreement had been reached between Austria-Hungary and Turkey. The sky was still overcast, "but I trust from the example of conciliation, which both Austria and Turkey have shown . . . it will be helpful in the settlement of the remaining controversies." Cf. Knaplund, *op. cit.*, p. 111.
86. This had reference to a speech by the Prime Minister Milovanovic in the Skuptschina [Servian Parliament] in which he declared that Austria-Hungary had done little more than make slaves of the Servian population of Bosnia-Herzegovina. Aehrenthal demanded an apology and got it. Cf. Schmitt, *op. cit.*, p. 145 ff.
87. Br. D., V, 503. Enclosure in Cartwright's dispatch of 6 January 1909.
88. *Ibid.*, 508. Cartwright to Grey, 7 January 1909.
89. A.D., I, 881. Telegram to London, 12 January 1909. Stieve, F., *Die Tragödie der Bundesgenossen*, p. 57 ff summarises Aehrenthal's complaints against Great Britain.
90. A.D., I, 892. Telegram from London, 14 January 1909.
91. *Ibid.*, 896. Telegram to London, 16 January 1909.

92. Wittrock, *op. cit.*, p. 274, believes that, although Aehrenthal did not credit the story about Noel Buxton's millions, he did believe that English agitators were at work and that British money was being spent in Servia for this purpose.

93. A.D., I, 903. Telegram from London, 18 January 1909.

94. *Ibid.*, 892. Telegram from London, 14 January 1909. In a speech in the House of Commons on 22 January 1909, Grey said:

"No doubt this feeling (for Turkey) and the force of events placed us in an attitude not sympathetic to the Austrian action of last autumn. When pending questions in the Near East have been settled I trust that want of sympathy will pass away. That is our desire. But in Austria we have been unduly and publicly accused of a deliberate play of malevolence. I do not attach much importance to these accusations. But I cannot allow the gross charges made against us to pass without saying that it would be under the mark to call the gross charges that have been made against us misrepresentations. They are sheer inventions, and the harm they do is not so much in the resentment caused here as in the fact that until they are not only discontinued but disbelieved in the country of their origin, they create a state of feeling there, which is a barrier to cordial relations between the public opinion of the two countries—a barrier which is not in our power but only in theirs to remove."

Cf. Knaplund, *op. cit.*, p. 112.

95. Br.D., V, 522. Private letter from Hardinge to Nicolson, 20 January 1909.

96. *Ibid.*, 570. Nicolson to Grey, 14 February 1909.

97. *Ibid.*, 571 and 576. Telegrams from Nicolson to Grey, 15 and 17 February 1909.

98. A.D., I, 963. Telegram to London, 5 February 1909.

99. Cf. Nintchitch, *op. cit.*, II, p. 110 ff, and Wittrock, *op. cit.*, p. 320 ff for a full description of Servian preparations and provocations.

100. Br.D., V, 555. Cartwright to Grey, 3 February 1909.

101. *Ibid.*, 592. Grey to Cartwright, 19 February 1909. Quoted by Gooch, *op. cit.*, II, p. 52 ff.

102. *Ibid.*, 583. Grey to Goschen, 18 February 1909, enclosed is a Memorandum dated 11 February 1909 by Sir C. Hardinge reporting his conversation with the German Imperial Chancellor, Prince von Bülow, the day before.

103. *Ibid.*, 604. Telegram from Grey to Cartwright, 24 February 1909. Cf. also Grey, *Twenty-five Years*, I, pp. 186-187.

104. *Ibid.*, 592. Cartwright to Grey, 20 February 1909.

105. *Ibid.*, 598. Goschen to Grey, 23 February 1909.

106. *Ibid.*, 597. Whitehead to Grey, 23 February 1909.

107. *Ibid.*, 603. Grey to Cartwright, 24 February 1909.

108. A.D., I, 1048. Telegram from London, 24 February 1909.

109. *Ibid.*, 1053. Telegram to London, 25 February 1909.
110. *Ibid.*, 1054. Instructions to London, 25 February 1909.
111. Br.D., V, 621. Grey to Nicolson, 27 February 1909.
112. *Ibid.*, 624. Nicolson to Grey, 28 February 1909.
113. For these Franco-German negotiations, cf. Schmitt, *op. cit.*, p. 158 ff.
114. A.D., II, 1072. Telegram from Aehrenthal to Mensdorff, 27 February 1909.
115. Br.D., V, 643. Grey to Cartwright, 2 March 1909.
116. A.D., II, 1097. Circular Telegram from Aehrenthal, 3 March 1909. Cf. also Wittrock, *op. cit.*, p. 451.
117. *Ibid.*, 1107. Mensdorff to Aehrenthal, 4 March 1909.
118. Br.D., V, 657. Cartwright to Grey, 6 March 1909.
119. *Ibid.*, 659. Grey to Cartwright, 8 March 1909. Cf. also A.D., II, 1109. Aehrenthal to Forgach, 5 March 1909.
120. *Ibid.*, 647. Grey to Goschen, 3 March 1909. Cf. also A.D., II, 1087. Telegram from London, 2 March 1909.
121. *Ibid.*, 634. Grey to Whitehead, 1 March 1909. Enclosed is the Servian Declaration of 27 February 1909.
122. *Ibid.*, 653. Whitehead to Grey, 4 March 1909. Enclosed is a "Proposed Circular to the Servian Representatives at the Capitals of the Signatory Powers of the Treaty of Berlin." For Russian situation cf. *ibid.*, 664. Nicolson to Grey 10 March 1909.
123. Cf. Schmitt, *op. cit.*, p. 153 ff.
124. The French text of the Servian Declaration is to be found in Br.D., V, 662. Gruič to Grey, 10 March 1909.
125. The words "as to the competent tribunal" are left out of Schmitt's translation. Otherwise the present English version follows that of Schmitt, *op. cit.*, p. 171.
126. Br.D., V, 667. Cartwright to Grey, 12 March 1909.
127. *Ibid.*, 674. Grey to Cartwright, 12 March 1909. Cf. also A.D., 11, 1193. Telegram from London, 12 March 1909.
128. For text of Servian Note, cf. A.D., II, 1220. Telegram from London, 15 March 1909. Cf. also Schmitt, *op. cit.*, p. 182, and Boghitschewitsch, *op. cit.*, II, 471.
129. A.D., II, 1235. Telegram to London, 15 March 1909.
130. *Ibid.*, 1220. Telegram from London, 15 March 1909.
131. Br.D., V, 683. Whitehead to Grey, 15 March 1909. Minutes on this dispatch. Cf. also *Ibid.*, 690. Nicolson to Grey, 15 March 1909, where Isvolsky is reported as saying that the Servian Note contained certain phrases which would have been better left out. Nicolson ended his account of Russia's attitude to Servia's demands with the words:

> "It is unfortunate that, as is I fear undoubtedly the case, Russia held out until recently hopes to Servia that she would obtain territorial compensations and that Russia would employ every diplomatic and pacific means to secure them for her. It would have been better, and perhaps

juster to Servia, if from the outset the true situation had been explained to her."

132. A.D., II, 1239. Note from the Foreign Office handed to the Austro-Hungarian Ambassador in London, 16 March 1909, and also No. 1236. Telegram from London of the same date.

133. *Ibid.*, 1237. Telegram from London, 16 March 1909.

134. *Ibid.*, 1252. Note from English Ambassador, 17 March 1909.

135. Br.D., V, 697. Grey to Cartwright, 16 March 1909.

136. A.D., II, 1278. Telegram to London, 17 March 1909.

137. *Ibid.*, 1278. Telegram to London, 19 March 1909.

138. The English text is to be found in Schmitt, *op. cit.*, p. 210 f. The French text as above is in A.D., II, 1280. Note for the English Ambassador in Vienna, 19 March 1909. The words contained in the final—third—paragraph of the text above were not intended to be included in the Servian Note, nor communicated to the Servian Government, but were only for the information of the British Cabinet. Cf. A.D., II, 1365. Telegram to London, 26 March 1909.

139. Br.D., V, 725. Grey to Cartwright, 20 March 1909, and also 721. Cartwright to Grey, 19 March 1909.

140. A.D., II, 1302. Note from the English Ambassador, 21 March 1909.

141. *Ibid.* Cartwright handed the Note to Aehrenthal on 21 March and an account of their subsequent conversation is given in a private letter from Aehrenthal to Cartwright, 22 March 1909, to be found in A.D., II, 1313, and also in Cartwright's long private letter to Grey on 1 April 1909 which is to be found in Br.D., V, 820. Aehrenthal maintained that it was Cartwright who made the proposal. Cf. also A.D., II, 1411. Telegram from London, 29 March 1909.

142. *Ibid.*, 1313. Enclosure I.

143. *Ibid.*, 1315. Telegram from London, 22 March 1909.

144. *Ibid.*, 1314. Mensdorff to Aehrenthal, 22 March 1909.

145. *Ibid.*, 1325. Telegram from London, 23 March 1909.

146. *Ibid.*

147. *Ibid.*, 1341. Telegram from London, 24 March 1909.

148. Br.D., V, 739. Grey to Cartwright, 22 March 1909. An English translation is to be found in Schmitt, *op. cit.*, p. 214.

149. *Ibid.*, 747. Cartwright to Grey, 23 March 1909.

150. A.D., II, 1324. Telegram to London, 23 March 1909. Lübbin, *op. cit.*, p. 59, does not think it was Aehrenthal's intention to humiliate Russia or Servia. He condemns Grey's conduct and speaks of his pedantry.

151. Cf. Schmitt, *op. cit.*, p. 186 ff, and Wittrock, *op. cit.*, p. 516 ff, among other writers.

152. Grey's tenacious determination to retain certain phrases in his draft even after Russia had accepted Aehrenthal's draft was doubtless due to the fact that he grudged Berlin a diplomatic victory. Cf. Wedel, *op. cit.*, p. 92.

153. Br.D., V, 758. Grey to Cartwright, 24 March 1909.

154. *Ibid.*
155. See p. 133.
156. A.D., II, 1353. English draft of Servian Declaration. Cf. also Schmitt, *op. cit.*, p. 215 ff.
157. *Ibid.*, 1358. Berchtold to Aehrenthal, 24 March 1909.
158. *Ibid.*, 1364. Telegram to London, 26 March 1909, and cf. also Br.D., V, 773. Cartwright to Grey, 26 March 1909.
159. *Ibid.*, 1365. Telegram to London, 26 March 1909.
160. For English text cf. Schmitt, *op. cit.*, p. 217.
161. See p. 133.
162. A.D., II, 1367. Austro-Hungarian Draft of a Servian Declaration. The third paragraph of Aehrenthal's first draft was omitted because it was only intended for Great Britain's information.
163. Br.D., V, 770. Grey to Goschen, 25 March 1909, and also 774. Grey to Cartwright, 26 March 1909. Grey ended his long account of a conversation with the German Ambassador, Count Metternich, with the words:

> "Count Metternich continued to maintain that we were obstructing peace by refusing recognitions. I, on the contrary, maintained that by giving unconditional recognition we should not be securing peace, but might simply be preparing the way for a settlement of the Servian and Montenegrin difficulties by force, to which method we should then indirectly be parties, whereas, if Austria promised peace, we should be quite ready to become partners in a general peaceful settlement by doing what Austria desired."

At the end of the telegram to Cartwright, Grey said:

> "H.M. Government have no wish to assert special interests of their own in the matter, which go beyond the facts of the case, but they cannot accede to the request which has been made without some assurance that they are not being placed in the position or made parties to the procedure described and that their assent will contribute to a peaceful and not a forcible solution of present difficulties."

164. *Ibid.*, 802. Cartwright to Grey, 20 March 1909.
165. A.D., II, 1379. Telegram to London, 27 March 1909.
166. Br.D., V, 781. Grey to Cartwright, 27 March 1909.
167. *Ibid.*, 771. Grey to the British Ambassadors at Paris, Rome, and St. Petersburg, 26 March 1909. The Italian and French Governments at once agreed to Grey's proposal.
168. That Aehrenthal did take into his calculations the possibility that in the last resort he might have to attain his end by force of arms cannot be doubted. Nevertheless it is no less certain that he wanted if at all possible to avoid war. He told the German Ambassador in Vienna, von Tschirsky, that the incorporation of Servia with the Dual Monarchy, or a partition of Servia between Austria-Hungary, Bulgaria, and Rumania was not, in his opinion, practicable nor in the

interest of Austria-Hungary. Cf. G.Pol., XXVI, Pt. II, 9493. Tschirsky to Bülow, 28 March 1909. Cf. also Schmitt, *op. cit.*, p. 225.

169. Br.D., V, 781. Grey to Cartwright, 27 March 1909.

170. A.D., II, 1398. Aide-Mémoire from the English Ambassador, 28 March 1909. Cf. also Br.D., V, 786. Grey to Cartwright, 27 March 1909.

171. Br.D., V, 794. Cartwright to Grey, 28 March 1909. Grey was also the recipient of the Emperor's thanks for his efforts for peace.

172. No attempt is made here to describe the negotiations that led up to the alteration of Article XXIX of the Treaty of Berlin. Agreement was only reached after lengthy negotiations that were chiefly carried on between Austria-Hungary and Italy. Clause 5 and Clauses 7-11 were abrogated. But Clause 6, which forbade the use of Antivari as a naval base, was retained in force.

173. A.D., II, 1394. Telegram to London, 28 March 1909. Hardinge expressed himself to Mensdorff in similar terms. Cf. 1397. Telegram from London, 28 March 1909.

174. A controversy arose out of this action inasmuch as the English, French, Italian, and Russian Ministers at Belgrade made a written communication to the Servian Government of Aehrenthal's assurance that he did not intend to place obstacles in the way of the free development, security, and independence of Servia. Aehrenthal protested against this action because he had never contemplated that an assurance intended for the Powers would be passed on to the Servian Government. Grey replied that he had understood that this assurance was to be given to the Servian Government.

On this subject cf. A.D., II, 1442. Aehrenthal to Mensdorff, 2 April 1909, and 1453. Mensdorff to Aehrenthal, 3 April 1909. Cf. also Schmitt, *op. cit.*, p. 227 and n. 3.

On the subject of the Servian Note of 31 March, cf. Gottschalk, E., *Die diplomatische Geschichte der serbischen Note vom 31 März, 1909*, in *Berliner Monatshefte*, X, 1932, p. 787 ff.

For the negotiations between the British and Austro-Hungarian Governments during the last days of March, cf. Wittrock, *op. cit.*, p. 540 ff.

175. A.D., II, 1434. Telegram to London, 1 April 1909.

176. British statesmen from the outset doubted the wisdom of settling highly controversial questions in a conference. But they changed their views from time to time in their desire to fulfil the wishes of other Powers. Neither Grey nor Hardinge attached much importance to the manner in which these questions were settled and continued to bring forward the idea of a conference whenever any of the other proposals for settling these questions encountered insuperable opposition. Cf. *Cambridge History of British Foreign Policy*, III, p. 405, and also Schmitt, *op. cit.*, Chapter VII, "The Abandonment of the Conference."

177. A.D., II, 1452. Telegram from London, 3 April 1909; and 1474. Telegram from London, 5 April 1909.
178   *Ibid.*, 1523 and 1524. Telegrams from Aehrenthal to Mensdorff, 15 and 16 April 1909.
179. *Ibid.*, 1542. Note from the British Embassy in Vienna, 17 April 1909.
180. Cf. Conrad von Hötzendorff, *Aus meiner Dienstzeit*, Vol. I, p. 162, who says that on 29 March 1909 mobilization was decided upon by a Council of Ministers presided over by Aehrenthal. In Conrad's opinion this was proof that Aehrenthal was reckoning with the possibility of war. It seems more likely that Conrad is exaggerating in making this statement.
181. For Conrad's plans in regard to Servia. Cf. Conrad, *op. cit.*, I, p. 78 ff. On the subject of the differences that arose between Conrad and Aehrenthal as to the limitations set to their individual authority, cf. Conrad, *op. cit.*, II, p. 218 ff., and also the present writer's article on "Conrad and Aehrenthal" in *Oesterreichischen Rundschau*, 1921.
      At the time of the Bosnian Crisis Count Berchtold was Austro-Hungarian Ambassador at St. Petersburg and an intimate friend of Aehrenthal's. In an essay which he wrote for General Steinitz's book, *Rings um Sazonoff*, he says on p. 45:
      "Aehrenthal never at any time expressed to me by word of mouth or in writing the notion of a complete subjection of Servia to Austrian influence or domination."
182. This is the view that is most widely held to-day. In his biography of his father, *Sir Arthur Nicolson, First Lord Carnock: A study in the Old Diplomacy*, Harold Nicolson writes on p. 303:
      "The Central Powers had secured a diplomatic victory more disastrous to themselves than any possible defeat."
      The present writer has already described the outcome of the Bosnian Crisis as a Pyrrhic victory in his earlier books, *England and the Great European Powers, 1821-1914*, p. 129, and *Austrian Foreign Policy, 1908-1914*, p. 32.
      An especially severe judgement upon Aehrenthal as a statesman has been passed by Wedel in his book *Austro-German Diplomatic Relations, 1908-1914*.

CHAPTER FOUR

1. A.D., II, 2157. Dispatch from Count Adam Tarnowski, London, 7 May 1910. Count Tarnowski (who acted as Chargé d'Affaires from time to time during Count Mensdorff's absence) wrote in this dispatch *inter alia*:
    "The feeling that is current here to-day about us does not arise directly out of the Crisis. It is rather an inevitable corollary of the only consequence of the Annexation that still persists, namely, the 'new impression' that has been spread abroad in this country 'about us'. To define this 'altered judgement' that has taken the place of that which

was entertained in England of Austria-Hungary before the Crisis is only possible within a few words by saying that formerly we [Austria-Hungary] were looked upon as a Power with whom it was unthinkable that Great Britain would go to war whereas to-day we are looked upon here as a possible enemy who in the event of war would support the only Power with whom Great Britain seriously contemplates the possibility of conflict—Germany." Tarnowski's words are also cited—though not quite literally—by Stieve, *op. cit.*, p. 59.

1A. Br.D., VI, 178. Cartwright to Grey, 29 April 1909, with Minute by Crowe and Grey, 8 May 1909.

2. A.D., II, 2157. Tarnowski to Foreign Ministry, 7 May 1909.

3. *Ibid.*, 2168. Instructions to London, 13 May 1909.

4. Br.D., IX/I, 19. Cartwright to Hardinge, private letter, 9 July 1909.

5. A.D., II, 1677. Report to the Emperor, 16 July 1909.

6. *Ibid.*, 1685 and 1694. Telegrams from London, 22 and 27 July 1909. King Edward VII also gave Mensdorff to understand that the German Emperor who was in Norway would say that he (King Edward) was taking the opportunity of his absence to invite himself to Ischl.

7. Br.D., IX/I, 48. Cartwright to Grey, 4 September 1909.

8. *Ibid.*, 56. Grey to Cartwright, 24 September 1909.

9. *Ibid.*, 38. Cartwright to Grey, 9 August 1909. The Austro-Hungarian Ambassador in Washington, Baron von Hegelmüller, who had been involved in 1880 in the dispute between Gladstone and Karolyi, also said the same thing. Karolyi wrote to Gladstone and the latter had then excused himself on the ground that he had been falsely informed.

10. *Supra.* Note 8.

11. *Ibid.*, IX/I, 212. Grey to Cartwright, 3 February 1911, and cf. also A.D., II, 2419. Tarnowski to Foreign Ministry, 20 January 1911.

12. In a Memorandum which he wrote at Abbazia on 6 March 1910 on the subject of his conversations in Berlin between 22-25 February 1910, with the German Emperor William II and the German Chancellor, Herr von Bethmann-Hollweg, Aehrenthal stated that he had said that since April 1909 British policy in regard to Austria-Hungary had been more conciliatory and that he could express himself as satisfied with the existing relations between the two countries. Cf. A.D., II, 2024. Memorandum by Aehrenthal. Cf. also A.D., III, 2445. Telegram to London, 4 February 1911.

13. Br.D., IX/I, 16. Cartwright to Hardinge, private letter, 24 June 1909, with a Minute by Sir Edward Grey.

14. *Ibid.*, 64. Hardinge to Cartwright, private letter, 4 October 1909. Hardinge ended his letter with these words: " . . . but I would sooner trust Aehrenthal than Isvolsky, and I prefer Aehrenthal because he is much the more clever . . ."

15. *Ibid.*, 127. Grey to Cartwright, 2 March 1910, and cf. also A.D., II, 1981. Telegram to London, 4 February 1910.
16. *Ibid.*, 134. Grey to Cartwright, 8 March 1910, and 135 and 136. Cartwright to Grey, 10 and 11 March 1910.
17. Aehrenthal complained of this article to Grey but soon afterwards said he did not want to make a fuss about it. Cf. *Ibid.*, 146. Grey to Cartwright, 29 March 1909, and 147. Cartwright to Grey 31 March 1909. Also *ibid.*, 136. Cartwright to Grey, 11 March 1909.
18. A.D., II, 1914. Telegram to London, 20 December 1909.
19. *Ibid.*, 2006. Private letter to London, 18 February 1910.
20. Br.D., IX/I, 165. Cartwright to Grey, 5 August 1910.
21. A.D., III, 2260. Aide-Mémoire from the English Ambassador, 28 September 1910.
22. *Ibid.*, 2289. Private letter from Aehrenthal to Mensdorff, 30 October 1910.
23. *Ibid.*, II, 2024. Memorandum by Aehrenthal of his conversations with the German Emperor and German Chancellor in Berlin, 22-25 February 1910, written at Abbazia, 6 March 1910.
24. *Ibid.*, III, 2541. Instructions to London, 9 June 1911.
25. *Ibid.*, 2668. Dispatch from Balmoral, 29 September 1911.
26. Br.D., I, 359. Lansdowne to Lord Currie, 3 February 1902 in which he said: " . . . if at any time an alteration of the *status quo* should become inevitable it would be their (British Government's) object that such alteration should not be of a nature to operate to the detriment of Italian interests." Cf. also 360. 7 March 1920, where the words used are: "that such alteration should be in conformity with Italian interests."
27. Cf. Giesl, *Zwei Jahrzehnte im nahen Orient*, p. 190, writes: "The Archduke (Francis Ferdinand) once said to me, 'Aehrenthal collaborates with Jews and Freemasons to prevent the Monarchy from holding a day of reckoning with Italy before it is too late'."
28. A.D., III, 2801. Telegram to London, 21 October 1911, and cf. also Br.D., IX/I, 290. Cartwright to Grey, 23 October 1911.
29. *Ibid.*, 2814 and 2818. Telegrams from London, 23 and 24 October 1911.
30. *Ibid.*, 2848. Telegram to London, 29 October 1911.
31. *Ibid.*, 2852. Telegram from London, 30 October 1911. Cf. also Br. D., IX/I. 297, Grey to Cartwright, 24 October 1911.
32. *Ibid.*, 3214, 3225, 3275, 3300. Telegrams from London, 12 and 15 January, 6 and 16 February 1912.
33. *Ibid.*, IV, 3315. Telegram from London, 26 February 1912, and 3326, Note from the English Embassy, 29 February 1912. For the policies pursued by the several Powers during the Balkan Wars, cf. Helmreich, E. C., *The Diplomacy of the Balkan Wars, 1912-1913*, where on pp. 473-495 will be found a bibliography of the very extensive literature upon this subject. Cf. also Schröder, Werner, *England, Europa und der Orient*. Both books were published in 1938.

34. *Ibid.*, 3342. Telegram from London, 1 March 1912.
35. *Ibid.*, 3361. Telegram to London, 7 March 1912.
36. *Ibid.*, 3507. Aide-Mémoire for British Embassy, 4 May 1912.
37. Br.D., IX/I, 528. Cartwright to Grey, 5 December 1911, with Minute by Grey.
38. *Ibid.*, 560. Nicolson to Cartwright, private letter, 18 March 1912. For the Austro-Hungarian and British Governments attitudes to the treaty of 14 March 1912 between Servia and Bulgaria, cf. Schröder, *op. cit.*, p. 90 ff.
39. *Ibid.*, 598. Grey to Cartwright, 23 July 1912.
40. A.D., IV, 3633. Instructions to London, 20 July 1912, drafted by Berchtold and marked "Highly Confidential". In the middle of June conversations took place between Grey's Private Secretary, Mr. (later Lord) Tyrrell, and Mensdorff in which the former assured the latter that Grey would give his warmest support for all measures for the preservation of the *status quo* in the Balkans. Cf. Schröder, *op. cit.*, p. 150 ff. Berchtold's hopes of holding further discussions with Grey over this matter were doomed to disappointment.
41. Br.D., IX/I, 622. Cartwright to Grey, 15 August 1912 and Editorial Note. 623, Note communicated by French Chargé d'Affaires, 15 August 1912. 627, Buchanan to Grey, 16 August 1912. 695, Buchanan to Grey, 3 September 1912. 698, Cartwright to Grey, 4 September 1912, with Minutes by Grey and Mallet.
42. *Ibid.*, 713. Grey to Cartwright, 10 September 1912, and Editorial Note.
43. *Ibid.*, 715. Cartwright to Grey, 11 September 1912, with Grey's Minute.
44. A.D., IV, 3869. Memorandum by Chief of the General Staff to the Emperor, 28 September 1912. 3928, Memorandum, Secret, 2 October 1912. Quoted by Gooch, *Before the War*, II, pp. 385-386.
45. *Ibid.*, 3973. Circular Telegram to Austro-Hungarian Embassies in Europe, 6 October 1912, with enclosure. Quoted by Gooch, *op. cit.*, II, p. 386. Count Hoyos, in the article he contributed to Steinitz, *op. cit.*, p. 68 ff, says that the Foreign Ministry never seriously considered the problem of a possible partition of the Balkans. Only at the eleventh hour was a Commission set up to study it, and it recommended the creation of an independent Albania and also that other questions should be left for decision by the Balkan peoples. In Hoyos' opinion Grey's conduct of the London Conference was strongly influenced by the state of Anglo-German relations.
46. Br.D., IX/II, 15. Cartwright to Nicolson, private letter, 10 October 1912. Cf. also A.D., IV, 4041. Dispatch from London, 11 October 1912.
47. *Ibid.*, 4087. Dispatch from London, 14 October 1912.
48. *Ibid.*, 4167. Dispatch from London, 25 October 1912.

49. *Ibid.*, 4170. Memorandum of the proceedings of a conference held in the Foreign Ministry, undated (between 25 and 30 October 1912). It is worthy of note that Berchtold did not deceive himself as to the intentions of the Great Powers. On 2 October 1912 he remarked in a memorandum:

> "We must not entertain any illusions that our action in the annexation of Bosnia-Herzegovina did not give the impulse for the creation of the Balkan League, and also that it aroused the mistrust of the Chancelleries of all the Great Powers against the Monarchy, which in its turn created a hitherto unknown community of understanding between them on the subject of their attitude towards our Eastern policy."

Cf. *ibid.*, 3928. Memorandum, 2 October 1912. Quoted by Gooss, *Das Werk des Untersuchungsausschusses der verfassungsgebenden deutschen Nationalversammlung des deutschen Reichstages. Erste Reihe. Die Vorgeschichte des Weltkrieges.* Vol X. Opinion of the expert witness, Dr. R. Gooss.

50. *Ibid.*, 4183. Note to Chief of the General Staff, 26 October 1912. Cf. also Giesche, Richard, *Der serbische Zugang zum Meere und die europäische Krise, 1912*, p. 17. This book is useful in studying the various stages of the question of Servia's access to the Adriatic.

51. *Ibid.*, 4215. Telegram from London, 31 October 1912.

52. *Ibid.*, 4227. Telegram from London, 1 November 1912.

53. G.Pol., XXXIII, 12399. Prince von Lichnowsky to the Foreign Ministry in Berlin, London, 19 November 1912.

54. Cf. Giesche, *op. cit.*, p. 37 ff.

55. Br.D., IX/II, 83. Cartwright to Grey, 1 November 1912.

56. A.D., IV, 4265. Report on a visit by the Turkish Ambassador to the Foreign Ministry, 4 November 1912.

57. A.D., IV, 4268. Telegram from London, 4 November 1912.

58. Br.D , IX/II, 134. Grey to Cartwright, 5 November 1912. The narrative above is based on the statements in this dispatch which fully coincide with the declaration made by the Austro-Hungarian Government in Berlin. Cf. Gooch, *op. cit.*, p. 389, and also A.D., IV, 4269. Telegram from London, 4 November 1912.

59. Sazonov, S. D., *Fateful Years, 1909-1916*, p. 73, says that the Russian Minister in Belgrade, M. Hartwig, after the victory of the Balkan allies, declared that among their demands was one for the partition of Albania between Servia, Montenegro, and Greece by which Servia would receive northern Albania, with the exception of Scutari (which was to go to Montenegro), and the whole Adriatic coastline from San Giovanni di Medua up to Skumbra, while Greece was to take southern Albania.

60. A.D., IV, 4321. Telegram from London, 8 November 1912.

61. *Ibid.*, 4333. Telegram from London, 9 November 1912.

62. *Ibid.*, 4359. Telegram to London, 10 November 1912.

63. *Ibid.*, 4369. Telegram to London, 11 November 1912.
64. *Ibid.*, 4370. Telegram from London, 11 November 1912.
65. *Ibid.*, 4404. Telegram from London, 13 November 1912. It was at this time that Nicolson expressed the opinion that the Servians had lost their heads because they had no right whatsoever to any part of Albania with the possible exception of the district adjoining the Sandjak of Novibazar. The British Ambassador at St. Petersburg, Sir George Buchanan, in reply to the Servian Minister's statement that Austria-Hungary's opposition to Servia's acquisition of a harbour on the Adriatic was only bluff, said that Great Britain had no intention of going to war over any such question, and that Servia might easily lose the fruits of her victory if she provoked Austria-Hungary to take up arms. Buchanan's remark met with Grey's approval. Quoted in Roloff, *England und der Balkankrieg, 1912-13*, in *Berliner Monatshefte*, December 1935, p. 1034 ff.
66. Br.D., IX/II, 165. Cartwright to Nicolson, private letter, 8 November 1912.
67. On this question, and also for the whole course of the negotiations over the delimitation of the southern frontier of Albania, cf. Stickney, Edith Pierpont, *Southern Albania or Northern Epirus in European International Affairs, 1912-1923* (Stanford University Press, 1926).
68. Br.D., IX/II, 192. Cartwright to Grey, 13 November 1912, and also 233. Cartwright to Grey, 19 November 1912, and 241. Cartwright to Grey, 21 November 1912.
69. A.D., IV, 4565. Dispatch from London, 22 November 1912. Cf. also Br.D., IX/II, 238. Nicolson thought that Berchtold acted with great dignity and displayed much moderation and forbearance. Also cf. Schröder, *op. cit.*, p. 186.
70. On Grey's attitude at this time the Russian Ambassador in London, Count Benckendorff, wrote:
    "When I drew Grey's attention to the solidarity of the Triple Alliance and asked him if he could tell me anything about England's attitude in case our efforts to prevent Austrian action were not successful, he replied after some moments' reflection that it was impossible for him to give a direct answer to a question referring to a possibility which since his interview with Mensdorff no longer appeared probable."
    Benckendorff's remarks are to be found in Dickinson, G. L., *The International Anarchy*, p. 338.
71. A.D., IV, 4542. Dispatch from London, 21 November 1912.
72. *Ibid.*, 4581. Telegram to London, 23 November 1912, and 4612, telegram from London, 25 November 1912.
73. Cf. Gooch, *op. cit.*, II, p. 312 ff.
74. G.Pol., XXXIII, 12447. Prince Lichnowsky to Foreign Ministry, 27 November 1912. Cf. also Giesche, *op. cit.*, p. 64.
75. Anxiety was felt in Paris over this understanding between the

German and British Governments. Hanotaux thinks that the Anglo-German understanding brought into existence a sort of secret Congress of Berlin that would deliberate in London. Cf. Hanotaux, G., *La guerre des Balkans et l'Europe, 1912-1913*, p. 181.

76. Br.D., IX/II, 311. Cartwright to Grey, 30 November 1912. Also cf. 297 and 310, Grey to Goschen. Telegrams of 28 and 29 November 1912.
77. *Ibid.*, 345. Grey to Cartwright, 6 December 1912.
78. *Ibid.*
79. *Ibid.*, 364. Grey to Cartwright, 9 December 1912.
80. Cf. Gooch, G. P., *History of Modern Europe*, p. 507.
81. Br.D., IX/II, 351. Cartwright to Grey, 12 December 1912.
82. A.D., V, 4924. Instructions to London, 15 December 1912. In the essay which he contributed years later to Steinitz, *op. cit.*, p. 47, Berchtold in writing of the policy followed by the Austro-Hungarian Government from the outset of the London Conference says:

"Nothing weighed more heavily on us in those days than the thought that the complete change that had taken place in the Balkans against our wishes might involve us in war. An impartial person will not doubt that at a time when a fundamental re-arrangement of the political configuration on our frontiers was in progress an empire of fifty million inhabitants, even though completely 'satiated' in a territorial sense, had definite and important—indeed vital—interests at stake. Nor would he doubt that the policy which necessity compelled us to pursue was not inspired by enmity towards our neighbour but solely by regard for our own security."

83. Cf. Grey, *Twenty-five Years*, p. 267, where he says that Mensdorff's "manner gave the impression of one who heard news that is almost too good to be true".
84. Br.D., IX/II, 391. Grey to Cartwright, 17 December 1912. Cf. also A.D., V, 4944. Telegram from London, 17 December 1912.
85. *Ibid.*
86. A.D., V, 4954. Telegram from London, 18 December 1912.
87. *Ibid.*, 4957. Telegram from London, 18 December 1912.
88. *Ibid.*, 4958. Telegram from London, 18 December 1912.
89. *Ibid.*, 4960. Telegram from London, 18 December 1912. Also cf. Br.D., IX/II, 394, Grey to Cartwright, 18 December 1912.
90. Br.D., IX/II, 400. Grey to Cartwright, 19 December 1912. Cf. also A.D., V, 4979. Telegram from London, 19 December 1912.
91. *Ibid.*, 403. Grey to Cartwright, 20 December 1912. Also cf. A.D., V, 4994. Telegram from London, 20 December 1912.
92. Br.D., IX/II, 407. Cartwright to Grey, 21 December 1912. Minute by Grey.
93. *Ibid.*, 406. Cartwright to Nicolson, private letter, 20 December

1912. At this time it was believed in Austria-Hungary that further attempts by Servia to extend her frontiers must be made an European question. The peace of Europe would then be threatened by a sword of Damocles which Servia could let fall whenever she chose. The Austro-Hungarian Government was anxious that a direct and unexpected provocation by Servia should not at this time compel them to make an end to this situation. The Austro-Hungarian Empire must of course reckon with the consequences arising out of a continuance of such conditions and certainly be on its guard. This would mean that Austria-Hungary must be armed to the teeth and therefore would unwillingly become the cause of an increased rivalry in armaments throughout Europe—a rivalry that had recently provoked Grey to a characteristic utterance in a public speech when he said: "Bleeding to death in peace time is worse than war." Cf. Schwendemann, *Grundzüge der Balkanpolitik Oesterreich-Ungarns, 1908-14*, in *Berliner Monatshefte*, May 1930, p. 213.

94. Br.D., IX/II, 416. Cartwright to Grey, 28 December 1912.
95. A.D., V, 5028. Telegram from London, Secret, 22 December 1912.
96. *Ibid.*, Report of a visit by the British Ambassador, Vienna, 11 January 1913. Cf. also 5270. Telegram to London, 8 January 1913, and 5375. Telegram from London, 13 January 1913. Cf. also Helmreich, *op. cit.*, p. 247 ff.
97. A.D., V, 5171. Telegram to London, 3 January 1913.
98. *Ibid.*, 5186. Telegram to London, 4 January 1913. Berchtold was prepared to give up Ipek, Ochrida, and Prisren.
99. *Ibid.*, 5195. Telegram to London, 4 January 1913.
100. *Ibid.*, 5216. Telegram to London, 4 January 1913.
101. *Ibid.*, 5384. Telegram to London, 14 January 1913.
102. Br.D., IX/II, 538. Nicolson to Cartwright, private letter, 21 January 1913.
103. *Ibid.*, 543. Grey to Cartwright, 22 January 1913. Cf. also A.D., V, 5488-9. Telegrams from London, 22 January 1913.
104. A.D., V, 5532. Telegram from London, 25 January 1913.
105. *Ibid.*, 5533. Telegram from London, 25 January 1913.
106. *Ibid.*, 5535. Telegram from London, 25 January 1913. Cf. also Br.D., IX/II, 559. Grey to Cartwright, 25 January 1913.
107. A.D., V, 5577. Telegram to London, 28 January 1913.
108. *Ibid.*, 5578. Telegram to London, 28 January 1913.
109. *Ibid.*, 5597. Telegram from London, 29 January 1913.
110. *Ibid.*, 5604. Dispatch from Berlin, 30 January 1913.
111. *Ibid.*, 5609. Telegram to London, 30 January 1913.
112. *Ibid.*, 5628. Dispatch from London, 31 January 1913.
113. *Ibid.*, 5630. Private Letter from Mensdorff, 31 January 1913.
114. *Ibid.*, 5644. Telegram to London, 1 February 1913.
115. Cf. Helmreich, *op. cit.*, p. 282 ff.
116. A.D., V, 5693. Telegram from London, 6 February 1913.

117.   *Ibid.*, 5694. Telegram from London, 6 February 1913.
118.   *Ibid.*, 5708. Dispatch from London, 7 February 1913.
119.   Br.D., IX/II, 613. Grey to Cartwright, 13 February 1913.
120.   Giesl, *op. cit.*, p. 234, says that the Archduke Francis Ferdinand
       told him before he left for London that he must insist upon
       Djakova belonging to Albania.
121.   A.D., V, 5801. Telegram from London, 14 February 1913.
122.   *Ibid.*, 5812. Telegram from London, 15 February 1913.
123.   *Ibid.*, 5855. Telegram to London, 18 February 1913. Cf. also
       Br.D., IX/II, 642. Grey to Cartwright, 20 February 1913,
       enclosing Mensdorff's *aide-mémoire.*
124.   A.D., V, 5889. Telegram from London, 21 February 1913.
125.   *Ibid.*, 5926. Report of a visit by the British Ambassador, 24
       February 1913, and also cf. Br.D. IX/II, 654. Cartwright to
       Grey, 24 February 1913, with Minutes.
126.   Br.D., IX/II, 663. Memorandum communicated by Count
       Mensdorff, 26 February 1913, and also cf. A.D., V, 5934.
       Instructions to Mensdorff, 5 February 1913.
127.   *Ibid.*, 650. Grey to Goschen, 23 February 1913.
128.   A.D., V, 6012. Telegram to London, 4 March 1913. Friedrich
       Stieve, *op. cit.*, p. 116, speaks of the marked lack of imagina-
       tion and the monotony revealed by Berchtold's fighting
       methods. "He was not a skilled and supple fencer who
       knows how swiftly to change his style of fighting and to
       confuse his opponent by the agility and variety of his move-
       ments. On the contrary he was a tenacious but monotonous
       fighter who always thrust in the same direction without
       noticing how far he was wide of the mark or that he was
       thereby assisting his opponent." I myself cannot assent to
       this harsh judgement.
129.   Br.D., IX/II, 655. Grey to Cartwright, 24 February 1913.
130.   A.D., V, 6024. Report on a visit of the German Ambassador in
       Vienna, 5 March 1913.
131.   Br.D., IX/II, 686. Grey to Cartwright, 6 March 1913, and also
       cf. A.D., V, 6044. Telegram from London, 6 March 1913.
132.   A.D., V, 6042. Telegram from London, 6 March 1913, and also
       cf. Br.D., IX/II, 686. Grey to Cartwright, 6 March 1913.
133.   A.D., V, 6069. Telegram to London, 8 March 1913.
134.   Br.D., IX/II, 691. Cartwright to Grey, 10 March 1913.
135.   A.D., V, 6132. Telegram from London, 13 March 1913.
136.   *Ibid.*, 6142. Telegram to London, 14 March 1913, and see also
       Br.D., IX/II, 721. Grey to Cartwright, 13 March 1913. A
       revelation of Berchtold's feelings at this time is to be found in
       his letter of 13 March to the German Secretary of State for
       Foreign Affairs, von Jagow (A.D., V, 6126), in which he says
       that after bitter struggles he has been successful in the Con-
       ference in securing the exclusion of Servia from the Adriatic
       and in the establishment of a viable Albania. True, Servia
       and Montenegro did not want to accept these decisions.
       "But if the Powers remained indifferent to the performances

of the Serbs and Montenegrins, Austria-Hungary might be compelled to put these arrogant young Slav States in their place." Cf. Gooch, *op. cit.*, II, p. 405.

137. Br.D., IX/II, 721. Grey to Cartwright, 15 March 1913.
138. A.D., V., 6145. Telegram from London, 14 March 1913.
139. *Ibid.*, 6202. Telegram from London, 18 March 1913.
140. *Ibid.*, 6161. Telegram from London, 15 March 1913.
141. Berchtold in the essay he contributed to Steinitz's *Erinnerungen an Franz Josef* states that it was due to Francis Joseph's direct intervention that Djakova was left to Servia, quoted by Gooch, *Recent Revelations of European Diplomacy* (4th Edition), p. 113. Cf. also Grey, *op. cit.*, p. 268, where he describes the joy that filled Mensdorff and himself when they knew that this question had found a solution. "He (Mensdorff) wanted peace, he knew that we all wanted peace, and the block was removed and the conference could go on again."
142. A.D., V, 6230. Telegram to London, 21 March 1913.
143. *Ibid.*, 6261. Telegram from London, 22 March 1913.
144. *Ibid.*, 6295. Telegram to Archduke Francis Ferdinand, 24 March 1913.
145. *Ibid.*, 6287. Telegram from London, 24 March 1913.
146. *Ibid.*, 6313. Telegram from London, 26 March 1913. Cf. also Br.D., IX/II, 751. Grey to Cartwright, 24 March 1913.
147. *Ibid.*, 6347. Telegram from London, 28 March 1913.
148. *Ibid.*, 6352. Dispatch from London, 28 March 1913, and 6378. Telegram to London, 30 March 1913, and cf. also Br.D., IX/II, 768. Aide-Mémoire communicated by Count Mensdorff, 31 March 1913.
149. *Ibid.*, 6379. Telegram to London, 30 March 1913.
150. *Ibid.*, 6388. Telegram from London, 31 March 1913, and cf. also Br.D., IX/II, 767. Grey to Cartwright, 31 March 1913.
151. In his speech in the House of Commons on 12 April 1913 Grey did not mention Scutari. This speech is printed in Asquith, H. H., *The Genesis of the War*, p. 274 ff.
152. Br.D., IX/II, 870. Cartwright to Grey, 22 April 1913.
153. Hanotaux, *op. cit.*, p. 286, remarks that after the capture of Scutari by Montenegrin troops if Montenegro retained possession of Scutari Austria-Hungary "n'a plus qu'a dire adieu à ses espérances Adriatiques." Berchtold had once more adopted Aehrenthal's policy and "avec une ingéniosité remarquable elle (Austria-Hungary) a jeté sur le tapis la conception d'une Albanie indépendante" (p. 287). For events at this time cf. Giesl, *op. cit.*, p. 242 ff where he prints extracts from his diary.
154. Br.D., IX/II, 877. Communication from Count Mensdorff, 23 April 1913.
155. *Ibid.*, 885. Grey to Cartwright, 24 April 1913, where Grey says Nicolson told Mensdorff that he doubted if British public opinion "would admit that the lives of British bluejackets should be endangered for the purpose of bring Montenegro

to reason". He added that large sections of public opinion thought the Government had gone far enough—possibly too far—in participating in the blockade. Also 899. Grey to Cartwright, 28 April 1913.

156. *Ibid.*, 915. Grey to Cartwright, 30 April 1913, and 927. Grey to Cartwright, 1 May 1913.

157. *Ibid.* Grey to Cartwright, 1 May 1913.

158. *Ibid.*, 942. Grey to Cartwright, 3 May 1913.

159. A.D., VI, 6870. Protocol of the Council of Ministers for Joint Affairs, Vienna, 2 May 1913.

160. *Ibid.*, 6894. Telegram to London, 4 May 1913.

161. Br.D., IX/II, 954. Grey to Cartwright, 5 May 1913.

162. Personally I cannot agree in so far as it concerns Grey with the condemnation expressed by Boghitschewitsch, *op. cit.*, III, p. 176, of the Entente's policy.

163. A.D., VI, 7096. Dispatch from London, 21 May 1913.

164. *Ibid.*, 7360. Telegram from London, 13 June 1913.

165. *Ibid.*, 7441. Dispatch from London, 21 June 1913.

166. *Ibid.*, 7621. Telegram from London, 4 July 1913.

167. *Ibid.*, 7548. Telegram to London, 29 June 1913.

168. *Ibid.*, 7689. Telegram from London, 8 July 1913.

169. *Ibid.*, 7775. Telegram from London, 15 July 1913.

170. *Ibid.*, 7830. Telegram to London, 18 July 1913.

171. Berchtold proposed the phrase "autorités nationales provisoire". The Russian and French Ambassadors objected strongly to any emphasis being laid on the nationalist element. The words reproduced above were finally agreed upon after long discussions. On this subject cf. *ibid.*, Nos. 7900, 7995, 8051, 8084, 8100 (telegrams from London between 21 and 29 July 1913) and 7929. Telegram to London, 22 July 1913.

172. *Ibid.*, 8143. Telegram from London, 31 July 1913. The text of the Statute for Albania is enclosed with 8147. Dispatch from London, 31 July 1913.

173. On the vexed question of the southern frontier of Albania cf. Stickney, *op. cit.*

174. A.D., V, 5471. Telegram to London, 21 January 1913.

175. *Ibid.*, 5743. Telegram to London, 10 February 1913.

176. *Ibid.*, 6217. Dispatch from London, 19 March 1913, with an enclosure laying down the proposed frontier.

177. *Ibid.*, 6334 and 6350. Telegrams from London, 27 and 28 March 1913.

178 *Ibid.*, 7067. Dispatch from London, 19 May 1913.

179. Br.D., IX/II, 1019. Grey to Cartwright, 30 May 1913. Cf. also AD., VI, 7209. Telegram from London, 30 May 1913.

180. Br.D., IX/II, 1051. Grey to Cartwright, 11 June 1913.

181. *Ibid.*, 1104. Grey to Carnegie (Chargé d'Affaires in Vienna) 3 July 1913, enclosing Memorandum concerning the question of the International Commission.

182. A.D., VI, 7807. Telegram from London, 17 July 1913, and 7895. Telegram to London, 21 July 1913.

183. *Ibid.*, 7829. Telegram to London, 18 July 1913.
184. *Ibid.*, 8121. Telegram to London, 30 July 1913.
185. Br.D., IX/II, 1190. Grey to Cartwright, 31 July 1913.
186. *Ibid.*, 1192. Grey to Cartwright, 1 August 1913.
187. *Ibid.*
188. *Ibid.*, 1195. Grey to Cartwright, 5 August 1913, and also cf. A.D., VII, 8229. Telegram from London, 5 August 1913.
189. *Ibid.* Also see p. 202.
190. Br.D., IX/II, 1207. Grey to Cartwright, 6 August 1913.
191. *Ibid.*, 1226. Grey to Cartwright, 8 August 1913. The draft submitted to the Conference of Ambassadors by Count Mensdorff read as follows:

"Les territoires sur lesquels s'étendront les travaux de la commission ne peuvent rester indéterminés. Ses limites seront à l'ouest les montagnes séparant la région côtière, attribuée à l'Albanie, jusqu'à Phtelia, de la vallée d'Argyrokastro. Au nordest la ligne frontière de l'ancien Kaza ottoman de Koritza. Entre ces deux régions la ligne indiquée dans le mémorandum présenté par M. Vénizélos à la réunion formera la limite septentrionale des travaux de la commission, tandis qu'au sud et sud-est ceux-ci s'étendront jusqu'à la ligne proposée par l'Autriche-Hongrie.

Il est dès à présent établi que la région côtière jusqu' à Phtelia, y compris l'île de Sasséno, la région située au nord de la ligne grecque, ainsi que l'ancien Kaza ottoman de Koritza, avec la rive ouest et sud du lac d'Ochrida, s'étendant du village de Lin jusqu'au monastère de Sveti Naoum font intégralement partie de l'Albanie."

192. *Ibid.* The draft went on to propose that:

"pour la conduite de ses travaux la commission procédera par sections en tenant compte de la conformation naturelle des vallées . . . pour les constatations ethnographiques on établira la langue maternelle de la population, savoir la langue parlée dans les familles, la commission ne tiendra aucun compte des tentatives de plébiscite ou d'autres manifestations politiques."

193. *Ibid.*
194. *Ibid.* Appendix V. Grey to Cartwright, 11 August 1913, reports the final meeting of the Conference.
195. *Ibid.*
196. Count Alexander Hoyos in his book *Der deutsch-englische Gegensatz und sein Einfluss auf die Balkanpolitik Oesterreich-Ungarns*, p. 35, puts forward the view that under Russian pressure the Conference delimited Albania's frontiers in such a manner as to make the viability of Albania questionable from the very outset. He says: "Austria-Hungary should have taken practical measures to protect at the beginning of the Balkan Wars her serious interests in any partition of the Balkans."
197. In his speech to the Reichstag on 7 April 1913, Bethmann-Hollweg paid tribute to Grey's work in these words:

"All Europe owes a debt of gratitude to the British Secretary of State for Foreign Affairs for the exceptional devotion and the spirit of conciliation with which he guided the London Conference and for the manner in which he was able again and again to effect compromises between opposing points of view." Quoted by Schröder, *op. cit.*, pp. 223-224.
The above quotation is taken from Grey, *op. cit.*, I, p. 271 ff. Grey expressed himself more fully in his speech in the House of Commons on 12 August 1913, but his argument was the same. He told the House that it was important for England that the Aegean Islands, of which the strategic importance was immense, should not fall into the hands of a Great Power. The Conference had passed a resolution to this effect. True, Italy was now in possession of some of the islands which, however, she had promised to return to Turkey after Turkey had fulfilled the stipulations of the Treaty of Lausanne. Cf. Knaplund, *op. cit.*, p. 218 ff.

198. A.D., VI, 8103. Telegram from London, 29 July 1913.

199. Cf. Helmreich, *op. cit.*, p. 419.

200. Br.D., X/I, 32. Cartwright to Grey, 6 October 1913.

201. *Ibid.*, 17. Cartwright to Grey, 24 September 1913.

202. Cf. Helmreich, *op. cit.*, p. 423 f.

203. Br.D., X/I, 38. Goschen to Grey, 16 October 1913, with Minute by Crowe. Grey sent a telegram to Goschen in the same sense on 18 October 1913, cf. 43.

204. A.D., VII, 8854. Circular Telegram to the Austro-Hungarian Embassies and Legations in Europe, 17 October 1913.

205. Br.D., X/I, 48. Grey to Goschen, 20 October 1913.

206. *Ibid.*, 51. Grey to Cartwright, 22 October 1913.

207. For the work of this Commission cf. G.Pol., XXXVI/I, p. 129 *passim*, where are reproduced the reports of the German delegate. Also cf. Boghitschewitsch, *op. cit.*, I, 373 and 378; G.Pol., XXXVI/I, 13971 and 13994, and Helmreich, *op. cit.*, p. 429.

208. Cf. G.Pol., XXXVI/I, pp. 131 ff, and also the report of the French delegate dated 19 December 1913 in D.D.F., III serie, IX, 40 annexe, as well as Helmreich, *op. cit.*, p. 429 ff, and Stickney, *op. cit.*, pp. 36 ff.

209. Cf. Helmreich, *op. cit.*, p. 431.

210. Br.D., X/I, 58. Grey to Bertie, 29 October 1913.

211. *Ibid.*, 59. Nicolson to Hardinge, 29 October 1913.

212. Cf. Fay, B., *The Origins of the World War I*, p. 464 (for Greek policy). Also G.Pol., XXXVI/I, 13990. Aide-Mémoire handed by Goschen to the German Foreign Ministry, 19 November 1913; D.D.F., III serie, VIII, 497; Helmreich, *op. cit.*, p. 431.

213. G.Pol., XXXVI/I, 14020, and Notes. Also cf. Helmreich, *op. cit.*, p. 431, and Stickney, *op. cit.*, p. 40.

214. Br.D., X/I, 102. Grey to Bunsen, 27 December 1913, with Editorial Note.
215. *Ibid*, 100. Bunsen to Grey, 24 December 1913.
216. *Ibid*. See Crowe's Minute on this dispatch.
217. *Ibid*., 104. Memorandum for circulation to the Cabinet, 6 January 1914.
218. Cf. Helmreich, *op. cit.*, p. 433.
219. *Ibid*., p. 434.
220. A.D., VII, 9151. Dispatch from London, 2 January 1914, and 9159. Telegram to London, 5 January 1914.
221. *Ibid*., 9175. Telegram to London, 9 January 1914.
222. *Ibid*. Berchtold had thought of demanding Lemnos for Turkey but gave up the idea when he encountered opposition. Also cf. *ibid*., 9193. Telegram from London, 14 January 1914, and Br.D., X/I, 203.
223. *Ibid*., 9239. Dispatch from London, 24 January 1914, and Br.D., X/I, 211, where the drafts of the Notes to Greece and Turkey are to be found.
224. Br.D., X/I, 211. Also cf. Helmreich, *op. cit.*, 435.
225. A.D., VII, 9272. Memorandum of a conversation between Berchtold and the Greek Prime Minister, M. Venizelos, 30 January 1914.
226. *Ibid*., 9344. Telegram from London, 12 February 1914, and 9345. Private Letter and Memorandum from the British Ambassador in Vienna, 12 February 1914.
227. Cf. Helmreich, *op. cit.*, p. 435 ff.
228. Br.D., X/I, 123. Elliott to Grey, 8 March 1914.
229. *Ibid*. Minutes to Elliott's dispatch by George Clerk and Crowe.
230. *Ibid*., 124. Grey to Bunsen, 10 March 1914.
231. On this question cf. Br.D., X/I and A.D., VII and VIII in general. Also cf. Helmreich, *op. cit.*, p. 437 ff and Stickney, *op. cit.*, pp. 42 ff.

CHAPTER FIVE

1. No attempt is made here to give a bibliography of the literature relating to the events immediately preceding the outbreak of the First World War—see, however, Bibliography. The most important publications of which I have made use are listed in the Notes for this Chapter.
2. Br.D., X/II, 506. Grey to Bunsen, 6 May 1914. Grey expressed his deep pleasure at Berchtold's commendation of British policy. "It was things of that kind that gave one a little pleasure in public work."
3. For the conflict between Austria-Hungary and Servia see Bibliography, and also books listed in Notes to Chapter III. Also Schmitt, B., *The Coming of the War, 1914*, I, pp. 77-257, and Seton-Watson, *Serajevo*. At the end of 1913 Francis Joseph said to Count Czernin: "The Peace of Bucharest cannot last and we are drawing near to another war. May

God grant that it will only be a Balkan War." Cf. Czernin, O., *Im Weltkreig*, Second Edition, p. 11.

4. Br.D., XI, 14. Grey to Bunsen, 29 June 1914, and 15, Private Letter from Grey to Mensdorff, 29 June 1914. Henceforward all dates will refer to the year 1914 unless otherwise mentioned.

5. Anrich, E., *Die englische Politik im Juli 1914*, p. 12.

6. For all quotations from British newspapers throughout the text cf. Zimmermann, W., *Die englische Presse zum Ausbruch des Weltkrieges*. See Bibliography.

7. Count Johann Forgach was Austro-Hungarian Minister in Belgrade from 1907 to 30 April 1911, when he was transferred to Dresden where he remained until in October 1913 he became head of one of the divisions of the Foreign Ministry in Vienna. Forgach was an exceptionally forceful, gifted, and ambitious man who never concealed his inimical feelings towards Servia. He exercised great influence over Berchtold. For Forgach's work and personality cf. Szilassy, I. von, *Der Untergang der Donaumonarchie*, p. 255, and Dumaine, *La dernière ambassade de France en Autriche*, p. 88.

8. Count Hoyos said: "Servia should be destroyed." He favoured marching into Servia without any preliminary diplomatic negotiations or warnings. Cf. Fischer, E., *Die historischen 34 Tage*, p. 75.

9. Br.D., XI, 29. Bunsen to Nicolson, Private Letter, 3 July.

10. *Ibid.*, 40. Bunsen to Grey, 5 July.

11. *Ibid.* Minute by Nicolson.

12. *Ibid.*, 41. Grey to Rumbold, Chargé d'Affaires at Berlin, 9 July. The German Ambassador in London, Prince Lichnowsky, according to Grey, was in a very confident mood and cheerfully declared that he saw no grounds for pessimism. Cf. Dickinson, *op. cit.*, p. 429.

13. A.D., VIII, 10118. Protocol of the Council of Ministers for Joint Affairs held on 7 July 1914. For Tisza's attitude at this time there is much information in his correspondence which has been published in the Hungarian language and of which an abridged German translation was made by O. von Wertheimer. Cf. too Fraknoi, *Tisza und die Entstehung des Weltkrieges*; Angyal, D., *Graf Tisza* in *Neue Oesterreichische Biographie*, Bd., I; Marczali, *The Papers of Count Tisza* in the *American Historical Review*, January 1924. In reply to Marczali's question as to what thoughts arose in his mind after the assassination of the Archduke Francis Ferninand, Tisza replied:

"My whole being revolted against the horrors of war. Religion and patriotism alike commanded me to avert this infernal trial from humanity and our country." Quoted by Gooch, *Revelations of European Diplomacy*, III Edition, p. 90.

14. Br.D., XI, 40. Bunsen to Grey, 5 July.

15. *Ibid.*, 46. Bunsen to Grey, 11 July.

16. *Ibid.*, 55. Bunsen to Grey, 13 July.

17. A.D., VIII, 10215. Dispatch from Berlin, 12 July.
18. *Ibid.*, 10335. Dispatch from London, 27 July.
19. Cf. Spender, J. A., *Life, Journalism and Politics*, Vol. II, pp. 9-10, and Franckenstein, Sir George, *Facts and Features of My Life*, p. 148.
20. Quoted by Schmitt, *op. cit.*, p. 422. On the subject of further attempts to induce Mr. Wickham Steed of *The Times* to adopt a more favourable attitude towards Austro-Hungarian policy cf. Schmitt, *op. cit.*, p. 423.
21. Br.D., XI, 58. Bunsen to Grey, 18 July, where Bunsen quotes this article. Hermann Lutz in *Die europäische Politik in der Julikrise*, p. 22, reproaches Grey with not having made proper use of this article in Belgrade.
22. *Ibid.*
23. *Ibid.* Minute by Grey.
24. *Ibid.*, 56. Bunsen to Nicolson, Private Letter, 17 July.
25. *Ibid.*, 50. Bunsen to Grey, 16 July.
26. *Ibid.*, 65. Bunsen to Grey, 16 July.
27. The most influential considerations were undoubtedly Germany's assurance of support and Servia's conduct. It is nevertheless possible that there was another reason suggested by Gooch, *Before the War*, II, p. 418, n. 1, namely, "misrepresentations by Berchtold".
28. A.D., VIII, 10393. Protocol of the Council of Ministers for Joint Affairs held in Vienna on 19 July 1914. Quoted by Gooch, *op. cit.*, p. 418.
29. Cf. Zimmermann, *op. cit.*, p. 35.
30. A.D., VIII, 10337. Dispatch from London, 17 July.
31. Cf. Zimmermann, *op. cit.*, pp. 33 ff. Also Anrich, *op. cit.*, pp. 116 ff.
32. Cf. Grey, *op. cit.*, I, p. 312, where he says: "I knew it to be very doubtful whether the Cabinet, Parliament and the country would take this view (to side with France)."
33. Roloff in his article *Englands Anteil an der Kriegsschuld* in *Kriegsschuldfrage*, October 1928, like many German historical research students, condemns Grey's attitude in July 1914 and declares (p. 917) that Grey must have known from the Servian Minister in London, and the British Minister in Belgrade, that Servia would refuse any independent investigation into the participation of Servian citizens in the conspiracy against Francis Ferdinand, and certainly any alteration in her policy, as well as any suppression of nationalist associations in Servia and censorship of the Servian Press. While this contention is correct it does not furnish any reason why Grey should not have continued to hope that he would be able to break Servia's opposition if he were able to induce Austria-Hungary to moderate her demands and Russia to bring pressure to bear upon Servia—after all that was the aim for which he was working.
34. Br.D., XI, 67. Grey to Buchanan, 20 July, and also Grey, *op. cit.*, p. 309, where he writes:

"For the first weeks (of July) the attitude of the Government in Vienna was neither extreme nor alarmist. There seemed to be good reason to hope that, while treating the matter as one to be dealt with by Austria alone, they would handle it in such a way as not to involve Europe in the consequences."

35. Br.D., XI, 68. Grey to Rumbold, 20 July.

36. From the beginning to the end Grey never altered his opinion. Cf. Lichnowsky, Prince, *Auf dem Wege zum Abgrund*, I, pp. 35-36, where he writes:

"Grey would never allow Germany to destroy or even to weaken the French. The corner-stone of English foreign policy was that France must be maintained as a Great Power to serve as a counter-balance to Germany, and that Western Europe should not fall into a state of dependance upon Germany that would result in the extension of German power to the English coast."

37. The *entente* with France without any formal alliance was regarded by many members of the British Cabinet as a grave error on Grey's part. Lord Loreburn in *How the War Came*, p. 19, writes: "At last it was transformed into the equivalent of an alliance without the needful security and advantages that an open alliance would bring with it."

38. Br.D., XI, 66. Lord Granville to Grey, Paris, 18 July (received 20 July), with Minute by Nicolson.

39. *Ibid.*, 76. Buchanan to Grey, 22 July.

40. *Ibid.* Minutes on this telegram from Buchanan by Clerk, Crowe, and Nicolson.

41. *Ibid.*, 77. Rumbold to Grey, 22 July, with Minutes by Grey and Crowe.

42. Cf. Anrich, *op. cit.*, p. 143.

43. On 21 July Bunsen sent the main points in the Note as announced in the *Neue Freie Presse*. But his dispatch only reached Grey on the 24th, cf. Br.D., XI, 88. Bunsen to Grey, 21 July.

44. The majority of Austro-Hungarian newspapers approved of the Government's action. Cf. Scott, *op. cit.*, p. 66 ff. There were, however, newspapers—not only Czech and Southern Slav—that were not in agreement with the ultimatum. *Die Arbeiterzeitung* wrote on 24 July: "Such demands one State has never before made to another . . . every one of these demands is a denial of the independence of Servia." Cf. Scott, *op. cit.*, p. 65.

45. Cf. Pribram, A. F., *Austrian Foreign Policy*, p. 63.

46. A.D., VIII, 10535. Instructions to London, Secret, 23 July. On 28 July Lichnowsky reported that the members of the Austro-Hungarian Embassy, including Mensdorff himself, in conversation with members of the German Embassy, and with Lichnowsky himself, had never made any secret of the fact that Austria-Hungary was bent upon the overthrow of Servia and that the Note was deliberately drawn up in such a manner that it must be rejected. Only yesterday Mensdorff

said to him that in Vienna they wanted war. They had also said that it was intended to give portions of Servia to Bulgaria and also presumably to Albania. If these statements had any foundation in fact, they were incompatible with Berchtold's repeated assurances that the integrity of Servia would be respected. On Lichnowsky's dispatch Bethmann-Hollweg commented: "The ambiguity on the part of Austria is intolerable." Cf. Rumbold, Sir Horace, *The War Crisis in Berlin, July-August 1914*, p. 166.

47. *Ibid.*, 10536. Telegram to London, 23 July. In the Circular Note to the Powers the Austro-Hungarian Ambassadors and Ministers were told to represent the Note (to Servia) as a *fait accompli* and not to permit any discussion of it. Cf. Gooss, *Das Wiener Kabinett und die Entstehung des Weltkrieges*, p. 109.

48. *Ibid.*, 10537. Telegram from London, 23 July. Since Grey spoke of an ultimatum to Servia, Mensdorff was immediately instructed by telegram to tell Grey that the *démarche* in Belgrade was not to be looked upon as a formal ultimatum. If it produced no results before the expiry of the time-limit, then diplomatic relations would be broken off and military preparations would be begun. *Ibid.*, 10599. Telegram to London, 24 July.

49. Mensdorff tried to explain his Government's action in the matter of the time-limit by saying that Servia made deliberate use of delaying tactics and thereby rendered it imperative to set a time-limit for her reply. Several weeks had now gone by since the murder of the Archduke without Servia making any effort to trace the assassins. Cf. Br.D., XI, 86. Grey to Bunsen, 24 July.

50. A.D., VIII, 10600. Telegram from London, 24 July.

51. *Ibid.*, 10601. Telegram from London, 24 July. Also cf. Br.D., XI, 86 and 91. Grey to Bunsen, 23 and 24 July where greater emphasis is laid on the necessity for regarding Russia's wishes.

52. The French Ambassador in London, M. Paul Cambon, favoured this course. Cf. Br.D., XI, 98. Grey to Bertie, 24 July. Also cf. Montgelas, Count, *Leitfaden zur Kriegsschuld-Frage*, p. 105, and Fay, *The Origins of the World War*, II, pp. 370 ff.

53. Br.D., XI, 98. Grey to Bertie, 24 July, and 99. Grey to Rumbold, 24 July.

54. *Ibid.*, 100. Communication by the German Ambassador, 24 July, with Minutes by Grey, Crowe, Nicolson, and Clerk.

55. Seton-Watson, *op. cit.*, pp. 118-124, and Schmitt, *op. cit.*, I, p. 177n.

56. Pribram, *England and the International Policy of the European Great Powers*, 1871-1914, pp. 129 ff.

57. Cf. Oncken, H., *Greys Kampf um den Eintritt Englands in den Weltkrieg* in his book *Natur und Geschichte*, p. 442. Also cf. Grey, *op. cit.*, I, p. 5, where he asserts:

"I have never, so far as I recollect, used the phrase 'Balance of Power'. I have often deliberately avoided the use of it, and I have never consciously set it before me as something to be pursued, attained and preserved."

58. Cf. Montgelas, Max, *British Foreign Policy under Sir Edward Grey*, p. 58, and Trevelyan, G. M., *Grey of Fallodon*, p. 169, where he writes:

"Though Grey listened well to everyone who had a right to advise him, he was master in his own house, he was not the mouthpiece of the Foreign Office opinion. He did not follow Nicolson in his demand for alliances or Eyre Crowe in his emphatic anti-Germanism."

59. *The Times* wrote *inter alia*: "But should there arise in any quarter a desire to test our adhesion to the principles that inform our friendships and that thereby guarantee the balance of power in Europe, we shall be found no less ready to vindicate them with the whole strength of the Empire than we have been found ready whenever they have been tried in the past. That, we conceive, interest, duty and honour demand from us. England will not hesitate to answer to their call." Quoted in Willis, *England: The Holy War*, p. 17.

60. Cf. Zimmermann, *op. cit.*, pp. 43 ff, and Willis, *op. cit.*, pp. 30 ff.

61. Grey, *op. cit.*, I, pp. 312-313. Also quoted by Schmitt, *op. cit.* II, pp. 34 ff.

62. Br.D., XI, 101. Buchanan to Grey, 24 July. Minute by Grey. Churchill at once went to the Admiralty where he made a note of certain matters to be borne in mind in event of an outbreak of war. Cf. Churchill, Winston S., *The World Crisis*, I, p. 193.

63. Br.D., XI, 87. Communication by the Servian Minister, 23 July.

64. *Ibid.*, 102. Grey to Crackenthorpe (British Chargé d'Affaires in Belgrade), 24 July.

65. *Ibid.*, 116. Grey to Rumbold, 25 July.

66. *Ibid.*, 122. Rumbold to Grey, 25 July.

67. *Ibid.*, 104. Communication by the Austrian Ambassador, 24 July.

68. *Ibid.*, 125. Buchanan to Grey, 25 July.

69. *Ibid.*

70. *Ibid.*, 116. Grey to Rumbold, 25 July.

71. *Ibid.*, 132. Grey to Buchanan, 25 July. This dispatch was not included in the Blue Book at Grey's express direction (cf. Editorial Note to the dispatch) because Benckendorff's view of Grey's proposal differed from that subsequently taken by the Russian Government and therefore Grey thought it would be "kinder" to Benckendorff "not to publish this fact". Grey, *op. cit.*, I, p. 317, prints this dispatch. Lutz, *op. cit.*, p. 110, thinks that the dispatch was omitted from the Blue Book because on 31 July Grey realized that Russia had been too hasty in ordering general mobilization and also because he thought it better to conceal his own pro-Russian attitude.

72. *Ibid.*, 125. Buchanan to Grey, 25 July.

73. *Ibid.*, 135. Bunsen to Grey, 25 July.
74. The Servian answer is printed in Br.D., XI, Appendix B, and by Schmitt, *op. cit.*, II, pp. 483 ff.
75. A.D., VIII, 10781. Telegram to London, 26 July. The majority of Austro-Hungarian newspapers declared that the Servian reply was inacceptable. Cf. *Neue Freie Presse* and *Pester Lloyd* 27 July. The *Pester Lloyd* wrote:

> "that the Note was intended to convey the false impression that the Servian Government was ready in larger measure to fulfil the demands of Austria, but that in point of fact it was filled with a spirit of insincerity which made it clear that the Servian Government had no earnest intention of putting an end to its culpable tolerance of the intrigues against the Dual Monarchy."

   Cf. Scott, *op. cit.*, p. 72. The *Wiener Fremdenblatt* said that the ultimatum had only made the minimum demands and there could therefore be no question of negotiations. Cf. Goebel, *op. cit.*, p. 74.
76. Cf. Beazley, R., *Some Causes of the Great War*, p. 15.
77. Cf. Schmitt, *op. cit.*, I, p. 538.
78. Br.D., XI, 171. Communication by the Servian Minister, 27 July, with Minute by Crowe and Clerk.
79. A.D., VIII, 10813. Telegram from London, 27 July. Cf. Grey, *op. cit.*, I, p. 311, where he writes: "The Servian answer went further than we had ventured to hope in the way of submission."
80. *Ibid.*, 10812. Telegram from London, 27 July. On 26 July Asquith wrote in his diary: "The news this morning is that Servia has capitulated in the main point, but it is very doubtful if any reservation will be accepted by Austria who is resolved on a complete and final humiliation. The curious thing is that on many, if not most, of the points Austria has a good and Servia a very bad case, but the Austrians are quite the stupidest people in Europe. There is a brutality about their mode of procedure which will make most people think that this is a case of a big Power wantonly bullying a little one." Cf. The Earl of Oxford and Asquith, *Memories and Reflections, 1852-1927*, II, pp. 5-6.
81. Cf. Anrich, *op. cit.*, pp. 251 ff, and Zimmermann, *op. cit.*, pp. 62 ff.
82. Br.D., XI, 139. Nicolson to Grey, undated, but probably 26 July.
83. *Ibid.*, 144. Nicolson to Grey, Private Letter, 26 July.
84. Bethmann-Hollweg expresses the same opinion in his *Betrachtungen zum Weltkreig*, I, p. 144, where he writes:

> "This was nothing else than an intervention by the Great Powers in the Austro-Servian dispute . . . it was an attempt by the Triple Entente to bring the Austro-Servian dispute before the judgement seat of Europe—better said, before their own judgement seat."

Prince Lichnowsky did his utmost to explain the change in Grey's attitude. On 27 July he telegraphed to Berlin that in Grey's opinion "the Austro-Russian conflict cannot be separated from the Austro-Servian, as the former is based on the latter . . . An understanding between Austria and Russia depends on the settlement of the Austro-Servian quarrel." Quoted by Schmitt, *op. cit.*, II, p. 7n.

85. Br.D., XI, 176. Grey to Goschen, 27 July.

86. A.D., VIII, 10813. Telegram from London, 27 July. On 26 July Mr. Winston Churchill, First Lord of the Admiralty, and Prince Louis of Battenberg, First Sea Lord, had resolved on their own responsibility not to disperse the Fleet. Grey approved their action. On the morning of 27 July a public announcement was made of this decision. Cf. Churchill, *op. cit.*, I, p. 197 ff. In conversation with Mensdorff, Grey sought to minimize the importance of the action and said "that we should not have thought of calling-up reserves or taking any step of a menacing character, but that our naval forces having been collected for manoeuvres, we could not, when there was a possibility of a European conflagration, choose this moment for dispersing it". Cf. Br.D., XI, 238. Grey to Bertie, 28 July.

87. Br.D., XI, 166. Bunsen to Grey, 26 July.

88. *Ibid.*, 175. Bunsen to Grey, 27 July.

89. *Ibid.*, 170. Buchanan to Grey, 27 July. Minute by Crowe. Lutz, *op. cit.*, p. 136, says that a report reached London on the morning of 27 July from the British Military Attaché in Vienna that 5 August was looked upon as the earliest date for the opening of hostilities. Conrad had in mind 12 August. Bunsen also indicated 5 August (Br.D., XI, 166. Bunsen to Grey, 26 July). Nevertheless, this news was not conveyed to St. Petersburg, although Buchanan had already on the evening of 26 July reported that Russia had started mobilizing against Austria-Hungary (Br.D., XI, 155. Buchanan to Grey, 26 July).

90. Cf. Churchill, *op. cit.*, I, p. 199. And also cf. Hammond, *op. cit.*, p. 177, where Lloyd George is reported as saying to the Editor of the *Manchester Guardian*, C. P. Scott, that "as to the European situation there could be no question of our taking part in any war in the first instance. He knew of no Minister who would be in favour of it."

91. Cf. Schmitt, *op. cit.*, II, pp. 116-117. In his *Memorandum on Resignation, August, 1914*, Morley writes on p. 2: "He (Grey) ended in accents of unaffected calm and candour." Lloyd George, *War Memoirs*, I, p. 72, says "Grey never definitely put before the Cabinet the proposition that Britain should in that event declare war. He never expressed a clear and un-equivocal opinion either way." This is true, but the statements by Grey reproduced in the text show clearly what he thought. To force a decision was still far from his intention.

92. Br.D., XI, 190. Parliamentary Debates, House of Commons, 27 July 1914. The decisive sentences run:
    " . . . it is, of course, a proposal in which the co-operation of all four Powers is essential. In a crisis so grave as this, the efforts of one Power alone to preserve the peace must be quite ineffective . . . the moment the dispute ceases to be one between Austria-Hungary and Servia and becomes one in which another Great Power is involved, it can but end in the greatest catastrophe that has ever befallen Europe at one blow, no one can say what would be the limit of the issues that might be raised by such a conflict, the consequences of it, direct and indirect, would be incalculable."
    Also quoted in *The Cambridge History of British Foreign Policy*, III, p. 493.
93. Br.D., XI, 185. Goschen to Grey, 27 July.
94. Cf. Asquith, H. H., *op. cit.*, p. 191. Tyrrell said that Grey regretted having used the expression "conference" because all he had in mind was an exchange of ideas between himself and the Ambassadors of the three Great Powers. Cf. A.D., VIII, 10894. Telegram from London, 28 July. Bertie said that the discussions in London should be described as "consultations" and not as a "conference" in order to obviate giving Vienna the impression that Austria-Hungary was to be treated like a small Balkan State (Br.D., XI, 191. Bertie to Grey, 27 July). On the subject of the success or failure that might have resulted from a conference opinions differed at the time and have continued to differ ever since. Grey, *op. cit.*, I, pp. 321-322, holds firmly to the belief that a conference would have made a solution to the crisis possible and that therefore Germany was responsible for the war. Trevelyan, *op. cit.*, pp. 248 ff, quotes from a letter written by Grey to a friend in the autumn of 1915 in which he (Grey) says that the more he reflects upon the matter the more terrible does it appear to him that Germany should have refused in July 1914 to take part in a conference. Servia had accepted nine-tenths of Austria's demands and the remaining points could have been swiftly and easily settled by a conference. He added: "The refusal of a conference decided the fate of peace or war for Europe." Mr. Winston Churchill, *op. cit.*, I, p. 201, is of the same opinion and writes: "Had such a conference taken place there could have been no war. Mere acceptance of the principle of a conference by the Central Powers would have instantly relieved the tension." Contrary opinions are held not only by German but also by French and British historians like Fabre-Luce, Renouvin, Dickinson (cf. Lutz, *op. cit.*, p. 123) who have voiced the view that such a conference would have turned out badly for the Central Powers. Jagow, G. von, *Ursachen und Ausbruch des Weltkrieges*, pp. 119 ff, thinks that as a

consequence of the position of the two Powers, France and England, *vis-à-vis* Russia, and also of the anti-Servian attitude of Italy, all previous experience goes to prove that Germany would have found herself virtually isolated in a conference in her defence of Austro-Hungarian interests. Cf. also his *England und der Kriegsausbruch*, pp. 21 ff.

95. Cf. Jagow, *England und der Kriegsausbruch*, p. 36.

96. Cf. Swain, J. W., *Beginning the Twentieth Century*, p. 354.

97. Br.D., XI, 175. Bunsen to Grey, 27 July.

98. Cf. Zimmermann, *op. cit.*, pp. 83 ff.

99. Br.D., XI, 206. Telegram from Sazonoff to the Russian Ambassador in London, 27 July.

100. *Ibid.*, 196. Buchanan to Grey, 27 July.

101. Cf. Grey, *op. cit.*, pp. 322 ff.

102. Br.D., XI, 175. Bunsen to Grey, 27 July, with Minute by Crowe in which he wrote: "If Austria proposes neither to annex nor to crush Servia nor to deprive her of her independence, then it is difficult to know what meaning to attach to the alternative of obtaining guarantees for the future." Crowe overlooked the fact that the purpose of the proposal was to make it possible for Servia to safeguard her prestige by making this declaration to the Great Powers instead of to the Austro-Hungarian Government. The guarantee intended for Austria-Hungary was the changed political attitude of Servia to her great neighbour. Many historians have thought that the Italian proposal was especially well-designed to have produced a peaceful solution to the crisis. Cf. Lutz, *Lord Grey und der Weltkrieg*, p. 381n.

103. A.D., VIII, 10871. Note from the German Ambassador in Vienna, 28 July.

104. Br.D., XI, 175. Bunsen to Grey, 27 July.

105. *Ibid.*, 676. Bunsen to Grey, 1 September. In the course of this long dispatch, Sir Maurice de Bunsen writes:
    "On the 24th July the note [to Servia] was published in the newspapers. By common consent it was at once styled an Ultimatum. Its integral acceptance by Servia was neither expected nor desired, and when on the following afternoon, it was at first rumoured in Vienna that it had been unconditionally accepted, there was a moment of keen disappointment. The mistake was quickly corrected, and as soon as it was known later in the evening that the Servian reply had been rejected and that Baron Giesl had broken off relations at Belgrade Vienna burst into a frenzy of delight, vast crowds parading the streets and singing patriotic songs till the small hours of the morning . . . Now the flood-gates were opened, and the entire people and press clamoured impatiently for immediate and condign punishment of the hated Servian race. The country certainly believed that it had before it only the alternative of subduing Servia or of submitting sooner or later to

mutilation at her hands . . . So just was the cause of Austria held to be that it seemed to her people inconceivable that any country should place itself in her path . . ."

106. Br.D., XI, 227 and 230. 28 July.
107. Foreign Office opinion was opposed to an immediate declaration of neutrality. Cf. Br.D., XI, 250. Bunsen to Grey, 28 July, with Minutes by Crowe and Nicolson.
108. Cf. Zimmermann, *op. cit.*, pp. 78 ff, and also Anrich, *op. cit.*, pp. 322 ff. *The Manchester Guardian* wrote on 29 July that "if Austria-Hungary only wants to humble Servia, and does not seek territorial gains, she should be content with the occupation of Belgrade in which case the declaration of war will only lighten the task of those who are seeking to mediate and to make peace". [This is not a literal transcription of *The Manchester Guardian's* words. It is the translation of a German version that gives the general purport. Tr.]
109. Fay, *op. cit.*, II, pp. 393 ff, where a record of these negotiations will be found.
110. Br.D., XI, 248. Bunsen to Grey, 28 July.
111. *Ibid.*, 239. Nicolson to Buchanan, Private Letter, 28 July. Nicolson was strongly pro-Russian and in this letter he also wrote:
    "What has preoccupied, and I confess has troubled me very much, is satisfying Russia's very natural request as to what we should do in certain eventualities . . . We, of course, living under such conditions as we do here, when no Government practically can take any decided line without feeling that public opinion amply supports them, are unable to give any decided engagements as to what we should or should not do in any future emergencies, but I think we have made it perfectly clear that in any case neither Germany nor Austria could possibly rely with any certainty upon our remaining neutral . . ."
    Also cf. Rumbold, *op. cit.*, p. 224.
112. Br.D., XI, 231. Rodd to Grey, 28 July.
113. In conversation with Lichnowsky, Grey emphasized that he could not make any such proposal to Vienna because the Austro-Hungarian Government refused to take part in any negotiations over the Austro-Servian conflict.
114. *Ibid.*, 246. Grey to Rodd, 29 July.
115. *Ibid.*, 248. Bunsen to Grey, 28 July.
116. *Ibid.*, 249. Goschen to Grey, 28 July. Minutes by Crowe, Clerk, and Nicolson.
117. *Ibid.*, 266. Grey to Goschen, 29 July.
118. *Ibid.*, 276. Buchanan to Grey, 29 July.
119. *Ibid.*, 281. Goschen to Grey, 29 July.
120. *Ibid.*, 285. Grey to Goschen, 29 July.
121. *Ibid.*
122. *Ibid.*, 288. Parliamentary Debates, 29 July.
123. *Ibid.*, 295. Bunsen to Grey, 29 July.

124. *Ibid.*, 293. Goschen to Grey, 29 July, with Minute by Crowe, 30 July.

125. *Ibid.*, 303. Grey to Goschen, 30 July, and 309. Grey to Buchanan, 30 July.

126. *Ibid.*, 305. Goschen to Grey, 30 July.

127. *Ibid.*, 302. Buchanan to Grey, 30 July, enclosing telegram from Sazonoff to Benckendorff, 30 July, and also cf. Editorial Note.

128. *Ibid.*, 309. Grey to Buchanan, 30 July. Cf. Sazonov, *Sechs schwere Jahre*, pp. 243 and 257.

129. *Ibid.*, 335. Grey to Buchanan, 31 July. At Lichnowsky's instigation Grey refrained from introducing any mention of the Vienna Ultimatum into the final text of his telegram to Buchanan and instead only spoke of negotiations over the duties and penalties to be laid upon Servia.

130. *Ibid.*, 335. Grey to Buchanan, 31 July.

131. *Ibid.*, 311. Bunsen to Grey, 30 July.

132. *Ibid.*, 265. Bunsen to Grey, 29 July.

133. A.D., VIII, 11064. Telegram from London, 30 July.

134. *Ibid.*, 10974. Dispatch from London, 29 July.

135. *Ibid.*, 11065. Telegram from London, 30 July.

136. *Ibid.*, 11026. Telegram from Emperor William II to Emperor Francis Joseph, 30 July.

137. Cf. Schmitt, *op. cit.*, II, pp. 202 ff.

138. A.D., VIII, 11135. Communication from the German Embassy in Vienna of a telegram from King George of England to Prince Henry of Prussia, 30 July.

139. *Ibid.*, 11118. Telegram from Emperor Francis Joseph I to the German Emperor William II, Schönbrunn, 31 July.

140. *Ibid.*, 11203. Protocol of a Council of the Ministers for Joint Affairs held in Vienna on 31 July 1914.

141. *Ibid.*, 11155. Telegram to London, 31 July.

142. *Ibid.*, 11156. Telegram to London, 31 July.

143. *Ibid.*, 11159. Telegram from London, 31 July.

144. Br.D., XI, 340. Grey to Goschen, 31 July.

145. A.D., VIII, 11159. Telegram from London, 31 July. Even the *Reichspost* that had been foremost in championing war with Servia wrote on 30 July—the sincerity of its remarks is open to question:

"England to-day has the peace of Europe in her hands and she administers this precious treasure with dignity and care. The formula proposed by Sir Edward Grey for the adjournment of warlike action against Servia has been overtaken by events and necessities, but the most important purpose of the English proposal remains, now as before, active, and it is a great satisfaction to public opinion to perceive that England and Germany in large measure united are working together for the attainment of this goal."
Cf. Scott, *op. cit.*, p. 87.

146. Br.D., XI, 393. Buchanan to Grey, 31 July.

147. *Ibid.*, 340. Grey to Goschen, 31 July. Cf. Anrich, *op. cit.*, p. 431.
148. Cf. Montgelas, *op. cit.*, p. 150.
149. Br.D., XI, 412. Grey to Bunsen, 1 August. Bunsen believed that Berchtold was sincere in making this statement. In his final dispatch of 1 September (676) he wrote:

> "Austria, in fact, had finally yielded, and that she herself had at this point good hopes of a peaceful issue is shown by the communication made to you on the 1st August by Count Mensdorff to the effect that Austria had neither 'banged the door' on compromise nor cut off the conversations."

150. Berchtold wrote in his essay published in Steinitz, *op. cit.*, p. 54, that it was untrue that at the close of July 1914 the Austro-Hungarian Government refused any discussion with the Russian Government. He continues:

> "From the outset we took up the standpoint that the guarantees which we had to demand from Belgrade were absolutely essential for our security and consequently could not be made the subject of subsequent negotiations. This standpoint nevertheless did not exclude the continuance of the *pourparlers* begun with St. Petersburg since we attached the greatest importance to the achievement of an understanding with Russia. That there was sincerity behind these intentions is shown by the further course of the conversations in which we said that we were ready not only to negotiate with Russia on the widest basis over all latent differences but also especially over the text of the Note (to Servia)." This is how the situation appeared to the Foreign Minister's backward glance. But it does not correspond with the course he actually followed in those days.

151. Cf. Schmitt, *op. cit.*, II, pp. 468 ff.
152. Br.D., XI, 591. Grey to Rodd, 4 August.
153. *Ibid.*, 672. Grey to Bunsen, 12 August, and also cf. Schmitt, *op. cit.*, II, p. 470.
154. Cf. Zimmermann, *op. cit.*, p. 93.
155. Cf. Grey, *op. cit.*, II, pp. 233 ff, and Dickinson, *op. cit.*, p. 476. The above quotation is taken from Dickinson.
156. Cf. Burton, J., *The Life and Letters of Walter H. Page*, I, p. 305, where Page says:

> "Poor Mensdorff does not know where he is. He is practically shut up in his guarded embassy weeping and waiting the decree of fate."

When he handed over the charge of Austro-Hungarian interests to Page:

> "Mensdorff denounced Germany and the Kaiser, he paraded up and down the room wringing his hands. He could be pacified only by the suggestion from the American that perhaps something might happen to keep Austria out of the war."

157. Cf. Dickinson, *op. cit.*, p. 477. "Never has an empire resigned

before the disruptive forces of nationality. Always it had fought. And I do not believe there was a state in existence that would not under similar circumstances have determined, as Austria did, to finish the menace, once for all, by war."

158. Trevelyan, *op. cit.*, pp. 150-151, says that Grey later reproached himself for not having brought pressure to bear directly upon Austria instead of through Germany to induce her to reach a peaceful settlement of the Austro-Servian issue. But Trevelyan is right in doubting whether Vienna "would have listened to the direct representations of England if more strongly urged. It seems highly unlikely in the light of everything we now know of their policies and temper during the crisis."

159. Erich Brandenburg holds this point of view cf. *Die englische Politik beim Ausbruche des Weltkrieges* in *Zeitschrift für Politik*, Bd. 17, p. 385 ff, and in *Memoiren Greys* in *Historische Vierteljahrschrift*, Bd. 23, p. 222 ff. More recently he has again written on the same subject in *Grey und Englands Politik vor dem Weltkrieg* in *Berliner Monatshefte*, August 1931, pp. 631 ff. English newspapers also gave expression to this point of view. *The Times* wrote on 31 July 1914: "It is not merely a duty of friendship, it is an elementary duty of self-preservation." Cf. Willis, *op. cit.*, p. 20.

160. Opinions on this subject are divided. Not only were leading statesmen in France and Russia of this opinion in the years preceding the outbreak of the First World War, but also subsequent critics from other countries. On 28 February 1922, Sir Austen Chamberlain said in the House of Commons:

"Suppose that an engagement (with France) had been made publicly in the light of day. Suppose it had been laid before this House, and approved by this House, might not the events of those August days of 1914 have been different? If our obligations had been known and definite it is at least possible, and I think it is probable, that war would have been avoided in 1914."

Quoted by Morel, E. D., *The Secret History of a Great Betrayal* p. 13. Trevelyan, *op. cit.*, p. 250, quotes an unpublished memorandum of April 1915 as follows:

"What Herr Ballin [who made an attempt to mediate during the last days of July 1914 in London] said was apparently that I (Grey) was indirectly responsible for the war because I had not pledged this country definitely either to support France and Russia or not to support them. In the former event Austria would have given way, in the latter France and Russia would have given way."

161. In this same memorandum Grey went on to say:

"This was not true, but what it suggested to me was how far Herr Ballin was from understanding what democratic government meant. The idea that one individual sitting in a room in the Foreign Office could pledge a great democracy definitely by his word in advance either to take part in a great war or to abstain from taking part in it is absurd."

162. For example Francis Hirst wrote in the *Daily Chronicle* on 29 July 1914 "that in the city one is glad to learn—and I believe the same is true of businessmen all over the country—that one opinion prevails. 'It is no concern of ours' is the general cry. The greatest of British interests is peace. The folly and wickedness of fighting for Russia against Germany are no less clear than the folly and wickedness of fighting for Germany against France." Cf. Scott, *op. cit.*, p. 248.

163. On this subject cf. Oncken, H., *Die Sicherheit Indiens: Ein Jahrhundert englischer Weltpolitik.*

164. See p. 233.

165. Cf. Taube, Mikhail Aleksandrovich, Baron, *Der grossen Katastrophe entgegen. Die russiche Politik der Vorkriegszeit und das Ende des Zarenreiches, 1909-1917*, p. 358.

166. Cf. Grey, *op. cit.*, I, p. 334. "I felt that if the country went into such a war it must do so wholeheartedly with feeling and conviction so strong as to compel practical unanimity."

167. *Ibid.*, I, p. 336 ff.

168. The question as to whether Russia had more cause to fear England, or England to fear Russia, has received many different answers. Lutz, *op. cit.*, p. 103, says that Russia had more cause to fear Great Britain. On the other hand Morley in his *Memorandum on Resignation, August 1914*, p. 6, says:

"Have you ever thought what will happen if Russia wins? If Germany is beaten and Austria is beaten, it is not England and France who will emerge pre-eminent in Europe. It will be Russia. Will that be good for western civilization? I, at least, do not think so. If she says she will go to Constantinople or boldly annex both northern and neutral zone in Persia, or insist on railways up to the Indian and Afghan frontier, who will prevent her?"

Roloff, *op. cit.*, p. 996, is certainly right in saying: "It was fear of Russia and of Germany that decided English policy." The pro-Russian British Ambassador at St. Petersburg, Sir George Buchanan, constantly warned his Government against the revenge that would be taken by Russia if she were to be abandoned by Great Britain. In a private letter to Nicolson (who shared Buchanan's views) written on 3 August 1914, he says *inter alia*:

"I should venture to submit with all respect that if we do not respond to the Emperor's [Nicholas II's] appeal for our support, we shall at the end of the war, whatever be its issue, find ourselves without a friend in Europe, while our Indian Empire will be no longer secure from attack by Russia."

Cf. Dengler, A., *Der englische Botschafter Sir George Buchanan und seine Stellung zu Deutschland*, pp. 109-110.

BIBLIOGRAPHY

The books to which reference has been made in the Notes have not been included in this Bibliography, which is only intended to afford the reader a short survey of the literature of the subject.

CHAPTER ONE

This short survey of the diplomatic relations between Austria and England from their beginnings up to the year 1813 is based upon the detailed account to be found in my study of *Die Oesterreichischen Staatsverträge England* which was published in two volumes during the years 1907-13. In the Notes to these two volumes are to be found the titles of the works dealing with this period. For the years 1814-1908 the chief works that I consulted are as follows:

ENSOR, R. C. K. England, 1870-1914.
SETON-WATSON, R. W. Britain in Europe, 1789-1914.
— Disraeli, Gladstone and the Eastern Question.
STOJANOVIC. The Great Powers and the Balkans, 1875-78.
TEMPERLEY, H. The Life of Canning.
TEMPÉRLEY and PENSON. The Foundations of British Foreign Policy, 1792-1902.
TREVELYAN, G. M. British History in the Nineteenth Century and After.
WARD and GOOCH. The Cambridge History of British Foreign Policy, 1783-1919. Vols. I-III.
WEBSTER, C. The Foreign Policy of Castlereagh.

German.

BRANDENBURG, E. Von Bismarck zum Weltkrieg. Eng. trans. From Bismarck to the World War.
HERRMANN, W. Dreibund, Zweibund, England, 1890-95.
ISRAËL, L. England und der Orientalische Dreibund. Eine Studie zur europäischen Aussenpolitik, 1887-1896.
ONCKEN, H. Das Deutsche Reich und die Vorgeschichte des Weltkrieges.
SRBIK, H. Metternich.
STERN, A. Geschichte Europas, 1815-1871.

CHAPTER TWO

Francis Joseph I.
ANDRASSY, JULIUS GRAF. Diplomatie und Weltkrieg, p. 232 ff. Eng. trans. Diplomacy and War. 1921.
FRIEDJUNG, HEINRICH. Historische Aufsätze. Franz Josef I, p. 493 ff.
KETTERL, EUGEN. Franz Josef.
MARGUTTI, ALBERT VON. The Emperor Francis Joseph and his Times.
PLENER, ERNST. Erinnerungen, Bd. III, p. 299 ff.
REDLICH, JOSEF. Franz Josef. Eng. trans. Emperor Francis Joseph of Austria.

REDLICH, OSWALD. Franz Josef I in *Neue Oesterreichische Biographie*, Bd. I.

SIEGHART, R. Die letzten Jahrzehnte einer Grossmacht.

SRBIK, H. VON. Franz Josef in *Historische Zeitschrift*. Bd. 144, p. 509 ff.

STEINITZ, E. VON. Erinnerungen an Franz Josef I. (With an essay by Count Berchtold.)

TSCHUPPIK, KARL. Franz Josef. Der Untergang eines Reiches.

Francis Ferdinand.

BARDOLFF, K. VON. Franz Ferdinand in *Kriegsschuldfrage*, July 1925.
— Soldat in alten Oesterreich.

CHLUMECKY, L. VON. Franz Ferdinands Wirken und Wollen.
— Franz Ferdinands Aussenpolitik in *Berliner Monatshefte*, 1934, p. 455 ff.

CZERNIN, OTTOKAR, GRAF. Im Weltkrieg. Eng. trans. In the World War.

GLAISE-HORSTENAU, E. VON. Franz Ferdinand in *Neue Oesterreichische Biographie*. Bd. III.

NIKITSCH-BOULLES, P. Vor dem Sturm.

SFORZA, COUNT CARLO. Gestalten und Gestalter des heutigen Europ. Eng. trans. Makers of Modern Europe.

SOSNOSKY, T. VON. Franz Ferdinand der Erzherzog-Thronfolger.

Aehrenthal.

BÜLOW, FÜRST VON. Denkwürdigkeiten. Bd. II, p. 235. Eng. trans. Memoirs.

CROZIER, P. L'Autriche d'avatt-guerre in *Revue de France*. 1921, April-June, p. 300 ff.

FRANCKENSTEIN, SIR GEORGE. Facts and Features of my Life, p. 72 and 79 ff.

FRIEDJUNG, H. Zeitalter des Imperialismus. Bd. II, p. 236 ff.

GOOCH, G. P. Before the War. Vol I, p. 369 ff and also the bibliography.

JONESCU, TAKE. Some Personal Impressions, p. 74.

MOLDEN, B. Graf Aehrenthal.

STEED, WICKHAM. Through Thirty Years.

SZILASSY, J. VON. Der Untergang der Donaumonarchie, p. 126.

Berchtold.

GOOCH, G. P. Before the War. Vol. II, p. 373 ff where the literature on the subject is given.

MONTS, ANTON, GRAF. Erinnerungen und Gedanken des Botschafters Anton Graf Monts, p. 248.

NAUMANN, VIKTOR. Profile, p. 221 ff.

SZILASSY, J. VON. Der Untergang der Donaumonarchie, p. 224.

Mensdorff-Pouilly.

The chief source from which to form a judgement upon Mensdorff's

diplomatic work are his dispatches as reproduced in the eight volumes of *Oesterreich-Ungarns Aussenpolitik 1908-1914.*
BÜLOW, FÜRST VON. Denkwürdigkeiten. Bd. II, p.36. Eng. trans. Memoirs.
JONESCU, TAKE. Some Personal Impressions, p. 95 ff.
SPENDER, J. A. Life, Journalism and Politics. Vol. I, p. 176.
SZILASSY, J. VON. Der Untergang der Donaumonarchie, p. 72.

Tisza.
ANGYAL, DAVID. Graf Stefan Tisza in *Neue Oesterreichische Biographie.* Bd. I.
ERÉNY, GUSTAV. Graf Stefan Tisza: Ein Staatsmann und Märtyrer.
GRATZ, GUSTAV. Graf Stefan Tisza in *Berliner Monatshefte*, Februar, 1936, p. 92 ff.
JONESCU, TAKE. Some Personal Impressions, p 167 ff.
NOWAK, K. Der Sturz der Mittelmächte.
WERTHEIMER, O. VON. Tiszas Briefe. With an introduction by Wertheimer.

Edward VII.
BLUNT, W. S. My Diaries. Vol. II, p. 33 and 320.
ECKHARDSTEIN, H. VON. Persönliche Erinnerungen an König Eduard. Aus der Einkreisungszeit.
ESHER, LORD. The Influence of King Edward, p. 12 and 30.
— King Edward VII and Foreign Affairs in "King Edward and other essays", p. 49 ff.
GREY OF FALLODON, VISCOUNT. Twenty-five Years. Vol. I, pp. 206 ff.
KENNEDY, A. L. Old Diplomacy and New, p. 117.
LEE, SIR SIDNEY. Edward VII.
MAUROIS, A. King Edward VII and his Time.
MORLEY, VISCOUNT. Recollections. Vol. II, pp. 331-332.
REDESDALE, LORD. Memoirs, pp. 171 ff.
RIDDEL, LORD. More Pages from my Diary, 1908-1914, p. 63.
RENNELL OF RODD, LORD. Social and Diplomatic Memories, 1902-1919.
SPENDER, J.A. Short History of Our Time, p. 128.

George V.
BOLITHO, HECTOR. King Edward VIII, pp. 232-234.
CHURCHILL, WINSTON. Great Contemporaries, p. 321 and 324 ff.
ESHER, VISCOUNT. Journals and Letters. Vol. III. 25 August 1910 and 23 May, 1914.
GORE, J. King George V.
GÖRLITZ, WALTER. George V.
HOWARD OF PENRITH, LORD. Theatre of Life. Vol. II, p. 611.
ROLOFF, GUSTAV. König Georg von England und der Ausbruch des Weltkrieges in *Berliner Monatshefte*, Oktober, 1931, p. 927 ff.
SFORZA, COUNT CARLO. Europe and Europeans, p. 181.
SOMERVELL, D. C. The Reign of King George V, p. 496.

Grey of Fallodon.

In addition to the two volumes of Grey's autobiography "Twenty-five Years" and his "Speeches on Foreign Affairs" (edited by Paul Knaplund) as well as the "British Documents on the Origins of the War 1898-1914" the following books may be mentioned here from among the extensive number that have been published on the subject of Grey's personality and work.

English.

ASQUITH, H. H. The Genesis of the War.
CHURCHILL, WINSTON. The World Crisis. Vol. I, p. 90 ff.
CONWELL-EVANS, T. P. Foreign Policy from a Back Bench, 1904-1918.
ESHER, VISCOUNT. Journals and Letters. Vol. II, p. 345.
FARRER, J. A. England under Edward VII.
FYFE, HAMILTON. The Making of an Optimist, p. 40 (very unfavourable to Grey).
GOOCH, G. P. Before the War. Vol. II. Grey.
KENNEDY, A. L. Old Diplomacy and New, p. 140 ff.
LEE, SIR SIDNEY. Edward VII.
MAURICE, SIR F. R. B. Haldane, p. 164.
MORLEY, VISCOUNT. Recollections. Vol. II, p. 245.
MURRAY, GILBERT. The Foreign Policy of Sir Edward Grey, p. 122 ff.
PERRIS, G. H. Our Foreign Policy and Sir Edward Grey's Failure, pp. 211 ff.
SPENDER, J. A. Men and Things, p. 5 ff and p. 113 ff.
— Life, Journalism and Politics. Vol. I, p. 169 ff.
SWAINE, J. W. Beginning the Twentieth Century, p. 274 ff.
TREVELYAN, G. M. Grey of Fallodon. For opinions of Grey by Gladstone (p. 67,) Lloyd George (p. 69), Algernon Law (p. 168), Arthur Balfour (p. 170), and Lord Robert Cecil (p. 309).

Foreign.

BOSDARI, A. Delle Guerre Balcaniche, p. 258.
FREIDJUNG, H. Der Zeitalter des Imperialismus. Vol. II, p. 83 ff.
KIRCHER, R. Engländer: Grey, p. 166 ff.
LUTZ, H. Sir E. Grey und der Weltkrieg, p. 48 ff where Lutz collects together different opinions of Grey and his policy.
MAUROIS, A. King Edward VII and his Time.
ROTHFELS, H. Zum Tode Lord Greys in *Berliner Monatshefte*, Oktober, 1933, p. 937 ff.

Asquith.

Apart from Asquith's own books—"The Genesis of the War" "Fifty Years of Parliament", "Memoirs and Reflections, 1852-1927"— the following may be mentioned:

CHURCHILL, WINSTON. Great Contemporaries, p. 137 ff.
ENSOR, R. C. K. England, 1870-1914, p. 42 ff.

KIRCHER, R.   Engländer: Asquith, p. 23 ff.
PETRIE, SIR C.   The Life and Letters of Sir Austen Chamberlain, p. 55.
RIDDEL, LORD.   More Pages from my Diary, 1908-1914.
SPENDER, J. A., and ASQUITH, CYRIL.   Life of H. H. Asquith Lord
    Oxford and Asquith.
OXFORD AND ASQUITH, MARGOT, COUNTESS OF.   More Memories.

Hardinge.
GALL, WILHELM.   Sir Charles Hardinge und die englische Vorkriegs-
    politik.
BOVERI, MARGRET.   Sir Edward Grey und das Foreign Office,
    p. 80 ff.

Nicolson.
NICOLSON, HAROLD.   Sir Arthur Nicolson, Bart., First Lord Carnock.
    A Study in the Old Diplomacy.
WEGERER, A.   Sir Arthur Nicolson und Englands Weg in den
    Weltkrieg in *Berliner Monatshefte*, Mai, 1930, p. 414 ff.
    Nicolson's dispatches from St. Petersburg and his instructions
    and minutes are to be found in "British Documents on the Origins
    of the War".

Crowe.
    Crowe's Minutes and memoranda are to be found in "British
Documents on the Origins of the War".
BOVERI, M.   Sir Edward Grey und das Foreign Office, p. 123 ff.
CHIROL, SIR V.   Fifty Years in a Changing World, p. 329.
CONWELL-EVANS, T. P.   Foreign Policy from a Back Bench, p. 46 and
    63 (critical of Crowe).
GREGORY, J. D.   On the edge of diplomacy, p. 255.
HEADLAM-MORLEY, J. W.   British Documents on the Origins of the
    War. Vol. XI, pp. VII/VIII.
LUTZ, H.   Deutsch-feindliche Kräfte in Foreign Office der Vor-
    kriegszeit.
— Eyre Crowe der böse Geist des Foreign Office.
NICOLSON, HAROLD.   Sir Arthur Nicolson, Bart., First Lord Carnock,
    p. 325.
THIMME, F.   Das Memorandum E. A. Crowes vom I, Januar 1907 in
    Berliner Monatshefte, August, 1929, p. 732 ff.

Goschen.
The Times.   In its obituary of Goschen on 2 May 1924, *The Times*
    wrote *inter alia*:
        "He was faithful, diligent and loyal, his manner was pleasant
        and unobtrusive, and he won the attachment of his colleagues;
        his general attitude was one of cool and practical commonsense."
BOVERI, M.   Sir E. Grey und das Foreign Office.

Cartwright.
Cartwright's dispatches are to be found in "British Documents on the Origins of the War".

BENECKENDORFF UND HINDENBURG, HERBERT VON. Am Rande zweir Jahrhunderte, p. 207.

CROZIER, P. L'Autriche d'avant-guerre in *Revue de France*, Mai, 1921, p. 576 ff.

LUTZ, H. Deutsch-feindliche Kräfte im Foreign Office der Vorkriegszeit, p. 21 ff.

SZEPS, JULIUS. Article in *Neuer Wiener Journal*, 19 August 1923.

Bunsen.
His dispatches are printed in "British Documents on the Origins of the War". Vols. X/2 and XI.

DUGDALE, E. T. S. Maurice de Bunsen. Diplomat and Friend, p. xi and 339 ff.

FREIBERG-EISENBERG, BARON VON. "Sir Maurice de Bunsen" in "Staatsmänner und Diplomaten aus den Vorkriegszeit" in *Berliner Monatshefte*, Juni, 1935, p. 494 ff.

DUMAINE, A. La dernière ambassade de France en Autriche, p. 101.

CHAPTER THREE

The primary sources for the following narrative of the diplomatic relations between Austria-Hungary and Great Britain at the time of the Bosnian Crisis are the great Austrian, English, and German collections of diplomatic documents:

Oesterreich-Ungarns Aussenpolitik 1908-1914. Bd. I and II.
British Documents on the Origins of the War 1898-1914. Vol V.
Die Grosse Politik der europäischen Kabinette 1871-1914. Bd. 26, 1 and 2.
The French collection of diplomatic documents—Documents diplomatiques Françaises, 2nd Serie—does not as yet include documents bearing on the Bosnian Crisis.

I have also made use of the documents published by Boghitschewitsch in his book *Die auswärtige Politik Serbiens 1903-1914*, Vols. I and II and of those contained in Siebert, B. von, *Diplomatische Aktenstücke zur Geschichte der Ententepolitik der Vorkriegsjahre*, Vol. I. Among the most important studies of the Bosnian Crisis are the following:

NINCIC, MOMTCHILO. La crise bosniaque 1908-1909 et les puissances Européens. 1934. Two volumes.

SCHMITT, B. The Annexation of Bosnia, 1908-1909. 1937.

WITTROCK, G. Oesterrike-Ungern i Bosniskakrisen 1908-1909. Uppsala. 1939 in Schrifter Utgivna av Kungl. Humanistska Vetenskaps-Samfundet J Uppsala. Bd. 133.

The following deal more specially with British policy:

GALL, WILHELM. Sir Charles Hardinge und die englische Vor-kriegszeit.
GOOCH, G. P. Before the War. Vol. I. Aehrenthal. Vol. II. Grey.
GOOCH, G. P., and TEMPERLEY, H. Cambridge History of British Foreign Policy. Vol. III, pp. 403 ff.
BURISCH, ING. Englands Haltung in der bosnischen Annexionskrise. 1935.
KUBISCH, E. England und die Annexionskrise 1908 und 1909.
LÜBBING, H. Englands Stellung zur bosnischen Krise. 1933.

CHAPTERS FOUR AND FIVE

References will be found in the Notes to Chapter Four to the books that I have read or quoted from in writing that chapter. For Chapter Five I have deliberately abstained from giving a bibliography because of the enormous extent of the literature in all languages relating to the outbreak of the First World War. The reader is advised to consult the bibliographies mentioned in the Preface while references are to be found in the Notes to this Chapter to all the books and articles of which I have made use.

TRANSLATOR'S NOTE

The outbreak of the Second World War silenced—at any rate temporarily—the controversy over the origins of the First World War. In the years that have elapsed since Professor Pribram completed this study few books have been published that have any direct bearing upon it or that contain much new information of importance. Of these few the following deserve mention:

The History of The Times. Vol. III. The Twentieth Century Test. 1884-1912. London. The Times Office. 1947. (Of especial interest for readers of the present study are the chapters—twenty-two and twenty-three—dealing with "The European Equilibrium, 1909-1912" and "Balkan Dangers".)

KÜHLMANN, RICHARD VON. Erinnerungen. Schneider. Heidelberg· 1949.

TAYLOR, A. J. P. The Habsburg Monarchy, 1809-1918. New Edition. London. 1949.

INDEX

policy, guiding principle of (1914), 260 and *n.*; Press, 108, 112-13 and *n.*, 114, 116-17, 120-1, 148, 152, 218, 221, 224, 234, 240-1, 244, 258; public opinion, 148-50, 167, 192 *n.*, 193, 229, 233-4, 247-8 and *n.*
Browne, Gordon, 113 *n.*
Buchanan, Sir George, 225-6, 231-2, 236, 243 *n.*, 252 and *n.*; Grey and, 168 *n.*, 252 and *n.*; letter to Nicolson (3 August 1914), quoted 262 *n.*; Nicolson's letter to (28 July 1914), quoted 248 and *n.*
Bucharest, 71; Treaty of, *see under* Treaties.
Buchlau, 95, 96 *n.*
Budapest, 102, 112 *n.*, 130, 169, 170, 219, 222, 228; Treaty of, *see under* Treaties.
Bülow, Bernhard, Prince von, 123 and *n.*, 141.
Bulgaria, 52, 54, 184, 204; and Austria-Hungary, 108-9, 135, 163, 165, 217; and Great Britain, 54; and Russia, 165, 167; and Servia, 110 *n.*, 142 *n.*, 160 and *n.*, 195, 201, 229 *n.*; and Turkey, 104, 106, 108, 110 *n.*, 122, 131, 163, 195, 201; defeat of (1913), 195, 201; independence of, 97-8, 100, 102, 108, 117-18, 131, 135; *status quo* in, 54.
Bulgarians, the, 165, 167.
Bulgo-Servian Treaty (1912), *see under* Treaties.
Bund, the, 47, 49.
Bundestag, 47.
Bunsen, Ernest de, 90.
  Sir Maurice de, 226 *n.*; arrives in Vienna, 207; Berchtold and, 91, 220-1, 244, 246-7 and *n.*, quoted, 257 *n.*; career of, 90; character of, 90-1; on situation in Vienna (July 1914), quoted 219, 238, 243 and *n.*, 247 *n.*
Buol, Count, 42.
Burgundy, 2.
Buxton, Noel, 113 *n.*, 121 and *n.*

Cambon, Jules, 250.
  Paul, 104, 176, 178, 181, 183, 192, 194 *et seq.*, 197 and *n.*, 199 *et seq.*, 231 *n.*, 242; Grey and, quoted 208-9.
Cambrai, 16.
Campo-Formio, Peace of, *see under* Treaties.
Canning, George, 33, 38; Metternich and, 35-6.
Capet, House of, 2.
Capitulations, 104, 109.
Carl Emmanuel of Savoy, 21.

Carlos, Don, 16, 38.
Carlsbad Decrees, 33.
Carol I, King of Rumania, 215, 217.
Cartwright, Sir Fairfax, *aide-mémoire* (1909), quoted, 142-3; and Aehrenthal, 90, 116-18, 120, 132-3 and *n.*, 134, 137, 139-41, 145, 149-51, 152-3, 159-60, 207; and Berchtold, 90, 162, 166, 171, 173, 186, 188, 207; and Clémenceau, 116; and Edward VII, 89; and Grey, 113 *n.*, 122-3, 133 *n.*, 134, 138, 140 *n.*, 152, 160, 175-6, 186, 192 *n.*; and Nicolson, 168, 177 *n.*, 181; and Pichon, 116; career of, 89; character of, 89-90; recall of, 207; views on Bosnian Crisis, 144-5; views on Servia, 168, 177.
Castellerizo, 212, 214.
Castlereagh, Viscount, Metternich and, 31-5, 79.
Catholic Church, 65.
Catholics, Roman, 190.
Cavour, Count, 44.
Central Empires, *also* Central Powers, 35, 47, 52-3, 67, 73, 75, 83, 85, 92-3, 145 *n.*, 146, 217, 221, 244 and *n.*
Cettinje, 105, 188 *et seq.*
Chamberlain, Sir Austen, quoted 260 *n.*
Charles I, 5 *et seq.*
Charles II, 7, 9.
Charles II, King of Spain, 9-11.
Charles V, Emperor, 4.
Charles VI, Emperor, 12 *et seq.*
Charles VIII of France, 2.
Charles X of France, 37.
Charles, Archduke (son of Ferdinand I), 4.
  (son of Leopold I), 9 *et seq.*
Chataldja Line, 165.
Chaumont, Treaty of, *see under* Treaties.
Chotek, Countess, 65.
Christian IX of Denmark, 46.
Churchill, Winston Spencer, and mobilization of British Fleet (1914), 242 *n.*, quoted 235 and *n.*; on Grey, 81; on Grey's proposed conference (1914), quoted 244 *n.*
Clarendon, Earl of, 43, 48-9.
Clémenceau, Georges, 116.
Clerk, George (later Sir George), quoted, 240.
Commons, House of, 15, 47, 70, 78-9, 97 *n.*, 109 *n.*, 150, 151, 152, 189, 191 *n.*, 205 *n.*, 218, 220, 243 and *n.*, 251, 260 and *n.*
Compromise (*Ausgleich*) of 1867, 76.
Concordat of 1855, *see under* Treaties.

9/23

DATE DUE

NOV 7	1972		

GAYLORD   PRINTED IN U.S.A.